HEALTH
NAVIGATION
SERIES

Series Editor: Richard Riegelman

PRINCIPLES OF
HEALTH
NAVIGATION

Understanding Roles and Career Options

Karen Marie Perrin, PhD, MPH, CPH

Associate Professor
Assistant Dean of Undergraduate Studies
College of Public Health
University of South Florida
Tampa, Florida

JONES & BARTLETT
LEARNING

World Headquarters
Jones & Bartlett Learning
5 Wall Street
Burlington, MA 01803
978-443-5000
info@jblearning.com
www.jblearning.com

Jones & Bartlett Learning books and products are available through most bookstores and online booksellers. To contact Jones & Bartlett Learning directly, call 800-832-0034, fax 978-443-8000, or visit our website, www.jblearning.com.

Substantial discounts on bulk quantities of Jones & Bartlett Learning publications are available to corporations, professional associations, and other qualified organizations. For details and specific discount information, contact the special sales department at Jones & Bartlett Learning via the above contact information or send an email to specialsales@jblearning.com.

40277-3

Production Credits
VP, Executive Publisher: David D. Cella
Publisher: Michael Brown
Associate Editor: Nicholas Alakel
Associate Editor: Danielle Bessette
Associate Production Editor: Rebekah Linga
Senior Marketing Manager: Sophie Fleck Teague
Manufacturing and Inventory Control Supervisor: Amy Bacus

Composition: Integra Software Services Pvt. Ltd.
Cover Design: Kristin E. Parker
Rights & Media Specialist: Merideth Tumasz
Media Development Editor: Shannon Sheehan
Cover Image: © Jim Barber/Shutterstock
Printing and Binding: RR Donnelley
Cover Printing: RR Donnelley

Library of Congress Cataloging-in-Publication Data
Names: Perrin, Karen M., author.
Title: Principles of health navigation : understanding roles and career
  options / Karen (Kay) M. Perrin.
Other titles: Health navigation series.
Description: Burlington, MA : Jones & Bartlett Learning, [2017] | Series:
  Health navigation series
Identifiers: LCCN 2016030075 | ISBN 9781284090765 (pbk.)
Subjects: | MESH: Patient Navigation | Community Health Workers | Vocational
  Guidance | Community Health Services
Classification: LCC R690 | NLM W 84.7 | DDC 610.69–dc23 LC record available at
  https://lccn.loc.gov/2016030075

6048

Printed in the United States of America
19 18 17 16   10 9 8 7 6 5 4 3 2 1

CONTENTS

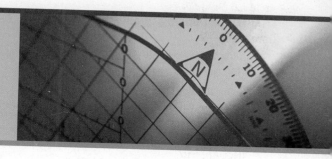

Health Navigator Applied Associate Degree and Academic Certificate Programs

"Health Navigator" is the term used by the Association of Schools and Programs of Public Health (ASPPH) and the League for Innovation in the Community College (League) for applied associate degrees and academic certificate programs that prepare students for employment in existing and emerging fields such as community health worker, patient navigator, and health insurance navigator. These programs also benefit employers and practitioners by offering opportunities for employees to obtain academic credentials that reflect the knowledge, skills, and abilities gained through job experience. As recommended by the Society for Public Health Education (SOPHE), Health Navigator programs should be designed to transfer to bachelor's Health Education degree programs should a graduate wish to do so.

The need for individuals with the skills to help patients obtain and maximally benefit from community services, clinical care, and health insurance is becoming a major issue in the increasingly complex and expensive U.S. health system. Those with Health Navigator training may assist individuals with limited health literacy as well as the elderly with accessing community services and implementing prevention. They may facilitate access to care and follow-up for sick and complicated patients with cancer, HIV, and a range of other complex and chronic health problems. In addition, Health Navigators can assist with identifying and enrolling patients in health insurance plans including those available through the Affordable Care Act exchanges, Medicaid, Medicare, as well as through community health centers.

The recommended Health Navigator applied associate degree program includes 30 semester credit hours of general education as well as 30 semester credit hours of coursework in the following areas:

- **Public Health Core:** 1) Population & Personal Health; 2) Overview of Public Health; and 3) Health Communications
- **Health Navigator Core:** 1) Prevention & Community Health; 2) Accessing and Analyzing Health Information; 3) Healthcare Delivery Systems; 4) Health Insurance
- Experiential learning
- Elective coursework allowing students to tailor their education to specific jobs in the field

This coursework can also form the centerpiece of academic certificate programs designed for nurses and allied health students as a complement to their clinical education. Certificate programs are well-suited for individuals with workforce experience and/or an academic degree who seek to augment their academic portfolio with a Health Navigator credential. Detailed course content outlines are available at www.league.org/ccph/ as part of the *Community Colleges and Public Health* report.

While this need has existed for a long time, until recently it has not been met through paid positions with well-defined roles. This is rapidly changing as a result of the growing commitment to develop specific Health Navigator positions and to integrate these positions into the healthcare and public health systems. Moreover, new funding mechanisms as part of Medicaid, Medicare's 30 day hospital readmission policy, and the Affordable Care Act have dramatically increased demand for employees with Health Navigator credentials. Salaries for Health Navigator graduates range from $30,000 to $55,000 per year. The Department of Labor estimates that by 2022 the demand for Community Health Workers—the only Health Navigator-related job classification it currently tracks—will increase by at least 25 percent

THE HEALTH NAVIGATION SERIES

ROM JONES & BARTLETT LEARNING

he NEW Jones & Bartlett Learning *Health Navigation* series meets the full range of Health Navigation education ompetencies of the League for Innovation in the Community College based on the Association of Schools and Programs Public Health (ASPPH) Community Colleges and Public Health report.

eveloped under the editorial direction of Richard K. Riegelman, MD, MPH, PhD, this series of three textbooks and ccompanying digital learning materials is designed for Health Navigator associate degree and certificate programs ading to employment as community health workers, patient navigators, and/or health insurance navigators.

Principles of Health Navigation

by **Karen Marie Perrin**, PhD, MPH, CPH University of South Florida, College of Public Health

This text will provide an overview of the content and knowledge competencies expected as part of health navigation education including health services delivery and health insurance, care of the individual, and accessing and analyzing health information competencies.

Navigating the U.S. Health System

by **Nancy Niles**, PhD, MS, MPH, Lander University
Available Spring 2017

This text will comprehensively cover the knowledge competency in healthcare delivery and public health expected as part of health navigation education in the United States.

Navigating Health Insurance

by **Alexis Pozen**, PhD, and **James Stimpson**, PhD, MA, Both of the CUNY School of Public Health
Available Spring 2017

This text will comprehensively cover the health insurance knowledge competencies needed to understand health insurance and serve as a health insurance navigator.

Each title will serve as a free-standing text designed for a 3 semester hour course. Together the series will cover the required course work recommended for health navigation associate degree and academic certificate programs by the ASPPH Community Colleges and Public Health report.

PROLOGUE

Principles of Health Navigation and the Jones & Bartlett Learning Health Navigation series

The health system in the United States has become increasingly complex. It would be difficult to design a more complex health system if one tried. In addition, potential interventions for prevention, treatment, and rehabilitation have become increasingly diverse, effective, and costly.

Little progress has been made in recent years in simplifying the health system. Therefore, the need to help individuals navigate the health system cries out for attention. The health navigation education movement aims to prepare health navigation professionals to help make the system work.

The need for health navigation education was front and center in the *Community Colleges and Public Health* report of the Association of Schools and Programs of Public Health, plus the League for Innovation in the Community College. The Jones & Bartlett Learning *Health Navigation* series is an effort to build on the frameworks put forth in this report and to implement a comprehensive curriculum for academic certification programs and associate degree programs.

The need for health navigation education is broad and growing. A wide range of individuals, including families and caregivers, need help with health navigation. Vulnerable populations include those with limited health literacy, limited English fluency, age-related frailty, and increasingly complex conditions such as advanced cancers, HIV, cardiovascular disease, and advanced respiratory diseases. The health navigation professions need to be prepared to serve the needs of all these groups and more.

Health navigation education leads to employment, including an enormous array of job titles. Three key area of focus have been recognized as "community health workers," "patient navigators," and "health insurance navigators." In addition all health navigation professionals need knowledge and skills to access and analyze health information.

Principles of Health Navigation Karen Marie Perrin is the first book in the Jones & Bartlett Learning *Health Navigation* series. It provides an overview of health navigation, including prevention and community health, patient navigation, health insurance navigation, as well as accessing and analyzing health information. Dr. Perrin is the perfect person to author her third Jones & Bartlett Learning book. She has a lifetime of personal and professional commitment to making the health system work. As a public health professional, as well as a former nurse and wife of a patient with long-term chronic needs, she understands health navigation literally "inside and out."

Principles of Health Navigation can stand on its own as an overview of what health navigation is all about. It is the first of four books in the Jones & Bartlett Learning *Health Navigation* series. It will soon be joined by texts focusing on the health system, health insurance, and putting health navigation into practice. *Principles of Health Navigation* is accompanied by a wide array of ancillary materials for students and faculty. As the editor of the Jones & Bartlett Learning *Health Navigation* series and a contributor to *Principles of Health Navigation*, I am confident that you will find in this book just what you are looking for.

Richard Riegelman, MD, MPH, PhD
Editor, Jones & Bartlett Learning
Health Navigation series

CHAPTER 1

Healthcare Personnel

LEARNING OBJECTIVES

By the end of this chapter, students will be able to:

- Differentiate between direct contact health providers and those with limited or no patient contact
- Understand the essential educational requirements and duties of varied healthcare providers
- Explain how many healthcare providers work together to improve the health outcomes of patients

CHAPTER OVERVIEW

In the modern world of healthcare, there are numerous types of healthcare personnel. To introduce the topic of healthcare personnel, this chapter will present the first segment of a case study. After the case study, the chapter provides a description of healthcare professions divided into two major categories: limited or no patient contact and direct patient contact. For each health profession, the chapter includes educational requirements, locations of employment, and descriptions of the primary duties, annual salary, and professional organizations. The case study continues in segments throughout the chapter to show the reader examples of how numerous health professions intertwine to serve one individual, Katherine. Prior to starting with the case study, let us review the role of the health navigation professional. The chapter notes where health navigation professionals serve in the healthcare system. See **Box 1.1**.

CASE STUDY: PART ONE

Brief description: Katherine, age 53, is a white female who works full-time at the local community college. She is married to Michael, and they have two children: Rachel, who is 24 and works full-time as an elementary teacher while living at home with her parents; and Paul, who is 18 and a freshman at a state university about 5 hours from home. Michael is employed as a computer science technician. Katherine's mom died last year at the age of 90 from congestive heart failure, with a history of breast cancer at age 80. Her father died at age 82, 15 years ago, from an acute myocardial infarction (AMI). Katherine has never been hospitalized other than for childbirth.

September: Katherine and Michael, her husband, arrive at the outpatient surgery center at 5 a.m. The valet parking attendant opens the passenger door to help Katherine get out of the car. Michael walks around and exchanges the key for a valet ticket. They walk inside and meet the front desk clerk, who asks for Katherine's driver's license and insurance card. She verifies that Katherine is on today's schedule for a colonoscopy

BOX 1.1 Description of Health Navigation Professionals

Health Navigation Professional

Education	Associate's degree programs that include basic science, medical terminology and additional general education coursework.
	Preferred skills and experience: Experience with community programs and services; strong analytical skills, ability to work independently with little supervision and ability to handle concurrent projects; strong interpersonal skills, including professional telephone skills and ability to work with medical and support staff in a professional manner; must type and possess computer skills, with experience in Microsoft applications; must have experience in drafting letters, memos, and spreadsheet applications and have the ability and skills to format, distribute, and maintain health communications and reports; knowledge of office administration and the ability to create and maintain organized systems; experience in working with culturally diverse populations and knowledge of medical systems and community resources desirable.
Work Duties	A health navigator is a health professional who focuses on the patient's needs, including guiding patients through the healthcare system and working to overcome obstacles that are in the way of patient required care and treatment. Some of the responsibilities of the health navigation professional include organizing schedules and managing appointments for patients to ensure they receive services in a timely manner; facilitating communication among the patient, family members, and healthcare providers to ensure patient satisfaction and quality of care; managing healthcare records, informing the patient on financial aspects of care and linking patient to financial resources as needed; accommodating interpretive language services when needed, managing follow up visits, and ensuring continuation of care and linkage to community resources. In addition, the health navigation professional is involved with outside entities. Patients may have needs to arrange legal counsel, home health care, transportation, or specialty care outside the hospital setting. Health navigation professionals collaborate with diverse organizations and personnel to ensure the needs of the patient are met, are involved in patient education about their care, and foster patient understanding of treatment options.
Alternative Work	Health navigation professionals work in a variety of healthcare settings, but hospitals are the most common place of employment. Health navigation professionals may specialize in a certain area such as oncology or diabetic care. Patient navigators may work with patients of all ages, from infants to geriatric populations. The patient navigator also works closely with the healthcare providers and healthcare institution.
Salary	$44,000 average salary, depending on location, industry, experience, and benefits.[1] The employment outlook for health navigation professionals is good, because the Affordable Care Act created a need to ensure patient satisfaction and quality health care at an affordable cost.[2]
Hours	40-hour workweek; work is full-time or part-time; hours are 8- or 12-hour shifts; usually involves daytime work with some night and weekend shifts.

procedure and requests a credit card to process the co-payment insurance charge. Upon receipt of payment, she directs Katherine and Michael to the outpatient surgical waiting room. They wait a few minutes; then, the admitting registered nurse (RN) calls Katherine's name. She verifies her name, date of birth, and reason for visit. She places a plastic band on Katherine's wrist and asks if she has any allergies. Katherine states that she is allergic to penicillin. The RN writes "penicillin" on a pink armband and places it on Katherine's wrist. Another RN, Lisa, comes to get Katherine and Michael. She will be in the exam room during the colonoscopy. She instructs Katherine to change into a gown and place all of her clothing and belongings in a large plastic bag, which is given to Michael. Lisa starts an intravenous (IV) catheter in Katherine's arm, so the physician has access to a vein for medications during the procedure. Prior to starting the procedure, the anesthesiologist stops by Katherine's bed and asks a few more questions related to her medical history and allergies. She comes back in a few minutes and injects some relaxation medication into Katherine's IV tubing. Within an hour, the gastroenterologist is ready to perform Katherine's colonoscopy. She is wheeled into the exam room, the anesthesiologist injects quick-acting, short-term medication, and Katherine drifts off to sleep. This procedure usually takes about 20 minutes, but for Katherine the procedure lasted only 10 minutes. The RN moved Katherine back to her outpatient room where Michael was waiting. The anesthesia wore off quickly and the gastroenterologist stopped by to inform Katherine and her husband that he suspected that she had colon cancer. There was a blockage in her colon that did not allow him to examine the colon as the procedure is intended to do. He explained that he had removed three tiny pieces of the suspected tumor that was causing the blockage and had sent the tissue samples to the lab for a pathologist to confirm the colon cancer diagnosis. After the cancer diagnosis was discussed and Katherine's questions were answered, the gastroenterologist gave Katherine a referral to a colorectal surgeon to schedule a surgical procedure to remove the tumor.

© Courtney Keating/iStockphoto

The RN returned to her room and removed the IV. She told Katherine that she could get dressed. In a few minutes, the RN returned with Katherine's discharge summary papers, a paper copy of the referral for the gastroenterologist (colorectal surgeon), and a paper prescription for a stool softener and pain medication.

Although this case study explores various types of healthcare personnel, it also reveals the number of individuals that a patient encounters when receiving health care. More of this case study is presented near the middle and at the end of this chapter.

HEALTHCARE PERSONNEL

Using this case study, let us begin to explore various types of healthcare personnel. The list provided is not meant to be all-inclusive, but rather a descriptive sampling of healthcare employment opportunities. The list is divided into two categories: healthcare personnel with limited patient contact and healthcare personnel with extensive patient contact. Each category begins with entry-level positions and advances through the list to positions requiring higher levels of education. Because the health navigation professional is a relativity recent addition to the healthcare system, a description of how health navigation professionals supplement or stand alone in a variety of healthcare duties is provided. Throughout the chapter, the U.S. Bureau of Labor Statistics was used for salary information (www.bls.gov).

Limited or No Patient Contact

Hospital Billing Clerk*
*Entry level for Health Navigation Professional

Education	Entry-level position that requires completion of a coding certification program plus a 2-year associate's degree in health information technology.
Work Duties	Responsible for coding and entering medical records, communicating with insurance companies and billing patients; uses computer software and knowledge of insurance and billing practices to correctly translate verbal descriptions of diagnoses and procedures into numerical codes.
Alternative Work	Bill and Account Collector; Bookkeeping, Accounting, and Auditing Clerk
Salary	$33,450 median salary
Hours	40 hours per week; some evenings and weekends
Professional Organizations	American Health Information Management Association (www.ahima.org)

Medical Transcriptionist*
*Entry level for Health Navigation Professional

Education	Entry-level position that requires a 1-year certificate program or a 2-year associate's degree program.
Work Duties	Transcribes recordings made by physicians and other healthcare workers to produce medical records, regulatory documents, and other pieces of correspondence; documents are then returned for review, corrections, or signing.
Alternative Work	Hospital Transcriptionist; Dental Transcriptionist; Radiology Transcriptionist
Salary	$35,260 median salary
Hours	Self-employed; work at home; freedom to choose own hours
Professional Organizations	Association for Healthcare Documentation Integrity (AHDI), formerly the American Association for Medical Transcription (www.biotechmedia.com/AAMTrans-Maillist.html)

Medical Record and Information Technician*
*Entry level for Health Navigation Professional

Education	Associate's degree with specialized credentials and courses in coding systems, healthcare reimbursement, anatomy, physiology, and data systems.
Work Duties	Organize and maintain medical records by collecting information about patients, including test results, diagnoses, exam results, recommended treatments, prior medical history, and other relevant data; records must be well organized; security and accuracy of the records is essential because small mistakes could result in a large liability.
Salary	$37,710 median salary
Hours	40 hours per week
Professional Organizations	Professional Association of Health Care Coding Specialists (PAHCS); the Board of Medical Specialty Coding (BMSC); the American Academy of Professional Coders (AAPC); and the National Cancer Registrars Association (NCRA)

Ophthalmic Laboratory Tech

Education	Ophthalmic laboratory technicians complete on-the-job training, though there are courses available at technical institutes for certificates in ophthalmic technology; students learn customer service through equipment maintenance for creating contact lenses and glasses.
Work Duties	Ophthalmic laboratory technicians make glasses and contact lenses based on the optometrists' instructions.
Work Alternative	Some ophthalmic technicians create telescope lenses and binoculars.
Salary	The salaries for ophthalmic technicians range from $18,487 to $38,555.[3]
Hours	40 hours per week; some evenings and weekends
Professional Organizations	None at this time

Medical and Clinical Laboratory Science Professions

Education	Associate's degree with specialized credentials and courses to carry out laboratory tests and operate laboratory equipment under the supervision of a certified medical laboratory technologist. Bachelor's and master's degrees are available in a variety of laboratory science professions. Graduate degrees focus on research and leadership skills for supervisory and management careers.
Work Duties	Maintain all laboratory equipment; prepare the laboratory equipment and specimens for tests; collect patient's body fluids for lab tests and analysis; analyze and record test results; issue reports that utilize graphs, charts, and narratives; perform blood counts and blood tests; assist medical laboratory technologists in less complex laboratory tests and procedures. Possible professions include Blood Bank Specialist, Clinical Genetic Technologist, Clinical Laboratory Sciences, Cytotechnologist, Hematology Technician, Histologic Technician, Histological Technologies, Medical Laboratory Technologies, Phlebotomy, and Renal and Dialysis Technician.
Work Alternative	Various health care facilities, including hospitals, medical offices, research laboratories, health clinics, veterinary laboratories, medical diagnostic laboratories, and biotechnology companies.
Salary	$33,619–$41,000 median salary
Hours	40 hours per week; some evenings and weekends
Professional Organizations	American Medical Technology (www.americanmedtech.org/default.aspx)

Medical Staff Services*
*Entry level for Health Navigation Professional

Education	High school diplomas for entry-level positions; however, most employers prefer candidates with associate's or bachelor's degrees in business administration or a related field; courses include health information science, management principles, medical terminology, and health care law.
Work Duties	Ensure health care staff is compliant with regulatory requirements; responsible for coordinating credentialing processes and maintaining databases of physician information, as well as other administrative duties; required to be familiar with relevant government regulations and be responsible for monitoring compliance.
Work Alternative	Health care office manager, medical credentialing specialist, medical staff coordinator
Salary	$41,755–$64,665 range
Hours	40 hours per week

Medical Facilities Management

Education	Entry-level positions are available after completing a degree at the undergraduate level; many positions require a master's degree; some medical facilities managers have degrees in engineering or architecture, while others have a degree in health administration.
Work Duties	Ensure that health care facilities, such as surgical centers, clinics, public health organizations, and hospitals, are properly cleaned, maintained, and supplied; oversee implementation of new technology and energy efficiency initiatives.
Work Alternative	Facilities maintenance director, facilities administrator, certified facilities manager, facilities coordinator
Salary	$93,290 median salary
Hours	40 hours per week

Medical Ethics and Bioethics

Education	Educational requirements include a master's or doctoral degree in bioethics, applied ethics, or a law degree in health care ethics. Some degrees have clinical practicum requirements for students to gain experience. A degree in medical ethics or bioethics can lead to a position creating health care policies, working in hospital administration, teaching bioethics at the postsecondary level, or working as a medical professional.
Work Duties	Medical ethicists and bioethicists work in large hospitals, law offices, and universities. Their work focuses on the emerging questions related to the latest advances in medicine, science, and technology.
Work Alternative	Additional career options include Bioethics Programs, Medical Ethics Programs, Health Care Consultant, Health Care Lawyer, Hospital Administrator, and Legal Nurse Consultant
Salary	The median annual salary for medical ethicists and bioethicists is $68,800.[4]
Hours	40 hours per week with some evenings and weekends
Professional Organizations	There are no specific professional organizations; however, most ethicists join professional associations closely related to their field of expertise.

CASE STUDY: PART TWO

On the way home from the outpatient center, Katherine's husband dropped off the two medication prescriptions at the pharmacy. The pharmacy technician logged the paper prescriptions into the computer, and the pharmacist filled the prescription. With the medication in hand, Michael took Katherine home. She felt tired, but was not experiencing any pain. She took a nap and then called to schedule an appointment with Dr. Smith, the colorectal surgeon recommended by the gastroenterologist who performed the colonoscopy. The medical assistant scheduled the appointment for the next week.

When Katherine returned to work the following day, she talked to a coworker who recommended another colorectal surgeon, Dr. Williams,

in the same office. Katherine called the office back and asked the medical assistant from the previous day about the difference between the two surgical techniques.

She learned that Dr. Smith did not use the laparoscopic procedure for colon cancer and that Dr. Williams used only the laparoscopic procedure for colon cancer. Because the laparoscopic procedure involved three tiny half-inch incisions and only 2 days in the hospital and the standard procedure involved a 6-inch incision and 4 days in the hospital, Katherine decided to select the laparoscopic procedure. Dr. Williams did not have any surgery appointments open for 2 weeks, but Katherine decided to wait the extra week for the laparoscopic procedure.

October: Prior to the day of surgery, Katherine had to go to the hospital for a chest X-ray, blood

© DragonImages/iStockphoto

clerk told Katherine that her surgical co-payment was $150. Fortunately, Katherine and Michael are both employed, so they had sufficient money to pay the $150 co-payment required by her insurance policy for any surgical procedure. After making the payment, she was given directions to the lab, so she could have her blood drawn prior to surgery. The lab technician took Katherine's paperwork and directed her to sit in one of the chairs. The lab technician wrapped a tourniquet around Katherine's arm, inserted a needle into her arm, and withdrew two vials of blood. The lab technician placed the computer label with Katherine's name and date of birth on each vial. Both vials were delivered to the laboratory hospital courier to send it to the laboratory for processing. The medical technologist in the laboratory processed the blood and sent a final computer report to the surgeon's office. Katherine's next stop for the day was the Department of Radiology. The same basic procedure was conducted here as well. The radiology technician took her paperwork and instructed Katherine to follow her into a room for the chest X-ray. There was no need to remove any articles of clothing for the chest X-ray. Katherine put down her purse, stepped up to the X-ray machine, held her breath when instructed to do so, and in a few seconds was told that she was finished and could leave. Katherine had completed the preoperation requirements, so she found her way back through the maze of hallways to the parking valet and left the hospital.

work, and pre-authorization for the procedure through her health insurance provider. During the course of this hospital visit, she encountered the valet parking attendant and the hospital information clerk who had given directions to the preadmission clerk. The preadmission clerk verified that Katherine's health insurance policy had agreed to authorize payment for her surgery, and then the

Extensive Patient Contact

Medical Office Assistant*
*Entry level for Health Navigation Professional

Education	There are no formal education or training requirements for medical assistants; 1-year programs lead to diplomas or certificates, while associate's degree programs require 2 years.
Work Duties	Perform a variety of administrative tasks key to the overall functioning of a doctor's office, including office administration, medical terminology, insurance billing, and basic back-office clinical duties.
Salary	$27,420–$30,740 range
Hours	40 hour per week
Professional Organizations	American Association of Medical Assistants (www.aama-ntl.org)

Certified Nursing Aide (CNA)

Education	Six-week to 3-month training programs are located in medical facilities, vocational schools, and community colleges. Once the requirements for certification are met, a certified nursing assistant credential (CNA) is awarded. Courses include medical terminology, geriatric care, nutrition, rehabilitation, vital signs, mental health, patients' personal care needs, patient rights, and responding to medical emergencies.
Work Duties	Assisting patients with eating, bathing, and dressing; taking some vital signs (e.g., respiration rate, temperature, blood pressure), making beds, noticing any changes in the physical or emotional state of a patient, and notifying a nursing supervisor.
Work Alternative	CNAs work in hospitals, skilled nursing facilities, long-term care facilities, and in home health care.
Salary	$24,890 median salary
Hours	40-hour workweek: 8-hour shifts including days (7 a.m.–3 p.m.), evenings (3 p.m.–11 p.m.), and nights (11 p.m.–7 a.m.).
Professional Organizations	The federal government provides oversight on the certification of nurse aides.

CASE STUDY: PART THREE

Monday arrived—the day of Katherine's surgery. Michael and Katherine arrived at the hospital at 6 a.m., as stated on the paperwork that was given to her at the preadmission appointment. They parked the car and walked into the main hospital lobby. A large sign reading "INPATIENT ADMISSION" marked the entrance for admission. A receptionist verified Katherine's name, date of birth, and requested a copy of her health insurance card. Again, Katherine received a plastic identification (ID) bracelet with her name, date of birth, hospital barcode, and admitting physician's name and hospital number. Upon completion of the verification process, Katherine and Michael were asked to take the elevator to the third floor. As they stepped off the elevator, another large sign directed them to the surgical waiting room. Michael was asked to wait in this area while Katherine was prepared for surgery. Katherine was told to change into a hospital gown, paper booties, and a hair cap. The presurgical RN checked her ID bracelet and then explained that after she started the intravenous line in Katherine's arm, Michael would be able to stay at Katherine's bedside until it was time for surgery. Michael sat next to Katherine's bed for over an hour, waiting for Dr. Williams, the surgeon. While they waited, the anesthesiologist came by, performed a brief history and physical exam, and asked Katherine a few questions related to her past experience with surgery and anesthesia. Because Katherine had never had any anesthesia prior to her colonoscopy, she did not have much information for the anesthesiologist.

About 8:30 a.m., Dr. Williams arrived in the presurgical area. He reintroduced himself to Katherine and Michael and gave a brief overview of her surgery and the laparoscopic procedure. He introduced Nancy, the circulating RN during the surgery, and Eileen, the RN ("scrub nurse") assisting with the surgery. Then he asked Katherine to sign the surgical consent form; Eileen witnessed her signature. The presurgical nurse gave Katherine the IV medication prescribed by the anesthesiologist, and then Michael gave her a kiss and was escorted back to the waiting room. By this time, their daughter had arrived to wait with her father while her mother was in surgery.

The surgery lasted about 2 hours. Dr. Williams was assisted by Eileen, the RN scrub nurse. The title "scrub nurse" is used because this RN wears a sterile gown, gloves, and mask and stands next to the surgeon during the operation. The scrub nurse hands sterile surgical instruments to the surgeon. The other RN, Nancy, is the circulating nurse in the operating room. Her position involves handling non-sterile items, such as non-sterile plastic bottles to collect tissue samples, using the phone or intercom system, and moving the surgical lights, as needed. Dr. Williams sent 3 tissue samples from the colon tumor that was removed and 16 lymph nodes to pathology. The pathologist, a board-certified medical physician, specializes in diagnosing tissue, bone, muscle, and forensic types of medical conditions. After Dr. Williams completed the surgical procedure and closed the tiny puncture wounds from the laparoscopic procedure, Katherine was moved to the post-anesthesia recovery area. Because her vital signs (temperature, pulse, respirations, blood pressure) were stable, Michael was allowed to visit for a few minutes and then return to the waiting room. Katherine was moved to her hospital room. She was groggy, but awake with minimal pain. Because Katherine was in a private room, Michael was able to spend the night and get some sleep on the couch in her room. The next morning, Katherine was able to eat clear liquids (Jell-O, broth, ginger ale) and walk a bit in the hallway. Dr. Williams stopped by her room in the afternoon and told Katherine that he had been able to remove the colon tumor and blockage. He told

her that the pathology report would be available on Friday. Of course, Katherine was eager to learn about the pathology report, because this report was needed to determine whether the cancer had spread to her lymph nodes or to another organ in her body. After a quick physical examination, Dr. Williams told Katherine that she could plan on going home on Wednesday. She walked a little in the halls and took a few naps. By Wednesday morning, she felt better. The certified nurse's aide recorded her vital signs in the morning and again around noon. Dr. Williams stopped by after lunch and wrote her discharge orders. The staff nurse RN reviewed Katherine's discharge orders, including the need to rest for the next few days, to eat several small meals each day for a few days, and avoid high-fiber foods to allow her colon to rest; she gave Katherine a prescription for pain medication. Michael arrived and Katherine was taken by wheelchair to valet parking, where their car was waiting. Because Katherine had pain medication left over from the colonoscopy, they did not fill this prescription for additional pain medication.

Allied Health Positions*
*Mid-level for Health Navigation Professional depending on job description and duties

Education	Some of these professionals may have 6 months to 2 years of training after high school, while others required a 4-year bachelor's and master's degrees. Allied health careers include emergency medical technicians (EMTs), paramedics, sonographers, radiology technician, health educators, dietitians, medical librarians, and dental hygienists.
Work	Because the field of allied health is so diverse, the careers are also diverse. However, most individuals in allied health work closely with patients and other health care providers. For example, a radiology technician works closely with physicians to provide accurate imaging for diagnosis, including X-rays, magnetic resonance imaging (MRI), and computed tomography (CT). EMTs and paramedics transport patients and perform emergency procedures as allowed by state laws. Dietitians and health educators work directly with patients with or without referrals from health care providers. Most allied health workers are employed by a hospital or closely linked community health care service, such as clinics.
Work Alternative	Some allied health professionals work as private consultants, such as dietitians and health educators. Others are employed in schools, universities, large corporations, and manufacturing industries.
Salary	Salary range is varied due to the number of professions linked to the classification of allied health.
Hours	40 hours per week; some evenings and weekends
Professional Organizations	Each allied health classification has a unique professional organization to serve the needs of their members.

Health Navigation Professional

Education	Associate's degree programs that include basic science, medical terminology, and additional general education coursework.
	Preferred skills and experience: Experience with community programs and services; strong analytical skills, ability to work independently with little supervision, and ability to handle concurrent projects; strong interpersonal skills, including professional telephone skills, and ability to work with medical and support staff in a professional manner; must type at least 45 w.p.m. and possess computer skills, with experience in Microsoft applications; must have experience in drafting letters, memos, and spreadsheet applications and have the ability and skills to format, distribute, and maintain health communications and reports; knowledge of office administration and ability to create and maintain organized systems; experience in working with culturally diverse populations and knowledge of medical systems and community resources desirable.
Work Duties	A health navigator is a health professional who focuses on the patient's needs, including guiding patients through the health care system and working to overcome obstacles that are in the way of patients receiving required care and treatment. Some of the responsibilities of the health navigation professional include organizing schedules and managing appointments for patients to ensure they receive services in a timely manner; facilitating communication among the patient, family members, and health care providers to ensure patient satisfaction and quality of care; managing health care records, informing the patient on financial aspects of care, and linking the patient to financial resources as needed; accommodating interpretive language services when needed, managing follow-up visits, and ensuring continuation of care and linkage to community resources. In addition, the health navigation professional is involved with outside entities. Patients may have needs to arrange legal counsel, home health care, transportation, or specialty care outside the hospital setting. Health navigation professionals collaborate with diverse organizations and personnel to ensure the needs of the patient are met, are involved in patient education about their care, and foster patient understanding of treatment options.
Alternative Work	Health navigation professionals work in a variety of health care settings, but hospitals are the most common place of employment. Health navigation professionals may specialize in a certain area such as oncology or diabetic care. Patient navigators may work with patients of all ages, from infants to geriatric populations. The patient navigator also works closely with the health care providers and health care institution.
Salary	$44,000 average salary; depends on location, industry, experience, and benefits (www.simplyhired.com/salaries-k-health-care-navigator-jobs.html). The employment outlook for health navigation professionals is good because the Affordable Care Act (www.hhs.gov/healthcare/rights/law/index.html) created a need to ensure patient satisfaction and quality health care at an affordable cost.[3]
Hours	40 hour workweek; work is full-time or part-time; hours are 8- or 12-hour shifts; usually involves daytime work with some night and weekend shifts.

CASE STUDY: PART FOUR

On Friday, Katherine called the oncology office to receive any news regarding the pathology report. She was told that Dr. Williams was not in the office, and she would have to wait until Monday. After a frustrating weekend of waiting for the pathology report, she called the office again on Monday. This time she was told by the office staff that they had not yet received the pathology report. Katherine decided that because she had a follow-up appointment on Wednesday, she would wait and talk to the surgeon, Dr. Williams.

Michael drove Katherine to the appointment so he could be there when she heard the pathology report. As Katherine was expecting, the pathology report stated that the colon cancer had spread to two of her lymph nodes near her groin. Her colon cancer was ranked Stage III.

Cancer is staged as Stage I (localized to one part of the body and can be surgically removed), Stage II (locally advanced and treatment is required), Stage III (locally advanced, depends on the type of cancer and whether positive lymph nodes are above or below the diaphragm), and Stage IV (cancer spread or metastasized to other organs or throughout the body).[5] Dr. Williams referred Katherine to Dr. Clark, an oncologist, for cancer treatment. Once again, she called to make an appointment and was told that the first available appointment was in 3 weeks. The office staff person told her that the appointment delay was fine, because the oncologist would not start any cancer treatment until about 6 weeks after surgery, so the patient has adequate time to heal.

The day of her appointment finally arrived, and Katherine and Michael went to Dr. Clark's office to discuss her treatment options. However, Dr. Clark did not offer many options. He told her that she needed chemotherapy because radiation would not be appropriate for her Stage III pathology report. She asked a few questions and signed some informed-consent forms. Before leaving the office, Regina, the office nurse, met with Katherine and Michael to go over some additional details. Regina explained that on the following Monday, Katherine was scheduled for an outpatient procedure at the hospital. A physician specializing in intervention radiology would place a plastic port with access to her vein on the upper-left side of Katherine's chest. The port would allow her to receive chemotherapy medication without having to start an intravenous line in her arm every other week. The port would be located under the skin to decrease the chance of infection. The nurse would be able to palpate (feel) the end of the port when placing a needle through the skin and into the port. Regina also explained that Katherine would be coming into the oncologist's office every other Monday for 6 months for a total of 12 rounds of chemotherapy. Katherine was scheduled for what the nurse called "slow chemotherapy infusions," and she went on to explain the schedule. On the first Monday, Katherine would come to the office and receive 1 liter of glucose fluid through her port access. This liter

© CaroleGomez/iStockphoto

of fluid would ensure that Katherine was well hydrated prior to receiving the chemotherapy medication. The nurse would disconnect the tubing from the liter of fluid and connect the tubing to the chemotherapy medication.

This technique will save Katherine from getting a needle inserted into her port access twice. The chemotherapy tubing is then connected to a small pump device (about the size of a deck of cards) that contains the chemotherapy medication. The pump delivers small doses of medication every few minutes for the next 48 hours. Katherine will return to the oncology office on Wednesday afternoon to be disconnected from the empty chemotherapy pump. On alternate Mondays, Katherine has a standing appointment for blood work to be drawn. This appointment will be fast and easy, because blood will be drawn from her port and thus does not involve any needle sticks in her arm. On the following Monday, if Katherine's lab results are within normal range, the chemotherapy pump will be reconnected, and the process will be repeated for 6 months. Before the patient education session concluded, Regina asked Katherine and Michael if they had any additional questions and talked a little about the side effects of chemotherapy. She explained that each individual reacts differently to the chemotherapy medications. Finally, Regina introduced them to Terri, the health navigation professional employed by Dr. Clark. Regina explained that Terri coordinates all aspects of patient care in the office. After Regina left, Terri went on to explain her role in the office. She told them that the phone number on her business card is her direct line. They will no longer have to navigate the phone tree when calling the main office number. Terri said that she is the first point of contact for all patients receiving chemotherapy at Dr. Clark's office. If she does not know the answer to Katherine's or Michael's questions, she will locate someone who has the correct answer. They can call her during regular business hours, but she might have to call them back after hours when she finds the answers to their questions. She calls herself "the stress buster" of the office. She wants every patient on chemotherapy to know that they do not have to go through the treatment with stress from unanswered questions. She can also arrange resources, such as health insurance options (e.g., in-network and out-of-network fees, co-payments), support groups, home health equipment rentals, meal delivery services, and safe and effective home remedies for the usual side effects of chemotherapy. Terri asked Katherine and Michael if they had any immediate questions; then, she handed them several of her business cards and reminded them to call her any time that they have a question.

Mental Health Services*
*Entry level for Health Navigation Professional with additional training

Education	Educational programs in mental health services lead to all levels of credentials. There are entry-level jobs that require a high school diploma and vocational certificates up to graduate and doctorate degrees. For example, mental health services technicians and psychiatric aides assist individuals with mental and/or behavioral disabilities. This position requires a high school diploma, and in some states additional training and licensure are needed. At the bachelor's level, mental health and substance abuse social workers complete training in the field and meet certification requirements. At the master's degree level, social workers have a bachelor's and master's degree in social work and complete an internship to become a license clinical social worker. Also at the master's level are counseling psychologists and mental health and substance abuse social workers serving specific populations, such as the elderly or adolescents. At the doctoral level, clinical psychologists serve as licensed practitioners in clinical settings or in private practice.
Work Duties	Mental health services professionals help individuals with psychological disorders to live functional lives by teaching them daily living skills and assisting them with social, recreational, educational, and occupational activities. Specific duties include assessing and diagnosing illnesses and developing and maintaining treatment plans. Mental health services occupations include mental health and substance abuse social workers, counseling psychologists, and psychiatric aides, who are also known as psychiatric assistants or technicians. Many graduates of mental health services programs work in hospitals or residential and rehabilitation facilities.
Work Alternative	Occupations that provide mental health services help individuals with mental or behavioral disabilities or illness to live a functional life. A wide variety of degree programs and career choices exist in this field, including clinical pastoral counseling, community health services, genetic counseling, marriage and family counseling, medical social work, mental health counseling, mental health services technician, psychotherapist, psychoanalysis, and substance abuse counseling.
Salary	As of 2013, the median salary for mental health workers was $44,420. The level of educational attainment determines increased salary.
Hours	The hours are usually 8-hour, 10-hour, or 12-hour shifts. Because many healthcare facilities are open 24 hours/7 days per week, mental health workers work all shifts and all days of the week.
Professional Organizations	Professional organizations vary by specialization.

Registered Nurse and Advanced Registered Nurse Practitioner

Education	A 4-year bachelor's degree program is the most common educational path for a registered nurse (BSN). Some community colleges offer 2-year associate degrees in nursing (AND). The 2-year associate degree limits where the graduates work, but they can enroll in a bridge program to obtain their 4-year BSN degree. A graduate degree is required for licensure as an Advanced Registered Nurse Practitioner (ARNP).
Work Duties	Most nurses work in hospitals, including specialty areas such as surgical areas, intensive care, burn unit, labor and delivery; and ambulatory care centers, outpatient clinics, and private physician offices. ARNPs may work independently depending on the state licensure requirements, while others work in collaboration with physicians.
Work Alternative	Nurses also work at universities and schools, employee wellness clinics, corporate settings, and worker's compensation clinics in manufacturing and industry.
Salary	In 2013, the average annual salary for BSN registered nurses was $68,910 and for an ARNP was $92,670.
Hours	The hours are usually 8-hour, 10-hour, or 12-hour shifts. Because many healthcare facilities are open 24 hours/7 days per week, nurses work all shifts and all days of the week.
Professional Organizations	American Nursing Association (www.nursingworld.org); National League of Nursing (www.nln.org.)

Body Movement and Therapies

1. Physical Therapy, Occupational Therapy, and Speech, Hearing, and Language Therapy

Education	Most fields of physical, occupational, or speech therapy require a graduate degree. However, physical therapy offers an associate degree for a physical therapy assistant that allows an individual to work in the field while continuing his or her education.
Work Duties	Most therapists work in hospitals and work directly with patients. Outpatient clinics, home healthcare agencies, and private practices employ therapists with graduate degrees in their field of expertise.
Work Alternative	Therapists also work within school districts, universities, employee wellness clinics, corporate settings, worker's compensation clinics, long-term care facilities, geriatric facilities, and wound-care clinics.
Salary	In 2012, the median annual physical therapy assistant salary was about $53,000. The average salary for a physical therapist was $64,958 per year.[6] The average salary for a speech therapist was $53,498 per year[7] and for an occupational therapist was $75,400.[7]
Hours	The hours are usually 8-hour, 10-hour, or 12-hour shifts. Because many healthcare facilities are open 24 hours/7days per week, therapists work day/evening shifts and 7 days a week.
Professional Organizations	American Physical Therapy Association (www.apta.org); American Speech, Hearing, and Language Association (www.asha.org/default.htm); American Occupational Therapy Association (www.aota.org.)

2. Kinesiology and Exercise Science Professionals

Education	Exercise science and kinesiology are closely related fields and are used interchangeably with one another. Required education ranges from associate's to doctoral degrees. Kinesiology and exercise science professionals study the basics of mechanics and anatomy related to the movement of the body.
Work Duties	Most individuals in this field focus on injury prevention, nutrition, sports psychology, athletic training or motor skills in schools, universities, sports facilities, and fitness centers. Graduate-level degrees offer professionals the ability to conduct research and develop policies related to injury prevention.
Work Alternative	Other types of employment include personal trainers and involvement with all ages of sporting activities, ranging from little league to the Olympics.
Salary	In 2013, the median annual income was $43,180 for a professional in kinesiology and exercise science.
Hours	40 hours per week; some evenings and weekends.

Professional Organizations	Association for the Advancement of Applied Sport Psychology (AAASP) (www.appliedsportpsych.org); American Kinesiology Association (www.americankinesiology.org); National Collegiate Athletic Association (www.ncaa.org); National Academy of Sports Medicine (www.nasm.org); United States Olympic Committee (https://teamusa.org.)

3. Massage Therapy

Education	Many states require formal training and licensure to work as a massage therapist.
Work Duties	Massage therapists manipulate the soft-tissue muscles throughout the body to reduce stress, improve circulation, treat injuries, and promote general health in a patient. Most massage therapists work part-time are self-employed, and work by appointment. Some massage therapists work for franchised locations that offer various types of massages and facial services.
Work Alternative	Some massage therapists are employed full-time and work in settings such as sports and fitness centers, hospitals, and nursing homes.
Salary	Massage therapists earn a median annual salary of $40,400; however, the massage therapists that are employed in healthcare facilities earn up to an annual salary of $55,700.
Hours	Because the work of a massage therapist is physically demanding, most massage therapists do not work more than 40 hours per week.
Professional Organizations	National Certification Examination for Therapeutic Massage and Bodywork (NCETMB) or the Bodywork Licensing Examination (MBLEx) offer certification for massage therapists. State licensing boards decide which certifications and examinations to accept.

Physician's Assistant (PA)

Education	Physician assistant (PA) programs are available at the associate's, bachelor's, and master's degree levels, but a master's degree program is the most common path for mandatory physician assistant licensure.
Work	Most PAs work in hospitals, outpatient clinics, or in group or private physician offices. States grant the PA license and regulate their scope of practice, which varies across states.
Work Alternative	PAs work within school districts, universities, and employee wellness clinics.
Salary	In 2012, the median salary for a physician assistant was $90,930.[8]
Hours	The hours are usually 8-hour, 10-hour, or 12-hour shifts. Because many healthcare facilities are open 24 hours/ 7 days per week, PAs work all shifts and any day of the week depending on their place of employment.
Professional Organizations	American Academy of Physician's Assistants (www.aapa.org.)

Pharmacist

Education	Becoming a pharmacist requires a 4-year bachelor's degree with a strong science background and admission into a college of pharmacy for another 4 years after the bachelor's degree. Upon graduation from pharmacy school, the individual is eligible to sit for the pharmacy license exam. After receiving a medical license, the individual may work as a pharmacist or select a pharmacy specialty for his or her residency. Depending on the area of specialty, the residency ranges from 2 to 5 years. Beyond residency training, physicians complete a 1- or 2-year fellowship to specialize further in their selected area of interest. For example, a radiologist wishes to further his or her training by specializing in oncology (cancer) radiology. Therefore, it is possible to have 12–15 years of education after completing high school.
Work	Physicians are generally employed in the healthcare system.
Work Alternative	Physicians also work in healthcare administration, law offices, political arenas, universities, and research institutions.

Salary	Salaries range from $175,000 to more than $1 million annually, depending on the specialty and geographic location.
Hours	The hours are usually 8-hour, 10-hour, or 12-hour shifts. Because many healthcare facilities are open 24 hours/7 days per week, nurses work all shifts and all days of the week.
Professional Organizations	The American Medical Association (ama-assn.org) is the primary medical organization, but there are national associations for all of the medical specialties.

Physician

Education	Becoming a physician is a long, intense educational process. The first step is a 4-year bachelor's degree with a strong science background. Admission into a college of medicine is extremely competitive and expensive. Medical school is 4 years after the bachelor's degree. Upon graduation from medical school, the individual is eligible to sit for the medical license exam. After receiving a medical license, individuals select a medical specialty for their residency. Depending on the area of specialty, the residency ranges from 3 years to 5 years. For example, family practice is a 3-year residency, while radiology is a 5-year residency. Beyond residency training, physicians complete a 1- or 2-year fellowship to specialize further in their selected area of interest. For example, a radiologist wishes to further his or her training by specializing in oncology (cancer) radiology. Therefore, it is possible to have 12–15 years of education after completing high school.
Work	Physicians are generally employed in the healthcare system.
Work Alternative	Physicians also work in healthcare administration, law offices, political arenas, universities, and research institutions.
Salary	Salaries range from $175,000 to more than $1 million annually, depending on the specialty and geographic location.
Hours	The hours are usually 8-hour, 10-hour, or 12-hour shifts. Because many healthcare facilities are open 24 hours/7 days per week, nurses work all shifts and all days of the week.
Professional Organizations	The American Medical Association (ama-assn.org) is the primary medical organization, but there are national associations for all of the medical specialties.

© Jim Barber/Shutterstock

Summary

In summary, this chapter provided a detailed description of numerous types of healthcare personnel. The healthcare professions were divided into two major categories: no or limited patient contact and direct patient contact. For each health profession, the chapter described the educational requirements, location of employment, and a description of the primary duties, annual salary, and professional organizations. The case study explained the interactions between the team members, the patient, and the family.

Student Activity

It is your turn to create the end of the story. Write a minimum of 1000 words describing the final chapter of Katherine's cancer chemotherapy. Using the established healthcare personnel, describe their continued role in caring for Katherine and supporting Michael.

References

1. Simply Salary. *Average health care navigator salaries.* Retrieved January 31, 2016, from http://www.simplyhired.com/salaries-k-health-care-navigator-jobs.html.
2. Careersinpublichealth.net. *Patient navigator careers.* Retrieved December 18, 2014, from http://www.careersinpublichealth.net/careers/patient-navigator.
3. Pay Scale. *Optical laboratory technician salary.* Retrieved December 18, 2014, from http://www.payscale.com/research/US/Job=Optical_Laboratory_Technician/Hourly_Rate.
4. Salary.com. *Clinical ethicists salaries.* Retrieved December 18, 2014, from http://www1.salary.com/Clinical-Ethicist-salary.html.
5. National Cancer Institute. *Cancer staging.* Retrieved December 18, 2014, from http://www.cancer.gov/cancertopics/factsheet/Detection/staging; last updated May 3, 2013.
6. Pay Scale. *Physical therapist salary.* Retrieved December 18, 2014, from http://www.payscale.com/research/US/Job=Physical_Therapist_%28PT%29/Salary.
7. Pay Scale. Speech therapist salary. Retrieved December 18, 2014, from http://www.payscale.com/research/US/Job=Speech_Therapist/Salary.
8. *U.S. News & World Report. Physician assistant: Salary.* Retrieved December 19, 2014, from http://money.usnews.com/careers/best-jobs/physician-assistant/salary.

PART 1

Prevention and Community Health

CHAPTER 2

Preventive Health Care through the Life Span

LEARNING OBJECTIVES

By the end of this chapter, students will be able to:

- Define and describe the role of health navigation professional in the healthcare system
- Differentiate among the different levels of preventive care
- Explain the difference between observable and calculated risks

CHAPTER OVERVIEW

This chapter begins by introducing the concept of health navigation professionals and their role in the complex healthcare system. Building on this knowledge, the discussion moves into a description of levels of prevention, including primary, secondary, and tertiary care across the life span. Finally, the chapter explores the concepts of risk, risk assessment, and evidence-based recommendations.

HEALTH NAVIGATION PROFESSIONALS

The profession of health navigation began in 1990, when Dr. Harold Freeman developed the first patient navigation program in Harlem, New York, to reduce health disparities related to cancer diagnosis and treatment among poor and uninsured individuals.[1] Dr. Freeman identified healthcare barriers facing the community as financial (e.g.,

no health insurance, low income); communication and information (e.g., English as a second language, low literacy skills); healthcare system issues (e.g., missed appointments, lost results); and fear, distrust, and emotional barriers.[1] See **Box 2.1**.

Since 1990, several government-funded programs have been developed to study the effect and value of health navigation. During this period, several attempts were made to develop a patient's bill of rights. A patient's bill of rights was considered by the US Congress in 2001 as a list of guarantees for those receiving medical care, including having their medical decisions made by a doctor; seeing a medical specialist; going go to the closest emergency room; and receiving information, fair treatment, and autonomy over medical decisions. In 2001, the bill (Bill S.1052) was passed by the Senate in a vote of 59–36; it was then amended by the House of Representatives and returned to the Senate, where it ultimately failed to pass.

In 2005, President George W. Bush signed the Patient Navigator and Chronic Disease Prevention Act, which provided additional funding for research on the effectiveness of health navigation professionals. The evidence shows that patient navigation can increase participation in cancer screening;[2] can reduce the time from abnormal finding to point of cancer diagnosis;[2, 3] and the modest cost of health navigation offsets the

BOX 2.1   Role of the Health Navigation Professionals

© gradyreese/iStockphoto

As the newest career in the field of public health, health navigation professionals play an important role in assisting individuals and their caregivers through a complex healthcare maze. Health navigation professionals may be employed by a hospital, a community clinic, a private practice group of healthcare providers, or work as self-employed consultants. Regardless of the place of employment, health navigation professionals assist individuals to enhance their quality of life by increasing the understanding of their medical condition, including medications, lab tests, and treatment procedures. Although health navigation professionals do not provide direct services, they assist with the coordination of care, such as arranging home health, medical appointments, and transportation; they also answer questions related to filing health insurance forms and paying health bills. Most importantly, health navigation professionals serve as the communication liaison between healthcare providers and individuals and their caregivers.

savings due to the high cost of advanced cancer treatment.[1] In 2012, the American College of Surgeons required that cancer programs have a patient navigation process for all patients. Most recently, patient navigation was included in the Affordable Care Act as well as the intention to fund patient navigation professionals under Medicaid.[1] It is noted that the term "patient navigation" has evolved into the broader and more inclusive term of "health navigation professional." Throughout this text, the inclusive term of "health navigation professional" is used. See **Box 2.2**.

The health navigation profession has been defined by the Patient Advocate Certification Board (PACB), which has written ethical standards, including the following topics: the role of an advocate, transparency and honesty disclosure, protection of confidentiality and privacy, fostering autonomy, provision of competent services, avoidance of impropriety and conflict of interest,

avoidance of discriminatory practices, and continuing education and professional development.[4] This organization has incorporated and plans to develop a certification exam in the future.[5] Take the time to explore the PACB website (http://pacboard.org).

With this historical information in mind, let's explore two examples of how health navigation professionals improve lives in various situations. A navigator is defined as an individual who provides directions for others. Whether the navigator is steering a boat, assisting a customer in a grocery store, or guiding an individual through the healthcare system, each situation requires specific knowledge and skill to perform their assigned duties. Without a skillful navigator, the individuals are likely to get lost. The case studies in **Box 2.3** illustrate a few of the many possible roles for health navigator professionals, including community clinics, disease-specific organizations (e.g., American Cancer Society, American Heart

BOX 2.2 Principles of Health Navigation Professionals

1. Promote a timely movement of an individual through the complex healthcare system.
2. Eliminate barriers to timely care in all phases of the healthcare system.
3. Work to integrate all aspects of the healthcare system.
4. Define the navigator's scope of work from other healthcare providers.
5. Deliver navigation services at a cost-effective price that is comparable with skill and training.
6. Determine the most appropriate level of skill required for navigation.
7. Define the points at which navigation begins and ends.
8. Connect segmented healthcare systems for continuum of care.
9. Coordinate who is responsible for overseeing all phases of navigation through the healthcare system.

Data from: Freeman H.P. (2013). The history, principles, and future of patient navigation: Commentary. *Seminars in Oncology Nursing,* 29(2), 72–75.[1]

Association, March of Dimes, National Kidney Foundation), and hospitals and other residential facilities (e.g., assisted-living facilities, rehabilitation centers, memory care centers).

As a health navigation professional, you will be assisting individuals searching for resources, information, and answers to their specific questions. The first steps of the investigative process

BOX 2.3 Examples of Health Navigation Professional Roles

Case Study One: Memorial Hospital employs eight health navigation professionals to assist patients and family members with questions prior to discharge. Each day, the health navigation professional receives a list of patients who are scheduled for discharge within 1 or 2 days. Each patient is visited and given the opportunity to ask any questions related to their upcoming discharge. The health navigation professional writes down the questions; investigates the answers, resources, or services; writes a summary note in the patient medical record to alert the rest of the healthcare team regarding the questions; and goes back to the patient with updates on the progress. The role of the health navigation professional is not to offer health or medical advice or information, but rather to offer guidance and assistance.

Case Study Two: The county health department primary care clinic employs six health navigation professionals to serve the needs of their patients and family members. During each clinic, two health navigation professionals are stationed at a desk in the waiting room to assist patients with intake information such as forms, health insurance, co-payments, and language barriers. Two navigators are stationed in the clinic exam room hallway. This allows the healthcare providers to have a health navigation professional step into the exam room as needed to hear the patient's questions regarding the follow-up appointments, medication changes, treatment schedules, and health education questions. After the patient exits the exam room, the health navigation professional invites the individual to step into a nearby private cubicle to discuss, explain, and answer their questions and the questions that their family or friend may have. The last two health navigation professionals are stationed at the check-in desk to assist patients with scheduling convenient times for follow-up appointments, treatments, lab work, and answering questions such as directions, bus routes to the treatment clinic, and ways to get discounts on prescription medications. Each day, the health navigation professionals rotate to stay current on all aspects of the clinic services.

Case Study Three: ABC Company employs about 800 individuals in a variety of job levels ranging from factory workers to administrators. Due to the large number of young workers with limited experience, ABC Company decided that the young workers would benefit from the services of a health navigation professional to assist the personnel office because the young workers have many questions about their benefits, including health insurance options. The health navigation professional is available 3 days per week to answer questions related to health insurance, such as definitions of terms (e.g., co-payment, deductibles, out-of-pocket expenses, and reimbursement), flexible spending, PPO versus HMO, and many more. On the other 2 days, the health navigation professional provides compliance training, lunch health topic seminars, and various other duties.

are similar. When individuals have a question, they use the available tools (e.g., signage, websites, phone calls, insurance policies) to attempt to solve the problem. If the tools do not solve the problem, the individual asks questions (e.g., phone operator, store clerk, neighbor, friends, family members, or complete strangers) to resolve the problem. The same is true in health care. If individuals have a simple medical concern or symptom, they may ask a friend or family member for an opinion. As individuals gain opinions, they begin to explore other information sources (e.g., websites, books, pamphlets) to increase their knowledge. If the symptoms persist or worsen, they seek health care. At this point, the services of a health navigation professional become useful.

Upon entry into the healthcare system, the individual receives care but may also leave with additional questions regarding the treatment plan and follow-up appointments. For complex health conditions, if these escalating questions become more and more confusing, the individual may lack understanding to the point of frustration and withdraw from further testing or treatment. This action begins a downward cycle of disease progression. When a health navigation professional is employed to intervene at the first appointment, the medical condition is less likely to escalate into a serious condition due to lack of adequate communication. Health navigation professionals provide the opportunity for individuals to receive understandable medical information, ask multiple questions on all aspects of the medical condition, and assist with navigating the healthcare system with a partner—the health navigation professional. This process reduces the barriers to receive treatment, decreases the fear, and improves communication for better outcomes. Research has shown that health navigation services contribute to beneficial outcomes across the cancer care continuum.[6]

LEVELS OF PREVENTIVE CARE

The goal of preventive care is to avoid an illness from ever happening. When an illness does occur, the goal becomes to prevent those circumstances from getting worse. In the following discussion, the topics of primary, secondary, and tertiary prevention are introduced. The activities performed at each stage are attempts to keep the illness or injury from becoming more severe. For example, if individuals do not rest and treat their flu symptoms, the virus will increase in severity until a hospitalization may be required. As you will learn in this section, the activity at each level of prevention is performed to prevent progression to a higher level of severity. Primary prevention is deterrence of illness or disease before it occurs. Secondary prevention relates to screening for risk factors and early intervention or treatment of the disease. Finally, tertiary prevention centers on treatment to control severe symptoms and prevent further complications of disease and rehabilitation. In summary, the easiest way to remember the three levels of prevention are prevention, treatment, and rehabilitation.[7] See **Figure 2.1** and **Figure 2.2**.

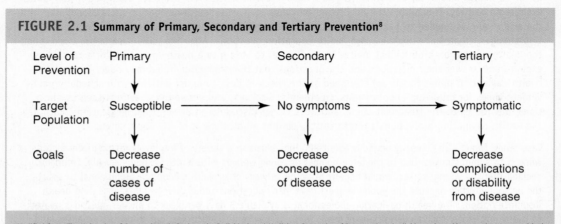

FIGURE 2.1 **Summary of Primary, Secondary and Tertiary Prevention[8]**

Level of Prevention	Primary	Secondary	Tertiary
Target Population	Susceptible →	No symptoms →	Symptomatic
Goals	Decrease number of cases of disease	Decrease consequences of disease	Decrease complications or disability from disease

FIGURE 2.2 Cumulative Lives Saved by Seatbelts[9]

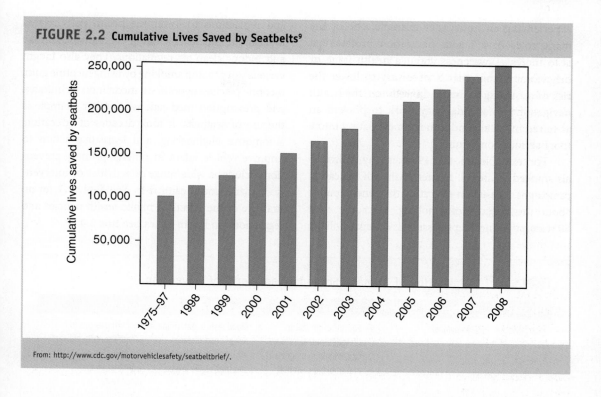

From: http://www.cdc.gov/motorvehiclesafety/seatbeltbrief/.

Now let's delve into a more detailed description of the three levels of prevention. When possible, it is easier to prevent illness from occurring than to treat the illness. It is also easier to treat the illness than to provide rehabilitation from advanced morbidity. Ideally, the entire healthcare system would benefit by focusing more attention on prevention. However, the responsibility is not solely on the healthcare system to keep individuals healthy. Prior to becoming patients, individuals must take personal responsibility for making positive lifestyle and behavior choices if they wish to maintain optimal health to the best of their ability. Throughout the healthcare system, all team members, including health navigation professionals, find opportunities to work in all levels of preventive care and with all types of individuals, as illustrated in the next section.

Primary Prevention

The simplest way to remember primary prevention is to visualize a river.

At the base of the river, many healthcare providers are pulling sick and injured individuals

© Aliaksandr Nikitsin/iStockphoto

from the river and treating them one at a time. As more and more individuals come down the river in need of treatment, the healthcare providers get overwhelmed with so many sick and injured individuals. Soon, a few individuals walk upstream to determine why so many individuals are falling into the river. These people are public health professionals who study primary prevention. Their goal is to protect healthy individuals and communities from acquiring a disease or experiencing an injury. For example, one of the many roles of a health navigation professional is to increase awareness about a health issue or behavioral change that is necessary to lower the risk of acquiring a disease. In addition, the health navigation professional may work to prevent an acquired medical condition from escalating into a more serious condition.

For example, in the 1960s, many individuals smoked cigarettes. Numerous health education campaigns focused on educating the general public about the hazards of smoking. Over the next 50 years, public health professionals changed policies

and regulations to lower the health risks related to cigarette smoke, including secondhand smoke and indoor clean air regulations. They also taught various ways to stop smoking by using nicotine gum, nicotine patches, hypothesis, meditation techniques, and prescription medications. Another example is the use of seatbelts. It took decades of education, automotive engineering, and legislative action to improve vehicle safety. In general, primary prevention includes a wide range of activities or interventions that reduce health risks. See **Table 2.1** for an example of the effects of public health policies and regulations on health issues. See **Box 2.4**.

TABLE 2.1 Application of Primary, Secondary and Tertiary Prevention

Disease	Intervention level	Primary	Secondary	Tertiary
Heart disease	Individual	Education on healthy lifestyles: nutrition, exercise, weight management and smoking cessation	Blood tests to determine risk of heart disease including cholesterol and triglyceride levels	Follow-up exams to identify severity of heart disease: physical examination and blood tests
	Population	Public service announcement related to prevention of heart disease: nutrition, exercise, weight management and smoking cessation	Organized heart healthy screening programs	Implementation of health care services to improve access to quality care
Infectious diseases: hepatitis C	Individual	Counseling on safe drug use to prevent hepatitis C virus (HCV) transmission; counseling on safer sex	Screening for HCV infection of patients with a history of injection drug use	HCV therapy to cure infection and prevent transmission
	Population	HCV prevention includes safer sex practices, programs to discourage needle sharing among intravenous drug users, etc.	Establish a universal testing system for HCV in high risk groups	(Similar to primary prevention): ensuring close control of high risk sites such as tattoo parlors that have been associated with outbreaks
Type II Diabetes	Individual	Education about appropriate diet and exercise	Free or low-cost diabetes screening	Referral to specialized endocrinology clinics
	Population	Build positive healthy lifestyle environment (walking and biking paths, clean air quality control)	Neighborhood recreation centers to promote healthy lifestyle for families	One-stop clinics for comprehensive care services

Data from The Association of Faculties of Medicine of Canada (2015). AFMC Primer on Population Health. Chapter 4: Basic Concepts in Prevention, Surveillance, and Public Health. Accessed on January 1, 2015.

BOX 2.4 Primary Prevention

What Is Primary Prevention?

Access to ongoing health care, wellness programs, immunizations, mental health services, and dental and eye examinations

Availability of long-term knowledge, support, and skills needed to make positive behavioral changes

Incorporation of positive environmental changes that promote health and wellness in communities (e.g., sidewalks, bike paths, playgrounds, community gardens, and improved outdoor air quality)

What Is Not Primary Prevention?

One-time health fairs with limited follow-up for healthcare services

Health classes filled with knowledge but not linked to skills and support

Changes are linked to high-income neighborhoods rather than improving the quality of the entire community

Primary prevention lowers health risk by changing behaviors, products, or the environment. When risk reduction is built into a product design, consumer behavior is altered with minimal behavior change from the individual. For example, because all new cars are equipped with side airbags, consumers gain additional driving safety without altering their driving habits. This type of protection is easily remembered by thinking about the Three E's.

Education

Health education increases awareness about health and wellness. For example, public service announcements and billboards increase awareness about healthy eating, regular exercise, sunscreen protection, breast feeding, oral health care, and smoking cessation. Community classes are offered on a variety of health and wellness topics. Healthcare providers advise individuals to seek regular wellness exams, participate in screening tests, and receive recommended immunizations. Product warning labels educate about pesticide and hazardous chemical exposure as well as safety precautions when operating equipment.

Keep in mind that knowledge does not equate to behavior change. For instance, if an individual attends a weight reduction seminar or joins a weight loss program, this does not necessarily suggest the individual will lose weight. Behavior change is a complex process that occurs over time and involves numerous steps. For example, individuals can describe the health benefits associated with regular exercise, but that knowledge is not necessarily linked to their personal behavior. When healthcare providers advise individuals to lose weight to lower their cardiac health risks, it does not automatically render lifestyle changes in diet and exercise. Many other factors, such as age, gender, health risks, culture, faith-based beliefs, socioeconomics, education, workplace, and living conditions influence how, when, and why individuals may or may not choose to change their health behaviors. Behavior change is never as simple as teaching an individual about the advantages of healthy behaviors and expecting a sustainable change. Remember this concept by thinking about your own health. How many times have you tried and failed to lose the same 10 pounds? How many times have you tried and failed to exercise 3 times per week over the course of 6 months? It is no different for individuals who are in need of changing their behavior to improve their health. The important message is to keep trying until the behavior change becomes a daily lifestyle routine instead of a daily task.

Engineering

The design of products and equipment is instrumental in improving safety and reducing injury, disability, and death. For example, automobile safety has improved greatly over the last 40 years due to the engineering design of seatbelts, airbags, bumper construction, type of tires, dashboard back-up monitors, steering wheel controls, adjustable head rests, padded dashboards, and child car seats. Engineers have also redesigned workplace environments to reduce repetitive motions that wear out joints and cause back injuries. The redesign of toys and sports equipment has shown a reduction of injuries in children as well as in professional sports. Finally, our homes are safer due to the engineering of bathroom safety bars, child safety gates, stove burner knobs placed along the back of the stove instead of the front, smoke alarms, and safety caps on household cleaning products and medication bottles. Without the involvement of engineering, the educational component is not effective. If the safer product is not available, there is no point in increasing awareness about the need to reduce potential injuries.

Enforcement

National, state, and local regulations and laws change to enforce adherence to new safety policies for the good of individuals or entire communities. Some such regulations are controversial. Mandatory motorcycle helmet use is an example. Some individuals feel that this law should be mandatory, while others feel that such a law is an infringement on personal rights. Other new laws, such as "no texting while driving," have more support among the general driving population and are based on new technology. In addition, there are numerous federal agencies created for the primary purpose of safety regulation. The Occupational Safety and Health Association (OSHA) oversees all aspects of employee and workplace safety regulations. The Food and Drug Administration (FDA) regulates and inspects food and drug safety from product development to consumer consumption. The Environmental Protection Agency (EPA) inspects and regulates all environment hazards and safety measures inside and outside.

SECONDARY PREVENTION

Secondary prevention can occur after the disease or injury occurs, but before an individual may be aware that anything is wrong. The goal of secondary prevention is discovering and treating a disease or injury. The intervention used for secondary prevention is to stop or slow the progress of illness in the earliest stages of the disease or to limit a long-term disability in the case of an injury.[10]

Secondary prevention also includes medical tests and screening procedures to detect and treat pre-clinical pathological changes. For example, a colonoscopy is a screening procedure to detect colon cancer and is often the first step in early intervention procedures that are cost-effective and life-saving before waiting until symptoms appear. Another example of secondary prevention is a routine fasting blood test for individuals over the age of 40 to detect Type 2 diabetes at an early stage.

For some diseases, such as skin cancer, there is a clear distinction between primary and secondary prevention. For example, sunscreen is used to avoid skin cancer from ever developing. Sunscreen and regular skin cancer screening is recommended for individuals with known skin cancer risk factors (for example, being very pale). However, the lines between primary and secondary intervention are less clear in musculoskeletal disorders, such as back pain. Because back injuries are difficult to prevent, the major focus for primary prevention of back pain is through using correct body alignment when lifting heavy objects. After a back injury occurs, secondary prevention focuses on muscle strengthening exercises to prevention further injury and pain.[10] See **Box 2.5** to practice your skills.

TERTIARY PREVENTION

Tertiary prevention is directed at individuals with noticeable symptoms of the disease or injury. The goal is to prevent further damage or injury,

BOX 2.5 Practice Skills

Answer the following questions about primary and secondary prevention.

Mr. Smith is a former smoker who was diagnosed with hypertension and chronic obstructive pulmonary disease (COPD). His healthcare provider gave him a prescription for an inhaler to improve his breathing function. A primary prevention need for Mr. Smith is:

a. Having the health navigation professional review the side effects of his medications
b. Scheduling a spirometer (breathing function test) measurement
c. Receiving an annual influenza immunization

Mrs. Williams is an obese 65-year-old woman with diabetes. She works full-time as an administrative assistant in an elementary school. A secondary prevention for Mrs. Williams is:

a. Obtaining a routine mammogram
b. Receiving an annual influenza immunization
c. Attending a diabetic cooking class

Answers: C—Receiving an influenza immunization is primary prevention
A—Obtaining a routine mammogram is secondary prevention

reduce pain, slow the progression of the disease or injury, prevent the disease or injury from causing further complications, and rehabilitate as much as possible to improve quality of life. A health navigation professional may assist with navigation services, communication, understanding, and resources at any point along the continuum of level of preventive care. For example, when an individual experiences a myocardial infarction (heart attack), tertiary prevention provides immediate acute clinical treatment to reduce the risk of additional heart muscle damage. After the individual is stable, then rehabilitation begins to alter the individual's lifestyle to improve bodily function, longevity, and quality of life. Rehabilitation may include weight loss and improved nutrition, smoking cessation, muscle strengthening exercise, aerobic activity, and the initiation of other positive health behaviors. Overall, the key of tertiary prevention is to improve the quality of life.[10]

Tertiary care also includes stopping or delaying the progression of an established disease or learning to control the pending consequences. Here are two examples. First, if an individual is diagnosed with an autoimmune disease such as

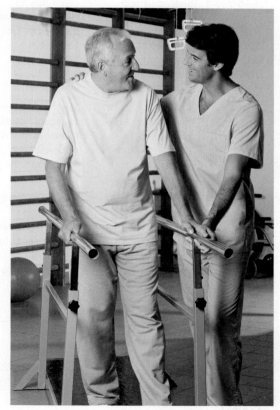
© Tyler Olson/Shutterstock

rheumatoid arthritis, it is important to achieve and maintain a healthy weight. Excess weight strains muscles, joints, and ligaments and reduces mobility and quality of life. Generally, tertiary care is focused on minimizing the consequences of the disease or injury.[8] Second, an individual with long-term Type 2 diabetes may have decreased blood flow to a lower extremity, such as a toe or foot. When blood flow is decreased, vascular and tissue damage occurs. Amputation is needed when the damaged tissue is severe. After the individual recovers from the surgical amputation, rehabilitation focuses on balance, mobility, and quality of life using a prosthetic lower extremity.

Tertiary prevention treatment involves supporting individuals in their current health status, improving their quality of life, and reducing any further deterioration caused by their noncommunicable disease or injury status. See **Box 2.6**.

RISKS AND RISK ASSESSMENT

Now that you understand the three levels of prevention, we will now explore the concept of risk assessment. In other words, how likely is it that an individual will acquire a specific disease in the future? The simple definition of risk is a situation involving exposure to danger. There are two types of risks: observable and calculated.

BOX 2.6 Practice Skills

	Individual	Family and Friends	Community	Society
Health Condition: Type 2 Diabetes Caused by Obesity	Individualized education about connection between obesity and chronic health conditions	Learn how to support positive dietary changes to achieve a healthy weight among family and friends	Public service announcements to inform citizens about negative health consequences of obesity	Promote healthy weight by building walking and biking paths in the community
	Quarterly hemoglobin A1C blood tests to determine blood glucose levels over time	Seek health care to request baseline to determine risk of developing diabetes in the future	Organize a health fair to encourage individuals to get screened for diabetes with a fasting glucose blood test	Improve access to quality, low-cost health care in the community
	Referral to an endocrinology healthcare provider to regulate insulin dosage	Encourage family members to attend healthcare appointments to learn how to offer support to individual with diabetes	Form partnerships with community healthcare providers to offer diabetic supplies to low-income individuals for free or reduced cost at local health department clinics	Solicit legislative action to improve healthcare coverage for all individuals

Health Condition Selected:

Health Condition Selected:

Observable risk is verifiable. For instance, the meteorologist reports that there is a 70 percent chance of rain tomorrow. Because rain causes slippery roads, you are increasing your chances of getting into a vehicle crash if you drive while it is raining. This activity would expose you to an observable risk. Each individual chooses the risks that he or she is willing or not willing to accept. Risks may include driving without a seatbelt, riding a bike without wearing a helmet, driving and texting, skydiving, drinking alcohol and driving, and many more risky behaviors. In terms of health risk assessment, there are numerous observable risks. Here are a few examples of reducing the risk of acquiring a disease: (a) frequently washing your hands; (b) maintaining an ideal weight; (c) obtaining an annual flu vaccine; (d) exercising daily; (e) obtaining recommended age-appropriate preventive screening tests; (f) eating healthy foods; and (g) incorporating other positive health choices into your lifestyle.

As a health navigation professional, it is useful to understand the probability of observable health risks. Here are three different examples explaining the concept of observable risks in making decisions about healthcare treatment options:

1. Based on years of observable research outcomes, the surgeon tells Mary that there is a 50 percent observable risk that the surgery *will not* improve her medical condition. In other words, there is a 50 percent observable risk that the surgery *will* improve her medical condition. Should Mary have the surgical procedure?
2. Based on years of observable research outcomes, the surgeon tells Harold that he has a 30 percent chance of living and a 70 percent chance of dying (observable risk) in the next 6 months unless he has the recommended surgery. Should Harold have the surgical procedure?
3. Based on years of observable research outcomes, Barbara is told by her oncologist (cancer specialist physician) that, for her type of cancer, the only chemotherapy treatment available offers her an

observable risk of a 60 percent chance of living (40% chance of not living) another 5 years. Should she receive the chemotherapy treatment? See **Box 2.7**.

Second, calculated risks are not observed, but, as the term implies, they are calculated with a mathematical formula. For example, you have a calculated risk of getting hit with a piece of space debris falling from a spacecraft. Even though this event has never happened, there is a calculated risk that it might happen at some point in the future, even though the event is highly unlikely. Another example is discussed on news broadcasts when a state lottery is approaching an excessive dollar amount. The news reporter states that individuals have a greater chance of getting struck by lightning than winning the multimillion-dollar lottery. The "chance" that the reporter is describing is a calculated risk. Yes, individuals do get struck by lightning and individuals do win multimillion-dollar lotteries; however, the calculated risk of either event actually happening is extremely low, given the millions of lottery tickets sold for one prizewinner.

Now, let us think about calculated risks from a health standpoint. For example, parents are caring for their child with the flu. If the parents *are not* frequently washing their hands, they are greatly increasing their calculated risk of acquiring the flu virus. Because each individual's immune system is different, it is impossible to observe (predict) with absolute certainty how each individual reacts to exposure of a specific virus, bacteria, or medical condition; therefore, it is a calculated risk. For example, Susan is given the opportunity to participate in a clinical research trial using a new chemotherapy drug. Her risks are calculated (not observed) because only a few individuals have ever received this chemotherapy drug for her type of cancer. Susan would prefer to hear from her physician that there is a 90 percent calculated risk cure rate rather than learning that there is only a 10 percent calculated risk cure rate.

In addition, the calculated risks of acquiring most diseases are not based on a single risk factor. In other words, a list of possible risk factors

BOX 2.7 Asking Health Risk Questions

As a health navigation professional, you may be asked to accompany individuals to their healthcare appointments. Generally, when individuals learn of a serious health condition, they need to make important decisions. Often, individuals are unable to formulate useful questions to ask on the spot. Possible sample questions that the health navigation professional might ask the healthcare provider for Mary, Harold, and Barbara follow. Because they need more information to make their decisions, you are asked to write two more sample questions that would also be useful to ask.

Mary:

Sample Question One: Are there other nonsurgical procedures, such as physical therapy, that might decrease the symptoms, because the surgery may or may not be successful?

Sample Question Two:

Sample Question Three:

Harold:

Sample Question One: If Harold does not have the recommended surgery immediately, when the medical condition becomes more serious over time, will the surgery remain an option?

Sample Question Two:

Sample Question Three:

Barbara:

Sample question: How fast does this type of cancer progress if Barbara chooses to delay starting the chemotherapy treatment for a few months?

Sample Question Two:

Sample Question Three:

increases the chances of acquiring a disease. For example, if an individual smokes two packs of cigarettes each day for 40 years and lives in a city with a high level of industrial air pollution, the risk of developing lung cancer is higher than for an individual who never smoked. For most diseases, there are multiple risk factors. Even though an individual may have every risk factor, there is no absolute certainty that the individual will develop the disease. On the other hand, an

BOX 2.8 Risk Factors for Developing Multiple Sclerosis (MS)

Variable	Risk Factor
Age	Most common between ages 15 and 60, but can occur at any age
Gender	Women are about twice as likely as men
Family History	Higher risk if a parent or sibling has had MS
Race/Ethnicity	White individuals are at highest risk of developing MS
Climate	MS is more common in cooler climates, such as southern Canada, northern United States, New Zealand, southeastern Australia, and Europe

Data from the Mayo Clinic (2014). Multiple Sclerosis: Risk Factors. Available at: http://www.mayoclinic.org/diseases-conditions/multiple -sclerosis/basics/risk-factors/con-20026689. Accessed on December 18, 2014. Last Updated on July 10, 2014.[11]

individual may have no risk factors and still develop the disease. See **Box 2.8.**

Controllable and Non-Controllable Health Risks

Now that you have a basic understanding of risks and risk assessments, we will explore health risks that are controllable and non-controllable. First, we investigate a few controllable health risks. Smoking cigarettes is controllable. An individual has a choice whether to smoke or not. If and when the individual wishes to stop smoking, there are many options (nicotine gum, patches, prescription medications, support groups, health education websites) available to assist with smoking cessation. Bike helmet use is another controllable risk. Individuals choose whether or not to wear a bike helmet when riding their bike. Not all examples are as easy to label as controllable risk.

Excessive weight gain is an example. The cause of obesity is complex and involves physical, social, medical, emotional, economic, and environmental issues. See **Table 2.2.**

The risk of heart disease is minimized by lifestyle choices that are controllable. Because cardiovascular disease has controllable and non-controllable factors, the discussion begins with the controllable side. As previously stated, there are multiple risk factors that increase or decrease an individual's risk of developing cardiovascular disease. It is important to know the key factors that are controllable to lower the risk of heart disease. See **Table 2.3.**

Now, we will explore health risks that are not controllable, such as genetic risks. Individuals do not have control over their genetic risks. However, if individuals have a strong family history of cardiovascular disease, they can modify their

TABLE 2.2 Causes or Consequences of Obesity

Variable	Causes or Consequences
Physical	Lack of physical activity; injury; decreased mobility
Social	Social stigma; isolation
Medical	Body systems: cardiovascular, endocrine, kidney, muscular-skeleton
Emotional	Depression; unforeseen life circumstances
Economic	Unemployment; discrimination
Environmental	Need for sturdy furniture, ramps, and slanted curbs for scooters and wheelchairs

TABLE 2.3 Controllable Risk Factors to Reduce Cardiovascular Disease

Controllable Risk Factors	Link to Cardiovascular Disease
Smoking	Smoking increases damage to cardiovascular system
Blood Pressure	Keeping blood pressure within normal limits (WNL) with or without prescription medications protects cardiovascular system
Cholesterol Level	Control cholesterol levels with diet or prescription medications
Overweight or Obesity	Weight management reduces risk of Type 2 diabetes
Physical Activity	Daily physical activity reduces risk of cardiovascular disease

controllable risks by improving nutritional intake; not smoking; and maintaining quality exercise and weight management to offset genetic risks that are not controllable. Keep in mind that not all genetic factors can be modified with positive lifestyle behaviors. For instance, an individual who is predisposed to breast cancer as determined by the BRAC1 genetic test may not be able to increase healthy lifestyle behaviors to reduce the overall risk of developing breast cancer. Another example would include specific diseases, such as sickle cell disease or hemophilic disease. Such diseases are linked to genetic factors with limited response to lifestyle modifications. However, unhealthy lifestyles behaviors can often exacerbate the non-controllable risk factors.

Other less controllable or non-controllable risk factors include environmental, occupational, and socioeconomic factors. Environmental factors involve long- and short-term exposure to poor water, indoor air, and outdoor air. If a community is downwind from a manufacturing factory that emits toxic fumes, then the entire population suffers from long-term exposure to toxins. On the other hand, workers at the World Trade Center following the September 11, 2001, terrorist attacks were exposed to countless toxins, chemicals, and poisons for a short time having long-term effects. In times of war, military personnel may be exposed to toxins for a short period of time with long-term negative health conditions. Occupational exposure encompasses

short- and long-term exposure, including chemical spills, asbestos, toxic fumes, etc. Healthcare workers may unexpectedly be exposed to diseases such as hepatitis without their knowledge.

Socioeconomic factors are less controllable, but also greatly impact health risks. If individuals have limited education and thus limited income, their ability to access quality health care is less controllable due to the lack of health insurance. If individuals with limited income reside in a geographical location with fewer healthcare facilities, they have little or no control over their options. Finally, individuals with fewer social support networks have greater health risks due to lack of socialization. For example, if an elderly person lives alone and no one visits daily, the elderly person is at-risk of experiencing a health crisis without care.

Let us take a slight detour to explore the term "victim-blaming." Victim-blaming is defined as blaming an individual for his or her circumstances without taking into account the surrounding contexts. For example, a victim-blaming comment about someone who did not graduate high school would be, "Well, it is her fault that she did not complete high school. She should have studied more." However, there is no way to know the reasons why an individual did not finish school. In this example, maybe the main breadwinner for the family became chronically sick and could not work, and this individual needed to quit high school to find a job to help pay household expenses. Other examples of victim-blaming may target obesity,

BOX 2.9 Examples of Victim-blaming Accusations

Accusation	Reality
That individual is obese because he simply eats too much food.	Obesity involves many variables besides caloric intake, including physical mobility, depression, grief, stress, abuse, unemployment, medications, and other health challenges.
Those people should go get a job instead of begging for money on the street corner.	Homelessness is complex problem. Homeless individuals do not have any way to bathe and obtain clean clothes that would be acceptable to seeking employment.
Anyone can graduate from high school if they try and study a little.	A high school diploma is difficult to achieve. If the student is homeless, has an undiagnosed learning disability, or has limited access to food, academic achievement becomes difficult or unobtainable.
I do not know why my neighbor stays in that relationship.	Intimate partner violence is more complex than merely telling the abused individual to pack up and leave the situation. The individual may be financially dependent or lack the emotional strength to leave the situation.
That individual would feel better if he would take his medication instead of skipping doses.	The individual may not have enough money to buy the correct amount of medication, so he or she takes the medication every few days to reduce rather than eliminate the symptoms. The individual may not understand the need to take the medication regularly.
Individuals should stop using the hospital emergency department as an urgent care clinic.	Many individuals do not have health insurance or money to pay for an appointment at an urgent care clinic, so they go the emergency department to access the healthcare system.

domestic violence, homelessness, unemployment, criminal action, mental illness, lack of health care, and the list goes on. Take a few minutes to think of other social topics leading to victim-blaming comments and discrimination. See **Box 2.9**.

Now that you are familiar with the concept of victim-blaming, you have a better understanding of the complexity of the many factors that influence an individual's health. In fact, many health conditions begin prior to conception and include factors that are not associated with genetics. For instance, the status of the mother's health, nutritional status, stress, poverty, and lack of access to prenatal care affect the health of the fetus. The negative factors that influence the health of the fetus continue to have a negative influence into childhood. For example, one study reports that children from low-income communities develop academic skills more slowly than children from higher education and income communities.[12] Another study revealed that academic skills are related to the child's home environment. For instance, if a child lives in a household where the adults have low educational achievement and high chronic stress, these factors negatively affect a child's ability to learn prior to attending school.[13] Inadequate elementary education early in life also increases dropout rates later and thus perpetuates the cycle of poverty in communities, while improving early intervention programs reduces some risk factors for low-income children.[12] In today's society, individuals jump into victim-blaming judgments that lead to false accusations and assumptions.

Risk Assessments

Now let us investigate some risk assessment tools. Keep in mind that risk assessment tools or calculators are often compiled from data sources taken from across the entire population. A risk assessment should never be interpreted as a definitive outcome. For example, if the risk assessment tool suggested that an individual is at low risk for developing a specific type of cancer, it is exactly that: a suggestion. It does not mean that the individual with the same risk factors will never develop a specific type of cancer. It merely means that after reviewing the data collected from the entire population, individuals with the same risk factors did or did not later develop a specific type of cancer. Risk assessment tools are never used to make a medical diagnosis at any time.

Among the most famous long-term and multigenerational studies is the Framingham Heart Study (FHS). FHS began in 1948, when individuals in Framingham, Massachusetts, were followed over a very long period of time. Researchers began publishing research articles from the population data in 1951; since that time, thousands of articles have been published. The primary purpose of FHS is to research the genetic and environmental factors that influence the development of cardiovascular disease. FHS is among the most important public health studies in U.S. history.[15] If you wish to determine your personal risk of heart disease, go to the National Institute of Health website (*http://cvdrisk.nhlbi.nih.gov /calculator.asp*).

Evidence-Based Recommendations

Evidence-based recommendation is a concept used in health care to illustrate that the latest and most recommended procedure or treatment is used for a specific health condition. Over the past several decades, treatment recommendations have changed due to changing recommendations from the latest scientific findings. For example, in the past, cancer treatment began with surgery and then was followed by radiation and/or chemotherapy. This sequence is not always the case today. For some cancers, one of the latest treatment suggestions includes an approach called *intraoperative radiation therapy (IORT)*. With IORT, a dose of radiation is delivered directly to the affected tissues inside the body during the surgical procedure. For other cancers, intensity modulated radiation therapy (IMRT) is used to deliver a precise 3-dimensional dose of radiation directly to the tumor and surrounding tissue.[16] Another study shows that giving chemotherapy and radiation therapy before surgery helps to reduce the risk of the cancer reoccurrence in 5 years.[17] Finally, even in the realm of behavioral medicine, many evidence-based changes have shown the danger of smoking and secondhand smoke, while other research continues to provide mixed results, such as for drinking coffee and consuming eggs.[18-21] In summary, it is always important to verify the most current evidence-based recommendation available when researching any lifestyle behavior or health condition. See **Box 2.10**.

BOX 2.10 Student Activity: Fact or Fiction

As a health navigation professional, you may be asked questions about various health topics. For this activity, select three health topics. Using a variety of websites, find information from two websites supporting your selected topic and two websites refuting your selected topic. Because research is always adding to medical knowledge, there are no absolute correct or incorrect answers. The purpose of this activity is not to find the correct answer, but rather to illustrate how and why individuals get confused with health information.

Here are a few examples of possible health topics:

Is drinking coffee helpful or harmful?

Is it better to eat butter or margarine?

How far do you have to walk to lose weight?

Does consuming 81 mg of aspirin each day reduce risk of heart disease?

What is the duration of aerobic exercise needed to achieve health benefits?

© Jim Barber/Shutterstock

Summary

In this chapter, the concept of health navigation professionals and their role in the complex healthcare system was introduced. Building on this knowledge, the discussion defined and described the levels of prevention, including primary, secondary, and tertiary care across the life span. Finally, the chapter explores the concept of risks, including observable and calculated risks as well as controllable and non-controllable health risks and evidenced-based recommendations.

Case Study

With an understanding of the concepts presented in the chapter, you are able to apply your knowledge to the following case study and then answer the questions.

Ralph, age 72, was diagnosed with moderate hypertension and mild coronary artery disease (CAD) about 5 years ago due to some blockage in two of the arteries supplying blood to his heart. His physician prescribed two types of medication: one for the hypertension and one for CAD. Ralph is overweight, recently stopped smoking, and has pain in his left knee from an old football injury in college. Ralph remains employed as a math professor at a small liberal arts college in the Midwest. His wife, Marilyn, died from breast cancer about 9 months ago. Ralph took a 6-month leave of absence to care for Marilyn prior to her death. Hospice offered home health services to assist Ralph with Marilyn's daily care needs. Since going back to work, Ralph finds that he is depressed and struggles to find joy. He misses Marilyn and worries that no one will take care of him if he gets sick because they never had children. Ralph used to walk every morning before going to work,

but it snowed last week. Ralph stopped walking, because he is afraid of falling. Recently, he noticed that he has a nagging cough, but no other upper respiratory cold or flu symptoms. Before the breast cancer, Marilyn was the nursing director at a small ambulatory care clinic. Because Ralph had a flexible schedule, he did most of the cooking and enjoyed trying new recipes. Lately, he has no desire to cook and does not enjoying eating alone. When he looked at his mail last week, he noticed a postcard advertising a health navigation service. He saved the card and thought this service might be useful for him, even though he had never heard of a health navigation professional. Because Marilyn was a nurse, he always let her take care of their medical needs. He decided that he probably needed to get a physical exam. While he was caring for Marilyn, he neglected his own health needs, which is common among family members who serve as primary caregivers for their loved ones. Ralph decided to call the phone number on the postcard and learn more about the health navigation service. In addition, he scheduled an appointment for a complete physical with his internal medicine physician. He had been going to this physician for years, but he really did not know how to talk to Dr. Schwartz. After all, Marilyn usually asked all of the questions and talked in medical terms that Ralph did not care to understand.

Questions

1. Describe one example for each of the levels of prevention that pertain to Ralph's case study.
2. Using the risk assessment tool provided in the chapter, discuss an estimate of Ralph's

current risk for developing a serious cardiac condition in the future.

3. As a health navigation professional, describe how you would define your role to Ralph when he calls your office.

4. List four questions that you could ask Dr. Schwartz if you were invited to accompany Ralph to his medical appointment.

References

1. Freeman, H. P. (2013). The history, principles, and future of patient navigation: Commentary. *Seminars in Oncology Nursing, 29*(2), 72–75.

2. Paskett, E. D., Harrop, J., & Wells, K. J. (2011). Patient navigation: An update on the state of the science. *CA: a Cancer Journal for Clinicians, 61*(4), 237–249.

3. Byers, T. (2012). Assessing the value of patient navigation for completing cancer screening. *Cancer Epidemiology Biomarkers & Prevention, 21*(10), 1618–1619.

4. Patient Advocate Certification Board. (2015). *Ethical standards for a board certified patient advocate (BCPA)*. Retrieved January 25, 2016, from http://pacboard.org /documents/PACB-EthicalStandards-final-08.21.15.pdf.

5. Patient Advocate Certification Board. *Decisions and documents*. Retrieved January 25, 2016, from http://pacboard .org/decisions.

6. Crane-Okada, R. (2013). Evaluation and outcome measures in patient navigation. *Seminars in Oncology Nursing, 29*(2), 128–140.

7. Goldston, S. E. (Ed.). *Concepts of primary prevention: A framework for program development*. Sacramento, CA: California Deparment of Mental Health, 1987.

8. The University of Ottawa. *Categories of prevention: Society, the individual, and medicine*. Retrieved December 14, 2011, from http://www.med.uottawa.ca/sim/data /Prevention_e.htm.

9. The Association of Faculties of Medicine of Canada. *AFMC primer on population health*. Chapter 4: Basic concepts in prevention, surveillance, and public health. Retrieved December 18, 2014, from http://phprimer.afmc .ca/Part1-TheoryThinkingAboutHealth/Chapter4Basic ConceptsInPreventionSurveillanceAndHealthPromotion/ Thestagesofprevention.

10. Institute for Work and Health. *What researchers mean by primary, secondary, and tertiary prevention*. Retrieved December 18, 2014, from http://www.iwh.on.ca/wrmb /primary-secondary-and-tertiary-prevention.

11. The Mayo Clinic. *Multiple sclerosis: Risk factors*. Retrieved December 18, 2015, from http://www.mayoclinic.org /diseases-conditions/multiple-sclerosis/basics/risk-factors /con-20026689; last updated July 10, 2014.

12. Morgan, P. L., et al. (2009). Risk factors for learning-related behavior problems at 24 months of age: Population-based estimates. *J Abnorm Child Psych, 37*(3), 401–413.

13. Aikens, N. L., & Barbarin, O. (2008). Socioeconomic differences in reading trajectories: The contribution of family, neighborhood, and school contexts. *J Educ Psychol, 100*(2), 235.

14. Palardy, G. J. (2008). Differential school effects among low, middle, and high social class composition schools: A multiple group, multilevel latent growth curve analysis. *Sch Eff Sch Improv, 19*(1), 21–49.

15. The American Heart Association. *Heart attack risk assessment*. Retrieved December 18, 2014, from http://www.heart .org/HEARTORG/Conditions/HeartAttack/Heart AttackToolsResources/Heart-Attack-Risk-Assessment _UCM_303944_Article.jsp; last updated October 24, 2014.

16. Johns Hopkins Colon Cancer Center. *Stage III radiation therapy*. Retrieved January 2015 from http ://www.hopkinscoloncancercenter.org/CMS/CMS_Page .aspx?CurrentUDV=59&CMS_Page_ID=A1BC933B -CD98-4368-87DD-551E2599F180.

17. Breastcancer.org. *Chemo and radiation before surgery seems to reduce risk of recurrence for certain breast cancers*. Retrieved January 25, 2015, from http://www.breastcancer .org/research-news/20101105b; last updated November 5, 2010.

18. National Cancer Institute. *Harms of smoking and health benefits of quitting*. Retrieved January 25, 2015, from http://www.cancer.gov/cancertopics/factsheet/Tobacco /cessation; last updated January 12, 2011.

19. American Cancer Society. *Secondhand smoke*. Retrieved January 25, 2015, from http://www.cancer.org/cancer /cancercauses/tobaccocancer/secondhand-smoke; last updated February 11, 2014.

20. Lopez-Garcia, E., et al. (2008). The relationship of coffee consumption with mortality. *Ann Intern Med, 148*(12), 904–914.

21. Lee, A., & Griffin, B. (2006). Dietary cholesterol, eggs and coronary heart disease risk in perspective. *Nutrition Bulletin, 31*(1), 21–27.

CHAPTER 3

Role of Public Health Institutions in Healthcare Delivery

LEARNING OBJECTIVES

By the end of this chapter, students will be able to:

- Define public health and explain the core functions and essential services
- Describe the public health activities of several federal agencies
- Describe the notifiable disease surveillance system
- Understand how state, county, and local agencies work with federal agencies

CHAPTER OVERVIEW

This chapter describes how public health fits into the healthcare structure of the U.S. federal government. Before introducing the various public health institutions and agencies, it is important to understand the basic concepts of public health. After defining public health, the discussion explores the core functions and essential services of public health. Once the purpose of public health is understood, we investigate how federal government agencies contribute to the overall health and safety of the U.S. population. Finally, there is discussion concerning how state, county, and local governmental agencies coordinate with federal agencies to provide essential services to preserve the public's health.

WHAT IS PUBLIC HEALTH?

The simplest way to remember the basic definition of public health is to think of a river. At the bottom of the river, physicians, nurses and other healthcare providers rescue individuals to provide necessary treatment, such as in a clinic or hospital setting. If you look up the river, public health professionals are creating policies and programs to keep individuals from falling into the river. Public health is focused on the prevention of illness and injury and maintenance of the health of the population. For instance, seatbelt laws keep passengers safe; clean indoor air quality laws allow workers protection from secondhand smoke exposure; and federal inspections keep food and medications safe for the public. For a formal definition of public health, we look to the definition given by the Association of Schools and Programs of Public Health: Public health protects and improves the health of individuals, families, communities, and populations, locally and globally.[1]

With an understanding of the definition of public health, let us explore the 3 core functions of public health and the 10 essential services of public health. The 3 core functions of public health are assessment, policy development, and assurance. According to the Institute of Medicine

TABLE 3.1 Core Functions and Essential Services of Public Health

Three Core Functions	Ten Essential Services
Assessment	1. Monitor health status to identify and solve the community health problem. 2. Investigate the health problem and determine possible risks and hazards within the community.
Policy Development	3. Inform, educate, and empower individuals about the health issue. 4. Mobilize community partners, resources, and necessary actions to identify and solve the health problem. 5. Develop policies and plans that support individual and community efforts to address the problem.
Assurance	6. Enforce laws and regulations that protect health and ensure safety. 7. Link individuals to needed health services and assure the provisions of health services when otherwise unavailable. 8. Assure a competent health workforce to provide services and address the problem. 9. Evaluate effectiveness, accessibility, and quality of healthcare personnel and population-based healthcare services. 10. Conduct research to discover new solutions to improve health issues.

Modified from: the Centers for Disease Control and Prevention (2011). Core Functions of Public Health and How They Relate to the 10 Essential Services. http://www.cdc.gov/nceh/ehs/EPHLI/core_ess.htm. Accessed May 31, 2015.

(IOM), assessment is the regular and systematic collection and analysis of the health status and needs of the population.[2] Policy development includes the creation of comprehensive public health policies based on scientific evidence in service to the public.[2] Assurance is the provision of services to the public either directly or through regulation of other entities.[2] Each of the core functions also has a number of essential services that are expected to be performed to accomplish the core functions of public health. The core functions are described further by the 10 essential services of public health. See **Table 3.1**.

After understanding the basics of public health, the discussion turns to a description of how public health agencies fit into the federal government structure to improve or protect the health and safety of individuals as well as entire populations. The information presented is useful for health navigation professionals when providing resources to individuals and caregivers.

U.S. FEDERAL STRUCTURE AND AGENCIES RELATED TO HEALTH

The U.S. government has three branches: the judicial (the Supreme Court), the legislative (the U.S. Congress, which is made up of the Senate and House of Representatives), and the executive

(The White House). The executive branch is led by the President of the United States. Under the president's control, a combination of 25 various departments, offices, and councils are responsible for the day-to-day administration and enforcement of federal laws. Many of the 25 departments are related to maintaining the health and safety of the people of the United States. The remainder of this chapter highlights a few of the federal government departments that focus of health and safety. It is also important to remember that under the federal government departments, similar departments are housed within each of the states. For example, the federal government includes the Department of Health and Human Services while each state government has a Department of Health, which handles statewide decisions. Although many similarities exist between federal and state policies and laws, it is not essential that the same policies be in place at the federal and state levels. For example, the federal government has a minimum wage policy. Whereas states may not set their minimum wages lower than the federal policy, they can vote to raise the state minimum wage to exceed the federal minimum. Each state can set the minimum wages that they believe are best for the workers in their geographical location, as long as the wages are not less than the federal minimum wage. This highlights a special facet of our government: States may make a number of laws and policies, but they are required to abide by federal laws, where applicable.

Department of Health and Human Services

The U.S. Department of Health and Human Services (HHS) has the mission to enhance and protect the health and well-being of all Americans and provide essential human services, especially for those least able to help themselves.[3] HHS fulfills its mission by providing for effective health and human services and fostering advances in medicine, public health, and social services. To fulfill this vast mission, HHS is divided into 11 divisions. Although the head of HHS is not the surgeon general, the Office of the Surgeon General of the United States is housed within HHS. The president gains public health information from the surgeon general, who is the leading spokesperson on matters of public health. Also housed within HHS, of which the surgeon general is the operational head, is the U.S. Public Health Service Commissioned Corps (PHSCC).[4] The U.S. Public Health Service

Commissioned Corps is an elite team of approximately 6700 full-time, highly trained public health professionals dedicated to promoting public health promotion and disease prevention programs while advancing the science of public health.[5] Driven by a passion for public service, these professionals serve on the front lines in the nation's fight against disease and poor health conditions. As one of America's 7 uniformed services, the Commissioned Corps fills essential public health leadership and service roles within the nation's federal government agencies and programs.[5] The Commissioned Corps emergency response teams are trained to respond to public health crises and national emergencies such as natural disasters, disease outbreaks, or terrorist attacks in the United States and internationally, such as Hurricane Katrina, the earthquake in Haiti, and the Deepwater Horizon oil spill in the Gulf of Mexico.[5]

HHS covers numerous health topics and specific populations from infants to the elderly. Whereas the scope of this vast department is beyond the capacity of this chapter, **Table 3.2** provides a brief description of each of the 11 divisions. The Centers for Disease Control and Prevention is also housed within the HHS.

TABLE 3.2　U.S. Department of Health and Human Services: 11 Divisions

Division	Description
Administration for Children and Families	Promotes the economic and social well-being of families, children, individuals, and communities through a range of educational and supportive programs in partnership with states, tribes, and community organizations.
Administration for Community Living	Provides general policy coordination while retaining unique programmatic operations specific to the needs of the elderly, individuals with disabilities, and their caregivers in order to maximize their independence, well-being, and health.[6]
Agency for Healthcare Research and Quality	Produces evidence and engaging partners to improve health care through research.[7]
Agency for Toxic Substances and Disease Registry	Serves the public by using the best science, taking responsive public health actions, and providing trusted health information to prevent harmful exposures and diseases related to toxic substances.[8]
Centers for Disease Control and Prevention	Protects America from health, safety, and security threats, both foreign and in the United States.[9]
Centers for Medicare and Medicaid Services	Achieves a high-quality healthcare system at lower costs and improved health through administration of the Medicare and Medicaid programs.[10]

Division	Description
Food and Drug Administration	Provides regulation and supervision of food safety, tobacco products, dietary supplements, prescription and over-the-counter medications, vaccines, medical devices, cosmetics, and foods and medicines for animals. They also update and inform patients, health professionals, scientists, researchers, and industry for staying safe and healthy.[11]
Health Resources and Services Administration	Improves access to health care by strengthening the healthcare workforce, building healthy communities, and achieving health equity. HRSA trains healthcare providers and improves access to health care in rural and underserved communities. They are also responsible for organ, bone marrow, and core blood donation.[12]
Indian Health Services	Provides federal health services to American Indians and Alaska Natives.[13]
National Institutes of Health	This agency is the primary agency responsible for health-related research and is made up of 27 institutes and centers, each with a specific research agenda, often focusing on particular diseases or body systems.[14]
Substance Abuse and Mental Health Services Administration	Leads public health efforts to advance the behavioral health of the nation and reduce the impact of substance abuse and mental illness on America's communities.[15]

Centers for Disease Control and Prevention

As noted in Table 3.2, the Centers for Disease Control and Prevention is a federal agency under the umbrella of the U.S. Department of Health and Human Services. The name of this agency was formerly the Centers for Disease Control (CDC). When the words "and Prevention" were added to more fully describe the agency function, the "P" was not added to the acronym; thus, "CDC" remains the correct abbreviation. The mission of the CDC is to keep the U.S. population safe from health, safety, and security threats at home and across the globe. The CDC is the nation's foremost health protection agency, whose mission is to save lives, protect people from health threats, and save money through prevention.[16] The CDC was founded in 1946 and is housed in Atlanta, Georgia.

The CDC is known as the health protection agency of the United States. However, CDC scientists also work with international partners to (a) respond to emergency health threats; (b) investigate and stop transmission of deadly disease outbreaks; (c) protect the U.S. food supply through testing; (d) improve the effectiveness of research laboratories; (e) collect critical data needed to develop prevention strategies against noncommunicable disease; and (f) advance the research to provide life-saving vaccines. The CDC employs more than 15,000 individuals over all 50 states and in more than 50 countries.[16]

In addition, the CDC is responsible for the prevention and control of communicable diseases. This type of tracking (surveillance) and study of diseases (epidemiology) includes more than 70 reportable communicable diseases. When a healthcare provider diagnoses one from a list of diseases (called a *reportable disease*), he or she is mandated to notify the CDC and the state health office so investigators are aware of the disease in a specific location. This type of disease tracking is important to the CDC, including (a) learning how disease is transmitted to people and where it might spread to next; (b) education about how to stop the spread of the disease, such as wearing a mask, no skin-to-skin contact (shaking hands), or protection from bodily fluids; (c) education about preventing disease, such as immunizations; and (d) education about how to manage symptoms and risks once the disease is contracted. For example, if one high school student has a positive tuberculosis test, the CDC and state officials alert everyone in the county of the disease outbreak, especially the parents of the students at the high school where the student with tuberculosis is enrolled. Alerting the public is essential for tracking how many people may also be potentially

BOX 3.1 Definitions Related to Reportable Diseases

Epidemic (also called an *outbreak*)	The occurrence of cases of a disease in excess of what would normally be expected in a defined community, geographical area, or season
Pandemic	The occurrence of cases of a disease that has spread throughout an entire country, continent, or the whole world

infected with tuberculosis. Without mandatory reporting, unaware public health officials are unable to stop the spread of the disease, identify individuals that may have been exposed, and treat and isolate other individuals who are infected. The mandatory reporting also improves scientific advances by collecting data related to an outbreak and incorporates such research into public health practice. See **Box 3.1** for definitions related to reportable diseases.

Table 3.3 gives examples of some of the mandatory reportable diseases. The term "mandatory reportable disease" means that if a healthcare provider, clinic, residential living facility (e.g., prison, assisted-living facility, school, resident hall, mental health institution), outpatient facility, hospital,

or place of employment is found to have come in contact with one of these illnesses, the institution is mandated by federal law to report the disease diagnosis to the CDC for tracking.

© KeithSpaulding/iStockphoto

TABLE 3.3 Nationally Notifiable Infectious and Noninfectious Diseases

Botulism	Foodborne botulism is a rare but serious illness caused by eating foods that are contaminated with a nerve toxin. Even taking a small taste of food containing this toxin can be deadly. Home-canned vegetables are the most common cause of foodborne botulism outbreaks in the United States.
Chlamydia trachomatis Infection	A common sexually transmitted infection (STI) that can infect both men and women. If left untreated, it can cause serious, permanent damage to a woman's reproductive system, making it difficult or impossible for her to conceive later on.
Dengue Virus Infections	Dengue is caused by any one of four related viruses transmitted by mosquitoes. There are not yet any vaccines to prevent infection with dengue virus, and the most effective protective measures are those that avoid mosquito bites. Although dengue rarely occurs in the continental United States, it is endemic in Puerto Rico and in many popular tourist destinations in Latin America, Southeast Asia, and the Pacific islands.
Diphtheria	Diphtheria is a respiratory disease that is spread (transmitted) from person to person, usually through respiratory droplets caused by coughing or sneezing. A person also can become infected with diphtheria by coming in contact with an object, like a toy, that has been contaminated with the bacteria that cause diphtheria.
Giardiasis	*Giardia* is a microscopic parasite that causes the diarrheal illness known as giardiasis. Though the parasite can be spread in different ways, water (drinking water and recreational water) is the most common method of transmission.

Gonorrhea	Gonorrhea is a sexually transmitted disease (STD) that can infect both men and women. It can cause infections in the genitals, rectum, and throat. It is a very common infection, especially among people ages 15–24 years.
Hepatitis A	Hepatitis A is an infection spread through the fecal–oral route. It has an incubation period of approximately 28 days, replicates in the liver, and is shed in high concentrations in feces from 2 weeks before to 1 week after the onset of clinical illness. Hepatitis A is a self-limited disease that does not result in chronic infection or chronic liver disease.
Hepatitis B	Hepatitis B virus infection is a short-term illness that occurs within the first 6 months after someone is exposed to the Hepatitis B virus. Hepatitis B virus is spread through blood or other bodily fluids (including through sexual contact). Acute infection may lead to chronic infection and remains in a person's body. Chronic Hepatitis B is a serious disease that can result in long-term health problems and even death.
Hepatitis C, Acute	Hepatitis C is a liver disease that results from infection with the Hepatitis C virus. It can range in severity from a mild illness lasting a few weeks to a serious, lifelong illness. Hepatitis C is usually spread when blood from a person infected with the Hepatitis C virus enters the body of someone who is not infected (either through sharing needles, transfusions, or poorly sterilized medical equipment). Acute Hepatitis C virus infection is a short-term illness that occurs within the first 6 months after someone is exposed to the Hepatitis C virus. For most people, acute infection leads to chronic infection.
HIV Infection (AIDS has been reclassified as HIV Stage III)	Human immunodeficiency virus (HIV) is transmitted through bodily fluids (such as through sexual contact, sharing of needles, and breast milk). This virus cannot be cured and is deadly. With effective treatment and management, individuals with HIV may live long, productive lives.
Influenza-Associated, Pediatric	Infants and children are at risk of becoming very ill from the influenza virus, which is thought to be spread through respiratory droplets from coughs and sneezing. From the time an individual is exposed to the flu, it takes an average of 2 days to become ill, during which time flu may be spread to other individuals. Unlike chickenpox, having the flu once does not mean the individual is protected from acquiring the flu this year. It is important to obtain the flu vaccine each year for adequate protection.
Legionellosis	Legionnaires' disease is caused by a type of bacteria found naturally in the environment, usually in water. The bacteria grow best in warm water, such as hot tubs, cooling towers, hot-water tanks, large plumbing systems, and decorative fountains. The bacteria are not spread from one person to another person.
Listeriosis	Listeriosis is caused by eating food contaminated with the bacterium *Listeria monocytogenes* and affects older adults, pregnant women, newborns, and adults with weakened immune systems.
Malaria	Malaria is a mosquito-borne disease caused by a parasite. People with malaria often experience fever, chills, and flu-like illness. If left untreated, they may develop severe complications and die.
Measles	Measles starts with fever, runny nose, cough, red eyes, and sore throat, which is followed by a rash that spreads over the body. The measles virus is a highly contagious virus and spreads by air through coughing and sneezing. A vaccine is available for measles, mumps, and rubella (MMR).
Meningococcal Disease	Meningococcal disease is caused by bacteria and includes infections of the lining of the brain and spinal cord (meningitis) and bloodstream infections (bacteremia or septicemia). It is spread through the exchange of respiratory and throat secretions like spit (e.g., by living in close quarters, kissing). Meningococcal disease can be treated with antibiotics, but quick medical attention is extremely important. Keeping up to date with recommended vaccines is the best defense against meningococcal disease.
Mumps	Mumps is a contagious disease caused by a virus and starts with a few days of fever, headache, muscle aches, tiredness, and loss of appetite, followed by swelling of the salivary glands. A vaccine is available.
Pertussis	Pertussis, also known as *whooping cough*, is a highly contagious respiratory disease and is known for uncontrollable, violent coughing that often makes it hard to breathe. Pertussis most commonly affects infants and young children and can be fatal, especially in babies less than 1 year of age. A vaccine is available.
Rabies, Animal	Rabies is a preventable viral disease of mammals most often transmitted through the bite of a rabid animal. The vast majority of rabies cases reported to the CDC each year occur in wild animals like raccoons, skunks, bats, and foxes. The rabies virus infects the central nervous system, ultimately causing disease in the brain and death.

Rubella	Rubella is a contagious disease caused by a virus. The infection is usually mild with fever and rash. Though symptoms vary by age, rubella causes a rash that starts on the face and spreads to the rest of the body, low fever (less than 101 degrees), swollen glands, and aching joints.
Salmonellosis	Salmonellosis is an infection caused by the bacteria *Salmonella. Salmonella* is found in contaminated, under-cooked food and poor kitchen hygiene. Every year, *Salmonella* is estimated to cause 1 million illnesses in the United States, with 19,000 hospitalizations and 380 deaths. Most persons infected with *Salmonella* develop diarrhea, fever, and abdominal cramps 12 to 72 hours after infection. The illness usually lasts 4 to 7 days, and most people recover without treatment. However, in some, the diarrhea may be so severe that the patient needs to be hospitalized.
Severe Acute Respiratory Syndrome	Severe acute respiratory syndrome (SARS) is a viral respiratory illness caused by a coronavirus. In 2003 there was a global outbreak that spread to more than 2 dozen countries in North America, South America, Europe, and Asia before it was contained.
Shigellosis	Shigellosis is an infectious disease caused by bacteria. Shigellosis is a foodborne illness most often caught through improperly handled food and preparation. Symptoms include diarrhea, fever, and stomach cramps starting a day or two after an individual is exposed to the bacteria and resolves in 5 to 7 days. The spread of *Shigella* is stopped by frequent and careful hand-washing with soap and taking other hygiene measures.
Syphilis	Syphilis is a sexually transmitted infection that can cause long-term complications if not treated correctly. In adults, there are three stages: primary, secondary, and late syphilis. You can get syphilis by direct contact with a syphilis sore during vaginal, anal, or oral sex. Syphilis can also be spread from an infected mother to her unborn baby.
Tetanus	Tetanus is an acute, often fatal, disease caused by an exotoxin produced by bacteria. It is characterized by muscle stiffness, generalized rigidity, and convulsive spasms of skeletal muscles. Tetanus is most often caused by close contact with bacteria-harboring animals or by experiencing a cut or puncture of a rusty metal object (like a nail).
Toxic Shock Syndrome	Toxic shock syndrome is a potentially fatal disease caused by a bacterial toxin. The illness can be caused by the use of an infected contraception sponge, diaphragm, or tampon; after a surgery; or a cut or burn to the skin. Toxic shock syndrome typically begins suddenly with high fever, vomiting, and profuse watery diarrhea, sometimes accompanied by sore throat and headache The disease progresses to hypotensive (low blood pressure) shock within 48 hours, and the patient develops a diffuse rash with nonpurulent conjunctivitis. Urine output is often decreased, and patients may be disoriented or combative. The adult respiratory distress syndrome or cardiac dysfunction may also be seen.
Tuberculosis	Tuberculosis (also referred to as *TB*) is a disease caused by bacteria that usually attack the lungs, but may attack any part of the body such as the kidney, spine, and brain. If not treated properly, TB can be fatal.
Typhoid Fever	Typhoid fever is a life-threatening illness caused by the bacteria *Salmonella typhi*. Typhoid is spread by eating or drinking food or water contaminated with the feces of an infected person. In the United States, it is estimated that approximately 5700 cases occur annually. Most cases (up to 75%) are acquired while traveling internationally. Typhoid fever can be prevented through food safety procedures and can usually be treated with antibiotics.
Vancomycin-Resistant *Staphylococcus aureus*	Vancomycin-resistant Enterococci are specific types of antimicrobial-resistant bacteria that are resistant to vancomycin, the drug often used to treat infections caused by enterococci. Enterococci are bacteria that are normally present in the human intestines and in the female genital tract and are often found in the environment. These bacteria can sometimes cause infections. Most vancomycin-resistant Enterococci infections occur in hospitals.
Varicella	Chickenpox is a very contagious disease caused by the varicella-zoster virus. It causes a blister-like rash, itching, tiredness, and fever. Chickenpox can be serious, especially in babies, adults, and people with weakened immune systems. It spreads easily from infected people to others who have never had chickenpox or received the chickenpox vaccine. Chickenpox spreads in the air through coughing or sneezing. It can also be spread by touching or breathing in the virus particles that come from chickenpox blisters.

BOX 3.2 U.S. Measles Outbreak in 2015

Due to lack of mandatory vaccination programs, measles remains a common disease in many countries, including Europe, Asia, the Pacific, and Africa. As a result, it is not uncommon for international travelers to bring measles into the United States. This was the situation in January 2015; international travelers with measles came to the United States and visited the Disney theme park in California. During the visit, the measles virus was spread to unvaccinated U.S. individuals who were also visiting the theme park. Because the time of exposure to the development of the rash symptom is several days, U.S. individuals who had been infected with the measles virus did not show any symptoms until they returned home to various states. Therefore, from January 1 to May 1, 2015, 169 people from 20 states and the District of Columbia were reported to have measles.[17] Of the 169 cases, 117 (70%) cases were part of a large multi-state outbreak linked to theme park in California.[17] Travelers with measles continue to bring the disease into the United States, and then the disease spreads to a U.S. community where groups of people are unvaccinated.

Modified from the Centers for Disease Control and Prevention (2015). Measles Cases and Outbreaks. Available at: www.cdc.gov/measles/cases-outbreaks.html. Accessed May 31, 2015.

The CDC National Notifiable Diseases Surveillance System (NNDSS) is a nationwide collaboration that enables all levels of public health professionals (local, state, territorial, federal, and international) to share health information to monitor, control, and prevent the occurrence and spread of state-reportable and nationally notifiable infectious and some noninfectious diseases and conditions.[16] See **Box 3.2** to know about the measles outbreak of 2015. See Table 3.3 for a few examples of the reportable diseases that are likely to be diagnosed in the United States. The next section describes in detail a few of the more common notifiable diseases in the United States. As a health navigation professional, it is important to be at least familiar with the concept of reportable diseases.

2015 Measles Cases in the United States: January 1 to May, 2015

Modified from the Centers for Disease Control and Prevention (2015). Measles Cases and Outbreaks. Available at: www.cdc.gov/measles/cases-outbreaks.html. Accessed May 31, 2015.

Mandatory Reportable Diseases

This section explores two of the mandatory reportable diseases, so the health navigation professional can gain a basic understanding of the disease and mode of transmission. As a health navigation professional, it is important to know how to protect your clients and how to protect yourself. Here is a brief description of mandatory reportable diseases.

1. HIV (Human Immunodeficiency Virus).

HIV is a noncurable infection transmitted through bodily fluids; if left untreated, HIV can cause severe illness and eventual death. In the past, HIV and AIDs were commonly referred to as the same illness. HIV was thought to be the infection that turned into Acquired Immune Deficiency Syndrome, the disease. However, in 2009, the acronym "AIDS" was reclassified as "HIV Stage III."[18] The risk factors for HIV transmission vary according to the method of transmission.

Sexual contact. Individuals at greatest risk are those who do not practice safer sex by always using a condom; those who have multiple sexual partners; those who participate in unprotected anal intercourse; and those who have sex with a partner who has the HIV infection and/or other sexually transmitted diseases (STDs).

Transmission in pregnancy. High-risk pregnant women include women sexually active with bisexual men and intravenous drug users. The chances of transmitting the disease to the fetus (unborn infant) are higher in women in advanced stages of HIV. Breast feeding increases the risk of HIV transmission as HIV can be passed into breast milk. The rate of pediatric HIV transmission in the United States had decreased substantially because of HIV testing and improved drug treatment for infected mothers; less than 1 percent of HIV cases now occur in children under age 15.[19] In the developing world, mother-to-infant transmission still remains high.

Exposure to contaminated blood. Risk of HIV transmission among intravenous drug users increases with the frequency and duration of intravenous use, frequency of needle sharing, number of people sharing a needle, and the rate of HIV infection in the local population. With effective blood screening techniques, HIV transmission through blood transfusions is rare in the developed world. However, contaminated blood is still a significant source of infection in the developing world.

Needle sticks or body fluid splashes among healthcare providers. Transmission through these sources accounts for fewer than 0.3 percent of all HIV infections in the United States due to the emphasis on using universal safety precautions (e.g., use of gloves, face shields, proper disposal of needles).[20]

Reproduced from CDC. Retrieved from: http://www.cdc.gov/hiv/default.html/

2. Influenza-Associated Pediatric Mortality.

The CDC collects data year-round and reports on influenza (flu) activity in the United States each week from October through May. The U.S. influenza surveillance system consists of five separate categories: (a) laboratory tracking from laboratories across the country; (b) doctor visits for flu-like symptoms; (c) 122 cities report pediatric deaths through the Nationally Notifiable Disease Surveillance System with confirmation of laboratory tests; (d) hospitalization tracking of laboratory confirmed influenza-associated cases in children and adults; and (e) state and territorial reports of influenza activity and degree of severity.[26]

In the United States each year, more than 200,000 individuals are hospitalized from seasonal flu-related complications.[26] Flu seasons are unpredictable and can be severe. Some individuals, such as elderly adults, young children, pregnant women, and individuals with certain health conditions, are at high risk for serious flu complications. The best way to prevent seasonal flu is by getting a flu vaccination each year. Immunity sets in about 2 weeks after vaccination. The peak of the flu season is from late November through March.

As a health navigation professional, it is important to recognize the seasonal flu symptoms. Mainly, the flu is different from a cold; flu symptoms appearing suddenly. The flu is a respiratory disease and not a stomach or intestinal disease. See **Box 3.3**. The influenza virus is spread from individual to individual and is thought to be spread through respiratory droplets from coughs and sneezing. From the time an individual is exposed to the flu, it takes an average of 2 days to become ill. The flu is not like chickenpox. Even though an individual may have had the flu in a previous year, it does not mean that he or she is

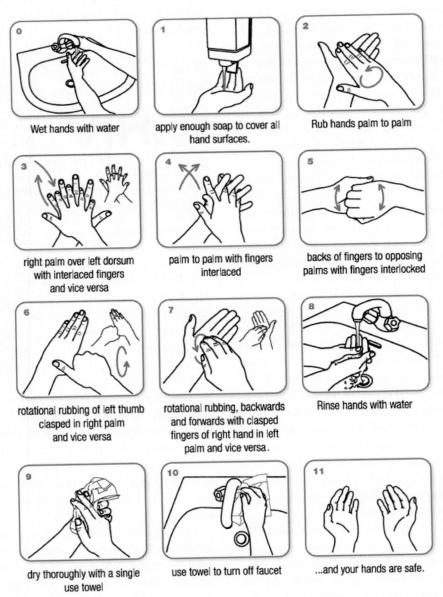

0 — Wet hands with water

1 — apply enough soap to cover all hand surfaces.

2 — Rub hands palm to palm

3 — right palm over left dorsum with interlaced fingers and vice versa

4 — palm to palm with fingers interlaced

5 — backs of fingers to opposing palms with fingers interlocked

6 — rotational rubbing of left thumb clasped in right palm and vice versa

7 — rotational rubbing, backwards and forwards with clasped fingers of right hand in left palm and vice versa.

8 — Rinse hands with water

9 — dry thoroughly with a single use towel

10 — use towel to turn off faucet

11 — ...and your hands are safe.

Reprinted from Clean Care is Safer Care, Clean hands protect against infection, retrieved from http://www.who.int/gpsc/clean_hands_protection/en/ Copyright (2016).

BOX 3.3 Symptoms of the Flu

Individuals with the flu have some or all of these symptoms:

- Fever (not everyone has a fever with the flu)
- Cough
- Sore throat
- Runny or stuffy nose
- Body aches
- Headache
- Chills
- Fatigue
- Sometimes diarrhea and vomiting

Centers for Disease Control and Prevention (2014). The Flue: What to Do If You Get Sick. http://www.cdc.gov/flu/takingcare.htm. Accessed May 31, 2015.

protected from acquiring the flu this year. It is important to obtain the flu vaccine each year for adequate protection. Due to complications of the flu, it can often make a chronic medical condition more severe (e.g., congestive heart failure (CHF), asthma, or diabetes).[26]

Individuals who acquire the flu and have mild symptoms should avoid contact with others except to receive medical care. If needed, the healthcare provider may prescribe antiviral drugs to treat the flu. These drugs reduce the symptoms and may prevent serious complications. The CDC recommends staying home for at least 24 hours to keep from infecting others. When returning to work or social functions, it is important to cover coughs and sneezes with a tissue and wash hands often to keep from spreading the flu virus to others.[27]

Department of Homeland Security

Now that you have a general understanding of the Department of Health and Human Services, the discussion moves to another federal agency having a focus on health and safety. Within the U.S. Department of Homeland Security is housed the Federal Emergency Management Agency (FEMA). The purpose of FEMA is to plan, prepare, and mitigate natural disasters (e.g., hurricanes, earthquakes, floods, lightning strikes, forest fires, tornadoes, mudslides, volcanoes) and human-caused catastrophes (e.g., terrorists; technological, environmental, and accidental hazards and pandemics). The goal of FEMA is to teach individuals and communities how to plan ahead and prepare for an unexpected disaster.[28]

As a health navigation professional, you may be asked to teach classes on how to prepare for a disaster in your community. Because disasters affect all individuals, it takes everyone (youth, parents, and community members) to help prepare. The information provided in **Figure 3.1** from the FEMA website shows adults, children, business owners, and entire communities how to plan for a disaster. It is best to plan for a disaster rather than react when the disaster is pending. This website is a valuable tool. The topics explored in Figure 3.1 include being informed, making a

FIGURE 3.1 Planning and Preparing for a Disaster

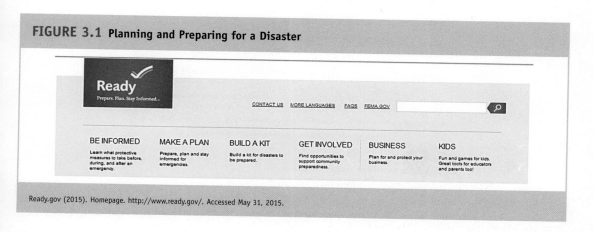

Ready.gov (2015). Homepage. http://www.ready.gov/. Accessed May 31, 2015.

plan, building kits, and getting involved for adults, kids, and businesses.

As a health navigation professional, it is important to plan for adverse events for yourself, your family, and individuals in your case load. Keep in mind that families may not be together when a natural or man-made disaster strikes. It is important to plan in advance for all types of situations. In addition, cell phone and Internet services are often disrupted during adverse events. By posing a few questions, individuals and families will begin to realize how the situation becomes complex quickly. Here are a few questions to consider:

Where will the family members meet?

How will each individual travel to a safe place?

How will individuals contact one another if mobile phone service is interrupted?

How you will get back together?

Have you investigated the emergency plans at places where the individuals spend time, such as work, day care, school, commuting, and organizations?

What you will do in different situations?

Of course, there are no correct or incorrect answers to any of these questions, but the questions are intended to start a conversation. See **Figure 3.2**.

FIGURE 3.2 Family Communication Plan from the CDC

Reproduced from Ready.gov (2015). Family Communication Plan. http://www.fema.gov/media-library-data/a260e5fb242216dc62ae380946806677/FEMA_plan_child_508_071513 .pdf. Accessed May 31, 2015.

When making an emergency kit, several types of kits may be considered. Will the kit be used at home or for an evacuation? It is important to include a collection of basic items needed for individuals in the household in the event of an emergency. The kit needs to be assembled in advance for emergency preparedness. If evacuation is necessary with limited notice, the kit needs to be ready with essential items. In some situations, there could be time to purchase and assemble the necessary supplies. The key items for an emergency kit include a sufficient quantity of any items needed to survive for at least 72 hours, including water, food, medications, diapers (adult or baby sizes), blankets, and flashlight and radio with extra batteries. Emergency workers on the scene focus on caring for the sick and injured. Households without electricity, gas, water, sewage treatment, and telephones may not have services restored for hours, days, or weeks depending on the circumstances and range of damage.[29] Communities come together with courage and compassion, while asking, "How can I help?" For example, prior to a disaster, communities are known to fill bags with sand to stop floodwaters, hose down the roofs of neighbors to save a home from an approaching forest fire, and transport the elderly to safe shelters during a pending hurricane. Entire communities can participate in programs and activities to make their families, homes, and communities safer from risks and threats. However, it is important for community leaders to train volunteers prior to any threat or danger, so the volunteers are prepared to increase the support of emergency response agencies during disasters. Major disasters overwhelm first-responder workers and agencies, so training volunteers improves community impact.

STATE, COUNTY, AND LOCAL HEALTH ORGANIZATIONS

Because you now have a greater understanding of the federal government agencies, it is time to discuss coordination with the state, county, and local government agencies to provide essential services that preserve the public's health. Generally, the federal government gets involved when state resources are not sufficient to cope with a specific health issue, such as a natural disaster. For example, it is common to hear on a media broadcast that the governor of the state is requesting federal assistance immediately after a disaster or weather emergency. In all cases, the purpose of the federal response is to augment the resources of state and local communities.

Because disasters happen in local communities and impact individuals and families, it is important to remember that citizens look to local government to lead immediate response efforts and guide the long-term recovery. FEMA and state officials coordinate the first response only. The local community oversees all four phases of emergency management: (a) preparedness, (b) response, (c) recovery, and (d) long-term recovery.[30]

SCENARIO: PREPARING FOR A DISASTER

Nancy is a health navigation professional who lives in Daytona Beach, Florida. Although she has lived in Florida since high school, she knows that many retired individuals move to Florida each year. Currently, Nancy is employed as a health navigation professional with a home health organization. During the last staff meeting, her supervisor discussed the importance of preparing their clients for the upcoming hurricane season between the months of June and November. Prior to the meeting, Nancy's supervisor asked her to prepare some community resources and websites to share with the other health navigator professionals. Besides assembling a packet of information for each employee, she gave a few examples from previous hurricane seasons and stressed the importance of preparing yourself, your family, and your clients. Here are two of her stories.

First story: Nancy had an elderly client living alone with her two dogs on 10 acres of land a few miles outside of town. Mrs. Williams, age 78, was in excellent health, still drove her car to church and the grocery store, but had trouble with her knees due to arthritis. She never bothered to convert her landline phone to a mobile phone. As the hurricane threatened the coast of Florida, Mrs. Williams was too afraid to drive in the rain to the grocery store to stock up on supplies. The hurricane turned, so a direct hit to Daytona Beach was avoided. However, the rain continued to drench the area for several days, and many trees fell and damaged power lines. This happened on Mrs. Williams's property. Her power and phone lines went down between her home and the barn where she parks her car. Nancy had made a home visit a few days before the hurricane threat. She had given her a packet of information about preparing for hurricanes, but Mrs. Williams said that she had lived in that house for 47 years and she did not need to prepare for the hurricane. As a result of two trees falling on the wires, Mrs. Williams was without power and phone service for 4 days. Because it was July, it was hot and humid. Because Nancy was busy with her own family and several other clients, she alerted the local fire department to check on Mrs. Williams. Due to heat exhaustion and dehydration, Mrs. Williams was transported to the local hospital for 1 day of observation. Her dogs were taken to a neighbor's home until she was discharged.

Second story: Harold Jones, age 67, single, lives in an adult congregate living facility (ACLF). He is obese and has hypertension, congestive heart failure, mild dementia, and intermittent anxiety attacks. He states that he has no living relatives. Prior to the pending hurricane, the ACLF staff announced to the 12 residents that everyone would be required to evacuate the home. Nancy had met Mr. Jones during his most recent hospitalization. While walking to the park, he had tripped over a sidewalk crack and had fallen. Due to his overall medical condition, Nancy was called to help Mr. Jones navigate his health care. After getting to know him, she talked to his physician, because he continued to tell her that he had lost his anti-anxiety pills and wanted another prescription. The doctor agreed with Nancy and gave Mr. Jones another prescription. However, this time Nancy explained that the pills would be given to the ACLF for safety. Although this scenario was unplanned, it turned out that Mr. Jones was accurate. His anxiety medication had been lost. But when it came time to evacuate, Mr. Jones was able to fully cooperate because Nancy had taken the time to get to know him in the hospital and had secured a new prescription by reporting the situation to his doctor.

Environmental Protection Agency (EPA)

The third federal agency that focuses on the health and safety of the U.S. population is the Environmental Protection Agency (EPA). Unlike the Department of Health and Human Services and the Department of Homeland Security, the Environmental Protection Agency is an independent agency within the federal government structure with the mission to protect human health and the environment (e.g., clean air and water, proper sanitation, safe indoor air quality) by writing and enforcing regulations based on laws passed by Congress. The EPA was created in the 1970s by President Nixon for "America to pay its debt to the past by reclaiming the purity of its air, its water, and its living environment." The headquarters of the EPA are located in Washington, D.C., but there are 10 regional offices and 27 laboratories throughout the United States. The agency conducts environmental assessment, research, and education. The primary responsibility of the EPA is to maintain and enforce national standards under the regulation of the environmental laws. It delegates some permitting, monitoring, and enforcement responsibility to individual states and the federally recognized tribes. The EPA has the power to enforce fines, sanctions, and other measures. The EPA collaborates with industries and state, county, and local government agencies to prevent environmental pollution and monitor prevention programs and energy conservation efforts.[31] See **Figure 3.3.**

Environmental Protection Agency (EPA)

FIGURE 3.3 Environment Protection Agency Website

MyEnvironment

Location [   ] [go]

Enter a location such as address, zip, city, county, waterbody, park name, etc. (e.g., 22207, Arlington, VA or Difficult Run).

Reproduced from Environmental Protection Agency (2015). My Environment. http://www.epa.gov/. Accessed May 31, 2015.

Under the EPA, several different agencies focus on air, land and clean-up, lead, asbestos, pesticides and toxic substances, waste, and water. For the purpose of this discussion, the works of two EPA agencies are explored: (a) outdoor air quality data and monitoring; and (b) poison control centers These EPA agencies provide valuable resources for health navigation professionals, patients, and caregivers.

First, the EPA monitors air pollution daily in more than 400 cities and maintains "real-time" maps that are displayed each hour. See Figure 3.3. The hourly tabulations are validated through the quality assurance procedures monitoring organizations used to officially submit and certify data on the EPA Air Quality System (AQS). See **Figure 3.4**. This information allows healthcare professionals, students, parents, teachers, and coaches to track the air quality in their communities. You may be asking yourself why health navigation professionals need to know about daily air quality. See **Box 3.4**.

Second, the EPA is closely associated with the American Association of Poison Control Centers (AAPCC) and the 55 national poison control centers that monitor the incidences of poisoning and their sources, including household products, chemicals at work or in the environment, drugs, and animal and insect bites. See **Figure 3.5**. The AAPCC is dedicated to advancing the healthcare role and public health mission through information, advocacy, education, and research.[32] Each of the poison control centers provides free, 24-hour professional advice to anyone in the 50 states, Puerto Rico, the Federated States of Micronesia, American Samoa, the U.S. Virgin Islands, Guam, and if needed, American soldiers serving overseas. All poison centers have the same telephone number (1-800-222-1222) and are staffed by pharmacists, physicians, nurses, and poison information providers who are toxicology specialists.[32] About 20 percent of calls come from healthcare facilities, because healthcare providers rely on poison centers for expert advice on poisoning cases.[32]

In addition, since 1983, the AAPCC has worked closely with the National Poison Data System (NPDS). Data are continually uploaded to NPDS from all AAPCC member poison centers every 8 minutes to provide a near real-time snapshot of poisoning conditions nationwide.[33] These surveillance techniques are used for all common poisonings and toxic environmental concerns, as well as a wide variety of noncommon occurrences ranging from food or drug contaminations to biological warfare agents, and focus on events of public health significance.[33]

FIGURE 3.4 EPA AirNow Website

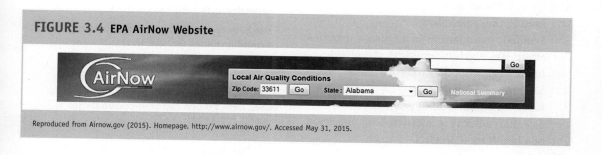

Reproduced from Airnow.gov (2015). Homepage. http://www.airnow.gov/. Accessed May 31, 2015.

BOX 3.4 EPA Air Quality

Ms. Blackstone, age 72, has allergies and chronic obstructive pulmonary disease (COPD) from 35 years of cigarette smoking. She has continuous oxygen delivered by a nasal cannula (plastic tubing running from a portable oxygen tank to her nose). Over the past few months, you have had time to get to know Ms. Blackstone. She has shared with you that her favorite weekend activity is to attend her grandson's little league baseball games. You know that spending time outside when the pollen and air pollution levels are high would be dangerous for her COPD. On Friday, you check the air quality index (AQI) for the weekend. You make a quick phone call to Ms. Blackstone to alert her of the potential risk of a hospital readmission if she attends her grandson's baseball game on Saturday. Although she is disappointed, she appreciates your phone call and decides that seeing the game is not worth a possible hospital readmission.

FIGURE 3.5 American Association of Poison Control Centers

Reproduced from: http://aapcc.org/.

Let us explore some of the recent poison hazard trends that have been identified by NPDS data as being useful to the daily practices of health navigation professionals as they gather resources for themselves, their clients, and caregivers.[34]

E-cigarette devices and liquid nicotine
Energy drinks
Prescription painkillers
Synthetic marijuana, which causes dangerous effects like psychotic episodes and seizures
Intentional arsenic poisoning in coffee
Melamine in dog food
Salmonella (bacteria) in peanut butter
Selenium toxicity associated with ingestion of a health food product

In addition, NPDS data is used to identify injury patterns through product safety monitoring.[34] For example, when portable generators are used incorrectly, carbon monoxide can seep into living spaces and kill the occupants. Carbon monoxide poisoning is the most common poison-related cause of hospitalization and death in the wake of hurricanes. It is called a "silent killer" because there are no odors and few symptoms that signal a problem. When people use generators improperly—too close to homes, in garages, or outside bedroom windows—carbon monoxide can seep in and sicken or even kill.[35] See **Box 3.5**.

BOX 3.5 Important Safety Tips for Using Portable Generators[36]

Generators:

Carefully follow the manufacturer's safety instructions for portable generators.

Never use portable generators indoors, in garages, or near open windows.

Do not siphon gasoline by mouth to fill a generator with fuel.

Use battery-operated (or battery-backup) carbon monoxide alarms. Be sure to test the batteries.

If you experience sleepiness, dizziness, headaches, confusion, or weakness or if your carbon monoxide alarm goes off, immediately seek fresh air and call your poison center at 1-800-222-1222.

FIGURE 3.6 EPA Safer Product Standards

See **Figure 3.6** and **Figure 3.7** for additional websites related to EPA product safety standards.

Consumer Product Safety Commission (CPSC)

Like the EPA, the U.S. Consumer Product Safety Commission (CPSC) is an independent agency that was created in 1972 (Public Law 92-573; 86 Stat. 1207, October 27, 1972) and reports to Congress and the president.[37]

Currently, the CPSC addresses lead, toy safety, and third-party testing of all manufactured consumer products made in the United States as well as imported products (not agricultural products or food). When unsafe products are identified, the CPSC has the authority to order a product recall and proceed with civil and criminal penalties. The CPSC hosts the SaferProducts. gov. website for consumers with information on product recalls. Overall, the CPSC administers and enforces several federal laws, regulations, mandatory standards and bans, recall guidance, and voluntary standards. It is possible for consumers to check products for safety.

First, the federal statute laws authorize CPSC to protect the public against injuries and death from consumer products.[38] For example, these federal statues regulate the safety of electrically operated toys, cribs, rattles, pacifiers, bicycles, and children's bunk beds. In addition, the statues require certain hazardous household products to have warning labels, flammable fabric notices, poison prevention packaging, and refrigerator safety information.[38] A specific example pertaining to the elderly is the 1995 memo regarding flammability of nightwear. See **Figure 3.8**.

FIGURE 3.7 Find Safer Choice Products

FIGURE 3.8 1995 Meeting Log: Flammability of Nightwear for the Elderly

LOG OF MEETING

SUBJECT: Flammability of Nightwear for the Elderly

DATE: January 23, 1995

PLACE: CPSC, Bethesda, Maryland

Non-COMMISSION ATTENDEES: See attached list

COMMISSION ATTENDEES: See attached list

LOG ENTRY SOURCE: James F. Hoebel, CPSC

SUMMARY OF MEETING:

Chairman Brown welcomed the participants, and expressed her concern over the problem of people over 65 who are burned by fires involving nightwear. She emphasized that the CPSC is data-driven, and that there are too many deaths in such fires.

CPSC staff noted that about 20-30 million people are now over 65 years old, and that up to 40 million will be when the "baby boomers" get there.

Reproduced from the Consumer Product Safety Commission (1995). Log of Consumer Product Safety Meeting on Flammability of Nightwear for the Elderly. Available at: http://www.cpsc.gov//PageFiles/98497/elderlynightwear.pdf. Accessed May 31, 2015.

At this point, a health navigation professional is probably wondering why it is necessary to learn so much about consumer safety agencies and products. Review the safety alert information in **Table 3.4.** Keep in mind that grandchildren frequently visit the homes of their grandparents. It is important for all homes to be childproof and safe for elderly residents and guests of all ages.

According to the Centers for Disease Control and Prevention, one out of three older adults (those ages 65 or older) falls each year, but less than half talk to their healthcare providers about it.[39] Falls are

TABLE 3.4 Home Safety Alerts

Hazards	Solutions
Home Fires	Install AFCIs (arc fault circuit interrupters) for protection from fires resulting from unsafe arcing and sparking in home wiring.
Room Humidifiers	Clean room humidifiers to reduce health problems resulting from mold.
Older Brass Connectors	Replace connectors on old appliances to prevent fires, explosions, injuries, and death.
Portable Electric Space Heater	Keep portable space heaters at least 3 feet from beds, sofas, curtains, and other items that can burn. Turn the space heater off at night.
Hot-Water Burns	Avoid tap water scalds. Keep water heater temperature at 120 or less degrees Fahrenheit.
Extension Cords and Power Strips	Do not overload extension cords and power strips to avoid a serious fire hazard.
Fall Risks	Remove small rugs, increase lights and night lights, remove cords in walking pathways, install gripper bars in bathroom, install bed rails, keep emergency numbers in several locations, repair tile cracks inside and outside, and repair torn carpet.

Modified from The Consumer Product Safety Commission. (2015). Safety Guides: Home. Available at: http://www.cpsc.gov/en/Safety-Education/Safety-Guides/Home/. Accessed on July 1, 2015.

the leading cause of both fatal and nonfatal injuries. Falls can cause moderate to severe injuries, such as hip fractures. More than 95 percent of hip fractures are caused by falls, with the rate for women is almost twice the rate for men.[39] People age 75 and older who fall are four to five times more likely than those age 65 to 74 to be admitted to a long-term care facility for a year or longer.[39] Rates of fall-related fractures among older women are more than twice those for men.[39] Fortunately, falls are a public health problem that is largely preventable. In 2013, 2.5 million non-fatal falls among older adults were treated in emergency departments and more than 734,000 of these patients were hospitalized.[39] The direct medical costs of falls, adjusted for inflation, were $34 billion.[39]

In addition, health navigation professionals need to have ideas to share with elderly individuals on how to reduce the risk of falling. A few examples are (a) participating in Tai Chi, an excellent form of exercise for the elderly, because it increases leg strength and improves balance but does not put undue burden on their bodies; (b) requesting that a physician or pharmacist review prescription and over-the-counter medications to identify medications with side effects that may cause dizziness; (c) scheduling an annual eye examination with an ophthalmologist to check for vision changes or eye disease (e.g., glaucoma, macular degeneration, cataracts); (d) installing grab bars in the bathroom and improving lighting in stairways and throughout residences; and (e) getting periodic screening and treatment for osteoporosis.[39]

One last item for the consumer to consider is the selling and purchasing of used and recycled products. The CPSC's laws and regulations apply to all individuals who sell or distribute consumer products, including thrift stores, consignment stores, charities, yard sales, and flea markets. Sellers and buyers may not be aware that the used product has been recalled. Used products may have caused injuries and deaths and been the subject of numerous recalls. Resellers should closely examine items prior to resale to ensure product safety and compliance with federal laws. It is recommended that sellers and buyers review the "Reseller's Guide to Selling Safer Products."[40] The CPSC office recommends the "when in doubt, throw it out" policy, especially for infants, children, and the elderly.

© RiverNorthPhotography/iStockphoto

See **Box 3.6** for examples of recalled products that might affect families including infants, children, and elderly. For instance, when grandchildren are visiting over the holidays, grandparents may visit neighborhood garage sales to purchase inexpensive items (e.g., infant carrier, crib, car seat) so that the parents do not feel obligated to bring or rent infant and child items during their stay. Although this sounds like a cost-saving idea, it can prove to be extremely dangerous. Adult children may also have the same idea when elderly parents visit their home. Adult children may purchase high toilet seats, bed rails, and walkers to make the parent visit more accommodating. Again, this presumed good idea might lead to a dangerous fall or unintended injury for the elderly guest.

BOX 3.6 Examples of Recalled Products

Electric Portable Heaters	Infant gates, carriers, swings, and walkers
Portable Generators	Infant high chairs
Smoke Alarms	Strollers
Bed Rails	Infant bedding and accessories
Shower Seats	Car seats and booster seats
Motorized Scooters	Toys

Modified from: The Consumer Protection Safety Commission (2015). Voluntary Standards. Available at: http://www.cpsc.gov/en/Regulations-Laws--Standards/Voluntary-Standards/. Accessed May 31, 2015.

Summary

This chapter described how public health fits into the healthcare structure of the U.S. federal government. Public health was defined, including core functions and essential services. In addition, several federal departments and agencies were described, including how their services contribute to the overall health and safety of the U.S. population.

Student Activity

See **Table 3.5**. Select a public health topic that you have seen change in your lifetime (e.g., mandatory seatbelt laws, indoor air quality, no smoking areas, change in marijuana use, new vaccinations, etc.). Answer the questions in each box.

TABLE 3.5 **Practice Skills Related to Public Health Core Functions and Essential Services**

Three Core functions	Ten Essential Services
Assessment	1. How would you monitor the health status of your topic? For example: In 2012, XXXX individuals died in vehicle crashes as a result of not wearing a seatbelt. 2. What are the possible risks and hazards within the community?
Policy Development	3. How were individuals taught about this health issue? 4. How did communities take action to solve this health problem? 5. What type of polices were developed to address the health problem?
Assurance	6. What, if any, laws were changed to protect the health of individuals related to this topic? 7. What services are available to help individuals improve their health related to this health issue? 8. Is this health issue related to training healthcare workers? 9. How has this program been evaluated to determine its effectiveness? 10. What research has been done on this topic to improve the health issue?

References

1. Association of Schools and Programs of Public Health. *Discover: What is public health?* Retrieved May 15, 2015, from http://aspph.org/discover.
2. The Committee for the Study of the Future of Public Health. (1988). *The future of public health.* Washington, DC: Institute of Medicine.
3. U.S. Department of Health and Human Services. *HHS strategic plan.* Retrieved May 18, 2015, from http://www.hhs.gov/about/strategic-plan/index.html.
4. Commissioned Corps of the U.S. Public Health Service. Mission and core values. Retrieved May 18, 2014, from http://www.usphs.gov/aboutus/mission.aspx; last updated February 3, 2014.
5. U.S. Department of Health and Human Services. *U.S. public health service commissioned corps.* Retrieved June 3, 2015, from http://www.surgeongeneral.gov/about/corps.
6. Administration for Community Living. Retrieved May 18, 2015, from http://www.acl.gov/About_ACL/Organization/Index.aspx.Organization; last updated October 22, 2014.
7. Agency for Healthcare Research and Quality. *AHRQ research conferences.* Retrieved May 18, 2015, from http://www.ahrq.gov/news/events/conference/index.html.
8. Agency for Toxic Substances & Disease Registry. Retrieved May 18, 2015, from http://www.atsdr.cdc.gov.
9. Centers for Disease Control and Prevention. *Mission, role, pledge.* Retrieved May 18, 2015, from http://www.cdc

.gov/about/organization/mission.htm; last updated April 14, 2014.

10. Centers for Medicare and Medicaid Services. Retrieved May 18, 2015, from www.cms.org.

11. U.S. Food and Drug Administration. Retrieved May 26, 2015, from http://www.fda.gov.

12. Health Resources and Services Administration. *About HRSA*. Retrieved May 18, 2015, from http://www.hrsa.gov/about/index.html.

13. Indian Health Services. *Agency overview*. Retrieved May 18, 2015, from http://www.ihs.gov/aboutihs/overview; last updated February 3, 2015.

14. National Institutes of Health. *About NIH*. Retrieved May 18, 2015, from http://www.nih.gov/about; last updated February 2, 2015.

15. Substance Abuse and Mental Health Services Administration. *About us*. Retrieved May 18, 2015, from http://www.samhsa.gov/about-us.

16. Centers for Disease Control and Prevention. *CDC fact sheet*. Retrieved May 18, 2015, from http://www.cdc.gov/about/resources/facts.htm; last updated April 24, 2014.

17. Centers for Disease Control and Prevention. *Measles cases and outbreaks*. Retrieved June 3, 2015, from http://www.cdc.gov/measles/cases-outbreaks.html; last updated June 2, 2015.

18. Centers for Disease Control and Prevention. *National notifiable diseases surveillance system (NNDSS)*. Retrieved May 18, 2015, from http://wwwn.cdc.gov/nndss; last updated May 6, 2015.

19. Centers for Disease Control and Prevention. HIV/AIDS: *Pregnant women, infants and children*. Retrieved May 18, 2015, from http://www.cdc.gov/hiv/risk/gender/pregnantwomen/index.html; last updated January 10, 2010.

20. Centers for Disease Control and Prevention. *HIV/AIDS*. Retrieved May 26, 2015, from http://www.cdc.gov/hiv/default.html; last updated May 19, 2015.

21. Centers for Disease Control and Prevention. *Hepatitis C FAQs for the public*. Retrieved May 18, 2015, from http://www.cdc.gov/hepatitis/C/cFAQ.htm; last updated April 15, 2015.

22. Centers for Disease Control and Prevention. *Hepatitis B FAQs for the public*. Retrieved May 18, 2015, from http://www.cdc.gov/hepatitis/B/bFAQ.htm#overview; last updated March 6, 2015.

23. World Health Organization. *Hepatitis A*. Retrieved May 18, 2015, from http://www.who.int/mediacentre/factsheets/fs328/en; last updated June 2014.

24. Centers for Disease Control and Prevention. *Hepatitis B information for the public*. Retrieved May 18, 2015, from http://www.cdc.gov/hepatitis/B; last updated March 1, 2013.

25. Centers for Disease Control and Prevention. *Hepatitis B: Vaccine information statements*. Retrieved May 18, 2015, from http://www.cdc.gov/vaccines/hcp/vis/vis-statements/hep-b.html; last updated June 18, 2013.

26. Centers for Disease Control and Prevention. *Seasonal influenza Q&A*. Retrieved May 18, 2015, from http://www.cdc.gov/flu/about/qa/disease.htm; last updated August 14, 2014.

27. Centers for Disease Control and Prevention. *The flu: What to do if you get sick*. Retrieved May 18, 2015, from http://www.cdc.gov/flu/takingcare.htm; last updated August 14, 2014.

28. Federal Emergency Management Agency. About the agency. Retrieved May 18, 2015, from http://www.fema.gov/about-agency; last updated January 31, 2015.

29. Federal Emergency Management Agency. *Ready: Build a kit*. Retrieved May 18, 2015, from http://www.ready.gov/build-a-kit; last updated September 2, 2014.

30. Public Management. *Disaster recovery: A local government responsibility*. Retrieved June 25, 2015, from http://webapps.icma.org/pm/9102/public/cover.cfm?title=disaster%20recovery%3a%20%20a%20local%20government%20responsibility.

31. Environmental Protection Agency. *Our mission and what we do*. Retrieved May 18, 2015, from http://www2.epa.gov/aboutepa/our-mission-and-what-we-do; last updated October 6, 2014.

32. American Association of Poison Control Centers. *About AAPCC*. Retrieved May 18, 2015, from http://www.aapcc.org/about.

33. American Association of Poison Control Centers. *National poison data system*. Retrieved May 18, 2015, from http://www.aapcc.org/data-system.

34. American Association of Poison Control Centers. *Uses for NPDS data*. Retrieved May 18, 2015, from http://www.aapcc.org/data-system/uses-npds-data.

35. American Association of Poison Control Centers. *Alerts*. Retrieved May 18, 2015, from http://www.aapcc.org/alerts.

36. American Association of Poison Control Centers. *Carbon monoxide*. Retrieved May 28, 2015, from https://www.youtube.com/watch?v=Q990dmgMb_M.

37. United States Consumer Product Safety Commission. *About CPSC*. Retrieved May 31, 2015, from http://www.cpsc.gov/en/About-CPSC.

38. United States Consumer Product Safety Commission. *Regulations, laws and standards*. Retrieved May 31, 2015, from http://www.cpsc.gov/en/Regulations-Laws--Standards/Statutes.

39. United States Consumer Product Safety Commission. *Statutes*. Retrieved May 18, 2015, from http://www.cpsc.gov/en/Regulations-Laws--Standards/Statutes.

40. Centers for Disease Control and Prevention. *Falls among older adults: An overview*. Retrieved May 18, 2015, from http://www.cdc.gov/HomeandRecreationalSafety/Falls/adultfalls.html; last updated March 19, 2015.

PART 2

Introduction to Health Care and Health Insurance

CHAPTER 4

Inpatient Healthcare Services

LEARNING OBJECTIVES

By the end of this chapter, students will be able to:

- Define a number of different inpatient clinical care settings
- Understand the role of the health navigation professional in inpatient health care

CHAPTER OVERVIEW

Healthcare services are vast and complex for patients, caregivers, and healthcare providers. One way to divide healthcare services is by inpatient healthcare services and outpatient healthcare services. This chapter focuses on the healthcare services that are provided to an individual in an inpatient unit. Inpatient services are provided when an individual is staying overnight in the facility. The chapter begins with a description of various types of hospitals and ends with a discussion of nonhospital residential facilities.

HOSPITALS

Although individuals know about the healthcare services offered at hospitals, they may not realize the numerous types of hospitals that exist. Generally, hospitals are defined as offering inpatient healthcare services for individuals in need of medical care. The personnel working within a hospital include (a) the clinical staff (e.g., physicians,

nurses, pharmacists, physical therapists) who care for and treat the patients; (b) nonclinical personnel (finance, technical, facilities maintenance and engineering, personnel and human resources, insurance, medical records and billing, food service, environmental services, safety officers, and others) who oversee the day-to-day operation of the hospital facilities; and (c) administrative staff (chief operation and finance officers, chief of medical staff, members of the board of directors, supervisors of departments and divisions) who develop the long-term strategic plan and maintain the certification and fiscal requirements. In addition, there are numerous ways to describe hospitals. Let us begin with the hospital size.

Small, Medium, and Regional Hospitals

There are small, medium/large, and regional hospitals. Small hospitals are located in rural communities, have fewer than 50 beds, and offer basic medical and surgical services with limited emergency department services. The purpose of a small emergency department is to treat, if possible, or stabilize an individual and then transport him or her via helicopter to the nearest regional medical center. Medium hospitals are located in larger communities and have less than 300 beds. This type of hospital may be free-standing or a satellite hospital for the larger regional hospital.

Some medium-sized hospitals are associated with religious organizations (e.g., Presbyterian Hospital, Jewish Community Hospital, Sisters of Mercy Hospital); are owned by corporations, such as Hospital Corporation of America (HCA); are county-owned (e.g., Sarasota Memorial Hospital, Denver General Hospital, Purdue County Hospital); or are privately owned by a group of investors (Doctor's Hospital, Women's Hospital, Edward White Hospital).

All of these various types of hospitals offer the same healthcare services, but the difference is based on their sources of revenue for funding and reimbursement. Typically, the revenue sources are invisible to the patients. However, the ownership (e.g., corporation, religious organization, county, or private owners) determines who gains or loses money from the hospital's annual profits or losses. These medium-sized hospitals offer full-service inpatient and outpatient medical treatments. For some midsized cities, this type of hospital serves most of the needs of the population. Regional hospitals are commonly, but not always, linked to universities with a medical school. Keep in mind that the name of the hospital may or may not reflect the name of the associated university. For example, Massachusetts General Hospital is linked to Harvard University College of Medicine. In addition, most medical schools have links to several hospitals in their geographical location. Regional hospitals offer highly skilled, specialized services, such an intensive care unit for trauma victims, solid organ (lung, heart, kidney, pancreas) transplants, on-site blood banking services, and adequate emergency department staff and multiple helicopter pads for recipient of numerous individuals with life-threatening injuries received in an industrial explosion or natural disaster. Finally, there is one additional way to categorize hospitals. Regardless of the size, some hospitals are "for-profit" and some are "not-for-profit." Unlike what this suggests, the actual meaning is a legal term relating to corporate laws and how the original hospital charter was written by attorneys and boards of directors.

Before moving into a discussion of specialized hospitals, let us explore the role of a health navigation professional employed in a hospital. See **Scenario 4.1.**

Specialty Hospitals

In addition to size as a way to categorize hospitals, there are specialized hospitals that serve a specific type of patient. The following discussion describes examples of specialized hospitals.

Pediatric Hospitals

Shriners Pediatric Hospitals   The Shriners, a national philanthropy organization, conducts research and provides specialized pediatric hospital care at no cost for children from the United States and around the globe. There are four types of specialized Shriner's Pediatric Hospitals: burn, orthopedics, spinal cord injury, and cleft lip and palate. Four Shriner's burn hospitals are located in California, Texas, Ohio, and Massachusetts. The first Shriner's Burn Hospital for Children opened in 1966 in Galveston, Texas. Children receive care for their burn injuries from the time of acute injury through rehabilitation and individual reconstructive needs throughout their childhood. Shriners has 17 orthopedic hospitals in the United States, plus 2

SCENARIO 4.1 Role of Health Navigation Professional in an Inpatient Hospital Setting

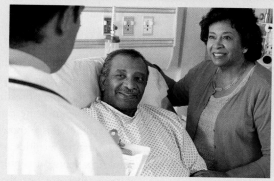

© Catherine Yeulet/iStockphoto

Roger Henley was admitted to a regional hospital 4 days ago with a hip fracture sustained by tripping in his driveway while retrieving the morning newspaper. Mr. Henley is 76 years old and is married to Mary, his wife of 48 years. She is also 76 and can no longer drive due to arthritis in her hands and spine. They do not have any children. Mr. and Mrs. Henley have owned a real estate agency for more than 20 years and they remain employed about 30 hours per week. They say that their work is enjoyable and keeps them active. Mary loves showing the homes for sale and Roger loves driving clients around their city. Upon admission after the fall in the driveway, Mr. Henley had surgery to repair his hip fracture. He has a moderate cardiac condition sustained from an acute myocardial infarction about 8 years ago. His cardiac condition is well controlled with medication, but has slowed his recovery from the hip surgery. Dr. Garcia, his surgeon, suggested that he receive physical therapy in a nearby rehabilitation facility, but Mr. Henley is not interested. He wants to receive physical therapy at home.

Dr. Garcia explained that the hospital's health navigation professional would coordinate the home health services needed for Mr. Henley's discharge to home. Deborah, the hospital's health navigation professional, stopped by Mr. Henley's room. Because Mrs. Henley was visiting, Deborah was able to explain the coordinated services provided by a health navigation professional to her. Because Mr. Henley's discharge is not planned for 3 days, Deborah has plenty of time to coordinate these needed services. She interviewed Roger and Mary to determine their immediate needs upon discharge. She also arranged a time with Mary to visit their home within the next day to see what other equipment Roger would need at home. After the home visit assessment, Deborah submitted her plan to Mr. and Mrs. Henley and Dr. Garcia. After they approved her plan, Deborah involved the hospital's home health agency, the outpatient physical therapist, and the hospital pharmacy. The day before his discharge, Deborah arranged for Mr. Henley's transportation home and the delivery of the rental home health equipment. Deborah knows that it is not useful for equipment to be delivered the day of discharge because the patient needs the wheelchair to get into the home and the high toilet seat and hospital bed upon arrival. It is disturbing to the patients and their family caregivers when the essential equipment does not arrive before the patient. Another advantage of delivering the equipment the day before discharge is that someone must be present at home to let the delivery person into the house and to sign the paperwork for the rented equipment. If the caregiver is at the hospital preparing the patient for discharge, then it is impossible to be at home to sign for the rented equipment. Deborah visits Mr. and Mrs. Henley at their home in the evening after he is discharged. She needs to ensure that they do not have any immediate questions regarding his care on the first night at home. After she answers their questions, she gives them her phone number and

© ULTRA.F/Getty Images

reminds them to call if they have any questions. Before leaving, she reviews his medications, tells them that the physical therapist will stop by in the morning for Mr. Henley's first home visit, and reminds them of his follow-up appointment with the surgeon in 3 days. Deborah visits every other day for the first week; then, the visits decrease to once a week for the next 3 months, then once per month for 6 months. By having Deborah assigned as the health navigation professional for Mr. Henley, Mrs. Henley feels confident caring for him at home. She knows that Deborah is available to answer questions and arrange appointments and home health services.

in Canada and 1 in Mexico. In addition, there are 3 Shriners pediatric spinal cord hospitals in California, Illinois, and New Jersey. Finally, there are 9 Shriners hospitals that specialize in the repair of cleft lip and palate in the United States.[1]

St. Jude Children's Hospitals The history of St. Jude Children's Hospital is interesting and quite remarkable. Danny Thomas was a struggling comedian in his early career. Because he was a devout Catholic, he prayed to St. Jude Thaddeus, the patron saint of hopeless causes. He vowed, "Show me my way of life and I will build you a shrine."[2] That prayer became a pivotal moment in his life as he went on to become one of the biggest stars of radio, film, and television of the 1950s. Making good on his promise, by 1955 Danny and a group of businessmen began raising funds for a children's hospital and research center in Memphis, Tennessee, with a focus on childhood cancer. In 1962, the St. Jude Children's Research Hospital opened its doors. From the first day of opening until today, "families never receive a bill from St. Jude for treatment, travel, housing or food—because all they should worry about is helping their child live."[2] Though Danny Thomas died in 1991, his legacy of saving the lives of children is ongoing.

St. Jude Children's Hospital offers a vast array of inpatient and outpatient services for children and their families, including clinics for long-term survivors of childhood cancer, genetic counseling and testing, cardiopulmonary services, dental services as part of the treatment plans, diagnostic imagining, endocrine services, eye clinic, chemotherapy, blood products and other medicines, pharmacy, social services and counseling for patients and families, child life services to manage stress and treatments, clinical nutritional counseling services, rehabilitation services, school programs, social work, and spiritual care services.

Long-Term Acute Care Hospitals (LTACH)

Prior to the development of LTACH facilities in the mid-1990s, patients who were on ventilators (a type of machine that helps patients who cannot breathe sufficiently on their own) moved from acute care hospitals to skilled nursing facilities (also known as a nursing home). Skilled nursing facilities are not suited to care for complex patients on ventilators, making patient outcomes that are less than ideal. LTACHs can be thought of as free-standing intensive care units. Long-term acute care hospitals improved patient outcomes at a lower cost because the nursing staff had adequate training and the facility was equipped to care for patients on ventilators. Prolonged ventilation is defined as one of the following: (1) more than 48 consecutive hours on a ventilator (not breathing without mechanical assistance); (2) more than 96 consecutive hours with tracheotomy (surgical placement of tube in trachea and mechanical assistance needed to breathe); or

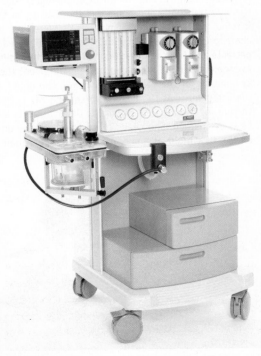

(3) more than 21 consecutive days with at least 6 hours of ventilation (ability to breathe without mechanical assistance for only a few hours) required each day. LTACH patients have mixed health outcome results, ranging from high 1-year mortality (death) rates with limited weaning success for removing the patient from the ventilator to full success in removing patients from their required ventilation. Other reports state high hospital readmission rates leading to high mortality rates. LTACH offer a variety of services, but the level, intensity, and quality of rehabilitative and pulmonary treatment plans of care vary from one location to another.[3, 4] Another study reported that patients on ventilators are usually older, sicker, and harder to wean from mechanical ventilation due to diagnoses of respiratory failure, chronic obstructive pulmonary disease, and pneumonia.[5] As the population ages, there is a greater need for LTACHs because there is an increased number of patients with respiratory distress syndrome; the cost of long-term care in a traditional hospital intensive care unit is prohibitive; and it is not a good use of hospital intensive care beds. Because medical care is able to keep individuals alive in intensive care units, the number of patients requiring mechanical ventilation (respirator) is increasing. However, they are too sick to go home or to a skilled nursing facility due to continued need for long-term acute care. Long-term respirators are also used by individuals with spinal cord injuries. Although some such individuals live at home with healthcare assistance, they frequently encounter respiratory infections that require admissions to hospitals and LTACHs for treatment.

Cancer Research Institutions

The primary purpose of a cancer institution is to conduct research while treating individuals with a cancer diagnosis. Many of these cancer institutions have the "National Cancer Institute" (NCI) designation in the title. This NCI designation means that the federal National Institutes of Health provides a substantial amount of federal grant dollars to fund the research being conducted at these national centers. Although these cancer institutions look like a typical hospital, they do not have emergency departments for treating noncancer-related injuries or illness. Additionally, there are a smaller number of hospital beds, because most of the space in the large buildings is occupied by high-level research laboratories and research offices. If individuals choose to receive their cancer treatment at a cancer institution, they are given extensive information about the clinical research trial protocols for their type of cancer diagnosis that are available at that institution. After signing the informed-consent documents, the individuals enroll in the appropriate clinical trial and receive the treatment prescribed in the research protocol. If the individuals do not wish to participate in clinical cancer research, they may be advised to seek cancer treatment at a non-NCI cancer institution. For example, a patient with a cancer diagnosis may seek standard of care at a regional hospital. Standard of care is defined as the best-known way that is typically used to treat a specific type of cancer. The extensive research has shown that a specific treatment or combination of treatment protocols (e.g., medication, radiation therapy, surgical technique) is currently proven to be the most effective and safe. However, if the standard of care is not working as expected or the type of cancer is too rare, the patient may decide to enroll in a research clinical trial at an NCI institute. In addition, there are cancer treatment centers that are not designated NCI institutions, but are hospital facilities that specialize in the care and treatment of patients with cancer. Some of these institutions advertise extensively and purport that they offer a holistic approach to cancer treatment. Whether an individual selects nonresearch standard of care treatment, clinical research protocols, or an alternative cancer care institution, it is advised that they explore the advantages and disadvantages of all options and obtain second options prior to making their final selection for cancer treatment.

RESIDENTIAL HEALTHCARE FACILITIES

The following section describes inpatient healthcare facilities that offer residential specific services, including rehabilitation, assisted-living and memory care centers, skilled nursing, palliative care, and hospice.

Rehabilitation Facilities

Rehabilitation facilities provide residential treatment for individuals who sustained an injury or surgical procedure requiring short-term convalescence, physical therapy, and occupational therapy. A few examples of individuals needing rehabilitation care include (a) an individual who sustained serious internal injuries and several fractured bones from a car crash; (b) military veterans returning from combat needing rehabilitation services to recover from wounds and possible amputations; and (c) an elderly individuals needing rehabilitation services after sustaining a serious fall or joint (e.g., shoulder, knee, hip) replacement surgery. All of these individuals are capable of recovering and returning to their place of residence after receiving care and therapy in a rehabilitation facility. Whereas the individual is not medically ill enough to remain a hospital patient, their immediate needs are unable to be met at home by their family, caregivers, or home healthcare services.

© Comstock/Stockbyte/ThinkStock

Assisted-Living Facilities

Assisted-living facilities provide nonmedical services to individuals who are no longer able to live independently. The staff assists with the activities of daily living (ADL), such as dressing, bathing, toileting, eating, and mobility. Assisted-living facilities do not provide medical care. Residents are responsible for taking their own medications with limited medical supervision and assistance. The residents have access to common living areas such as a television viewing/living room area, a common dining room, an activity/craft room, library, chapel, outside patio and gardens, as well as a private or shared

© Jupiterimages/Stockbyte/ThinkStock

bedroom with a bathroom. The staff provides assistance with bathing and assists in getting to the dining room whether by walking, using a walker or cane, or a wheelchair or scooter. It is common to encourage eating meals in the common dining room for socialization. However, it is possible for residents to have their meals brought to their bedroom periodically. Residents wear clothing of their choice and laundry services are available.

Memory care centers are a specialized type of assisted-care facility. Because of the increase of Alzheimer's disease and other memory loss diagnoses in the general population, there is a greater need for memory care centers to protect individuals with late-stage memory loss. Some memory care centers are attached to assisted-living facilities or skilled nursing facilities. In other communities, the memory care centers are free-standing facilities. In the early stages of memory loss, the family and other caregivers often provide care for their loved ones. However, as memory loss increases, some families find the responsibility to be overwhelming or find it unsafe for the individual to remain at home. For example, if adult children are employed full-time outside of the home, it is not possible to leave an elderly parent with late-stage memory loss at home alone. Some families cope by hiring a certified home health aide, but this arrangement has mixed results. The elderly parent may not recognize the home health aide and become frightened. In other situations, the elderly parent must have 24-hour supervision due to dangerous activities such as leaving a stove burner on, overflowing the bathtub, or leaving the house unattended and getting lost. Whatever the situation, some families determine that a residential environment outside of their home is required for the safety and well-being of their family member. Within the memory care centers, as with other assisted-living facilities, the staff provides assistance with the activities of daily living as needed. As memory diminishes for the individuals, the staff changes from assistance with ADL care to basic skilled nursing care to high levels of nursing care as the individual becomes bedridden with lack of bladder and bowel control and, finally, death as the brain is no longer able to function to support life.

Skilled Nursing Services

Skilled nursing facilities (also called *nursing homes*) offer a full range of nursing services, including 24-hour medication dispensing, wound care, diaper changes, nutritional supplements, extensive assistance with activities of daily living, as well as therapies (speech, occupational, physical). Individuals with advanced Alzheimer's disease or dementia are moved from assisted-living facilities to a skilled nursing facility as their condition worsens. For individuals who are bedridden, skilled nursing facility staff are trained to prevent decubitus ulcers (bed sores), urinary tract infections from indwelling catheters, and care of fragile skin. Meals are prepared to meet specific dietary needs for diabetics, blended meals for tube feeding needs, and calorie intake monitoring for individuals losing weight due to illness. Skilled nursing facilities are costly, but are often necessary for families unable to care for elderly family at home. There are private skilled nursing facilities for individuals who have purchased long-term care insurance and have sufficient finances to cover the cost of skilled nursing care. For individuals without long-term care insurance or adequate financial resources, there are public skilled nursing facilities for individuals with low income and who are Medicaid qualified. Both types of skilled nursing facilities are licensed under strict federal and state guidelines, including staffing ratios between nurses and patients, staff training, food preparation, safety standards and monitoring, and laundry services. However, the differences are noted at the level of staff salaries, availability of private

rooms, wide food choices, daily activities, extent of therapy services, and extra amenities such as beauty and barbershops, gift shop, lush grounds maintenance, and garden paths.

Palliative Care and Hospice

Palliative care is defined as an approach to medical care that improves the quality of life for individuals who have chronic long-term pain. Palliative care is not always related to a terminal illness. For example, an individual with a multiple sclerosis diagnosis (a degenerative muscle syndrome) lives for many years, but will experience intermittent episodes of pain that can be managed by palliative care. On the other hand, an individual with a bone cancer diagnosis lives with progressive pain and finds relief with palliative care before, during, and after cancer treatment. Palliative care focuses on quality of life while working in conjunction with the appropriate course of treatments that are intended to prolong life, such as surgery, chemotherapy, or radiation therapy. Both individuals have progressive illnesses and thus may or may not choose to move from palliative to hospice care at some point. Individuals facing the problems associated with painful or life-threatening illness receive relief of suffering by early identification, assessment, and management of pain and other problems including physical limitations, psychosocial issues, and spiritual guidance.[6] A support system team helps patients live as actively as possible and helps the family cope during the patient's illness. As the disease process advances, palliative care services are enhanced to manage pain and other symptoms, and the individual may move from palliative care to hospice care and maintain quality of life as desired.[6]

Individuals do not need to be receiving palliative care to move into hospice care. Individuals may choose hospice care when they have a limited life expectancy. However, hospice care is no longer reserved for the last 6 months of life because for many diseases there is no way to determine an individual's life expectancy. Whereas hospice patients usually have a cancer diagnosis, they can accept anyone regardless of age, type of illness, or ability to pay. These individuals may receive hospice services

© Wavebreakmedia/ iStockphoto

at home, in a community setting, or in homelike hospice facilities. Hospice offers comprehensive services to patients and support to their families.

The comprehensive care includes a care plan for pain management along with emotional, spiritual, and practical support for the patient and their families. Hospice offers a team approach to care. Each team typically includes a physician, a nurse, a home health aide, a social worker, a chaplain, and a volunteer. The specially trained volunteers offer respite care for family members as well as meaningful support to the patient. The concept of hospice affirms life and regards dying as a normal process. The philosophy of hospice is to neither hasten nor postpone death. Death is unique for each individual, so the goal of the hospice team is to focus on a sensitive and responsive approach for each individual and their family.[7]

Summary

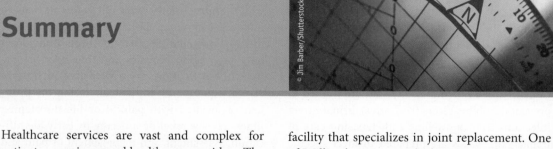

© Jim Barber/Shutterstock

Healthcare services are vast and complex for patients, caregivers, and healthcare providers. The focus of this chapter was on various types of inpatient healthcare facilities. The chapter began with a description of various types of hospitals and ended with a discussion of nonhospital residential facilities, including rehabilitation, assisted living, skilled nursing, palliative care, and hospice.

Student Activity

Health navigation professionals encounter various individuals in need of services. For this student activity, select one type of outpatient facility. Write a 200-word scenario for the facility that you selected to illustrate how the services of a health navigation professional would be utilized.

Example

William is a health navigation professional who works full-time at a corporate physical therapy

facility that specializes in joint replacement. One of William's primary job duties is to find transportation for the elderly patients who attend physical and occupational therapy at this facility. When he started this position, William spent time learning the kinds of transportation available for the elderly patients, including bus routes with accommodation for individuals with disabilities, taxi van service, retirement home bus services, transportation through home health services, and volunteer drivers (community networks, retired volunteer services). William also checked into possible transportation payment sources, such as Medicare, Medicaid, and supplemental insurance. After he made a complete list of available transportation services, William noticed that there was always some waiting time for patients, so he took this opportunity to get to know the patients and their families. He would inquire about their social support and perhaps other needs that may not have been addressed through physical therapy, such as pet care, grocery shopping, or preparing meals. As a health navigation professional, William looked at the whole person and made sure that each individual had the services needed for daily activity and social interaction.

References

1. Shriners Hospitals for Children. Retrieved June 8, 2015, from http://www.shrinershospitalsforchildren.org.

2. St. Jude Children's Research Hospital. *How St. Jude began.* Retrieved June 29, 2015, from https://www.stjude.org/about-st-jude/history/how-we-began.html.

3. Criner, G. J. (2012). Long-term ventilator-dependent patients: New facilities and new models of care. The American perspective. *Revista Portuguesa de Pneumologia,* 18(5), 214–216.

4. Criner, G. J. (2002). Care of the patient requiring invasive mechanical ventilation. *Respiratory Care Clinics of North America,* 8(4), 575–592.

5. The World Health Organization. *WHO definition of palliative care.* Retrieved May 31, 2015, from http://www.who.int/cancer/palliative/definition/en.

6. Peñuelas, O., Frutos-Vivar, F., Fernandez, C., Anzueto, A., Epstein, S. K., Apeztequiz, C., Gonzalez, M., et al. (2011). Characteristics and outcomes of ventilated patients according to time to liberation from mechanical ventilation. *American Journal of Respiratory and Critical Care Medicine,* 184(4), 430–437.

7. National Hospice and Palliative Care Organization. *Hospice care.* Retrieved May 31, 2015, from http://www.nhpco.org/about/hospice-care.

funding from local tax revenue for the local health and human services, the state covers a portion of the fiscal responsibilities of the county health services. Some larger departments of health provide medical services, whereas smaller departments with little funding refer individuals to medical services available in other locations in the county.

Federally Qualified Health Center

Federally Qualified Health Centers (FQHCs) offer important healthcare services in rural and underserved areas. See **Figure 5.1**. More than 22 million Americans receive care at a FQHC and approximately a third are rural residents.[1] An FQHC qualifies for federal support as a health center if the FQHC meets the following criteria: (a) offers services to all individuals, regardless of ability to pay; (b) establishes a sliding fee discount program; (c) is a nonprofit or public organization; (d) is community based, with the majority of the governing board of directors composed of its patients;

(e) serves a medically underserved area or population; (f) provides comprehensive primary care services; and (g) has an ongoing quality assurance program.[1] FQHCs have a unique reimbursement designation from the Bureau of Primary Health Care and the Centers for Medicare and Medicaid Services of the U.S. Department of Health and Human Services. This designation is significant for several health programs funded under the Health Center Consolidation Act (Section 330 of the Public Health Service Act). FQHCs and certain Tribal organizations qualify for enhanced reimbursement from Medicare and Medicaid.[1]

Hospital-Owned Outpatient Clinics

In some cities, hospitals are operating their own outpatient clinics. The purpose of these clinics is to offer primary care to individuals with or without health insurance instead of having the individuals rely on the emergency department for nonemergency medical services. Some outpatient

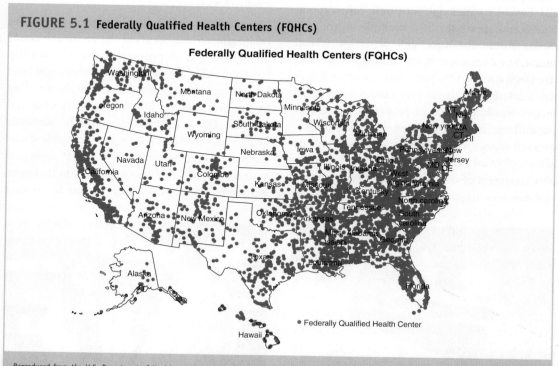

FIGURE 5.1 Federally Qualified Health Centers (FQHCs)

clinics are located near the hospital. If an individual is receiving medical care at the outpatient clinic, but is diagnosed with a more serious medical condition, he or she is transported to the hospital emergency department for treatment. Because the hospital emergency department offers the most intensive and expensive care for critically ill or injured individuals, it is not appropriate to use the emergency department to treat primary injuries, cold and flu symptoms, headaches, and mild forms of noncommunicable diseases. Instead, the hospital can offer the same services at the community outpatient clinics at a reduced cost and with limited wait times. These outpatient clinics offer appointments and walk-in services for convenience. Generally, the clinics have extended hours of operation (8:00 a.m. to 8:00 p.m.) to serve working families. These outpatient clinics are open 5, 6, or even 7 days per week depending on the needs of the community.

Urgent Care Clinics

Urgent care clinics (walk-in clinics) are usually owned by national, for-profit corporations. One corporation may own multiple urgent care clinics within the same city or across several states. The clinics are open about 12 hours per day (8:00 a.m. to 8:00 p.m.) and are open 7 days per week. Some urgent care clinics are located in free-standing buildings or shopping malls or within large discount department stores. Healthcare services offered at urgent care clinics include school physical examinations, treatment of allergies, treatment of cold and flu symptoms, radiology services to diagnosis minor unintentional injuries (such as sprained ligaments or minor broken bones), repair of a laceration with stitches, and the diagnosis of major medical conditions requiring a referral to a higher level of services, such as the emergency department at the local hospital. For example, an individual may go to an urgent care clinic with chest pain. The physician may diagnose the condition as an acute myocardial infarction and call an ambulance to transport the individual to the hospital. On the other hand, after conducting an **electrocardiogram (ECG)** and immediate blood tests, the diagnosis may not be linked to a cardiac diagnosis, but rather indigestion, anxiety, and stress. Individuals using an urgent care clinic may or may not have health insurance. Individuals without health insurance must pay for the initial visit prior to receiving services; if additional lab tests or X-rays are needed, then additional payment is required. Urgent care clinics do not offer reduced-cost care. If individuals do not have any method of payment, the staff refers them to the nearest emergency department.

PHARMACY

The most basic and simple type of outpatient healthcare service occurs at the pharmacy counter. For example, suppose you are leaving for a trip tomorrow. Your throat is a little sore and you have some sinus congestion. Because you are traveling by air, you ask the pharmacist what over-the-counter (OTC) medication would be advisable given your situation. For no cost, the pharmacist suggests a decongestant and a throat spray for your sore throat. She also reminds you that your symptoms are mostly likely caused by a viral

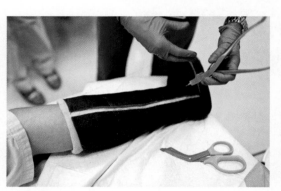

© Juanmonino/iStockphoto

© william87/iStock Photo

infection and that antibiotics would not improve your symptoms. She takes the opportunity to tell you to drink plenty of fluids and frequently wash your hands to avoid spreading the virus germs to others. This free service is available at any pharmacy. Recently, national pharmacy locations have begun adding other services such as vaccinations to reduce the chances of acquiring the flu, pneumonia, and shingles. The vaccines are provided for a nominal cost during a convenient walk-in service with little or no waiting. Pharmacists are also employed at hospitals, cancer treatment centers, corporate research institutions, and universities. However, your local pharmacy offers excellent, no-cost advice related to prescribed medications, over-the-counter medicines, and the interactions between medications.

OUTPATIENT AMBULATORY SURGICAL CENTERS (OASC)

Most cities have Outpatient Ambulatory Surgical Centers (OASC). The centers are owned and operated by a corporation, a local hospital, or a group of physicians. Because many surgical procedures are performed as outpatient services, it is no longer necessary to be admitted to a hospital. Examples of surgery performed in an OASC include breast cancer lumpectomy, placement of long-term venous ports for chemotherapy treatments, tissue and bone marrow biopsies, placement of several types of stents, simple realignment of bone fractures, colonoscopies, tubal ligation and vasectomies, foot and bunion surgeries, some dermatology and minor plastic surgery, cataract and Lasik eye surgery, and numerous other minimal risk surgeries. Patients have blood tests and radiology procedures completed a few days prior to the surgery, arrive early in the morning on their surgery day, and are ready for discharge by no later than 8:00 p.m. If complications occur, which are rare, the patient is transported to the nearby hospital for admission. In some situations, the OASC is specific to a surgical specialty. For example, a large 40+ orthopedic physician medical group builds an OASC only for their patients. All of the nurses and staff are employed, trained, and paid by the large physician

group. This model allows for ease of movement for patients, physicians, nurses, and staff during the day. In addition, the operating surgical rooms, equipment, and recovery rooms are specific to only orthopedic surgery. Another example is in the field of ophthalmology (the study of the eye). Similarly, the surgical operating room equipment is specific to only eye surgery and the physicians, nurses, and staff are trained for this unique type of surgical procedure.

OTHER OUTPATIENT SERVICES

Several other types of specific care are offered as outpatient services. This discussion provides examples of specific care services. Large cities offer a wide range of outpatient services, whereas small towns do not offer the same services due to the insufficient population needed to support such practices.

Dialysis Treatment

Two types of individuals with kidney disease need dialysis treatment. First, some individuals have sustained kidney damage from an unintentional injury, infections, chemotherapy, or a surgical procedure. Whereas their other injuries may heal properly, their kidneys remain damaged and require further treatment. These individuals continue to make urine, but their kidneys are not able to filter the toxins out of their blood adequately. They require dialysis treatment once or twice a week for a few months or until their kidneys regain normal function. Second, individuals with end-stage renal disease (ESRD) have permanent kidney failure and must remain on dialysis for

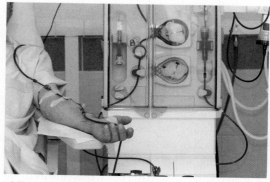

© Zeljko Bozic/Hemera/Thinkstock

the remainder of their life. The most common disease associated with ESRD is diabetes. Both Type 1 diabetes and Type 2 diabetes lead to ESRD if not controlled for a period of time. Some ESRD patients continue to produce small amounts urine, while others do not produce any urine. All dialysis patients need to closely control their fluid intake because any fluid that they consume remains in their body until their next dialysis treatment. For example, the average fluid intake limit for an adult with ESRD is less than one liter per day. All fluids are included in that measurement including water, milk, juice, and soda, but also the fluid in lettuce, soup, gravy, and sauces. The patients must also have limited amounts of sodium and potassium. Each patient is weighed prior to each dialysis treatment to determine how much fluid he or she gained since the last treatment and how much fluid needs to be removed. If the fluid gained exceeds one liter, the treatment takes longer and puts greater strain on the heart. Over time, dialysis patients develop heart failure. Over time, even patients who never exceed the fluid limit will sustain serious heart damage due to the extreme shift in body fluids and buildup of toxins.

Some dialysis patients may qualify for a kidney transplant. The transplant process is lengthy and involves one of three donation matches: (a) matched to a relative who is willing to donate a kidney; (b) matched to an individual who is willing to donate one of his or her two kidneys; or (c) matched to a person who designated a desire to be an organ donor on a driver's license at the time of death. The transplant process is beyond the scope of this discussion, but does remind the reader to consider becoming an organ donor. Hundreds of thousands of individuals receive dialysis treatment across the world each day.

Dialysis is an artificial kidney medical treatment that filters blood through a machine to remove excess fluid and toxins. There are two types of dialysis treatments. First, hemodialysis is a method in which the patient is connected to a dialysis machine with two large-bore needles. One needle is used to remove the blood from the body for cleansing, and the other needle is to return the cleansed blood back to the body. Individuals using

hemodialysis may receive services at a dialysis treatment center and are required to get dialyzed three times each week. If they fail to get a dialysis treatment, the excess toxins and fluids build up within their bodies and can lead to death. Individuals can also choose to receive home hemodialysis treatments. Because the home dialysis machine is smaller, these individuals must get dialyzed daily. Some dialysis patients choose to go to a dialysis center to have days off between the required treatments. In addition, home hemodialysis can represent a significant burden for family members or caregivers. It is usually not possible for individuals to connect themselves to the dialysis machine at home. They are encouraged to have a caregiver at all times. In addition, the dialysis center offers some social support aspects for patients on dialysis. At the centers, each individual is assigned a specific day (Monday, Wednesday, Friday or Tuesday, Thursday and Saturday) and a specific time. Therefore, the same individuals are receiving treatment at the same time and they get to know each other, creating supportive friendships. However, it should be noted that dialysis patients feel tired and experience flu-like symptoms most of the time due to the buildup of toxins in their blood. One patient described being on dialysis as "the day before dialysis you feel like you are getting the flu and the day of dialysis you feel like you have the flu." Dialysis patients never feel completely healthy. The process of cleaning the blood while connected to the dialysis machine takes about 4 hours for the average-sized individual. Obese individuals may be connected to the dialysis machine for up to 6–8 hours, depending on their body mass index. Dialysis centers offer comfortable lounge chairs with headphones, Internet access, and television screens. Some patients watch movies or use the Internet. However, most patients sleep during their dialysis treatment.

The second type of dialysis treatment is called *peritoneal dialysis*. This dialysis treatment is generally performed at home with a caregiver and requires the patient to be lying flat. For that reason, it is usually done during the night while the patient sleeps. This method involves having two tubes permanently and surgically placed in the abdominal cavity with access on the outside. The caregiver places several liters of exchange fluid into the abdominal cavity. The osmotic content of the fluid draws out the toxins and fluids from the blood. The fluid is removed after a few hours and clean fluid is replaced in the abdomen. This process takes 6–8 hours of cyclically exchanging and replacing the fluid throughout the night. This method does not require that patients have needles placed in their arm daily or every other day. However, this method is less effective in cleaning the blood and does require a caregiver each night to exchange the fluids.

Infusion Centers

Infusion centers were created by infectious disease physicians. The primary purpose of infusion centers is to allow patients to be discharged from the hospital and still continue their intravenous (IV) antibiotic medications. Patients are often discharged from a hospital with an infection acquired in the hospital or through the physician (iatrogenic) as a result of surgery, a wound infection, or a medical complication such as pneumonia. Whatever the cause, if the individual is able to be discharged from the hospital, there is no need to increase the length of stay or the hospital charges. These patients need the continued benefit of receiving intravenous antibiotics, because taking oral antibiotics would not be as effective for treating their infection. In these circumstances, the patients are given a referral to an infusion center. Prior to discharge, the physician writes the orders for the infusion center. It is up to the discharging nurse, patient, caregiver or health navigation professional to call the infusion center and arrange a day and time for infusion. Some patients need the medication every 12 hours, so they would go to the infusion center at 8:00 a.m. and 8:00 p.m. Other patients need the medication only once per day. In either case, the infusion centers are usually open 12 hours per day, 7 days per week. The patients may be discharged with their IV capped off, but remaining in their arm, while other patients have their IV removed at discharge and the

infusion center starts a new IV site every 4 days. It is not unusual for patients to need up to 28 days of IV antibiotics and, in some cases, the treatment may be extended for a few additional weeks. The infusion centers can also draw blood work, so the infectious disease physician can determine the effectiveness of the treatment on the patient's infection.

Similar to infusion clinics for antibiotic treatments, some large corporate cancer treatment centers offer chemotherapy infusion at small neighborhood clinics. Unlike the infectious disease infusion clinics, the chemotherapy clinics are usually only for the patients who receive their cancer medical care from the physicians associated with the large corporate cancer treatment center. Such clinics are generally in a convenient location and offer comfortable surroundings and lounge chairs, headphones, television screens, snacks, and social support for patients and families. Because some chemotherapy medications infuse slowly over 8 hours, patients appreciate the convenience and social support.

Wound Care Clinics

Wound care clinics serve patients with specific wound management needs, including decubitus ulcers (bed sores), small and deep tissue burns caused by unintentional injuries, wound infections, necrotic tissue linked to individuals with paralysis, and foot or leg ulcers related to diabetes. Although the causes of the wounds are varied, the

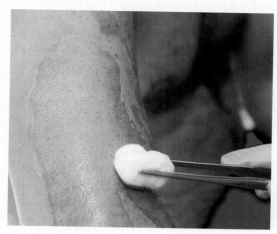
© choja/iStock Photo

treatments are similar and long-term. The individual may have been hospitalized with the initial wound for the initial treatment or it may have been necessary to perform surgery to debride (remove death tissue) the wound so healing could begin. A skin graft surgery may also have been performed, so healing could begin. Either way, the open wound or the skin-grafted wound needs daily medical oversight in an outpatient wound care clinic. Physicians who work in wound care clinics are generally dermatologists specializing in complex wound care. The patients are referred to wound care clinics upon hospital discharge or from an outpatient clinic visit. Wound care is needed daily for a few days or weeks. Then, as the healing progresses, the clinic visits are reduced to every few days until the healing is complete. For example, individuals with paralysis and in a wheelchair must be acutely aware of the condition of their skin. Because they are paralyzed, they do not have any feeling, so if an open wound begins due to rubbing from the edge of the wheelchair pad near their buttocks, the individual would not feel the wound discomfort signaling an issue. Without having a caregiver check their skin daily for red irritations, sores, or small breaks in the skin, a large wound can form and become infected in a few days. Wound care focuses on prevention. It is much easier to prevent a decubitus ulcer from ever forming. Excellent caregiving is required to maintain skin integrity for bedridden patients and includes turning the patient once per hour, applying skin protection ointment, changing the bed linens frequently, and frequently changing disposable diapers to keep skin clean and dry. In the case of wounds caused by lack of circulation, such as in the case of patients with diabetes and vascular medical conditions, the wound care physician works closely with a vascular surgeon to retain blood flow to the lower limbs for as long as possible. If the blood flow is reduced and vascular surgery cannot restore the circulation, the low limb becomes necrotic (dead tissue) and, unfortunately, may need to be amputated at the level of the limb where circulation remains adequate. For example, suppose for one individual the

tissue appears to be necrotic just above the ankle. However, the vascular surgeon determines that the blood flow reduction is actually just below the knee. The amputation is performed just below the knee in hopes of preserving the joint. Once the amputation is complete, the wound care physician is called to care for the surgical site of the amputation. It is essential for the wound to heal prior to fitting the prosthetic leg and beginning physical therapy. If the surgical site is not completely healed, the weight-bearing activity of physical therapy will disrupt healing and thus require another surgery. Also, wound care clinics provide outpatient services to individuals with severe burns after they have been discharged from the hospital.

Physical Therapy Outpatient Facilities

Physical therapy (PT) services are offered to patients in the hospital, in the home, and in outpatient facilities. Prior to discharge, the physical therapist begins to teach the patients a few basic exercises to improve their quality of life and strength. After an individual is discharged from the hospital following a surgical procedure, such as a shoulder, knee, or hip replacement, it is necessary to continue physical therapy at home for a few weeks. Unlike the daily physical therapy while in the hospital, the physical therapist comes to the home two or three times per week. As soon as the patients are able to gain sufficient mobility and strength, the physical therapy sessions are conducted in an outpatient physical therapy facility.

Other individuals begin their physical therapy sessions as outpatients. In either situation, physical therapists provide therapy treatments to assist individuals with injuries or illness to improve the ability to move (e.g., walk, use crutches, a walker or a cane, learn to move in a wheelchair) and manage their pain. All states require physical therapists to maintain national licensure. Outpatient physical therapy facilities are located near hospitals, clinics, or other convenient locations within a community, such as retail malls. The location is primarily based on ease of access and convenient parking because some individuals receiving physical therapy have limited mobility. The facilities are owned by corporations, hospitals, clinics, or private physical therapy companies. Physical therapy services are covered through health insurance, but most health insurance policies limit the number of physical therapy sessions covered in a 12-month period. Most individuals pay for some portion of their physical therapy as a fee-for-service. If they are unable to afford the cost to continue, physical therapists teach the individuals some exercises that can be performed at home. However, at-home exercise is less effective for complete recovery. Physical therapy is prescribed by healthcare providers to improve function, mobility, and recovery of joints and muscles in all parts of the body. Physical therapy includes active exercise, passive movement, exercise equipment, heat, ice, and massage.

TREATMENT CENTERS

There are several types of treatment centers. Some treatment centers offer only outpatient services, and some treatment centers offer both inpatient and outpatient services. As with other outpatient facilities, the types of centers are based on ownership including corporate, private, group, community, or nonprofit. Payment options for services include fee-for-service, private health insurance, or public funding such as Medicaid (health insurance for individuals with low income) or no-cost services.

Mental Health

Mental health treatment centers are owned by corporations, hospitals, community organizations, or private physician groups. Most treatment centers serve adolescents and adults. Children with mental health needs are admitted to hospital pediatric units. Eligibility of services for mental health treatment centers is divided by the individual's ability to pay for the services. First, some mental health treatment centers are strictly for individuals with health insurance that covers mental health services or who have adequate income to pay for services without health insurance coverage. Second, other mental health

© Wavebreakmedia/iStock Photo

treatment centers offer services to individuals with or without health insurance or the ability to pay for the services. Because most health insurance policies cover only a portion of mental health services and have limits on the number of days of services, many individuals seek treatment at community-based mental health treatment centers. Both types of mental health centers provide inpatient and outpatient services. Inpatient services are for individuals experiencing a crisis and are deemed as a risk to themselves or other people. Depending on the state laws, such individuals are placed in a protective environment, such as a comfortable private room, and given medication as prescribed to reduce their risks. Due to their mental health crisis, such individuals may be held against their will for a period of time until a licensed psychiatrist evaluates their mental status and prescribes appropriate treatment, length of stay, and medications. Outpatient services at mental health treatment centers include day treatment options; private, group, and family therapy sessions; community resources for education; food, housing, transportation, and health care. Because a large percentage of the homeless population have mental health challenges, some community mental health treatment centers provide day treatment options to offer support to the homeless. In the more private pay mental health treatment centers, services are similar, but the surroundings are more luxurious, private, and hidden from view or access of the general population. These treatment centers serve individuals such as movie stars or other wealthy individuals who wish to seek anonymous treatment and mental health services.

Drug Treatment

Drug treatment centers are similar to mental health treatment centers in that they offer inpatient and outpatient services. Drug treatment centers are also divided by type of patient funding, which is either fee-for-service, limited health insurance coverage or no health insurance, or another type of funding. Some drug treatment centers offer services specifically for adolescents, while other centers admit only adults. Drug treatment centers offer services for addiction of alcohol, street drugs, or prescription drugs. The supportive treatment begins with a detoxification process to wean individuals off the drugs by either "cold turkey" (stop all drugs immediately) or through a process over a few days. Either way, the goal is to assist the individual in moving from addiction to a life free of addiction.

Disordered Eating

Disordered eating treatment centers are similar to both mental health and substance abuse treatment centers. The services may be inpatient or outpatient and based on ability to pay. Generally, if the individual is not capable of paying for services, then the center makes referrals to community mental health centers. Some centers treat only adolescents, but most centers offer services to individuals over age 18. Disordered eating includes obesity, anorexia nervosa, and bulimia nervosa. The treatment is mental health therapy to gain a healthy perspective of food choices. Unlike substance addictions, individuals must eat to sustain life. Whether the purpose is weight loss or weight gain, the treatment includes individual, group, and family therapy sessions; exercise and yoga; healthy food choices; and a range of art, music, and meditation.

Summary

© Jim Barber/Shutterstock

This chapter described various types of outpatient facilities and services, including wellness and preventive services, several types of medical practices and clinics, pharmacy services, outpatient ambulatory surgical centers, and other outpatient services (e.g., dialysis treatment, wound care, infusion centers). Finally, there was a discussion about different types of outpatient treatment centers.

Student Activity

Health navigation professionals encounter various individuals in need of services. For this student activity, select two outpatient facilities. Write a 200-word scenario for each of the two facilities to illustrate how the services of a health navigation professional would be utilized.

Example

Linda is a health navigation professional with a specialization in geriatric care. She divides her full-time position between a corporate medical office in the morning and a rehabilitation facility in the afternoon. Both locations are owned by the same corporation. At the corporate medical office, she works as the liaison between the patients, their family members, and the staff to ensure the new patient is getting his or her immediate needs met and is satisfied with the care. Overall, her job is to do the little things where the staff may not have time. For example, Linda notices in Mr. Williams' EMR that he refusing to go to his physical therapy sessions. Because she has the time, she investigates why he refuses to go to physical therapy at 2:30 p.m. After a brief conversation, she learns that Mr. Williams' daily routine is to take a 1-hour nap from 2:00–3:00 p.m. each day. He explains that he would be glad to go to physical therapy in the morning, but no one asked him, so he just refuses. Linda talks to the physical therapist and he changes Mr. Williams' appointment from 2:30 p.m. to 9:30 a.m. A week later, Linda checks in with Mr. Williams. He is pleased to report that he has not missed physical therapy all week, is making good progress, and still enjoys his daily nap.

References

1. U.S. Department of Health and Human Services. *What are federally qualified health centers (FQHCs)?* Retrieved January 30, 2016, from http://www.hrsa.gov/healthit/toolbox /RuralHealthITtoolbox/Introduction/qualified.html.

CHAPTER 6

Health Insurance

LEARNING OBJECTIVES

By the end of this chapter, students will be able to:

- Explain the history of health insurance in the United States
- Differentiate between the health system in the United States and other countries
- Define the different types of available private insurance
- Define the different types of government insurance
- Understand important health insurance terminology

CHAPTER OVERVIEW

This chapter begins with a brief history of the U.S. health insurance system. After the historical background is understood, the discussion compares the health insurance system in other industrial countries to that of the United States. It will become obvious that there are no simple solutions to healthcare issues internationally. The next section describes the various types of health insurance available in the United States. This discussion illustrates the vast complexity across health insurance options and why it is so difficult to navigate the healthcare system. The chapter ends with two case studies that detail the reasons why individuals would benefit from the services of a health navigation professional.

HISTORY OF HEALTH INSURANCE IN THE UNITED STATES

Before exploring the current healthcare system in the United States, it is important to understand the historical background.

1847: The first healthcare insurance policy was offered by Massachusetts Health Insurance of Boston.[1, 2] At the time, when individuals needed medical services, they went to the hospital and paid cash. If they did not have the money, they did not receive care. This type of payment is called *fee-for-service*. This first health insurance policy was sold to individuals in the Boston area. It was a type of health savings account. Individuals who purchased the policy paid a weekly fee to the health insurance company. When an individual needed medical care, he or she paid cash for a portion of the care, and the health insurance company paid the remaining portion of the medical charges out of the individual's accumulated account.[1, 2]

1861: During the Civil War (1861–1865), early insurance policies offered coverage against accidents caused by train and steamboat travel.[1] This is the same concept as previously described. The workers paid into a fund, so that when they were injured on the job, there was money available to pay for their healthcare expenses.[1]

1890: Insurance companies issued the first individual disability and illness policies.[1] Again, individuals paid into a fund, so that if they became disabled, the cost of their medical expenses were paid or reduced.

1900: The physicians organized the American Medical Association (AMA) and determined that they would no longer provide free care to hospital patients. The railroad companies were the first to develop medical programs for their employees. During this same time, Europe was ahead of the United States in developing insurance programs.[3]

1910: The first employer-sponsored group disability policy was issued. However, this policy only replaced lost wages due to an inability to work, but did not pay for medical expenses.[2] Hospitals offered a variety of surgical operations, anesthesia, pain relief medications, and antiseptic cleanliness against germs. The American Association of Labor Legislation began to discuss the concept of "social insurance," which is similar to the retirement benefits of today. Employees paid into a fund and, upon reaching retirement, a monthly premium was paid to the individual. As is still common, the employees would need to work for one employer for a specific number of years and pay a set monthly fee to be eligible for monthly premiums in retirement. However, the concept fell apart in 1917 with the onset of World War I.[3]

1920: The income of physicians increased, and their prestigious status in society was established. The car manufacturing company General Motors signed a contract to provide health insurance to 180,000 workers, and the concept of employers offering health insurance to their employees began to spread into other industries. This event marked the beginning of linking employment to health insurance policies.[3]

1930: The Great Depression hit the United States and the political focus moved away from health insurance to providing unemployment insurance and benefits for the elderly. The Social Security Act was passed, but omitted any type of health insurance benefits. In 1932, the non-profit organization Blue Cross began to offer group health insurance plans to employers.[3] This strategy was successful because they negotiated

© Bettmann/Getty Images

discounted contracts with doctors and hospitals and, in return, promised increased volume and prompt payment to the healthcare providers.[1] This started the tradition that continues today. The employer negotiates the cost of the healthcare policy; then, the employer pays a portion of the monthly premium and the employee pays a portion of the premium.

1940: During World War II, the government placed wage and price controls on U.S. companies. To remain competitive, hire the best workers, and deal with collective employment bargaining agreements, companies began to offer health benefits as an incentive and a way to deal with the unions and employee collective bargaining agreements.[1,4] These incentives remain in place today.[5] President Roosevelt tried to pass an "economic bill of rights" that included the right to adequate health care, but the bill failed. President Truman tried without success to pass a national single payer health program for all citizens.[3]

1950: National healthcare expenditures were 4.5 percent of the gross national product (GNP). Since 2009, that percent has remained at 17.4 percent. The political attention moved to the Korean War and away from healthcare reform. The citizens who could afford health insurance purchased it, and the federal welfare services became responsible for the poor. However, in 1954, the Social Security Act was amended to include disability benefits.[1] In health care, vaccines became available to combat polio, and the first successful organ transplant was performed.[3]

1960: Because the price of hospital services doubled in the 1950s, generally, only individuals with employer-based health insurance could afford it. Unemployed and elderly individuals struggled to pay health insurance premiums. At this time in the United States, there were more than 700 insurance companies selling health insurance policies.[3] The successes of the health insurance industry were based on the fundamental principle of healthier groups receiving lower premiums.[4] Because there was a national concern about having too few doctors, the federal government began to pour money into universities to expand medical education. President Lyndon Johnson signed Medicare (elderly) and Medicaid (low income) health insurance into law.[3]

When Medicare and Medicaid were created, private sources paid for 75 percent of all healthcare costs. By 1995, individuals and employers paid about 50 percent of healthcare costs and the government paid the other half.[1] The passage of the Medicare and Medicaid law meant that the government was now in the business of health insurance.[5]

1970: The World Health Organization declared that smallpox had been eradicated.[6] The number of women entering medical school increased from 9 percent to 25 percent in this decade. Healthcare costs increased dramatically due to Medicare expenditures, increased hospital profits, greater use of medical technology, and medications. President Nixon reported that the U.S. healthcare system was in crisis. He attempted to pass a bill for national health insurance, but it

failed. He also declared a "War on Cancer," centralized cancer research, and increased funding within the National Institute of Health. The health maintenance organizations (HMO) were created.[3] An HMO is defined as "an organization that provides health care to people who voluntarily enroll, make regular payments to it, and who agree to use only the doctors, hospitals, and other services that belong to the organization." Member physicians are paid fixed periodic payments determined in advance and are allowed to make only limited referrals to outside (nonmember) specialists.[3] For example, an individual joins an HMO and pays a monthly health insurance premium. As a result, the individual can only make appointments with physicians who are on his or her HMO list and only be admitted into hospitals that have contracts with the HMO. For any health services received that are not on the approved HMO contract list, the cost of that health service becomes the responsibility of the patient and is not paid by the HMO. HMOs regulate the number of patients that each physician can have in his or her network. For example, HMO-contracted physicians get paid a set amount of money each month for each HMO member whether or not the member received health care. For the individual, HMO premiums are generally lower because the number of individuals paying into the fund is greater. HMO contracts regulate the number, degree of illness, and age of patients across geographic locations, so that there is a balance of pay and work across HMO physicians. The HMO Act of 1974 was thought to be the ideal way to control the rising healthcare costs, because it distributed the cost of health care across a large pool of patients paying into the policy. It was thought that the number of healthy individuals would offset the number of sick individuals and thus lower the overall cost for everyone. However, it only solved the problem for a short while and is no longer thought to be effective.[5]

1980: There was a shift toward privatization and consolidation of health care by corporations. For example, large corporations were buying small hospitals to gain control of healthcare–related businesses. President Reagan changed Medicare

© World History Archive/Alamy Stock Photo

costs to a payment system of diagnostic-related groups (DRGs) instead of by treatment. Private health insurance policies also changed to the DRG method of payment.[3] For example, if a patient had a cholecystectomy (removal of the gallbladder), the hospital was paid one set price for the procedure and a predetermined number of days in the hospital instead of being paid for each test, treatment, and days in the hospital. If the patient received fewer tests and had a shorter hospital stay, the hospital earned money. However, if the patient encountered complications and a longer hospital stay was required, the hospital lost money. The DRG payment system remains in place today. "Capitation" payments were created to standardize how physicians are paid by insurance companies. For example, one physician charges a patient's health insurance company $200 for an initial office visit whereas another physician could charge the same health insurance company $350 for the same type of office visit. The insurance company regulates the same payment rate for the same service for each physician in geographic locations regardless of what the physician submits as the charge. Therefore, even though one physician bills the insurance company $200 and another physician bills the insurance company $300, they both could get paid $182 for the same initial office visit based on the health insurance contract for that geographic region. The individual pays the difference between the negotiated rate of their insurance policy and what the physician charges. Using the same example, one individual may pay $50 of the $182 cost and another individual may pay $100 of the $182. Yes, indeed, it is complex and never appears to be fair across the population.

A good analogy of healthcare costs is the airline industry. For example, all 100 economy class passengers on the same plane are traveling nonstop from Atlanta to Miami. Some passengers bought their ticket 3 months ago and paid $200; some passengers used their frequent flyer points and traveled at no cost; while other passengers bought their tickets in the past 7 days and paid $400. Everyone on the plane has the same flight experience of free soft drinks and no food; the flight attendants have no idea what each passenger paid and, thus, treats each passenger with the same level of customer service. Regardless of ticket price, each passenger had the same "outcome" of the arrival time in Miami. The same is true in health care: The hospital staff has no idea what each patient is paying, so everyone is treated the same and experiences similar outcomes based on previous health condition rather than on ability to pay.

1990: The cost of health care rose to double the rate of inflation. In 1991, the rate of inflation was 4.2 percent. This meant that if an individual bought a chair in 1990 and paid $100 for the chair, in 1991 the same chair would cost $104.20. In health care, if the cost of childbirth in 1991 was $6000 and the same service cost $6504 in 1992, this would mean that inflation almost doubled from 4.2 percent to 8.4 percent in a 1-year period. Again, Congress failed to pass federal healthcare reform legislation. However, President Clinton did sign several key legislative bills that improved the health and well-being of the U.S. population including:

- The Family and Medical Leave Act (FMLA), which protects an employee's job while ill or caring for a family member
- The Childhood Immunization Initiative to improve the immunization rates of children less than 2 years of age
- The first-ever Comprehensive Plan to Reduce Youth Smoking
- The Health Insurance Portability and Accountability Act (HIPAA), which assures that personal health information is protected from unlawful review, but still allows the information to be shared with other healthcare providers to promote quality health[7]
- The Smoke-Free Federal Workplaces Administration, which improved indoor air quality, raised federal tobacco tax, and took the tobacco manufacturers to court for decades of deception about the dangers of tobacco
- In this decade, 44 million Americans (16% percent of the total population) had no health insurance. U.S. individuals infected with HIV/AIDS had a 60 percent mortality (death) rate.[3]

2000: Medicare was thought to be unsustainable and the current structure had to be changed. Due to rising costs of health insurance premiums, fewer employers covered any of the costs of health insurance for their employees. The number of direct-to-consumer pharmaceuticals and medical devices advertisements rose significantly in this decade.[3] The Human Genome Project was completed and identified all of the more than 100,000 genes in human DNA. The Human Genome Project changed how health care identified, diagnosed, and treated certain disease and medical conditions.[3]

2010: While President Barrack Obama was in office, he signed into law the Patient Protection and Affordable Care Act (PPACA), commonly known as the Affordable Care Act (ACA). The outcome of this act is still largely unknown, but it serves as an attempt to change the current and unsustainable healthcare system.[5] One important section of the ACA states that it is illegal for health insurance companies to discriminate against individuals with a pre-existing medical conditions, such as cancer or diabetes.

With an understanding of the historical events that shaped the current U.S. healthcare system, it is time to compare the United States with other industrialized nations.

INTERNATIONAL COMPARISON WITH THE U.S. HEALTH SYSTEM

Because all countries face unique situations, it is difficult to compare exact criteria from one country to another. However, two international organizations maintain and assess comparable data from numerous developed countries: (a) Organization for Economic Cooperation and Development (OECD), which is an international economic group composed of 34 industrialized developed countries, and (b) the World Health Organization (WHO), which compares data from 29 industrialized countries. These organizations make general comparisons; however, it is important to note that health systems are not limited to only improving health but also to protecting the population from illness and the cost of illness. Most countries attempt to distribute healthcare services and costs across the population. Distributing health services evenly across a population requires governments to utilize private and voluntary funding while attempting to offset low-income segments of the population. Depending on the overall economic status of the country, most healthcare systems depend on government support for funding and sustainability. See **Figure 6.1** to review the total health expenditures per capita among several industrialized countries.

Figure 6.1 illustrates the fact that the United States spends more than twice as much money per person on health care than the average of all other OECD countries. Based on OECD and the WHO data, let us explore some of the differences between the United States and other comparable countries.

In 2012, healthcare spending accounted for 16.9 percent of gross domestic product (GDP) in the United States. Among the OECD countries, the average was 9.3 percent and the United States was 16.8 percent. In most OECD countries,

© Mark Makela/Getty Images

FIGURE 6.1 Total Public and Private Health Expenditure per Capita, 2010[8]

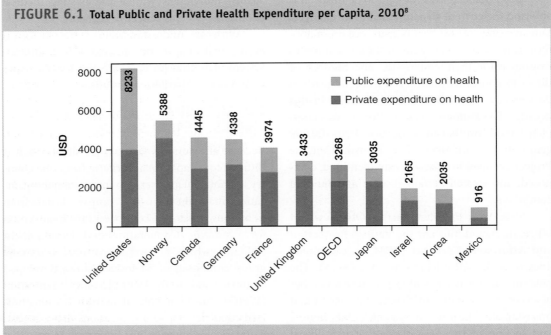

Data from: The Organization of Economic Cooperation and Development (2015). Health policies and data. Available at: http://www.oecd.org/health/. Accessed on February 8, 2015.

72 percent of health care is paid with public funding, but in the United States only 48 percent of health spending was publicly financed.[9] There are several apparent reasons for the higher cost of health care in the United States.

First, the U.S. healthcare system offers numerous advantages to individuals, albeit at a high cost. The United States leads the world in cancer treatment, with the highest survival rates in breast cancer and colorectal cancer. In the OECD countries, cancer treatment is available, but it may not involve the cutting-edge technology that is available at cancer research institution in the United States. On the other hand, the cutting-edge cancer treatment received at a cancer research institution does not guarantee a successful outcome or cancer remission. Also in the United States, insured patients have that shortest wait time for healthcare services compared with other OECD countries. In the United States, fewer than 20 percent of patients wait more than 4 weeks for a specialist appointment, and only 7 percent wait more than 4 months for elective surgery.[9] It is important to note that only insured individuals in the United States wait less time for healthcare services. The geographical location also determines the wait time for services due to lack of facilities and equipment. In addition, the United States leads the world in healthcare research and has the shortest drug approval processes for new drugs and treatments. The U.S. National Institutes of Health (NIH) conducts more clinical trials than any other country in the

© kasto80/iStockphoto

world. Finally, although the United States offers success stories of cutting-edge innovations and technology developed at research centers such as the Mayo Clinic and Johns Hopkins University, there is a struggle to implement successful innovations nationally.[10]

Second, in the United States, both physicians and patients demand more diagnostic tests and procedures. However, these tests and procedures are only available to individuals with adequate health insurance and income instead of equal access across the U.S. population. This demand creates a vicious and costly cycle of care. On the physician side, more tests are ordered out of fear of ligation and physician incomes increase if they do more interventions. For example, physicians can bill insurance companies for performing a skin biopsy, but they cannot bill for some preventive measures like counseling patients about controlling their hypertension. On the patient side, more and more patients request more tests and services because it is comforting to know that everything is being done to diagnose a medical problem and, if necessary, to treat it. If the patient has health insurance, the health insurance pays for the diagnostic test with little or no cost to the patient. Because there are so many types of health insurance contracts and policies, there is little incentive to decrease wasteful and expensive healthcare practices (on everyone's behalf—patients, physicians, and healthcare facilities). For example, when a patient does not have health insurance and is required to pay out-of-pocket for a nonrequired diagnostic test, they generally decline the service.

On the other hand, there are also high administrative costs. For example, administrative costs include (a) salaries of the health insurance claims clerks in medical offices, clinics, and hospitals; (b) the advertising costs that health insurance companies spend to gain new customers; (c) the premiums paid to the stockholders of health insurance companies; (d) the costs associated with the collection of debt for health services received; and (e) time spent calling in prescriptions, scheduling lab tests, arranging appointments for procedures, and calling the health insurance corporation for preauthorization for treatment. If the United States could trim some of the administrative costs by improving information and communications technology, it might be able to reduce overall costs. For example, in Sweden, all drugs are prescribed electronically from physician to pharmacist. This method decreases personnel costs, time, and medical errors[10] because the electronic medical records are merged; the healthcare provider enters the prescription, lab test, or procedure, and it is instantly submitted to the correct facility or individual for processing or authorization. This reduces costs of personnel employed to schedule and obtain authorizations for numerous individuals seeking healthcare services in medical offices, clinics, and hospitals.

Third, the United States has made great strides in reducing the proportion of adults who smoke cigarettes. In 2000, the rate of people who smoked every day was 19 percent, but by 2012 the rate had dropped to 14 percent.[9] This is the lowest smoking rate among OECD countries after Mexico, Sweden, and Iceland.[9] However, during

© nimon_t/iStockphoto

© Stockbyte/Thinkstock Images

© Grazvydas/iStock/ThinkStockphotos

the same time period, obesity rates among the U.S. adult population have increased from 30.9 percent in 2000 to 35.3 percent—the highest rate among OECD countries.[9] Mortality from diseases such as cardiovascular diseases and many cancers increases progressively once people become obese.

The United States has many lessons to learn from other countries about cost containment of healthcare services. At the same time, other countries look to the United States for the high success rates in medical and healthcare research and innovation. The United States would benefit from stronger policies related to lifestyle choices that lead to poor health outcomes, such as lessons learned by OECD countries related to higher prices and taxes on alcohol. There are no easy or quick-fix solutions, but best practices indicate that further research strives to improve health care for everyone.

Now, let us define the types of healthcare insurance that are available among the OECD countries. Of 33 developed nations, 32 offer their citizens some type of universal health care (also known as *socialized medicine*). Within universal health care, there are three types of health insurance: single payer, two-tier, and insurance mandates.

Single Payer: The government provides insurance for all citizens and pays all healthcare expenses except for co-payments and co-insurance costs. Healthcare providers may be public, private, or a combination of both.

Two-Tier: The government mandates catastrophic or minimum insurance coverage for all citizens, while allowing the purchase of additional voluntary insurance or fee-for-service care when desired. In Ireland and Israel, the government provides a core policy with the majority of the population paying for a supplement with private insurance.

Insurance Mandate: The government mandates that all citizens purchase insurance, whether from private, public, or nonprofit insurers. In some cases, the insurer list is quite restrictive, while in others a healthy private market for insurance is simply regulated and standardized by the government. In this kind of system, health insurance companies are not allowed to deny sick individuals, and individuals are required to purchase insurance to sustain the health insurance company. The information in **Table 6.1** shows that only 10 countries tackled the issue of developing a comprehensive healthcare system prior to the 1960s.

Most individuals assume that the United States does not have any form of universal health

TABLE 6.1 Comparison of Universal Health Insurance Plans

Single Payer	
Country	Year
Norway	1912
Japan	1938
United Kingdom	1948
Kuwait	1950
Sweden	1955
Bahrain	1957
Brunei	1958
Canada	1966
United Arab Emirates	1971
Finland	1972
Slovenia	1972
Italy	1978
Portugal	1979
Cyprus	1980
Spain	1986
Iceland	1990

Two-Tier	
New Zealand	1938
Netherlands	1966
Denmark	1973
France	1974
Australia	1975
Ireland	1977
Hong Kong	1993
Singapore	1993
Israel	1995
Insurance Mandate	
Germany	1941
Belgium	1945
Austria	1967
Luxembourg	1973
Greece	1983
South Korea	1988
Switzerland	1994

Data from: The True Cost Blog (2009). List of countries with Universal Health Care. Available from: http://truecostblog .com/2009/08/09/countries-with-universal-healthcare -by-date/. Last updated January 21, 2013. Accessed on February 8, 2015.[11]

care. However, that is not entirely true; each of the following examples is discussed in detail later in this chapter. Within the United States, three examples of universal health care are offered to limited populations, including the Veterans Health Administration, the military healthcare system, and the Indian Health Service. In addition, some individuals might also consider Medicare and Medicaid as possible forms of universal health care. However, Medicare requires a monthly premium for Part B coverage.

TYPES OF HEALTH INSURANCE

Before defining the various types of health insurance, let us provide an overview of health insurance in general. The basic concept is that each month an outside entity (e.g., government or an employer) or an individual pays a monthly premium (payment) to a health insurance company. Prior to signing an annual contract to pay the monthly premium each month, the outside entity or the individual reviews the annual contract to determine whether they agree with the terms of the policy. It is similar to a mobile phone contract. If the individual likes the data plan package, he or she signs the contract, pays a set monthly fee, and receives the phone service each month for 12 months. However, if individuals read the fine print on the mobile phone contract, they would know that if they exceed the set limit of digital data usage or time, additional fees will be attached to the monthly statement. If they fail to pay the full amount (monthly set fee and additional fees), the phone service is disconnected.

Now let us take that same example and apply it to health care. An employer negotiates healthcare insurance contracts for its employees through several different healthcare insurance companies. Just like phone contracts, each healthcare contract offers slightly different options. For example, one health insurance company may offer extensive prevention services (e.g., mammograms, vaccinations, tobacco cessation prescriptions), while another health insurance company may include physical therapy and mental health counseling. Generally, the employer negotiates with several health insurance companies and then offers its employees a choice of health insurance policies. It is up to each employee to carefully read each policy prior to signing the contract, because each policy is slightly different. It is up to the employees to ask questions to accurately determine the cost as well as which healthcare policy best serves their needs. The next section describes the various health insurance policies as well as the individuals eligible for each one.

Employment-Based Health Insurance

Employment-based health insurance is the simplest to understand. If individuals work for a company for a designated period of time (usually 90 days), then they are eligible to select a health insurance policy through their company. At this point, the employee meets with someone in the human resources department or attends a seminar to learn more about the available health insurance policy options. The main differences are related to the cost of the policy. Generally, employers pay a portion of the cost and employees pay the remaining portion. The size of the company and number of its employees typically determine how much the employer pays toward employee health insurance. For example, a small flower shop with 10 employees may contribute a set amount of $50 per month toward health insurance for each employee. In this case, the employee pays the remaining $150 for the selected policy. If the individual is employed by a large corporation, the employer may pay 80 percent of the total cost. Therefore, $160 is paid by the employer and $40 is paid by the employee for a similar $200 per month health insurance policy. The cost per month also varies by the number of family members that the employee wishes to include on the health insurance policy. The policies and costs vary from those that offer individual coverage only; individual and spouse coverage with additional costs per child; individual, spouse, and family coverage with no extra cost per child; and individual and family with no extra costs for spouse and children. In some cases, one spouse works for a small company, so that individual selects the single coverage option only, because his or her spouse works for a large corporation with great health insurance benefits at a lower cost for inclusion of the children.

There are two basic types of health care offered by employers: Health Maintenance Organizations (HMOs) and Preferred Provider Organizations (PPOs).

HMO

The HMO is defined as an organization that provides healthcare services to individuals who voluntarily enroll, pay monthly payments to the organization, and agree to use only the healthcare providers and hospitals that belong to the organization. The healthcare providers are paid fixed periodic payments determined in advance and are only allowed to make limited referrals to outside (nonmember) specialists. For example,

an individual joins an HMO and pays a monthly health insurance premium. As a result, the individual can only make appointments with physicians that are on their HMO list and only be admitted into hospitals that have contracts with the HMO. For any health services received that are not on the approved HMO contract list, the cost of that health service becomes the responsibility of the patient and is not paid by the HMO. HMOs regulate the number of patients that each physician has in his or her network. HMO contracts regulate the number and type of patients (e.g., degree of health or illness) across geographic locations, so that there is a balance of pay and work across the HMO physicians.

PPO

The PPO is defined as an organization that provides healthcare services to individuals that voluntarily enroll, pay monthly payments to the organization, and agree to use only the healthcare providers and hospitals that have agreed to service the PPO patients. In a PPO, individuals have greater healthcare options within a large network of healthcare providers and services. The providers are not paid a set payment for individuals, but rather bill the health insurance company for services provided. Through negotiated contracts, the health insurance company offers individuals discounted prices for the services of the healthcare providers, hospitals, and pharmacists.

Government Health Insurance

In the mid-1960s, the U.S. government developed and funded two types of government health insurance. Medicaid focused on the low-income population, while Medicare was created for the elderly. Most recently in 2010, the Obama administration created the Affordable Care Act to provide affordable health insurance for individuals without health care.

Medicare

In 1965, the federal government created and funded Medicare. In 1966, Medicare was implemented to provide health insurance for the elderly in the United States.[12] Medicare is a social insurance program funded at the federal level and focuses primarily on the older population. Three groups of U.S. citizens are eligible for Medicare health coverage: (a) most individuals older than 65; (b) individuals younger than 65 who have certain disabilities and illnesses; and (c) individuals of any age with kidney failure that requires dialysis or a kidney transplant.[13] As stated in the Centers for Medicare and Medicaid Services (CMS) website, Medicare is a health insurance program for people age 65 or older, people under age 65 with certain disabilities, and people of all ages with end-stage renal disease. The Medicare Program provides a Medicare Part A, which covers hospital bills; Medicare Part B, which covers medical insurance coverage; and Medicare Part D, which covers prescription drugs.

When Medicare was created, it had two sections: Medicare Part A and Medicare Part B. Medicare Part A covers portions of the costs of a hospital inpatient stay. Medicare Part B covers a portion of the costs for two types of healthcare services: (a) medically necessary services or supplies that are needed to diagnose or treat your medical condition and that meet accepted standards of medical practice; and (b) preventive services that prevent illness (e.g., flu and pneumonia vaccines) or detection of a disease at an early stage, when treatment is most likely to work best. Medicare Part C was developed and labeled as Medicare Advantage. Under the current Medicare program, Medicare Advantage plans are offered as an alternative to the traditional Medicare fee-for-service program.[14] In 2006, Medicare Part D was developed to cover a portion of prescription drug costs. Currently, the federally funded Medicare health insurance program helps to pay for medical and hospital services for more than 42 million people over the age of 65 or living with permanent disabilities.[12]

Medicaid

To understand Medicaid, it is easier to understand how Medicaid differs from Medicare. Medicaid is a program that is not solely funded at the federal level. States provide up to half of the funding for the Medicaid programs. In some states, counties also contribute funds. Unlike the Medicare entitlement program, Medicaid is a social protection program rather than a social insurance program and eligibility is determined largely by income. Whereas Medicare has no income eligibility requirements, Medicaid eligibility is limited by income and financial resources. Medicaid also covers a wider range of healthcare services for all ages than Medicare. Whereas Medicare focuses on the elderly, Medicaid serves millions of families, children, pregnant women, adults without children, and also seniors and people living with disabilities. Medicaid pays for services like medical office visits, prescription drugs, and preventive care. For children, there is a Medicaid program titled the Center for Medicaid and Children's Health Insurance Program (CHIP) Services (CMCS), while for individuals with disabilities and the elderly, Medicaid pays for a portion of long-term care services. Overall, Medicaid is the largest source of funding for medical and health-related services for U.S. citizens living in poverty.[15]

As of 2013, Medicaid has changed so that low income is no longer the only requirement to enroll in the program. Currently, eligibility is based on whether or not an individual fits into specific categories and includes low-income children below a certain age, pregnant women, parents of Medicaid-eligible children who meet certain income requirements, and low-income elderly. For the income status of elderly eligibility, there is a 5-year "look-back" period. The term "look-back" means that elderly individuals are not able to transfer large portions of their financial assets as a gift to another person, so that their assets are decreased enough to qualify for Medicaid.[16] For example, suppose a woman named Miriam is diagnosed with a long-term illness at age 70. She transfers the title to her home and the money in her saving account to her two children. At age 73, she needs to move into a skilled nursing facility. The penalty for this transfer of funds is calculated by dividing the average monthly cost of nursing home care in her geographical location into the amount of assets that she gave to her two children. Therefore, if Miriam gave her children $60,000 as a gift and the average monthly cost of a skilled nursing facility is $6,000, Medicaid officials divide

$6000 into $60,000 to obtain the answer of 10. Miriam is told that the number 10 represents the number of months that she is not eligible for Medicaid. Therefore, Miriam is without money for the skilled nursing facility due to the transfer of funds to her children, and she is unable to qualify for Medicaid for 10 months.

Keep in mind that Medicaid statutes and categories vary from state to state. Each state establishes its own eligibility standards; determines the type, amount, duration, and scope of services; sets the rate of payment for services; and administers its own program. For example, many states offer minimal dental care, such as pain relief services. Some state programs offer preventative care services and provide services for early diagnosis. Other states provide healthcare services for illegal immigrants for certain emergency situations. Most states offer Medicaid to any uninsured woman who has breast or cervical cancer, even if she does not meet income standards. In addition, Medicaid reimbursement to healthcare providers is a complex issue. Some states pay the healthcare providers directly as a fee-for-service payment, while other states offer healthcare providers a monthly payment similar to the health maintenance organizations (HMOs). Because each state offers slightly different Medicaid benefits, it is possible for a family on Medicaid in one state to move to the adjacent state and receive different Medicaid benefits. Within the same state, the legislatures may also change the eligibility and services to individuals or the reimbursement payment to healthcare providers. See **Box 6.1**.

National data indicate that Medicaid payments by percent for services include 49 percent for children, 22 percent for adults with no disabilities, 19 percent for individuals with disabilities, and 10 percent for the elderly. However, the average cost varies substantially by type of beneficiary. For example, because children are generally healthy, the Medicaid cost per child is low and many children are covered. On the other hand, elderly costs are high but a small percentage of the elderly population is eligible for Medicaid. As the U.S. population ages, the funding of long-term care through Medicaid is likely to increase. Currently, the Medicaid program pays about 41 percent of the total cost of nursing facility care. As the percentage of the elderly and disabled populations increases, so will the need for long-term care.[16]

BOX 6.1 Medicaid Healthcare Services (Benefits vary from state-to-state)

- Inpatient hospital services
- Outpatient hospital services
- Pregnancy-related services, including prenatal care and 60 days postpartum pregnancy-related services
- Vaccines for children
- Physician services
- Nursing facility services for persons ages 21 or older
- Family planning services and supplies
- Rural health clinic services
- Home health care for persons eligible for skilled nursing services
- Laboratory and X-ray services
- Pediatric and family nurse practitioner services
- Nurse-midwife services
- Federally qualified health center (FQHC) services and ambulatory services of an FQHC that would be available in other settings
- Early and periodic screening, diagnostic, and treatment (EPSDT) services for children under age 21

The Centers for Medicare and Medicaid Services (2015). Medicaid Data Sources – General Information. Available from: https://www.cms.gov/Research-Statistics-Data-and-Systems/Computer-Data-and-Systems/MedicaidDataSourcesGenInfo/index.html. Accessed on February 8, 2015.

MEDICARE AND MEDICAID

Some 8.3 million individuals are eligible for both Medicaid and Medicare.[15] Individuals with Medicare benefits and low incomes are also eligible for Medicaid benefits. For such individuals, their Medicare healthcare coverage is supplemented by services that are available under their state's Medicaid program. For individuals enrolled in both programs, Medicare pays first and Medicaid pays second.

Affordable Care Act

In March 2010, the Affordable Care Act (ACA) was signed into law. The ACA is based on the Patient Protection and Affordable Care Act (Public Law 111-148) and the Health Care and Education Reconciliation Act (Public Law 111-152). The law expands Medicaid coverage and services to millions of low-income individuals and families. However, states were able to decide whether or not they would expand their state program. Of the states that chose not to expand their Medicaid programs, their federal Medicaid funding remained the same. The ACA provides healthcare coverage for individuals and families through the insurance exchange system, which determines their eligibility, costs, and coverage through a convenient mail, fax, and phone, in-person or online process.

Veterans Administration

The largest integrated healthcare system in the United States is the Veterans Health Administration (VA), which is administered under the Department of Veteran's Affairs. It serves 8.76 million veterans in 1700 healthcare locations.[17] Health benefits are available for all seven branches of the Uniformed Services, including the Army, Navy, Air Force, Marine Corps, Coast Guard, Commissioned Corps of the Public Health Service, and the National Oceanic and Atmospheric Administration.[18] The VA provides eligible veterans hospital care and outpatient care services that promote, preserve, and restore health, including treatment, procedures, supplies, or services based on the accepted standards of clinical practice.[18] The VA health insurance is called TRICARE and offers three levels of coverage: Prime, Extra, and

© IPGGutenbergUKLtd/ istockphoto

Standard. TRICARE also offers home delivery pharmacy benefits, dental benefits, and a program for Medicare-eligible military retirees known as TRICARE for Life.[19]

- *TRICARE Prime*: Active-duty personnel are automatically enrolled in TRICARE Prime. They receive health care at a military treatment facility (MTF) or at the offices of TRICARE-contracted Civilian Medical Providers, called the Preferred Provider Network (PPN). It is necessary to pay an annual enrollment fee.[20]
- *TRICARE Extra*: There is no annual enrollment fee, but it is necessary to satisfy an annual deductible for outpatient care. It offers a discount on some health services, and the provider files the claims. It is not available overseas or to active-duty service members.[21]
- *TRICARE Standard*: This plan is the most flexible, but not available to active-duty service members. It is the fee-for-service

option that gives beneficiaries the opportunities to see any TRICARE-authorized provider. It allows the ability to seek care from civilian providers when military treatment facility (MTF) care is unavailable. Individuals file their own claims.[22]

Prison Health Services

The Federal Bureau of Prisons (BOP) is responsible for confining federal offenders in prisons that are safe, humane, cost-efficient, and secure. As part of these duties, "the BOP is responsible for delivering medically necessary health care to inmates in accordance with applicable standards of care."[23] As of 2014, the BOP housed 213,429 (14,344 females and 199,085 males) inmates in 112 BOP institutions.[24]

The Bureau employs licensed and professional staff to "provide essential medical, dental, and mental health services in a manner consistent with accepted community standards for a correctional environment."[23] Incarcerated men and women are often diagnosed with health, mental health, and substance abuse problems after receiving care from a correctional health provider.[25] Within the prisons, health promotion and education include effects of medications, infectious disease prevention and education, and information about noncommunicable diseases such as cardiovascular disease, diabetes, and hypertension. Other aspects of health, such as clean air, clean water, safe living conditions, and nutrition are also monitored and promoted.[23] For inmates with complex medical conditions, the Bureau operates several medical referral centers that provide advanced care.[23] Currently, the Bureau is exploring cost-cutting initiatives to reduce healthcare costs within the federal prison system. Such initiatives include installing the use of computer software for electronic medical records, use of technology for medical referrals to save transportation costs, and reviewing billing processes to validate healthcare costs.[26]

Indian Health Services (IHS)

The Indian Health Service (IHS) is an agency within the U.S. Department of Health and Human Services and is responsible for providing federal health services to American Indians and Alaska Native members of the 566 federally recognized Tribes across the United States. The IHS was established in 1787 based on Article I, Section 8 of the Constitution. The goal of the health services is "to ensure that comprehensive, culturally acceptable personal and public health services are available and accessible to American Indian and Alaska Native people."[27] Although comprehensive health services are available at IHS clinics, Tribal members are responsible for costs associated with medical ambulance transportation and any medical services received by a non-IHS medical provider.[28]

Special Types of Health Insurance and Benefits

Consolidated Omnibus Budget Reconciliation Act (COBRA)

In 1985, the **Consolidated Omnibus Budget Reconciliation Act (COBRA)** required most employers with group health insurance plans to continue to offer temporary group health insurance for their employees in special circumstances for a period of up to 18 to 36 months depending on the situation. Examples of the special circumstances include, but are not limited to, (a) losing health insurance due to termination or a reduction in work hours; (b) becoming disabled; (c) continued health insurance for spouses and dependents due to the employee's death, divorce, or legal separation; and (d) other qualifying events (e.g., covered employee becoming eligible for Medicare benefits).[29]

Workers' Compensation

Workers' compensation is a form of health insurance that provides replacement wages and pays medical expenses to employees injured while performing their job. Employers contribute to the workers' compensation fund. When an employee's injury is classified as eligible for workers' compensation, then the benefits are paid from that fund. Typically, injuries that are sustained on-the-job or that are in some way work-related are eligible for workers' compensation. Workers' compensation benefits vary across states including weekly

FIGURE 6.2 Example of Workers' Compensation: Florida

When an employee is injured at work, these three steps should be followed:
1. The employer should be notified immediately that an employee was injured on the job.
2. The hospital or physician should be told that the person was injured on the job, so that medical bills are filed properly with Workers' Compensation Insurance in their state.
3. If the injured employee encounters any excessive delays in treatment, the employee should contact the Division of Workers' Compensation in their state.

Data from: Florida Department of Financial Services (2015). Workers' Comp Works for You. Available at: http://www.myfloridacfo.com/Division/WC/pdf/WC-Broken -Arm-Poster-Final-March-2010.pdf. Accessed on June 29, 2015.

© Freer Law/Getty Images

payments in place of wages, compensation for economic loss (past and future), reimbursement or payment of medical expenses, and benefits payable to the dependents of workers killed during employment. Payment or reimbursement for pain and suffering and punitive damages for employer negligence are not available in workers' compensation plans.[30] See **Figure 6.2**.

Family Medical Leave Act (FMLA)

The Family Medical Leave Act (FMLA) allows eligible employees to take unpaid leave without losing their job for specified family and medical reasons with continuation of group health insurance coverage. Employers have specific guidelines for FMLA. For example, some employers allow employees to use their vacation or sick time to cover FMLA, so they maintain their full wages. Other employers allow their employees to take partial FMLA leave, such as a few hours per day or per week as needed for family or medical needs. Eligible employees are entitled to 12 weeks of leave in a 12-month period for the birth of a child and to care for the newborn child within 1 year of birth; the placement with the employee of a child for adoption or foster care and to care for the newly placed child within 1 year of placement; to care for the employee's spouse, child, or parent who has a serious health condition; a serious health condition that makes the employee unable to perform the essential functions of his or her job; any qualifying emergency need because the employee's spouse, parent, or child is in active-duty military; and 26 weeks of leave in a 12-month period to care for a spouse, child, or parent service member with a serious injury or illness (www.dol.gov/whd/fmla).

HEALTH INSURANCE TERMINOLOGY

The terminology related to health insurance is complex and filled with acronyms. See **Table 6.2**.

The following two case studies explain how the list of commonly used health insurance policy terms is used in day-to-day life.

TABLE 6.2 Health Insurance Terminology

Term	Definition
Co-Payment	A fixed fee or cost that individuals must pay prior to receiving specific medical services or treatments covered by their health insurance plan.
Diagnostic-Related Grouping (DRG)	A unit of description to classify patients by diagnosis, average length of hospital stay, and therapy received; the units are used to determine the payment received by healthcare facilities and providers to treat current and future inpatient procedures and services.
Deductible	Each individual enrolled in a health insurance plan must pay a set amount of medical charges each year before the health insurance benefits begin.
Explanation of Benefits (EOB)	Each individual enrolled in a health insurance plan receives, via email or postal mail, a document that explains the healthcare benefits, deductibles, co-payment responsibilities, and reasons for noncoverage of claims.
Flexible Spending Account	Some large employers offer employees the opportunity to have up to $2500 each year subtracted as a pre-tax deduction and added to a health savings account to be used for health expenses not covered by the employees' health insurance policy.
Health Maintenance Organization (HMO)	A type of group healthcare practice that provides health care to individuals who enroll and pay a fixed-price payment without concern for the amount or kind of services received.
In-Network	When individuals enroll in a health insurance policy plan, they receive a website that lists the contact information for healthcare providers in the healthcare plan network.
Out-of-Pocket	Amount of money that individuals must pay for health services or equipment that is not covered by their health insurance policies.
Preferred Provider Organization (PPO)	Individuals enrolling in a PPO health insurance policy have greater healthcare options within a large network of healthcare providers and services. The providers are not paid a set payment for individuals, but rather bill health companies for services provided. Through negotiated contracts, the health insurance company offers individuals discounted prices for the services of the healthcare providers, hospitals, and pharmacists.
Out-of-Network	Individuals receive healthcare services from a healthcare provider that is not on the list of approved providers covered by their health insurance policy plan. The individual must pay for the cost of the services received from nonapproved healthcare providers.

CASE STUDY ONE

Mr. and Mrs. Wilson are married, work full-time, and live in a northern metropolitan area. Mary, age 43, is the director of the Purchasing Department for the county school district, and James, age 45, is a mechanical engineer for a corporation that manufactures automotive parts. During the month of October, it is common for health insurance companies and employers to offer a process called "open enrollment" so employees can research, investigate, and select another type health insurance for the upcoming year, if they so desire. Prior to the open-enrollment period, the employer and health insurance companies have renegotiated the type of health plans that will be offered to the employees. The annual contracts are signed by employers and health insurance companies. Then, during the 6 weeks of open enrollment, employers allow health insurance companies with signed contracts the opportunity to offer seminars for employees to attend during the workday. Each health insurance company is promoting the advantages of its plan over the other plans being offered by the competitors. Ultimately, each vendor is selling its healthcare policy to the employees. Some vendors offer PPO policies, while other vendors offer HMO policies. Generally, the PPO policies are more expensive, but offer a wider range of health services, and there are more health providers in the network. On the other hand, the HMO policies are less expensive and offer quality care. Mary and James attended the open enrollment seminars at each of their companies to determine whether or not they should change their healthcare policy selection. They made the decision to purchase a PPO healthcare policy through Mary's company. The policies were more expensive at the corporation where James works, and the employer paid a lower percent of the costs.

The PPO healthcare policy that they selected through Mary's employer includes:

Monthly cost:	$400 = $250 paid by employer + $100 employee + $50 spouse.
In-network deductible:	No cost.
Co-payment:	$25 per office visit, radiology procedure, laboratory testing, $10 per prescription; $7 for generic prescription.
Out-of-network:	$750.00 out-of-network deductible.
Out-of-pocket:	$2,500 out-of-pocket deductible.

Their PPO policy went into effect on January 1. As expected, the flu season hit their city by the end of January. When Mary got sick with symptoms of a cough, vomiting, and high fever, she delayed going to the doctor because she felt too ill to leave their home. After 3 days, James stayed home from work and insisted that Mary go to the doctor. He looked online to see the location of the nearest doctor that was in the network of their new PPO health insurance policy. He called and they did not have any appointments available, so he called the next medical office on the list. After three calls, he took one look at his ill wife and decided to take her to the nearest walk-in clinic. He knew that Mary needed to be seen that day. James helped Mary get dressed and in the car.

When they arrived at the walk-in clinic, they were pleased to hear that there was only one person in line ahead of them. As they checked in, the receptionist asked for Mary's insurance card and driver's license as identification. The receptionist told James that the clinic was not part of their PPO network. At this point, James said that he did not care and would pay for the visit with a credit card. Because Mary was so sick, the nurse took her to an exam room, so she could rest. She also took Mary's temperature and blood pressure. Her blood pressure was lower than usual and her temperature was 101.9 (normal is 98.6 degrees). The doctor examined Mary and suggested that he test for influenza. He listened to her chest with his stethoscope and said that it sounded like she had pneumonia. After the nose swab and chest X-ray, the doctor returned to the exam room. He said that Mary had a positive flu test and the X-ray showed pneumonia in her left lung. He recommended that she be admitted to the hospital. James explained that they had a new PPO policy and wanted to make sure that Mary's admission was an in-network hospital.

As Mary waited in the exam room, James worked with the receptionist to review the PPO website for nearby hospital choices. After seeing two choices, the doctor called the admitting office of the closest hospital and told the Emergency Department that he was referring Mary to the hospital for a direct admission. He gave James a CD of Mary's chest X-ray and the results of the flu swab. This information eliminated the need to repeat the tests prior to admission. James gave the receptionist his credit card and was told that today's charges totaled $455 ($180 office visit; $200 chest X-ray; $75 flu swab). Although James was surprised at the charges, he was more concerned about getting Mary to the hospital as soon as possible, so he signed the receipt and took Mary to the hospital.

James took Mary to the Emergency Department prior to her hospital admission. James handed the clinic documents to the physician who had been contacted by the clinic physician. After a quick review of the notes, Mary was admitted to the infectious disease unit in the hospital. After Mary was settled into her hospital room, the admitting clerk came to Mary's room to complete the admission papers. Mary signed a few consent forms, provided employment and health insurance information, and received some information about James as her health surrogate in the event of her illness becoming more serious. The admitting clerk told James and Mary that the hospital co-payment was $200. Again, James handed the clerk his credit card. She swiped the card on her portable device and James signed the receipt. Over the next few days, Mary received intravenous antibiotics and started eating a soft diet. She was discharged after 4 days in the hospital. She stayed home for the rest of the week and then returned to work on Monday. Fortunately, James did not get the flu from Mary.

Over the next few weeks, Mary and James received various physician and hospital bills. They needed to pay $2500 out-of-pocket prior to receiving any benefits from the PPO health insurance policy. Because in the month of January, James paid $455 at the clinic and $200 at the hospital, the total payment was $655, so they had $1845 left to pay. Therefore, because the hospital bill for 4 days was approximately $27,000, Mary and James paid the $1845 and the remaining portion—$25,155—was paid by their PPO health insurance. Also, their next Explanation of Benefits (EOB) would show that their out-of-pocket deductive had been met for the year; however, their out-of-network was not yet fulfilled for the year. They still owe $295 ($750 – $55) to meet the out-of-network obligation.

© Ruslan Guzov/Shutterstock

CASE STUDY TWO

Dr. James, age 62, had chronic pain at the base of her left thumb. She ignored the pain for about 3 months, hoping that it would go away without medical intervention. Finally, in October, she decided that it was time to seek medical advice. Within the Department of Orthopedics, she was scheduled to see a hand surgeon, Dr. Garcia. He had the radiology technician take several X-ray views of her hand. Upon review of the X-rays, Dr. Garcia explained that she would benefit from a steroid injection in the thumb joint and eight sessions with an occupational therapist. She agreed with the injection and occupational therapy. The injection was tolerable because Dr. Garcia's physician assistant sprayed numbing medication on her hand during the injection. The following day, she scheduled her first appointment at Physical Therapy Associates. She was told that because the issue was with her hand, she would be seen by an occupational therapist rather than a physical therapist. At her first appointment, she was told that her co-payment was $10. She asked if that was the correct amount for occupational as well as physical therapy. She was told that it was the same co-payment cost.

Dr. James had a 30-minute appointment with the occupational therapist for 5 weeks.

Each week she asked about the co-payment and received the same response. After 5 weeks, Dr. James received a phone call from Physical Therapy, Inc. As she had suspected all along, she was told that the $10 co-payment was incorrect and that her health insurance policy did not cover occupational therapy visits. She was told that she owed $450 because they were offering a discount due to the unforeseen confusion. Each visit is usually $250, but Dr. James was being charged $100 – $10 for the co-payment or $90 × 5 visits = $450. This type of situation is common and the reason why it is important for individuals to continue to ask questions.

Summary

This chapter began with a brief history of the U.S. health insurance system. Then, the discussion moved to comparing the health insurance system in other industrial countries to that of the United States. This international comparison illustrated that there are no simple solutions to healthcare issues for any one country. The next section described the various types of health insurance available in the United States and why it is so difficult to navigate the healthcare system. The chapter ends with two case studies that show why individuals would benefit from the services of a health navigation professional.

Student Activity

Case Study One

1. What are some questions that employees might ask their health insurance representative during open enrollment to determine whether or not to change their health insurance?
2. List two advantages and two disadvantages for an HMO and a PPO health insurance plan.
3. Explain why Mary and James owed $1845 for the 4 days in the hospital.

Case Study Two

1. List three questions that Dr. James should have asked prior to her first occupational therapy appointment.
2. List two things that a health navigation professional could have done to prevent Dr. James from receiving the bill for the occupational services.

References

1. Northern California Neurosurgery Medical Group. *The history of health insurance in the United States.* Retrieved February 2, 2015, from http://www.neurosurgical.com/medical_history_and_ethics/history/history_of_health_insurance.htm; last updated November 10, 2013.
2. Health Insurance Association of America (1997). *Fundamentals of health insurance, Part A.* Washington, DC: Health Insurance Association of America.
3. Public Broadcasting Service. *Healthcare crisis: Who's at risk—Timeline.* Retrieved February 2, 2015, from http://www.pbs.org/healthcarecrisis/history.htm.
4. Erenthal, J. *History of health insurance.* Retrieved February 2, 2105, from http://echealthinsurance.com/health101/history-of-health-insurance.
5. Collaboration Health Care Inc. *History of health care: How we got to where we are.* Retrieved February 2, 2015, from http://www.collaborationhealthcare.com/library-and-resources/the-world-of-health-care/history-of-health-care-how-we-got-to-where-we-are.php.
6. The World Health Organization. *Smallpox.* Retrieved February 2, 2015, from http://www.who.int/topics/smallpox/en.
7. United States Department of Health and Human Services. *Summary HIPAA privacy rule.* Retrieved March 12, 2015, from http://www.hhs.gov/ocr/privacy/hipaa/understanding/summary/index.html.
8. Organization for Economic Cooperation and Development. (2015). *Total public and private health expenditure per capita, 2010.*
9. Organization for Economic Cooperation and Development. *OECD health statistics2014: How does the United States compare?* Retrieved February 2, 2015, from http://www.oecd.org/unitedstates/Briefing-Note-UNITED-STATES-2014.pdf.
10. World Health Organization. (2000). *World Health Organization assesses the world's health systems.* The World Health Report. Geneva, Switzerland: World Health Organization.
11. The True Cost Blog. (2009). *List of countries with universal health care.* Retrieved February 8, 2015, from http://truecostblog.com/2009/08/09/countries-with-universal-healthcare-by-date; last updated January 21, 2013.
12. The Henry J. Kaiser Family Foundation. *Medicare: A timeline of key developments.* Retrieved February 3, 2015, from http://kff.org/medicare/timeline/medicare-a-timeline-of-key-developments.

13. Centers for Medicare & Medicaid Services. *History*. Retrieved February 3, 2015, from http://www.cms.gov /About-CMS/Agency-Information/History/index.html; last updated June 13, 2013.

14. Jacobson, G., et al. *Medicare Advantage* 2015 *data spotlight: Overview of plan changes*. Retrieved February 3, 2015, from http://kff.org/medicare/issue-brief/medicare-advan tage-2015-data-spotlight-overview-of-plan-changes.

15. Centers for Medicare & Medicaid Services. *Medicaid: About us*. Retrieved February 3, 2015, from http://www .medicaid.gov/about-us/about-us.html.

16. Centers for Medicare and Medicaid Services. *Medicaid data sources: General information*. Retrieved February 8, 2015, from https://www.cms.gov /Research-Statistics-Data-and-Systems/Computer-Data -and-Systems/MedicaidDataSourcesGenInfo/index .html?redirect=/MedicaidDataSourcesGenInfo/04 _MdManCrEnrllRep.asp.

17. U.S. Department of Veteran's Affairs. *Veteran's Health Administration*. Retrieved February 8, 2015, from http ://www.va.gov/health.

18. Military.com. *Military medical benefits overview*. Retrieved February 3, 2015, from http://www.military.com/benefits /veterans-health-care/military-medical-benefits-over- view.html.

19. Military.com. *TRICARE benefits*. Retrieved February 3, 2015, from http://www.military.com/benefits/tricare.

20. Military.com. *TRICARE prime*. Retrieved February 3, 2015, from http://www.military.com/benefits/tricare /prime/tricare-prime-overview.html.

21. Military.com. *TRICARE extra*. Retrieved February 3, 2015, from http://www.military.com/benefits/tricare /extra/tricare-extra-overview.html?comp=700002277907 5&rank=6.

22. Military.com. *TRICARE standard*. Retrieved February 3, 2015, from http://www.military.com/benefits/tricare /standard/tricare-standard-overview.html?comp=700002 2779075&rank=7.

23. Federal Bureau of Prisons. *Medical care*. Retrieved February 3, 2015, from http://www.bop.gov/inmates/custody _and_care/medical_care.jsp.

24. Federal Bureau of Prisons. *About our facilities*. Retrieved February 3, 2015, from http://www.bop.gov/about /facilities/federal_prisons.jsp.

25. The Centers for Disease Control and Prevention. *Correctional health*. Retrieved March 15, 2015, from http://www .cdc.gov/correctionalhealth; last updated March 24, 2014.

26. United States Department of Justice. Office of the Inspector General. (2008). *The Federal Bureau of Prison's efforts to manage inmate health care*. Washington, DC: United States Department of Justice, 2008.

27. Indian Health Services. *Agency overview*. Retrieved February 3, 2015, from http://www.ihs.gov/aboutihs/overview.

28. Indian Health Services. *Eligibility*. Retrieved February 2015 from http://www.ihs.gov/aboutihs/eligibility.

29. Cobrainsurance.com. *When cobra?* Retrieved June 29, 2015, from http://ww1.cobrainsurance.com/when-cobra.

30. United States Department of Labor. *Workers' compensation*. Retrieved June 29, 2015, from http://www.dol.gov /dol/topic/workcomp/index.htm.

CHAPTER 7

Defining Quality in Health Care

LEARNING OBJECTIVES

By the end of this chapter, students will be able to:

- Define quality assurance in health care and understand its importance to individual health outcomes
- Describe the activities of major federal regulatory agencies
- Evaluate how healthcare effectiveness is measured
- Describe the role that insurance companies play in healthcare quality

CHAPTER OVERVIEW

In this chapter, health navigation professionals become acquainted with how their role is associated with the overall view of quality assurance in the healthcare system. First, the chapter introduces the important topic of quality in health care. Quality is defined as a high level of value or excellence (e.g., how good or bad something is). In health care, quality is linked to an organization's service delivery approach or underlying systems of care. There are four types of quality including quality control, quality assessment, quality improvement, and quality assurance. Next, the discussion provides information about the healthcare regulatory agencies that monitor the quality of health care, including licensure and accreditation. Next, the roles of the institutional review boards and bioethics committees are discussed as a way to protect the rights and welfare of individuals. Finally, the chapter concludes with an introduction to the roles of national and state insurance commissioners and how they regulate insurance fraud and malpractice.

DEFINING QUALITY

There are four types of quality (control, assessment, improvement, and assurance). Each type of quality is explored within the context of health care.

First, quality control describes the step-by-step processes in protocols and procedures used within an organization. For example, hospitals are required by law to train all employees annually on the topic of fire safety and evacuation procedures. If hospital administrators fail to require each employee to attend this training, the hospital's certification would be in jeopardy. This requirement mandates that training must be provided for employees on all shifts (day, evening, night, weekends) over several weeks to cover employees who miss a session of training. If a fire were to occur in the hospital, for example, every employee must know the procedures to contain the fire and, if necessary, evacuate patients to a safe zone. Along with required fire and safety training, other mandated training for all hospital employees includes standard universal precautions, which refers to avoiding contact with patients' bodily fluids by wearing nonporous articles such as medical gloves, goggles, and face shields. This practice was introduced in the mid-1980s.[1,2] Since 1996, the use of personal protective equipment has been recommended in all health settings, and all patients are considered to be possible carriers of blood-borne pathogens. The guidelines were changed to cover wearing gloves when collecting or handling blood and body fluids, wearing face shields when there was danger of blood splashing on mucous membranes, and disposing all needles and sharp objects in puncture-resistant containers. In addition, universal precautions are designed not only for healthcare workers (e.g., physicians, nurses, patients, healthcare support workers) who come into contact with patients or bodily fluids, but also staff and others who might not come into direct contact with patients.[3]

Second, quality assessment determines whether data were collected and analyzed accurately. For example, after universal precaution training has been completed, the sign-in sheets are checked against the employee roster to determine that, indeed, 100 percent of the employees completed the universal precaution training.[4]

Third, quality improvement involves utilizing systematic actions over time for the improvement of healthcare services and the health status of patients. To achieve continuous quality improvement, healthcare organizations focus on four key principles: (1) systems and processes, (2) quality of patient care and satisfaction, (3) teamwork across various departments and employees, and (4) use of data to verify quality improvement over time.[5]

© vm/iStockphoto

Fourth, quality assurance is a broad plan for maintaining quality in all aspects of a program, such as staff training, written protocols and procedures, data management, and data analysis. Quality assurance is used to prevent mistakes and defects. In health care, quality assurance verifies with confidence that the product (e.g., medication, surgical equipment, disinfectant solutions) or system (e.g., software used in the pharmacy that verifies that the correct medication is delivered to the correct patient or the finance department charges the patients' accounts correctly) meets the required specifications, features, and functionality that are appropriate for that product or system. For example, a patient does not want to learn that the hip joint used in his or her hip replacement surgery is being recalled by the manufacture for a defect. These quality safety assurances are tracked by consumer agencies, so consumers know that such products passed safety regulations tests. Even though quality assurances and regulations are in place, this does not mean that defective parts, medications, and systems do not appear in the healthcare system. When quality assurance is violated in health care, identifying and monitoring specific problems and developing corrective actions are essential.

This chapter explores various aspects of quality assurance, including national regulatory agencies, basic legal terminology, several types of informed-consent documents, and the concept of bioethics in healthcare practice. Throughout the chapter, health navigation professionals become acquainted with how their role is associated with the overall view of quality assurance. Keep in mind that quality assurance policies protect individuals as well as agencies. For example, if the hospital's automated laboratory devices are not calibrated for accuracy at the beginning of each shift, patients may receive too much or too little medication based on these inaccurate lab results. Quality assurance is vital at all levels of health care. The next section describes how the U.S. federal government standardizes quality assurance measurements, including accreditation, licensure, and certification. The discussion describes the two most commonly used national regulatory agencies: The Joint Commission and the National

Committee of Quality Assurance (NCQA). Both agencies enforce quality assurance by accreditation, which must be renewed every few years.

NATIONAL REGULATORY AGENCIES

The concept of national regulatory agencies in health care is relatively new. The earliest example was in 1910, when Abraham Flexner published a book related to standardization of medical education in the United States and Canada. Although *The Flexner Report* did not create a regulatory agency, it did have a direct influence on many current-day aspects of the American medical profession. Some of these effects include teaching a similar curriculum across all colleges of medicine and requiring students to pass a standardized board exam prior to obtaining medical licensure.[6]

Today, numerous healthcare regulatory agencies monitor the quality of health care. Keep in mind that if the national health regulatory agencies are performing their mission, then their work should be invisible to the general population. The national regulatory agencies oversee and enforce policies that protect the health of the population. For example, a hospitalized patient should feel confident that the instruments used during surgery have been properly sterilized based on federal regulatory guidelines. Of the numerous regulatory agencies, this discussion is focused on two agencies that provide oversight at the national level. These are The Joint Commission, formerly known as the Joint Commission on the Accreditation of Healthcare Organizations (JCAHO), and the National Committee of Quality Assurance (NCQA). Health navigation professionals need a basic understanding of these two accreditation agencies, because if they are employed in a hospital, clinic, medical office, or home health setting, their employer is required to renew one or both of these accreditations approximately every 3–7 years.

However, before delving into a discussion about regulatory agencies, a few terms need to be defined. It is useful for health navigation professionals to understand quality assurance terminology when working with healthcare providers, individuals, and their families.

Accreditation

Accreditation is a process of validation for professional associations, nongovernmental organizations (NGOs), and nonprofit organizations. First, professional associations (e.g., American Medical Association, American Public Health Association, National League for Nursing) were formed to unite and inform people working within the same occupation. Professional associations offer members the opportunity to network at conferences, forums, or through websites.[7] Second, NGOs (e.g., Mothers Against Drunk Driving) are commonly established by ordinary citizens. NGOs are funded by grants, foundations, businesses, or private individuals. Some NGOs are volunteer organizations to retain their charitable status, while others register for tax exemption based on recognition of social causes or special interest groups.[8] Third, nonprofit (also called not-for-profit) organizations are created for educational or charitable reasons (e.g., Habitat for Humanity, American Red Cross, United Way).

In nonprofit organizations, the shareholders do not benefit financially. Any profit earned by a nonprofit organization is retained and reinvested to pay its own expenses, operations, and programs. Nonprofit organizations apply for tax exempt status to avoid paying local taxes, such as sales taxes or property taxes. Most associations have by-laws or predetermined criteria to establish a standard of quality. Most U.S. hospitals are accredited by nonprofit, professional organizations, such as The Joint Commission (formerly, the JCAHO), which was created to assure the public that a facility has met the accrediting organization's standards.

© icholakov/iStock photo

Licensure

Licensure is the process of granting permission by a government agency to legally engage in a practice or activity. There are two types of licensure: individual and institutional. First, an individual fulfills certain required activities (e.g., completion of a course or degree, passing an exam, showing competence of a skill) and is granted a legal permit to engage in activities that are personal and cannot be transferred to another individual. For example, when individuals attempt to obtain their first driver's license, they must pass a vision examination, a written test, and a driving test. Upon successful completion of the tests, the clerk photographs the individual, so the license with their photo is unique and nontransferable. That person then has licensure to drive a vehicle. The same is true for a professional license, such as a nurse, medical doctor, hair stylist, barber, nail technician, and numerous other professions. Generally, the initial license is granted upon successful completion of a written or skills-based examination administered by the professional licensing board. An annual or bi-annual renewal is required along with a fee and, in most situations, proof of continuing education courses appropriate to the profession.

Second, institutional licensure is granted to any agency or organization providing a professional service to the public. For example, a restaurant is required to obtain an institutional license prior to opening and serving prepared food to the public.

During the restaurant inspection, the inspectors conduct numerous tests including, but not limited to, measuring the temperature of ovens, warming trays, refrigerators, freezers, and water used in the dishwasher. They test the cleaning and sanitation practices for the sinks, floors, countertops, tables, windows, and restrooms as well as the availability of soap and towels for frequent employee hand-washing. In a hospital setting, the institutional licensure inspection involves testing such items as the consistent temperature of machines that sterilize the surgical equipment, the bacteria count on hard surfaces (e.g., patient tray tables, intravenous poles and equipment, door handles), and the strength of the cleaning solutions used to clean operating rooms after each procedure. In a physical

© Arne Pastoor/iStockphoto

therapy clinic, inspectors verify the protocol to determine whether padded tables have been wiped down with antibacterial wipes after each patient or check the bacteria count on the hand weights used in treatment sessions. Finally, all license inspections receive protocols for all common procedures involving staff and patients, including fire alarms and emergency safety procedures, electronic medical records procedures to verify confidentiality and security of data, and verification of staff and patient safety to reduce back injuries and falls.

Certification

Certification is a process through which an organization recognizes that accreditation eligibility requirements have been met. Unlike licensure, where someone must become licensed in order to perform certain activities, certification is voluntary. For example, a nurse may pass a test to earn a certificate in Childbirth Education. The nurse must have a state license to work as a nurse, but her workplace does not require a childbirth educator certification. In another example, a farmer may pay a fee and pass an inspection to earn a certificate in organic gardening. However, the farmer must have a state-issued license to sell his produce, regardless of whether or not the produce carries organic certification. The same is true for organizations. A hospital may pass inspection to earn "Baby-Friendly" certification, which means the hospital promotes breastfeeding and other healthy-baby initiatives. However, they are not required to have this certification to provide maternal and infant health care.

Now that the terms have been defined, let's move to a discussion about national regulatory agencies.

THE JOINT COMMISSION

In 1951, the Joint Commission on Accreditation of Hospital Organizations (JCAHO) was initiated, but was not until 1965 that accreditation had any official impact. In 1965, the federal government linked the accreditation standards to whether or not the hospitals were allowed to participate in Medicare. Later in 2008, The Joint Commission's hospital accreditation program was linked to the U.S. Department of Health and Human Services in the Centers for Medicare and Medicaid Services (CMS).

Even with this change, The Joint Commission (which JCAHO is now known as) remains a private, nonprofit organization that continues to improve the safety and quality of U.S. health care provided. The Joint Commission assesses performance improvement and provides accreditation to healthcare organizations. It also sets standards and expectations for organization performance that are reasonable and measurable. The Joint Commission standards are developed with input from healthcare providers, patients, content experts, patients, employers, and government agencies. The standards are updated as needs change for patient safety, quality of care, positive health outcomes, or as new health laws and regulations are passed. The Joint Commission focuses on core measures. See **Table 7.1**.

TABLE 7.1 **Select Examples of the Joint Commission Core Measures**

Core Measures	Measured Objectives
Hospital Outpatient Department	Median time to transfer to another facility for acute coronary intervention
Venous Thromboembolism	Venous thromboembolism with anticoagulation
Stroke	Antithrombotic therapy by end of hospital Day 2 Discharged on statin medication Stroke education Assessed for rehabilitation
Surgical Care Improvement Project	Prophylactic antibiotic received within 1 hour prior to surgical incision Prophylactic antibiotics discontinued within 24 hours after surgery end time Cardiac surgery patients with controlled postoperative blood glucose Urinary catheter removed on postoperative Day 1 or postoperative Day 2 with day of surgery being Day Zero Surgery patients with perioperative temperature management Surgery patients who received appropriate venous thromboembolism prophylaxis within 24 hours prior to surgery to 24 hours after surgery
Children's Asthma Care	Use of systemic corticosteroids for inpatient asthma Home management plan of care given to patient/caregiver
Immunization	Pneumococcal immunization—Age 65 and older Pneumococcal immunization—High risk populations (age 6 through 64 years)
Pneumonia Measures	As of January 1, 2015, data collection for this measure is no longer required.
Heart Failure	As of January 1, 2015, data collection for this measure is no longer required.

Data from: The Joint Commission (2015). Core Measure Sets. Available at: http://www.jointcommission.org/core_measure_sets.aspx.[9]

NATIONAL COMMITTEE OF QUALITY ASSURANCE (NCQA)

In 1990, the National Committee of Quality Assurance (NCQA), "a non-profit organization dedicated to improving health care quality," was created.[10] NCQA provides an accreditation for health insurance companies. This accreditation is considered to be the most comprehensive research involving healthcare systems with the overall purpose to improve health insurance policies for individuals, physicians, and employers. NCQA is the most widely recognized accreditation program in the United States for healthcare providers and organizations.[11]

NCQA research evaluates health insurance policies and corporations at two levels: clinical performance and consumer experience. For example, NCQA collects satisfaction survey data from employees who purchase a specific health insurance policy. Keep in mind that health insurance corporations sell many different types of health insurance policies. If consumers rate their experience as poor (e.g., difficulty filing health insurance claims, being overcharged, poor telephone service interactions, long wait time to resolve problems), then the health insurance corporation or specific policy receives a low satisfaction score for customer satisfaction. In addition, NCQA reviews the billing data of health insurance corporations as well as specific types of health insurance policies for clinical performance (e.g., ordering unnecessary tests and procedures, overcharging for office visits, failing to resolve billing disputes). This would also lead to a low score.

So, how does a low score impact the health insurance company? Because NCQA is a national quality assurance organization, the scores of the health insurance corporation and their various health insurance policies are posted and available for review by employers and consumers. If a health insurance corporation reviews consistently low scores in several categories, then employers and consumers are less likely to purchase their policies.

Let us go back and examine the definition of clinical performance. NCQA uses a tool called the *Healthcare Effectiveness Data and Information Set*

(HEDIS) to evaluate clinical performance. HEDIS measures have been adopted for use by about 90 percent of U.S. health insurance corporations to measure performance on specific areas of care and service. Keep in mind that the HEDIS performance measures are linked to quality assurance. For example, if the health insurance corporation consistently denies payment for a prevention behavior (e.g., mammogram, colonoscopy, or vaccines), then its HEDIS performance measures would reflect a low score. The low score (poor quality assurance) is reported on the NCQA annual report. Consumers and employers review the NCQA quality rating scores and thus make decisions regarding whether or not to purchase a specific health insurance policy. In addition, the HEDIS data allow an equal comparison between health insurance policies, and the health insurance corporations use HEDIS data to improve health outcomes. See **Box 7.1**.

Second, for the consumer experience, the NCQA uses the Consumer Assessment of Healthcare Providers and Systems (CAHPS) survey to ask individuals to rate their experiences with health care related to the quality of the healthcare service, communication skills of the healthcare provider, distance to the healthcare provider's location by zip code, ease of access to healthcare services, customer service and coordination of care, and many other categories.[12]

BOX 7.1 Examples of HEDIS Measurements Used to Improve Health Outcomes

HEDIS measures used to improve health outcomes:

- Asthma Medication Use
- Persistence of Beta-Blocker Treatment after a Heart Attack
- Controlling High Blood Pressure
- Comprehensive Diabetes Care
- Breast Cancer Screening
- Antidepressant Medication Management
- Childhood and Adolescent Immunization Status
- Childhood and Adult Weight/BMI Assessment

The three most widely used CAHPS surveys are the Health Plan Survey, which covers experiences with health insurance usage and staff; the Clinician & Group Survey, which covers ambulatory care settings, healthcare providers, and staff; and the Hospital Survey, which covers experiences about care during an inpatient stay at a hospital facility. The other surveys include Home Health Care, In-Center Hemodialysis, Nursing Home, Surgical Care, American Indian, Dental Plan, and Experience of Care and Health Outcomes (ECHO) Survey.

The next section builds on consumer health information with a discussion of the operations of the State Insurance Commissioner's Office housed in each state, including insurance (e.g., health, home, vehicle) fraud and malpractice. The chapter concludes with the role of quality assurance committees and offices within healthcare organizations, including risk management and institutional review boards.

NATIONAL AND STATE INSURANCE COMMISSIONER'S OFFICE

The National Association of Insurance Commissioners (NAIC) is the U.S. standard-setting and regulatory support organization created and governed by the chief insurance regulators from all 50 states, the District of Columbia, and 5 U.S. territories. Through the NAIC, state insurance regulators establish standards and best practices with regard to insurance practices, conduct peer review, and coordinate their regulatory oversight. The NAIC mission is to assist state insurance regulators and serve the public interest through education.[13] NAIC and the state insurance regulators educate the public about insurance and consumer-protection issues, such as insurance fraud and malpractice. They provide web education programs in English and Spanish at www.insureuonline.org.

Insurance Fraud

Insurance fraud occurs when an insurance company, agency, adjuster, or consumer intentionally commits a deliberate deception to obtain an illegitimate gain. Insurance fraud happens during the process of buying, using, or selling insurance.[14]

Here are three examples of insurance fraud:

First, a fake insurance company commits fraud by collecting premiums from consumers for bogus policies with no intention of paying claims. Consumers need to check in advance to make sure that they are dealing with a legitimate, licensed insurer before signing an application for a policy (this can be done at www.naic.org/state_web_map.htm).

Second, an insurance salesperson commits fraud by collecting premiums from a customer and not sending the payments to the insurance company. The customer thinks that his or her premiums are being properly handled, while the insurance company thinks the policyholder is not paying premiums and eventually cancels the customer's policy.

Third, consumers commit insurance fraud by deliberately staging an accident, injury, theft, arson, or other type of loss that would be covered under an insurance policy; by exaggerating a legitimate claim; or by knowingly omitting or providing false information on an application.[14]

If insurance fraud is suspected, it is important to contact the state insurance department to file a complaint against the insurance company and/or visit www.naic.org to complete the form provided by the Online Fraud Reporting System (OFRS).[14]

Malpractice

Malpractice is defined as improper, unskilled, or negligent treatment of a patient by a healthcare provider (e.g., physician, dentist, nurse, pharmacist, home health aide, or other healthcare professional).[15] Negligence is the most common type of malpractice. To file a malpractice complaint or lawsuit, an individual must prove four elements: (1) A duty of care was owed by the physician (i.e., once a doctor agrees to treat a patient, he or she has a professional duty to provide competent care); (2) the physician violated the applicable standard of care (i.e., what other physicians in the same geographical location would do for a patient with a similar medical condition); (3) the person suffered an injury, such as a vehicle crash, and was not at fault or was not at fault for an injury sustained at his or her place of employment; and (4) the injury was caused by the substandard conduct or evidence or negligence, such as the physician was under the influence of drugs or alcohol. The burden of proving these elements is on the individual in a malpractice lawsuit.[15]

HEALTHCARE ORGANIZATION COMMITTEES RELATED TO QUALITY

Risk Management

In healthcare organizations, the responsibility of risk assessment is typically housed within the Office of Legal Affairs. The purpose of risk management is to improve safety and well-being for patients and staff and identify financial risks. First, patient safety is of utmost importance. Because individuals come to healthcare organizations to improve their health, strict protocols and procedures are in place to account for their safety at all times.

For example, disinfectant practices decrease the risk of infection, computer software programs are installed to decrease errors in dispensing medications, and measures are in place (e.g., slipper socks with plastic treads, grab bars in restrooms, call buttons at bedsides) to decrease falls and injuries.

Second, healthcare staff safety is another important issue. Even though healthcare workers are responsible for patient safety, they also need to have training regarding their own personal safety. For example, healthcare providers are trained to move patients properly to avoid back injuries. Long shifts, sleep disruption, and excessive overtime hours contribute to medical errors. Third, financial risk assessment deals with controlling the operating costs of the healthcare institution, including the costs associated with malpractice lawsuits and slip-and-fall injuries, and reducing costs of all aspects of health care (e.g., personnel costs, clinical quality improvement, building maintenance and improvements, technological upgrades). Last, risk identification is the process of finding potential hazards and reducing the risk prior to an adverse event

© sturti/iStockphoto

happening, which would improve patient care and lower healthcare costs.[16]

INSTITUTIONAL REVIEW BOARD (IRB) COMMITTEE

The purpose of the IRB Committee is "to assure, both in advance and by periodic review, that appropriate steps are taken to protect the rights and welfare of humans participating as subjects in the research. To accomplish this purpose, IRBs use a group process to review research protocols and related materials (e.g., informed consent documents and investigator brochures) to ensure protection of the rights and welfare of human subjects of research."[17]

The IRB is responsible for the following oversight functions:[18]

- Determine if the proposed activities involve human participant research (e.g., asking students to complete a survey about satisfaction with course content does not require IRB approval, but asking students to complete a survey about their eating and sleeping patterns does require IRB approval).

- Review, approve, and if necessary require modifications prior to initiation of all research activities.
- Require that informed-consent information given to participants is in accordance with appropriate laws, regulations, and international standards (e.g., primary language of participant, appropriate written and oral literacy level, understanding and comprehension of information).
- Require documentation of informed consent or waive documentation in accordance with federal and state laws and regulations for location of research sites.
- Notify researchers and institutions in writing of the IRB Committee's decision to approve or disapprove the proposed research activity, or of modifications required to secure IRB approval of the research activity.
- Conduct continuing review of research covered by the IRB guidelines at intervals appropriately associated with the degree of involved risk.
- Suspend or terminate approval of research that is not being conducted in accordance with the IRB's requirements or that is associated with unexpected serious harm to participants.

Keep in mind that the IRB Committee review's purpose is to assure that the rights and welfare of subjects are protected. A signed informed-consent document provides the prospective research participant with sufficient information to make an informed decision and agree to participate in the research. IRB review of informed-consent documents also ensures that the institution has complied with applicable regulations.[17]

Bioethics Committees

Before discussing the purpose of bioethics committees, let us begin with the definition of bioethics. Bioethics is the study of typically controversial issues that emerge from new technology or situations brought about by advances in medicine or biological research. The results of medical advances sometimes raise ethical questions. For example, the most common bioethical issues are caused by ethical decisions at the beginning and end of life. Some aspects of abortion and euthanasia are frequently debated in lower legal courts as well as the U.S. Supreme Court. The list of topics between the beginning of life and the end of life is endless; they include surrogacy, long-term storage of fertilized eggs (embryos), human genetic engineering, the allocation of scarce healthcare resources, organ donation, stem cell organ re-engineering, healthcare rationing, denial of care due to lack of health insurance, right to refuse medical care (e.g., vaccines or blood products) for religious or cultural reasons, and controversy of brain death versus prolonging life with mechanical support devices. Even among bioethicists (people who study these controversial issues), there is disagreement over the limits of the discipline and concern about the lack of final decisions because medical research continues to advance.

The history of human experimentation and the creation of bioethics is beyond the scope of this chapter, so our discussion begins in 1974 with the National Commission for the Protection of Human Subjects of Biomedical and Behavioral Research. This commission established the basic ethical principles to be used when conducting biomedical and behavioral research involving human subjects, human dignity, and the sanctity of life.

The Role of Bioethics Committees

All hospitals are required to have a bioethics committee with members representing various departments within the hospital, including, but not limited to, physician groups, nurses, social workers, administration, chaplains, other ancillary care services, community representatives, and an ethicist. The functions of the bioethics committees are (a) to advise on matters pertaining to ethical considerations within the hospital; (b) to provide forums for discussion regarding ethical issues associated with the hospital's medical, educational, and research objectives; (c) to increase awareness of ethical issues and concerns within the hospital through educational and informational programs and activities; (d) to serve as a resource for clinical ethical decisions; (e) to be available to patients, family members, and hospital staff for assistance and advice concerning ethical issues relating to patient care and to offer guidance and support to the individuals involved; and (f) to offer mediation to help in resolving intra-family or staff–family disagreements concerning the plan of care for the patient.[19, 20]

It is easier to think of bioethics as a shared and ongoing discussion rather than a final decision. It is an examination of ethical issues in all fields of health care, health science, and health policy. Although each healthcare discipline has its own ethical standards, the conversation is never over because the issues and technologies continue to change and challenge the ethical standards. Bioethics conversations take place in many locations, including classrooms, homes, hallways, media outlets, courtrooms, hospitals, research laboratories, and hospital rooms. These conversations must include individuals, families, caregivers, healthcare providers, scientists, attorneys, policy makers, and the general public. Traditional ethical standards need to be challenged and revised as science, technology, and policies are updated and accepted.[21]

For further valuable information about bioethics, visit this website: http://bioethics.od.nih .gov/general.html.

Summary

In summary, this chapter introduces the topic of quality assurance in health care, including a focus on the quality of activities and programs to assure quality of care, identify problems in delivery of care, monitor to decrease deficiencies, and develop corrective actions. This chapter also discusses various aspects of quality assurance, including national regulatory agencies and the concept of institutional review boards and bioethics committees in healthcare practice. Throughout this chapter, health navigation professionals became acquainted with how their role is associated with quality assurance in the healthcare system.

Case Study

Mary Williams, age 67, made an appointment to see Dr. Jackson, an orthopedic surgeon, regarding the arthritis in her left knee. It seems that the pain is increasing, and she is not ready to face a knee replacement at this time because she continues to work full-time as a high school art teacher. After making the appointment, the office receptionist instructed Ms. Williams to go to the office website to complete the patient history form prior to coming to the scheduled appointment. Ms. Williams completed the form as instructed.

On the day of the appointment, Ms. Williams arrived about 20 minutes early to sign in, pay her co-payment, and provide any other additional information. The medical assistant accompanied Ms. Williams to the back office to obtain her weight, blood pressure, and temperature; she also asked her about her current medications and the reason for her visit. Upon completion, Ms. Williams was directed to an

© Alexander Raths/Shutterstock

examination room. After Dr. Jackson went over her medical history, recent radiology reports, and examined her knees, she determined that Ms. Williams would be eligible for knee replacement. Because Ms. Williams stated that she was not interested in a knee replacement, Dr. Jackson suggested that she could receive an experimental gel injection into her knee to cushion her joint and give her about 12 months of pain relief.

Dr. Jackson gave Ms. Williams some pharmaceutical literature about the experimental gel injection. She also gave Ms. Williams the informed-consent document to read and sign if she was interested in trying the experimental gel injection. Dr. Jackson said that Ms. Williams should read the information and schedule another appointment with the office nurse to discuss any concerns that she might have regarding the experimental gel injection prior to making the decision.

Student Activity

1. As a health navigation professional, what questions would you advise Ms. Williams to ask prior to making the decision to receive or not receive the experimental gel injection?

2. List at least three questions that Ms. Williams should ask the office nurse during the appointment.

3. How would you advise Ms. Williams to make the final decision?

References

1. Centers for Disease Control. (1988). Update: Universal precautions for prevention of transmission of human immunodeficiency virus, hepatitis B virus, and other bloodborne pathogens in health-care settings. *MMWR. Morbidity and Mortality Weekly Report, 37*(24), 377.

2. Centers for Disease Control. (1985). Recommendations for preventing transmission of infection with human T-lymphotropic virus type III/lymphadenopathy-associated virus in the workplace. *MMWR. Morbidity and Mortality Weekly Report, 34*(45), 681.

3. Garner, J. S. (1996). Guideline for isolation precautions in hospitals. The Hospital Infection Control Practices Advisory Committee. *Infect Control Hosp Epidemiol, 17*(1), 53–80.

4. United States Environmental Protection Agency. *Quality assurance, quality control, and quality assessment measures.* Retrieved June 30, 2015, from http://water.epa.gov/type/rsl/monitoring/132.cfm; last updated in 2012.

5. United States Department of Health and Human Services. *Quality improvement.* Accessed June 30, 2015, from http://www.hrsa.gov/quality/toolbox/methodology/qualityimprovement/index.html.

6. Flexner, A. (1910). *Medical education in the United States and Canada: A report to the Carnegie Foundation for the Advancement of Teaching.* Stanford, CA: Carnegie Foundation for the Advancement of Teaching.

7. Santiago, A. *Professional association. About careers.* Retrieved June 30, 2105, from http://healthcareers.about.com/od/glossary/g/professional_gl.htm.

8. HumanRights.gov. *Fact sheet: Non-governmental organizations (NGOs) in the United States.* Retrieved June 30, 2015, from http://www.humanrights.gov/dyn/fact-sheet-non-governmental-organizations-ngos-in-the-united-states.html; last updated January 1, 2012.

9. The Joint Commission. *Core measure sets.* Retrieved June 30, 2015, from http://www.jointcommission.org/core_measure_sets.aspx.

10. National Committee for Quality Assurance. *About NCQA.* Retrieved June 30, 2015, from http://www.ncqa.org/AboutNCQA.aspx.

11. National Committee for Quality Assurance. *Health plan accreditation.* Retrieved March 19, 2015, from http://www.ncqa.org/Programs/Accreditation/HealthPlanHP.aspx.

12. Agency for Healthcare Research and Quality. *About CAHPS.* Retrieved March 19, 2015, from https://cahps.ahrq.gov/about-cahps/index.html.

13. National Association of Insurance Commisioners. *About the NAIC.* Retrieved June 30, 2015, from http://www.naic.org/index_about.htm.

14. National Association of Insurance Commisioners. *Insurance fraud: What is it and how do I report it?* Retrieved June 30, 2015, from http://www.naic.org/documents/consumer_alert_beware_insurance_fraud.htm; last updated August 2008.

15. Farlex. *The Free Dictionary: Medical malpractice.* Retrieved June 30, 2015, from http://legal-dictionary.thefreedictionary.com/Medical+Malpractice.

16. United States Department of Health and Human Services. *Clinical quality improvement.* Retrieved June 30, 2015,

from http://bphc.hrsa.gov/qualityimprovement/clinical
quality/qualityimprovement.html.

17. United States Food and Drug Administration. *Regulartory
information*. Retrieved June 30, 2015, from http://www
.fda.gov/RegulatoryInformation/Guidances/ucm126420
.htm; last updated June 24, 2014.

18. Cornell University Office of Reasearch Integrity and
Assurance. *Institutional review board for human participants: Human participants committee responsibilities*.
Retrieved June 30, 2015, from https://www.irb.cornell
.edu/responsibilities; last updated in 2007.

19. Cedars-Sinai Hospital Bioethics Committee. *The role of
the CSMC Bioethics Committee*. Retrieved March 19, 2015,
from http://www.cedars-sinai.edu/Patients/Programs-and
-Services/Healthcare-Ethics-/Bioethics-Committee.aspx.

20. The Brooklyn Hospital Center. *Bioethics*. Retrieved June
30, 2015, from http://www.tbh.org/about-us/ethics.

21. Michigan State University. *What is bioethics?* Retrieved
March, 19, 2015, from http://www.bioethics.msu.edu/index
.php?option=com_content&view=article&id=74&Ite
mid=71.

PART 3

Care of the Individual

CHAPTER 8

Individual Assessment

LEARNING OBJECTIVES

By the end of this chapter, students will be able to:

- Evaluate patients' specific healthcare needs
- Use information from family members and electronic medical records to understand patients' health status
- Describe how health disparities and social determinants of health influence health outcomes of an individual as well as a community
- Demonstrate communication techniques to assess patient health

CHAPTER OVERVIEW

This chapter introduces how a health navigation professional assesses an individual to identify and assist with his or her specific needs. Assessment information is obtained from the individual, caregivers (as appropriate), and the paper medical charts or electronic medical records (EMRs). Before the health navigation professional initiates a conversation with the individual, it is important to review the EMR, if it is available. The EMR provides the health navigation professional with a broad overview of the individual's health status, including past medical conditions and surgeries, allergies, current diagnoses and medications, and family health history. This EMR review gives the health navigation professional sufficient background information to initiate a conversation. The assessment

begins with the individual's life story, which explores all aspects of health disparities and social determinants of health that influence him or her. Throughout the life story conversation, the health navigation professional is gathering additional information related to the individual's current perception of his or her health status and current needs for improved quality of life. After the life story conversation, the health navigation professional returns to the EMR to investigate and verify the information provided during the conversation. If the EMR is not available, the health navigation professional verifies the information with the caregiver or family member.

LIFE STORY

Before a health navigation professional begins a conversation with an individual, it is essential to prepare for the interaction by reviewing the available background information about the individual. For example, if the individual is hospitalized or living in an assisted-living facility, the health navigation professional spends an adequate amount of time (e.g., 1 or 2 hours) reviewing the electronic medical record (EMR) to gain some insight into the individual's background, an understanding of the current medical condition, and past medical history.

The initial conversation begins with showing interest in seeking the individual's life story.

If the health navigation professional identifies an interesting tidbit in the EMR, it will help to start the conversation. It can be as simple as "I was reviewing your medical record and I noticed that your previous address was Michigan. Can you tell me why you recently decided to move to Arizona?" This type of open-ended question invites the individual to share his or her life story. On the other hand, if the health navigation professional begins the conversation with a question about the individual's medical condition or health issue, the individual assumes that the health navigation professional did not bother to read the EMR. The individual is less likely to form a communication partnership with the health navigation professional. Remember: It is better to delay a visit than to initiate a visit without gathering adequate information. See **Scenario 8.1**.

HEALTH OUTCOMES INFLUENCED BY SOCIAL AND CULTURAL NORMS

Once the conversation has been established as comfortable and casual, the health navigation professional begins to direct the conversation toward nonmedical factors that influence an individual's health, including the social and cultural aspects of the individual's life story. Typically, the EMR has limited information about such nonmedical factors, so the healthcare provider, including the health navigation professional, asks appropriate questions and listens as the individual tells his or her life story.

Usually, the EMR contains demographic information such as marital status, race/ethnicity, religious preference, and type of health insurance. Although the information is recorded, it fails to describe details. For example, if the marital status is marked "married," there is no information whether the individual has been married several times or once, the length of the marriage, or the quality of the marriage (e.g., loving kindness, domestic violence, infidelity, substance abuse). These subtle differences may impact the degree of support that the spouse provides to his or her partner during hospitalization and beyond as a caregiver. Before moving further into the discussion of social and cultural norms, it is important to explore the concept of health disparities.

HEALTH DISPARITIES

Whenever a health outcome is greater or less between different populations, this is what we call a *health disparity*. Health disparities are defined as the preventable differences in the burden of disease, injury, violence, or opportunities to achieve optimal health that are experienced by socially

SCENARIO 8.1 Health Communication

Mr. Ford had an appointment with his family practice physician. When he arrived at the medical office, the medical assistant weighed him, took his blood pressure, pulse, and temperature, and asked him the purpose of the visit. Mr. Ford explained that he had been coughing for a few days and having trouble

sleeping due to the cough; yesterday he stayed home from work due to a fever. The medical assistant recorded his information in the EMR and directed him to an examination room. The physician enters the room and asks, "What brings you to the office today?" Mr. Ford becomes annoyed because he is required to repeat the same information again, because the physician did not take the time to read what was recorded in the EMR.

This type of interaction is common and leads to poor communication between the healthcare provider and the individual.

© Steve Debenport/iStock Photo

disadvantaged populations[1] and the differences in health status between one population group in comparison to a more advantaged group due to issues of social justice and equity.[2] Health disparities adversely affect groups of individuals who experience obstacles to health.[3] The following list provides the social determinants that influence the health of an individual or group of individuals:[4, 5]

- Racial or ethnic group
- Religion or faith-based community
- Socioeconomic status
- Age
- Mental health status
- Disability status and special healthcare needs
- Cognitive, sensory, or physical disability
- Education and literacy level
- Sexual identity and orientation
- Physical environment (e.g., clean water, nonpolluted air, decent and safe housing)

- Adequate nutritious food
- Lifestyle behaviors (e.g., smoking, substance abuse)
- Occupation risks and hazards (e.g., hazardous chemical exposure, temperature)
- Affordable and reliable public transportation
- Geographic location (rural and urban)
- Access to health care and health insurance
- Other characteristics historically linked to discrimination or exclusion

Now, let us review some data to understand how social determinants of health impact the lives of individuals, populations, and communities. See **Table 8.1**.

After a careful review of Table 8.1, answer the questions in **Box 8.1**.

With a greater understanding of health disparities, let us describe in detail how a few of the social determinants of health impact of an individual or a community. The issues discussed

TABLE 8.1 Rural Life Expectancy Compared to Urban in Years of Age

Life Expectancy	Rural Counties	Urban Counties
All	76.8	78.8
Male	74.1	76.2
Female	79.7	81.3
White	77.2	79.2
Black	72.8	74.2
American Indian/Alaska Native	74.8	85.8
Asian and Pacific Islander	84.9	86.9
Hispanic	82.2	83.1

Health and Medical Issues	Rural Counties	Urban Counties
Low birth weight	8.3%	8.2%
Teen birth rate	49.5%	39.2%
Children overweight	25.0%	19.0%
Preventable hospital stays	84.0%	69.3%
Edentulism (total tooth loss) among persons 65 years of age and older	33.3%	28.8%

Modified from: Singh G.K. & Siahpush M. (2014). Widening rural-urban disparities in life expectancy, U.S., 1969–2009. *American Journal of Preventive Medicine*, 46(2), 19–29[6]; Rural Health Reform Policy Research Center. The 2014 Update of the Rural-Urban Chartbook. Princeton, NJ: Robert Wood Johnson Foundation[7]; Joens-Matre R.R., Welk G.J., Calabro M.A., Russell D.W., Nicklay E., & Hensley L.D. (2008). Rural-urban differences in physical activity, physical fitness, and overweight prevalence of children. *Journal of Rural Health*, 24(1), 49–54.[8]

BOX 8.1   Student Activity: Social Determinants of Health

Looking at Table 8.1, discuss the following questions:

1. As a health navigation professional, list some possible reasons why individuals living in an urban area live longer than individuals living in a rural area.
2. As a health navigation professional, discuss what factors might increase the rate of preventable hospital stays for individuals living in a rural community.
3. As a health navigation professional, explore the long-term consequences of edentulism among the elderly in rural and urban communities.
4. As a health navigation professional, identify some possible reasons for the increased rate of overweight children in rural communities.

include the influence of social support, cultural norms, and religious beliefs on health outcomes.

Social Support

Let us investigate how an individual copes with a health condition with and without social support. With information related to an individual's social support, the health navigation professional learns how to best assist the individual to solve pertinent issues involving their health needs and quality of life.

Social support is one of the most important factors in predicting an individual's overall well-being, physical health, mental health, and well-being across an individual's lifespan from childhood through old age.[9] Social support is also influenced by demographic variables, such as age, ethnicity, education, marital status, income, and geographical location. For example, if an individual is elderly and living alone in a rural location, it is likely that he or she will not have adequate social support because other elderly friends may

have difficulty finding transportation. In another example, if a spouse suddenly dies, the surviving spouse might experience loneliness and reduced social support if their previous social activities were typically structured with other married couples. See **Scenario 8.2**.

In addition, social support significantly predicts how well individuals cope with stress. Lack of social support is known to have a negative effect on physical and mental health. Individuals need to know that they are valued by others. Social support minimizes the negative aspects of an individual's life, boosts the immune system, and allows more focus on positive aspects.[10] Social support has been shown to have a positive effect on recovery in a variety of medical illnesses. For example, research has shown a strong association between social support and improved recovery from heart attacks (myocardial infarction and strokes)[11] as well as the considerable evidence that social support has a positive influence on recovery from hospitalization and medical procedures.[12] The Centers for Disease Control and Prevention (CDC) notes that social support is critical for elderly adults because they rely on family, friends, or organizations to assist them with daily activities, provide companionship, and care for their well-being.[9] Social support has also been consistently associated with greater medication adherence.[13] For example, if family and friends assist an individual with the practical aspects of purchasing the medication and filling the weekly pill box, the individual is more likely to take their medication as prescribed. Finally, the rise in the use of the

© YinYang/iStock Photo

SCENARIO 8.2 Social Support

© Susan Chiang/iStock Photo

Mary Randall, age 72, and Susan McKnight, age 73, have lived on the same street in Chicago and have been friends since high school. Mary's husband died about 2 years ago, and she has one daughter who lives in California. Because Susan's husband had died more than 10 years ago, and she understood what Mary was going through, she was able to offer social support by inviting Mary to social events and holiday activities.

Mary has two children: her son and his family live in the suburbs of Chicago; her other son is in the military and moves every few years. Most of Mary's and Susan's other friends have moved away, so most of their social activities are based at their church. Susan and Mary drive, but on the snowy days, they do not drive and merely walk to see each other. They both belong to the same Episcopal church, but the congregation is dwindling and the pastor has suggested a merger with another Episcopal church about 10 miles away. If this happens, Mary and Susan will no longer attend church services when driving is hazardous. In addition, Mary and Susan volunteer at the nearby elementary school as foster grandmothers. This activity gives them something useful to do three mornings per week, and they can walk to the school.

With regard to their health, Mary and Susan do not have the same doctor. Mary was diagnosed with diabetes a few years ago, but she keeps her blood glucose levels within normal limits through a healthy diet and walking for exercise. Susan is a breast cancer survivor of 15 years, so she is vigilant about getting lab tests and mammograms each year. However, they agreed to make all medical appointments in the morning and on days when they are not foster grandmothers, so that they can follow their medical appointments by going out to lunch. They enjoy their time together and the mutual support they give each other. Even though they talked about the fact that both of their homes are in need of repair, they do not wish to face the facts long enough to think about moving to a new location.

Several weeks ago, Mary tripped on the sidewalk outside the elementary school and bruised her hip, broke her right wrist, and several ribs. She needed to have surgery to repair her wrist and spent several days in the hospital to recover. Her daughter, Linda, came from California to care for Mary after she was discharged. During the visit, her daughter realized the disrepair of Mary's home and had a serious talk with her about moving to sunny California and living in a retirement community near Linda's home. If she moved, Mary would be close to her three grandchildren and could visit more than once per year. Mary was torn about the possible move, but knew that she could not continue to live in Chicago. When she told Susan about her decision, Susan disclosed that she, too, was thinking about moving into the home of her son. Susan had not wished to share the news while Mary was recovering, but they both decided that the time had come to progress to the next step in their lives.

Student Activity

1. Write a few questions that the health navigation professional may ask Mary at the first medical office appointment for her diabetes after she arrives in California.
2. After Susan moves to the Chicago suburbs, she finds that she is lonely and falling into depression. She goes to the university medical center for a checkup and encounters the health navigation professional. How should the health navigation professional begin the conversation with Susan?

Internet across the lifespan is likely to increase attention on the value of online support groups.[12]

Social support is more than merely having a few friends. Research has defined four types of social support. First, emotional support is associated with sharing life experiences and involves the provision of empathy, love, trust, and caring. For example, individuals with a supportive attachment to a spouse or life partner have an increased amount of social support and a companion for activities, conversation, and assistance. Second, instrumental support involves receiving needed tangible aid and services from close friends, colleagues, and neighbors. For example, there was a fire in an apartment complex. Robert's apartment was not burned, but there was smoke damage. His friends provided instrumental support by coming over to help clean the walls, remove damaged furniture, and make a trip to the thrift store to purchase a new couch. Third, informational support involves receiving advice, suggestions, and information that an individual can use to address problems. And fourth, appraisal support involves receiving information that is useful for self-evaluation purposes, such as constructive feedback, affirmation, and social comparison, especially when given by older individuals, mentors, or supervisors (e.g., teacher or parent).[10]

Given the strong connection between social support and improved health outcomes, the health navigation professional needs to explore with their clients and their caregivers the extent of the social support available to them. This information can be woven into the life story by asking about the level of social support used in the past. For example, "I noticed in your medical records that you are a recent widow. Can you tell me about how you are doing?" Gathering a social history should feel like a conversation for the individual rather than responding to another list of questions. Also this type of conversation allows the health navigation professional to determine if the information reported by the individual matches the information noted in the EMR. Individuals should feel comfortable enough with the conversation that they add additional information than what you asked. It is important to pay close attention to these extra comments. This information may prove to be valuable. The questions in Box 8.1 are suggestions with which to begin a conversation and build on the information that was obtained from the medical record. The health navigation professional should avoid asking a list of questions that limit conversation, such as simple "yes" or "no" questions. Remember, the purpose is to listen to the life story. It is always comfortable to ask a question, followed by "Could you tell me more about that?" See **Box 8.2**.

BOX 8.2 Examples of Questions for a Social Support Conversation

Place of Residence

Where do you currently live?
> How long have you lived there?
> How long do you plan to stay there?

If the individual lives in a home, you can ask a few related questions:
> Do you live alone or with others? Who else?
> Who is at home during the day? Night?
> Who cooks the meals?
> Are you a caregiver?

Is mobility a problem for you?
> Are you able to drive?
> Are the bus services convenient for you?
> What is your home like?
> Do you have to manage stairs?
> How do you manage the stairs?

Marital Status

What is the history of your marital status?
> How long have you been single? Married?
> Divorced? Widowed?

Is your partner healthy?
Do you have any children living at home?
Are your children healthy?

Employment

Do you work?
> Full-time or part-time?
> How long have you been retired?

What is/was your occupation?
What are your financial worries?
What is the status of your health insurance?

Miscellaneous Questions to Enhance the Conversation

Have you been abroad?
> If so, when? Where?

Do you have pets?
> Who is taking care of your pets now?

What are your concerns at this time?
How might I be able to help you with this concern?
Are there family members or friends available to assist you? Short-term? Long-term?

Cultural Norms

Cultural and social norms are defined as behavior patterns, values, attitudes, and beliefs of specific groups (e.g., ethnicity, age group, common language, geographical location). Individuals learn

© Susan Chiang/iStock Photo

cultural and social norms from parents, relatives, teachers, peers, and many other individuals whose common values, attitudes, beliefs, and behaviors take place in the context of their own organizational culture.[14] Generally, cultural and social norms are considered to be healthy, but this is not always the case. For example, being a member of a street gang might be considered a social norm in some large inner-city neighborhoods. However, the behavior of street gangs is not positive in most situations. Across various societies, there are conflicts and uncertainty about which cultural norms are or are not acceptable. Over time, cultural and social norms change to fit the society as it changes. For example, in the United States during the 1800s, it was unacceptable for women to wear dresses that showed their ankles. This is no longer the case with women's fashion. Most recently, the changing social norms related to same-sex marriage have changed and were legally upheld by the Supreme Court.

It is important to not compare norms as better or worse, but merely to make the comparison by seeing the differences. Norms are often so strongly ingrained in an individual's life that the individual fails to even recognize the behavior or value as a social or cultural norm that may be viewed differently by outsiders.[14, 15] See **Box 8.3**.

When health navigation professionals are working with individuals from a variety of cultures and social norms, it is important to clarify the meaning and understanding of words. A misunderstanding of cultural norms leads to miscommunication and errors. The simple definition of a cultural norm is what individuals generally do within a given culture, such as holidays, birth, wedding and funeral rituals, development

of laws, driving regulations, currency, weights and measures, and social ethics. Generally, cultural norms (also called *social norms*) are also defined as expectations about how people should behave and what negative consequences occur when individuals violate a social norm. For example, an individual receives a traffic citation and fine for exceeding the posted speed limit. Because uncertainly causes psychological stress, norms serve the purpose of allowing the individual to learn what to expect and prepare for the situation or activity. Norms are self-perpetuating and may or may not serve society over time. For example, until recently, the use of marijuana was considered a harmful and illegal behavior across society. However, medical research has shown positive effects of medical marijuana. Now numerous states have decriminalized medical marijuana and even encouraged the use of medical marijuana for palliative care. New norms can be incorporated into society. For example, consider rites of passage, such as high school prom or wedding receptions.[16]

Cultural norms may be depicted by clothing and by formal titles given to individuals to create or legitimize authority or cultural practices.[16] For example, in a hospital, an individual wearing a white lab coat with a stethoscope draped around the neck is assumed to be a physician. In a courtroom, the individual wearing a long black robe is assumed to be the presiding judge. On the street, an individual dressed in a police uniform is thought to be a law enforcement officer. Such clothing and appearances may or may not be accurate, and in some situations, the individual in the uniform may not fully uphold the duties and responsibilities of the uniform. In other situations, the individual maintains the appearance outside the work environment because the uniform serves as a "badge of honor" for recognition. For example, a hospital chaplain is not required to wear a black shirt and stiff white collar outside the hospital, but chooses to do so as a way to maintain respect in the community. It is merely a cultural norm for an occupation. In addition, titles have a tendency to be misunderstood across cultures. For example, in the United States, college professors with a PhD degree are addressed as "Dr. Smith." However, in the United States, a medical physician is also given the title "Dr. Smith." These identical titles could cause confusion. In European countries, individuals with a PhD degree are called professors and individuals with an MD degree are called doctors. Understanding language is dependent on the culture or country surrounding you.

In addition, cultural norms impact entertainment, humor, and personal space. As for entertainment, in one culture, loud laughter and teasing are expected and viewed as part of having a good time; other cultures may view the use of disrespectful language and aggressive behavior as offensive. One culture may enjoy drinking tea and playing board games, whereas another cultural would view this activity as lacking in excitement. Dancing in one cultural may be disallowed, while other cultures have ancient roots based on music, dance, and performance.[15]

For health navigation professionals, the concept of personal space is an important consideration. Individuals from some cultures stand very close when having a conversation, whereas others may need additional space between individuals. Some cultures encourage kissing on the check as a greeting of respect regardless of gender, whereas other cultural norms discourage touching altogether (particularly between the genders) as a form of personal greeting. The differences do not imply that one culture is better or worse than another culture. What is important is recognizing the differences without

assigning judgment as well as learning about cultures as a way to improve communication.[7]

Religious Practices

Closely related to cultural norms is the topic of religious practice. Even the concept of "religious practice" has various meanings, including spiritual views, faith-based community, or mindfulness meditation. Some individuals believe their religious practices occur with friends in a building, while others experience their spirituality alone in a forest. Religious practices influence how individuals go through their day-to-day lives as well as how they make decisions related to their healthcare decisions. In the United States, a wide spectrum of religious practices influences healthcare decisions. For example, individuals who practice the religious and cultural beliefs of the Amish are significantly different from what is considered the usual U.S. culture. The Amish do not generally practice preventive health care (e.g., immunizations, prenatal care, birth control) and instead use traditional healthcare providers from their faith-based community.[17] Although it is unlikely that a health navigation professional would encounter a practicing member of the Amish community, health navigation professionals will meet individuals with religious beliefs that are different from their own. Each individual will have specific religious beliefs and practices, and it is up to the health navigation professional to be aware of the various faith-based communities and respect the practices with judgment. For two examples of similarities between various religious beliefs and health practices, see **Table 8.2** for

© 2windspa/iStock Photo

TABLE 8.2 Similarities among Religions

	Historically Black Churches N = 1995	Catholics N = 8054	Mormons N = 581	Jehovah's Witnesses N = 215	Other Christians N = 129	Jews N = 682	Muslims N = 116	Buddhists N = 411	Hindus N = 257	National Total N = 35,556
Believe in God or Universal Spirit	90%	72%	90%	93%	82%	41%	82%	39%	57%	71%
More Than 1x Weekly Service Attendance	30%	9%	31%	71%	8%	6%	17%	8%	10%	15%
Frequency of Prayer: Daily	80%	58%	82%	89%	71%	26%	71%	45%	62%	58%
Frequency of Receiving Answers to Prayers: At Least Once a Week	34%	15%	32%	36%	29%	8%	31%	18%	13%	19%
Literal Interpretation of Scripture: Word of God	62%	23%	35%	48%	5%	10%	50%	8%	12%	33%
Religious Teachings: MORE Than One True Way to Interpret the Teachings of My Religion	57%	77%	43%	18%	82%	89%	60%	90%	85%	27%
Views of Religions: Many Religions Lead to Eternal Life	59%	79%	39%	16%	83%	82%	56%	86%	89%	24%
Importance of Religion in One's Life: Very Important	85%	56%	83%	86%	60%	31%	72%	35%	45%	56%

Data from: Ontario Consultants on Religious Tolerance (2003). Comparing Different Religions & Faith Groups. Available at http://www.religioustolerance.org/relcomp.htm. Retrieved on June 30, 2015[18]; and Pew Research Center (2014). The Religious Landscape Study. Available at: http://religions.pewforum.org/pdf/comparisons-all_beliefs.pdf. Retrieved on June 30, 2015.[19]

TABLE 8.3 Major Religions and Healthcare Decisions

	Buddhist	Hindu	Jewish	Protestant	Native American
Blood Transfusions and Artificial Reproductive Technology	Yes	No, artificial reproductive technology			Most nations allow blood transfusions; Navajos do not
Organ Transplants or Organ Donations	Yes	Yes	After death	Yes	Navajos do not
Healthcare Provider Same Gender as Patient	No	Preferred	Preferred	No	Preferred
Vegetarian or Vegan	No	Yes	No	No	
End-of-Life Decisions	Family	Family	Consult rabbi	Family	
Assisted Suicide		Yes	Yes		
Autopsy	Beliefs vary; must consult family	Yes	Only for legal issues or family concerns	Yes	Only for legal issues or family concerns
Abortion	Decision between patient/religious teacher/family	Yes	Yes	No universal agreement	Abortion practices vary
Artificially Prolonging Life	Based on wishes of the patient	No	Decisions made by patient/rabbi		No
Cremation	Yes	Yes	No	Yes	Yes
Artificial Insemination and Birth Control	Yes		Birth control questionable; consult rabbi		

Data from: Advocate Health Care (2014). Religious Beliefs and Healthcare Decisions. Available at: http://www.advocatehealth.com/beliefs. Retrieved on June 30, 2015.[20]

similarities among different religious beliefs and **Table 8.3** for health practices among different religious beliefs.

ELECTRONIC MEDICAL RECORD (EMR)

After reviewing the EMR for the first time and having a conversation with an individual regarding his or her life story, the health navigation professional returns to the EMR. This additional review allows the health navigation professional to verify whether the individual understands his or her health condition. For example, Ms. Hursting, age 73, described her medical condition during the life story conversation as "I have a little of the

© Sebastian Gauert/Shutterstock

sugar" (a common phrase for diabetes) and that she does not need to take any insulin injections.

However, the EMR states that Ms. Hursting's diabetes diagnosis requires daily insulin injections, and she has had multiple hospital readmissions due to being out of compliance with testing her glucose levels and refusing to comply with daily insulin injections. This information allows the health navigation professional to think of Ms. Hursting not as being noncompliant, but rather offers an opportunity to inquire about her understanding of her diabetes diagnosis; income available to purchase glucose testing strips, needles, and insulin; healthcare insurance options; transportation to clinic appointments as well as her social support; and cultural and religious practices related to a medical diagnosis. After a second conversation with Ms. Hursting, the health navigation professional has sufficient information to assist her with community referrals (e.g., Medicare supplemental insurance coverage, pharmaceutical discounts on diabetic supplies, free hospital-based diabetes and cooking classes, community elderly exercise classes, diabetic support groups).

To be most efficient in reviewing the EMR, it is useful to learn the standard format of the EMR. This EMR format helps the health navigation professional locate current medical information as well as the history of the individual's medical condition. Of course, each EMR system varies slightly, but generally after reviewing a few medical records, the system becomes familiar. Keep in mind that the EMR is used by the health navigation professional to gain and verify information. See **Table 8.4**.

TABLE 8.4 Typical EMR Format

Admission Data	Name
	Address, city, state
	Date of birth, ethnicity, and religious preference
	Health insurance policy information
	Contact person information: name, address, phone number, relationship
	Admission status: ambulance, direct admission from healthcare office, brought in vehicle to hospital emergency, scheduled admission
	Type of residence: private home, facilities: assisted living, skilled nursing, rehabilitation, mental health
	Preferred primary language
	Belongings brought to hospital: wallet, eyeglasses, hearing aids, dentures, clothing, shoes, identification and health insurance cards
Presenting Complaint	What brought you to the hospital today?
History of Presenting Complaint (e.g., pain) (*Hint*: SOCRATES is the acronym for this list.)	Site: Where is the pain located?
	Onset: How long have you had this pain? Is it constant, intermittent, or sudden?
	Character: How would you describe the pain, such as sharp, burning, dull?
	Radiation: Does the pain radiate anywhere?
	Association: Do you have other symptoms with the pain, such as sweating or vomiting?
	Time: How long does the pain last or is there a pattern?
	Exacerbating/relieving factors: Does anything make the pain better or worse?
	Severity: How severe is the pain with 0 being no pain and 10 being severe pain?

Past Medical History	Have you ever had this type of pain in the past?
	How was it resolved?
	Current medical conditions
	History of medical conditions
	Past surgeries
Medication and Allergy History	What prescription medications are you taking daily?
	Repeat questions for each medication: What is the dosage of this medication?
	How many times per day do you take this medication?
	What over-the-counter medications, vitamins, or supplements do you take daily? What is the dosage? How many times per day to you take it?
	Do you have any known allergies? Medications? Food? Seasonal pollen? Latex?
Family History	Do you have a family history of cancer, heart disease, or diabetes?
	Do you have any known genetic diseases in your family?
Social History	How many people live with you?
	Are you a caregiver for anyone?
	Are you employed outside of your home?
	Do you currently use any tobacco products? In the past?
	Do you currently use any illicit drugs? In the past?
	Have you ever tested positive for sexual infection? When? What?
Review of Systems (Multiple questions are asked by the physician as each system of the body is reviewed.)	Cardiovascular
	Respiratory
	Gastrointestinal
	Neurology
	Genitourinary and renal
	Musculoskeletal
	Psychiatry
Laboratory Test Results	Current and past lab results
Radiology Test Results	Current and past radiology test results (e.g., CT scan, MRI scan, PET scan, bone density, colonoscopy, mammography, cardiology stress tests, angiogram)
Patient Assessment	Daily patient assessment during hospitalization (e.g., wound care; catheter care; therapies: respiratory, speech, physical, occupational; dietetics and food intake; level of alertness; neurological checks; discharge planning; social work notes)
Physician Orders	All orders (e.g., medications, labs, radiology procedures)
Consultations	Notes from each consultation
Legal Documents	Healthcare surrogate documents: person chosen by patient to make health decisions when the patient is no longer capable of making decisions; advanced directives for end-of-life choices, such as no initiation of a feeding tube or ventilator for assisted breathing; Do Not Resuscitate (DNR) signed documents, if desired

Modified from: OSCE Skills (2015). History Taking. Available at:http://www.osceskills.com/e-learning/subjects/patient-history-taking/. Retrieved on June 30, 2015.

Summary

This chapter introduced how a health navigation professional assesses an individual to identify and assist with specific needs. The health navigation professional reviews the electronic medical record (EMR), if it is available, to obtain a general overview of the individual's health status. This EMR review is followed by initiating a conversation with the individual to listen to his or her life story and to explore all aspects of an individual's background (e.g., social norms, cultural impact, religious practices) that influence his or her health. Throughout the life story conversation, the health navigation professional gathers additional information related to the individual's current perception of his or her health and current needs for improved quality of life. After the life story conversation, the health navigation professional returns to the EMR to investigate and verify the information provide during the conversation. If the EMR is not available, the health navigation professional verifies the information with the caregiver or family member.

© leaf/iStock Photo

Case Study

Now, let us apply the information discussed in this chapter to a case study about Mrs. Jones.

Case Study One: Mrs. Jones, age 78, was brought to the hospital by ambulance after falling in her kitchen around 8:30 p.m. on Saturday after attending a monthly birthday celebration in her retirement community. The ambulance report stated that she became dizzy and was trying to sit down when she fell. She was able to reach her cell phone on the table to call 911. The EMR states that she was examined by Dr. Williams in the Emergency Department. No fractures were found after several radiology tests. She was admitted for observation and further tests. The laboratory tests revealed low potassium levels and slight anemia. The CT scans revealed a possible recent transient ischemic attack (TIA). The symptoms of a TIA are similar to a stroke and occur when blood flow to the brain is diminished for a brief period of time. Often, a TIA is a warning sign that a stroke may happen in the future if no intervention occurs (www.strokeassociation.org /STROKEORG/AboutStroke/TypesofStroke/TIA /TIA-Transient-Ischemic-Attack_UCM_310942 _Article.jsp#.VzjNv4-cGUk).

Mrs. Jones lives alone in her apartment in the retirement community, has never smoked, uses alcohol socially, has a normal body mass index (BMI), attends water aerobics four times per week and walks 1 mile each day, no longer drives, and remains involved in numerous social activities in her retirement community. Her husband of 54 years died 2 years ago, and she has two daughters and three grandchildren. Both daughters live out-of-state, but one is visiting this week. Mrs. Jones has no known allergies (NKA). Because Mrs. Jones has a medical history of hypertension, atrial fibrillation, and osteoporosis, each day she takes two prescription medications, Lasix and Coreg, as well as an over-the-counter (OTC) calcium supplement and a multivitamin. Her physician changed her prescription medications from Lasix to Dyrenium, kept Coreg the same, and added low-dose aspirin. The EMR states that she is scheduled for discharge in 2 days, and the health navigation professional has been called to conduct a home assessment.

After reading this EMR, the health navigation professional has some work to do. First, it is important to understand the medical terminology and medications. See **Box 8.4** for medications.

Student Activity

After reviewing medical history, Box 8.4, the student should answer the following questions:

1. Why did the physician change her medication from Lasix to Dyrenium?

2. Why did the physician add low-dose aspirin to Mrs. Jones' medication list?

Upon completion of her EMR review, the health navigation professional determines if time is ideal for a visit. For example, it is important to have a few questions answered: Does Mrs. Jones have any further tests scheduled for today? Are there any visitors in her room right now? How long will it be before lunch or dinner is delivered? Does she have a shared hospital room or a private room? Is she watching her favorite television series at this time?

After determining that it is a good time for a conversation with Mrs. Jones, it is also important for the conversation to be a good time for the health navigation professional. There is no point in arranging the ideal time for the patient if the health navigation professional has a personal conflict. Both individuals need to be engaged for trust to be established. It does not happen without planning and consideration.

Next, the health navigation professional needs to do a quick review of the setting in Mrs. Jones' room. Because Mrs. Jones has a private room, the health navigation professional can speak more freely during the conversation. If Mrs. Jones was sharing a room, the health navigation professional verifies whether Mrs. Jones is able to walk to a small conference room a few doors down the hall from her room. If that does not work, the health navigation professional could ask the nurse if Mrs. Jones could take a short ride in

BOX 8.4 Prescription Medication of Mrs. Jones

Lasix (generic name: furosemide): Reduces the amount of blood fluid; causes the kidneys to increase the salt and water that are passed in the urine, thereby lowering the amount of blood fluid and, as a result, lowering the blood pressure and causing a loss of potassium from the body.[21]

Coreg (generic name: carvedilol) is a beta-blocker and is used to treat heart failure and hypertension (high blood pressure).[22]

Dyrenium (generic name: triamtererene): Reduces the amount of blood fluid; causes the kidneys to increase the salt and water that are passed in the urine, thereby lowering the amount of blood fluid and, as a result, lowering the blood pressure. Do not cause a loss of potassium from the body.[23]

Low-dose aspirin is sometimes used to treat or prevent heart attacks, strokes, and chest pain (angina) and should be used for cardiovascular conditions only under the supervision of a physician.[24]

a wheelchair to a quite alcove with a few couches at the end of the hallway. Now, let us think about the setting in detail and ask a few questions prior to starting the conversation:

- Is Mrs. Jones experiencing any hearing loss? Review the EMR again for this information. If the hearing loss is in her left ear, sit on the right side of her bed. If Mrs. Jones normally wears a hearing aid, ensure that her hearing aid is in place prior to the conversation. Ask the nurse for assistance, if needed. It is not the role of the health navigational professional to place hearing aids.
- Does Mrs. Jones have dentures and are the dentures in her mouth? Without her dentures, she will likely be less willing to have a long conversation due to embarrassment and inability to speak clearly.
- Does Mrs. Jones speak English as her first language? If not, it will be necessary to coordinate the services of a translator prior to your visit.
- Does Mrs. Jones have difficulty speaking, perhaps from a previous stroke? If so, it may be necessary to use a medical picture board for ease of communication.
- Does Mrs. Jones wish to have her daughter present for the conversation? If so, then the time of her daughter's next visit would need to be coordinated.

Once the health navigation professional has the timing of the visit arranged, the arrangement of the room is explored. The health navigation professional needs to close the door and to sit on the correct side of the bed for optimal hearing. The bed should be in the lowest position, and the health navigation professional should face Mrs. Jones rather than facing the side of the bed. Keep in mind that over the past few days, many physicians, nurses, lab technicians, transporters, and environmental service workers have come into her room. She is likely to be tired, a bit confused, and eager to leave the hospital—especially if her physician has told her that she might be discharged in 1 or 2 days. The health navigation professional has a few moments to establish trust and communication with Mrs. Jones.

Now it is time to begin the conversation by introducing yourself. "Good afternoon, Mrs. Jones. My name is Sam Richards. I am a health navigation professional. Is this a good time?" (Pause and wait for a response.) If she responds positively, then the following question is: "Do you mind if I sit down, so we can chat for a few minutes?" Make sure that Mrs. Jones has time answer your question before proceeding. If you did your homework, this time should be suitable for both of you.

The next portion of the conversation begins with a simple statement: "Mrs. Jones, I read your medical history, so I am not going to be asking you any of those questions again. I would like for you to tell me about what concerns you about going home in a day or two." At this point, Mrs. Jones may need to complain about her physician or the night shift nursing staff. Without talking about the immediate things on her mind, she will be unable to focus on her thoughts about going home.

As the conversation continues, Sam needs to ask open-ended questions so the conversation is directed and purposeful. The questions asked are directed to issues that health navigation professional can address or resolve. For example, Sam should ask Mrs. Jones if she has grab bars in her shower, so she can get in and out of her shower with fear of falling. Also, the health navigation professional may call the retirement community in which Mrs. Jones lives to determine the availability, cost, and time frame for getting grab bars installed in her shower. This discussion may lead Mrs. Jones into sharing with Sam her overall fear of not being able to live independently in the future. Of course, the health navigation professional is not able to solve all of the upcoming problems, but he can take extensive notes and share the information with the appropriate hospital staff, such as the physicians, social worker, and discharge nurse. As a member of the healthcare team, the health navigation professional serves

TABLE 8.5 Summary of the Conversation between Mrs. Jones and Sam

Today's Date: August 21, 2016		
Action Item	Issue of Concern	Status and Date
1	Investigate getting grab bars installed in her shower.	8/21/16–Called retirement community to receive information.
2	Report to physician through the EMR that Mrs. Jones would like to get a prescription for a few weeks of outpatient physical therapy, so she can gain strength in her legs and improve her balance.	8/21/16–Entered EMR note to physician before leaving Mrs. Jones' room.
3	Request a registered dietician (RD) consult through the EMR for Mrs. Jones to review what foods should be eaten to improve her anemic status as shown on her blood work.	8/21/16–Entered EMR note to RD for consultation before leaving Mrs. Jones' room.
4	Schedule a time to meet with Mrs. Jones and her daughter, because her daughter was not available for this first meeting. Mrs. Jones gave Sam her daughter's cell phone number.	8/21/16–Left voicemail on Mrs. Jones' daughter's phone prior to ending the first meeting.
5	Report to physician through the EMR that Mrs. Jones requests a prescription to receive home health visits with the health navigation professional for a few weeks.	8/21/16–Entered EMR note to physician before leaving Mrs. Jones' room.
6	Schedule next time for next visit tomorrow with Mrs. Jones.	8/21/16–Next appointment is scheduled for 10:00 a.m. tomorrow.

as the bridge between the clinical staff and the patient. Health navigation professionals have the time to engage in extensive conversations with patients as well as continuing the conversation after the patient is discharged, so the rate of readmission can be reduced.

Before the conversation concludes, it is important for the health navigation professional to summarize the action items from the conversation. If Mrs. Jones is going to trust Sam in the future, she needs to know that the conversation was useful and her issues will be addressed. Sam types the summary into his tablet. After reviewing the summary of action items with Mrs. Jones, Sam sends the document to the printer at the nurses' station and gives Mrs. Jones a copy of the summary. See **Table 8.5** for a summary of the first conversation between Mrs. Jones and Sam.

References

1. Centers for Disease Control and Prevention. Health disparities. Retrieved January 31, 2016, from http://www.cdc.gov/healthyyouth/disparities/index.htm; last updated September 1, 2016.
2. Carter-Pokras, O., & Baquet, C. (2002). What is a "health disparity"? *Public Health Report, 117*(5), 426–434.
3. U.S. Department of Health and Human Services. (2010). The Secretary's Advisory Committee on National Health Promotion and Disease Prevention Objectives for 2020. Retrieved January 31, 2016, from http://www.healthypeople.gov/sites/default/files/PhaseI_0.pdf.
4. Healthy People 2020. Disparities. Retrieved January 31, 2016, from http://www.healthypeople.gov/2020/about/foundation-health-measures/Disparities.
5. Office of Minority Health. (2011). HHS action plan to reduce racial and ethnic health disparities: A nation free of disparities in health and health care. Retrieved January 31, 2016, from http://www.cdc.gov/minorityhealth/OMHHE.html.
6. Singh, G. K., & Siahpush, M. (2014). Widening rural–urban disparities in life expectancy, U.S., 1969–2009. *American Journal of Preventive Medicine, 46*(2), 19–29.

7. Rural Health Reform Policy Research Center. *The 2014 update of the rural–urban chartbook*. Princeton, NJ: Robert Wood Johnson Foundation.

8. Joens-Matre, R. R., Welk, G. J., Calabro, M. A., Russell, D. W., Nicklay, E., & Hensley, L. D. (2008). Rural–urban differences in physical activity, physical fitness, and over-weight prevalence of children. *Journal of Rural Health, 24*(1), 49–54.

9. Morbidity and Mortality Weekly Report. (2005). Social support and health-related quality of life among older adults–Missouri. *MMWR, 54*(17), 433–437.

10. Clark, C. M. Relations between social support and physical health. Retrieved June 30, 2015, from http://www.personalityresearch.org/papers/clark.html; last updated November 2005.

11. Ikeda, A., Iso, H., Kawachi, I., Yamagishi, K., & Inoue, M. (2008). Social support and stroke and coronary heart disease the JPHC study cohorts II. *Stroke, 39*(3), 768–775.

12. Petrie, K. J. *Social support and recovery from disease and medical procedures. International Encyclopaedia of the Social and Behavioural Sciences*, Oxford: Elsevier Science, 2002.

13. Scheurer, D., Choudhry, N., Swanton, K. A., Matlin, O., & Shrank, W. (2012). Association between different types of social support and medication adherence. *The American Journal of Managed Care, 18*(12), e461–e467.

14. National Central Regional Educational Laboratory. Cultural norms. Retrieved June 30, 2015, from http://www.ncrel.org/sdrs/areas/issues/envrnmnt/drugfree/sa1lk2.htm.

15. The Language Banc. Understanding cultural norms. Retrieved June 30, 2015, from http://www.thelanguagebanc.com/understanding-cultural-norms; last updated December 3, 2012.

16. PsychologyCampus. *Norms*. Retrieved June 30, 2015, from http://www.psychologycampus.com/social-psychology/norms.html; last updated 2008.

17. Adams, C. E., & Leverland, M. B. (1986). The effects of religious beliefs on the health care practices of the Amish. *The Nurse Practitioner, 11*(3), 58–63.

18. Ontario Consultants on Religious Tolerance. Comparing different religions and faith groups. Retrieved June 30, 2014, from http://www.religioustolerance.org/relcomp.htm; last updated March 2014.

19. Pew Research Center. The religious landscape study. Retrieved June 30, 2015, from http://www.pewforum.org/about-the-religious-landscape-study.

20. Advocate Health Care. Religious beliefs and healthcare decisions. Retrieved June 30, 2014, from http://www.advocatehealth.com/beliefs.

21. Drugs.com. *Lasix*. Retrieved Jun 30, 2015, from http://www.drugs.com/search.php?searchterm=lasix.

22. Drugs.com. *Coreg*. Retrieved June 30, 2015, from http://www.drugs.com/search.php?searchterm=Coreg&a=1.

23. Drugs.com. *Dyrenium*. Retrieved June 30, 2015, from http://www.drugs.com/search.php?searchterm=Dyrenium.

24. Drugs.com. *Aspirin*. Retrieved June 30, 2105, from http://www.drugs.com/search.php?searchterm=aspirin&a=1.

CHAPTER 9

Infectious Disease

LEARNING OBJECTIVES

By the end of this chapter, students will be able to:

- Differentiate between infectious and noncommunicable disease
- Understand the role of proper hygiene in preventing infectious disease
- Describe immunization as a successful primary prevention strategy
- Explain vaccine preventable disease

CHAPTER OVERVIEW

There are two major categories of disease: infectious and noncommunicable. Infectious disease is defined as being a disorder or illness caused by an organism, such as bacteria, viruses, fungi, or parasites. Infectious diseases are transmitted in one of four ways: (1) person to person (e.g., lack of hand-washing, lack of vaccinations); (2) bites from insects (e.g., mosquitos, flies) or animals; (3) acquired by ingesting contaminated food or drinking contaminated water; and (4) being exposed to organisms in the environment (e.g., swimming in a polluted lake).

Most infectious diseases begin with symptoms of a fever and feeling fatigued. Some infectious disease responds to rest and drinking plenty of fluids, while other infectious diseases may be life-threatening and require

hospitalization.[1] Historically, infectious diseases have been the major cause of disease, disability, and death. As public health measures (e.g., sanitation, hygiene, water treatment) improved, the rate of infectious disease decreased. In addition, as the development of antibiotics and vaccines became available, the rate of infectious disease decreased further across the globe. Today, infectious diseases remain a threat, but not to the extent as in the past.

Chronic (noncommunicable) diseases include cardiovascular diseases (e.g., heart attacks, stroke), cancers, diabetes, chronic respiratory diseases (e.g., chronic obstructive pulmonary disease, asthma), diabetes, and arthritis.[2] Most noncommunicable diseases are associated with poor lifestyle and behavioral choices, such as obesity, poor nutrition, tobacco use, and lack of sufficient exercise. Others may be caused by genetic risk factors.

This chapter begins with an overview of how to prevent the most common infectious diseases, including herd immunity and active and passive immunity. Next, types of infectious diseases are reviewed. The infectious diseases that are prevented and controlled with immunizations are followed by those that have no vaccine prevention (e.g., a vaccine for the common cold virus).

© Samo Trebizan/iStockphoto

© DKsamco/iStock/ThinkStock

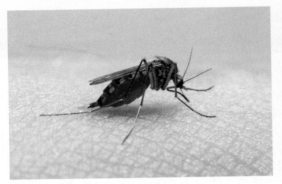
© k4d/iStockphoto

© Tim Hale/Photodisc/Getty Images

PREVENTION AND CONTROL OF INFECTIOUS DISEASE

As health navigation professionals, you may be asking why you need to learn how to prevent and control infectious diseases. The reason is simple. You will work closely with all types of individuals in numerous locations, including private homes, public clinics, hospitals, assisted-living facilities, and rehabilitation centers. As a result, you will be exposed to numerous infectious diseases. Understanding and reducing the spread of infectious diseases keeps you and others healthy.

The two most effective ways to prevent the spread of infectious disease are avoiding contact with the disease and vaccines (also known as *immunizations*). There are numerous ways to avoid contact and, thus, reduce the spread of infectious disease, including (a) avoiding ingestion of unsafe or untreated water; (b) using frequent and proper hand-washing techniques; (c) not sharing personal items (e.g., toothbrushes, towels, razors, nail clippers); (d) covering the mouth when coughing or sneezing; (e) using safe cooking practices (e.g., high temperature, proper refrigeration, separate cutting boards, clean countertops, washing fruits and vegetables); (f) traveling safely (verifying water safety, eating cooked foods, updating vaccines as advised); (g) safe sex practices (using condoms to limit transfer of bacteria and viruses from one individual to another); (h) being cautious regarding animals, including vaccinating household pets, avoiding handling wild animals (birds, snakes, mammals), eliminating places where wild animals can hide or build nests (rodents and other mammals), and covering trash cans with tight lids; and (i) watching the news regarding current events, such as recall of food items, outbreak of diseases (e.g., West Nile Virus, caused by mosquitoes), and use of insect repellant for insect-borne diseases.[3] Keep in mind that simply washing your hands frequently is among the greatest techniques to guard against the spread of diseases. See **Box 9.1.**

BOX 9.1 Proper Hand-Washing

© Mitarart/iStockphoto

© Monkey Business Images/Monkey Business/thinkstock

Many infectious diseases are spread due to lack of proper hand hygiene, including hand-washing and nail hygiene. For hand-washing to be effective, the individual must use soap and clean, running water. However, if soap and clean water are not accessible, it is effective to use an alcohol-based product (such as a gel or spray) containing at least 60% alcohol.[4] Appropriate hand hygiene includes diligently cleaning and trimming fingernails, which may harbor dirt and germs and can contribute to the spread of some infections, such as pinworms. Fingernails should be short, because longer fingernails harbor more dirt and bacteria. Individuals should avoid the following three behaviors: (a) biting or chewing their nails; (b) cutting their cuticles, because cuticles act as barriers to prevent infection; and (c) never ripping or biting a hangnail, but rather clipping hangnails with a clean, sanitized nail trimmer.[5]

Correct Way to Wash Your Hands

1. Wet your hands with clean, running (warm or cold) water and apply soap.
2. Lather your hands by rubbing them together with the soap. Be sure to rub the backs of your hands, between your fingers, and under your nails.
3. Scrub your hands for at least 20 seconds. Need a timer? Hum the "Happy Birthday" song from beginning to end twice.
4. Rinse your hands well under clean, running water.
5. Dry your hands using a clean towel or air dry them.

When to Wash Your Hands

Before preparing food, eating food, or treating a wound.

After using the toilet, changing a diaper, touching garbage, blowing your nose, coughing or sneezing, cleaning up pet food or pet waste.

Modified from the Centers for Disease Control and Prevention (2010). Keeping Hands Clean. Available at: http://www.cdc.gov/healthywater/hygiene/hand/handwashing.html. Last updated February 1, 2011.[6]

Before discussing how many infectious diseases are prevented and controlled by immunizations, it is important to understand how immunizations work and why constant vigilance is required to keep infectious disease rates low. Let us begin with the concept of herd immunity (also known as *community immunity*). Because it is not possible or safe for all individuals (e.g., infants, pregnant women, immunocompromised) to receive some vaccines, it is up to the rest of the community to receive the vaccine and thus protect the entire "herd" or the community. Herd immunity is defined as when there is enough of the population in a community who receives the immunization that the entire community is protected from the disease. When there are individuals who can receive a vaccine, but choose not to, they put themselves and others at risk of a disease outbreak occurring throughout the community. See **Figure 9.1**. In the top box, no one is immunized, and only a few individuals remain healthy

FIGURE 9.1 **Herd Immunity**[7]

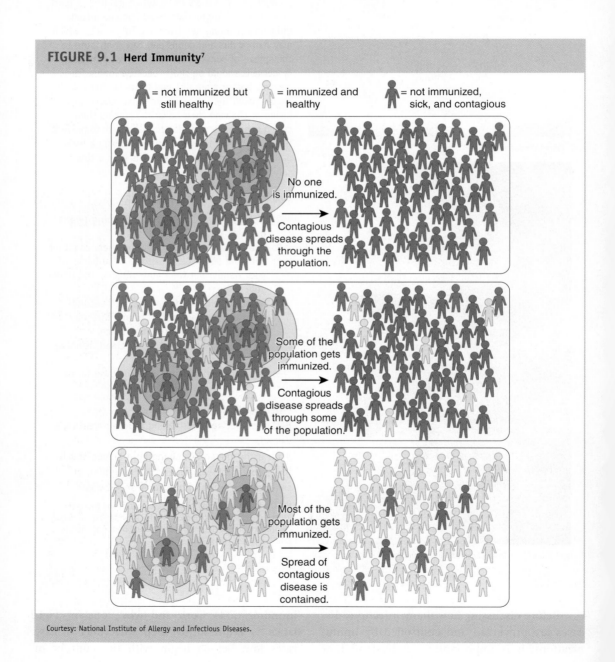

Courtesy: National Institute of Allergy and Infectious Diseases.

during a disease outbreak. The middle box shows only a few individuals receiving the vaccine, but not enough to protect the community. In the bottom box, most individuals are immunized, so the community is protected from the outbreak. The concept of herd immunity applies to the control of infectious diseases, such as influenza, measles, mumps, rotavirus, and pneumococcal disease. See **Box 9.2**.

Now that you have an understanding of herd immunity, let us define the two types of vaccines: passive and active.

Passive (also known as inactivated) immunity to infectious diseases vaccines occurs in two ways. First, passive immunization occurs when antibodies are transferred from mother to fetus during pregnancy. This protection lasts after the

baby is born if the mother is breastfeeding. Second, passive immunization is administered by injection of an inactivated (killed) virus in which the antibodies or specific elements of a virus are transferred to an individual so that the body does not need to produce these elements. This method of immunization begins to work very quickly, but it is short lasting because the antibodies are naturally broken down by the body and disappear over time. For example, the seasonal flu vaccine needs to be received every year, because the specific elements of the flu virus change every year. The body breaks down the elements, so the protection lasts for only one flu season.

Active immunity to infectious diseases occurs in two ways. First, immunity occurs naturally when individuals come into contact with

BOX 9.2 Measles Outbreak in California, 2014

© Yarinca/istockphoto

According to the California Department of Public Health, in 2014, there was a measles outbreak among Disneyland visitors in California, with nine people contacting confirmed cases of measles—all of whom visited Disneyland between December 15 and December 20. Measles spreads when an infected person coughs. Individuals near that individual are at risk of becoming infected if they haven't previously had the illness or at least two doses of the measles vaccine. The CDC recommends that children receive their first measles shot between age 12–15 months and a second shot between ages 4 and 6 years. Prior to the development of the vaccine, measles was nearly a universal disease of childhood. After the introduction of the vaccine, the rate of measles dropped dramatically. However, since 2012, the rates have started to increase: 55 cases in 2012; 187 cases in 2013; and 554 cases in 2014. This increase is due to (a) parents choosing to skip or space out their children's vaccines because of misguided concerns about vaccine safety; and (b) individuals infected in other countries who travel to the United States and are diagnosed after arrival. Because most parents today have not experienced measles, they do not understand the dangers that the disease poses to their children. Symptoms of measles include a fever, rash, cough, runny nose, and red eyes. Individuals are infectious for nine days, including time before and after the rash appears. There is no treatment, other than to keep the individual comfortable and hydrated. The dangers of measles include the following: 1 in 20 children with measles develops pneumonia, the most common cause of death from measles; about 1 in 1000 children with measles develops encephalopathy (swelling of the brain), which can lead to brain damage and deafness; and for every 1000 children with measles, 1 or 2 are likely to die.

Data from: Szabo, Lisa (2015). Measles Outbreak Linked to Disneyland. USA Today. Available at: http://www.usatoday.com/story/news/nation/2015/01/07/measles-outbreak-disneyland/21402755/. Last updated January 8, 2015.[8]

the virus, and their bodies create antibodies and other defenses against the virus. The next time the individual is exposed to the virus, his or her immune response against this virus is activated and fights off the infection. For example, prior to the development of the chicken pox vaccine, if individuals were exposed to the chicken pox virus, they developed the disease. After recovering from c hicken pox, if the individuals were exposed to the chicken pox virus again, they would not become ill again, because their bodies developed antibodies for immunity against the infection. Second, active immunity is obtained by an injection of the live virus vaccines that are prepared from attenuated strains of the virus. Attenuation is defined as altering an infectious virus so that the virus becomes harmless.[9] The attenuated virus is given usually by injection (i.e., polio vaccine is given orally) and multiplies in the body to provide continuous antibody stimulation over a long period of time. For example, individuals receiving the rotavirus vaccine at 2, 4, and 6 months have immunity protection for life. Other vaccines last for shorter periods of time (such as tetanus, which lasts approximately 5 years).

INFECTIOUS DISEASES: IMMUNIZATIONS AND DESCRIPTIONS

Before getting into this discussion, it is useful to discuss why knowledge about immunizations is important for health navigation professionals. Because health navigation professionals work with all ages of the population, it is essential that they understand how to keep themselves safe, healthy, and free of contagious diseases, and be able to provide guidelines for the communities in which they are employed. For example, if the health navigation professional is working with the elderly population, he or she would provide information about the need to update their DTaP (diphtheria, tetanus, and pertussis) immunizations. If the elderly person has grandchildren or is around children, the pertussis immunization stops the spread of whooping cough to children.[10] Let us begin with a list of infectious diseases that

TABLE 9.1 Infectious Diseases Prevented and Controlled with Immunizations

Chickenpox (Varicella)
Diphtheria, Tetanus, Pertussis (Whooping Cough) (DTaP)
Flu (Influenza)
Haemophilus Influenzae Type B (Hib)
Hepatitis A
Hepatitis B
Human Papillomavirus (HPV)
Japanese Encephalitis* (Ixiaro)
Leptospirosis*
Measles, Mumps, Rubella (MMR)
Meningococcal Disease (Neisseris Meningitides)
Pneumococcal Disease (Streptococcus Pneumonia)
    (PCV13–Pneumococcal Conjugate Vaccine OR
    PPSV23–Pneumococcal Polysaccharide Vaccine)
Polio* (IPV–Inactivated Poliovirus)
Rabies
Rotavirus (RV)
Shingles
Tuberculosis (TB) (BCG–Bacille Calmette-Guerin)**
Typhoid Fever*
Yellow Fever*

* Not common in the United States.

** Given to children under age 5 years in countries with highest rates of tuberculosis; not given to children in the United States.

are prevented or controlled by vaccines. See **Table 9.1**. Some of these diseases are commonly known in the United States, and others are more widely known internationally. In either case, it is important to note the abbreviations for the various diseases listed.

As noted in Table 9.1, immunizations are available for infectious diseases that are not common in the United States. Because health navigation professionals may work with immigrant and refugee populations, the CDC Yellow Book is a valuable resource. It is available online (www.cdc.gov/travel/diseases). It is also important to realize that there are many infectious diseases across the globe for which there are no available immunizations, including African Tick-Bite Fever, African Sleeping Sickness, Bird Flu, Dengue, Ebola, Encephalitis, HIV, Hepatitis, Malaria,

Scabies, Tuberculosis, West Nile Virus, and Zika. See **Figure 9.2**.

Next, let us discuss the vaccines recommended in the United States by the Centers for Disease Control and Prevention (CDC), especially for children between the ages of birth and 6 years of age. **Figure 9.3** illustrates the numerous recommended CDC immunization guidelines for children attending public school in the United States. Similar recommendations are enforced in most developed countries. *Note:* The abbreviations are defined in Table 9.1. In addition, the CDC has another recommended guideline for children 7 years to 18 years of age and for adults at the following two links:

www.cdc.gov/vaccines/who/teens/downloads/ parent-version-schedule-7-18yrs.pdf and www.cdc.gov/vaccines/schedules/downloads /adult/adult-schedule-easy-read.pdf.

With an understanding of herd immunity, types of vaccines, and the diseases prevented or controlled with vaccines across the globe, the last section of this chapter discusses numerous infectious diseases that are not prevented or completely controlled by immunizations.

FIGURE 9.2 CDC: The Yellow Book

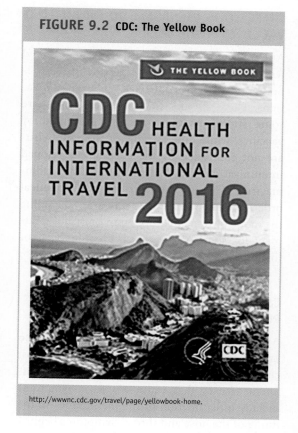

http://wwwnc.cdc.gov/travel/page/yellowbook-home.

FIGURE 9.3 Vaccine Recommendations for Children[11]

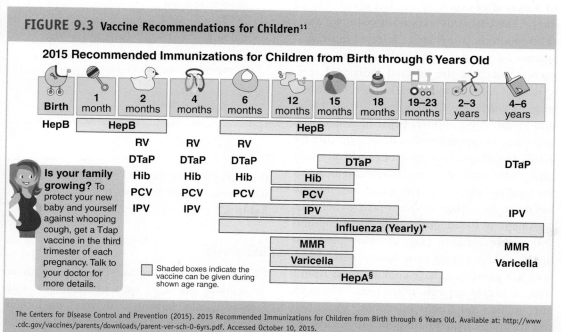

The Centers for Disease Control and Prevention (2015). 2015 Recommended Immunizations for Children from Birth through 6 Years Old. Available at: http://www .cdc.gov/vaccines/parents/downloads/parent-ver-sch-0-6yrs.pdf. Accessed October 10, 2015.

INFECTIOUS DISEASES: NO OR LIMITED VACCINES AVAILABLE

Although many infectious diseases are controlled with vaccines, a long list of infectious diseases is not prevented or controlled with immunizations. There are also infectious diseases where some strains of the virus are prevented by vaccines, while other strains of the same virus are not controlled by the currently developed immunizations (e.g., hepatitis, human papillomavirus). This section describes, in alphabetical order, common infectious diseases, including the mode of transmission, symptoms, and treatment for some of the most common types of infectious disease.[12]

© LittleBee80/istockphoto

Common Cold—Also Known as Upper Respiratory Infection (URI)

An upper respiratory infection (URI), also known as the *common cold*, is among the most common illness. There are more than 200 different viruses that cause a URI.[13] Symptoms include inflammation of the membranes in the lining of the nose and throat. Symptoms begin 1 to 3 days after exposure and last about 7 to 10 days.[13] The URI virus is transmitted in two ways: (a) through the air when an infected individual sneezes or coughs; and (b) by direct contact, such as touching the infected individual (e.g., shaking hands) or touching an object that was recently touched by the infected individual (e.g., doorknobs, toys, phones, pens, utensils). It is important to remember that there is no cure for a URI (cold) and that antibiotics will not help treat such a viral infection. Though medications are used to help relieve the symptoms, they do not make the URI go away any faster. Therefore, treatment is based on helping the symptoms and supportive care (e.g., drinking plenty of fluids, resting, staying away from others). However, it is possible to have complications from a cold, including ear infections, sinus infections, pneumonia, and throat infections. Some URI complications require antibiotics to resolve the infection. Most importantly, the best way to

prevent spreading the URI virus is to frequently wash your hands with soap and water.[13] See **Table 9.2**.

TABLE 9.2 Cold and Flu Symptoms

Cold Symptoms	Flu Symptoms
Low or no fever	High fever
Sometimes a headache	Commonly a headache
Stuffy and runny nose	Sometimes a runny nose
Sneezing	Sometimes sneezing
Mild, hacking cough	Cough, may progress
Slight aches and pains	Often severe aches and pains
Normal energy to mild fatigue	Exhaustion and fatigue
Sore throat	Sometimes a sore throat

Data from: Johns Hopkins Medicine (2015). Health Library: Upper Respiratory Infection (URI or Common Cold). Available at: http://www.hopkinsmedicine.org/healthlibrary/conditions/pediatrics/upper_respiratory_infection_uri_or_common_cold_90,P02966/.[13]

Giardiasis

Giardiasis is caused by bacteria. It is contracted by drinking untreated water contaminated with feces of infected animals. The symptoms include abdominal discomfort and prolonged, intermittent diarrhea. In the United States, individuals hiking

© Mike Powell/DigitalVision/thinkstock

in the back country are at risk of contracting giardiasis if they drink water from the streams, rivers, and lakes.

Hepatitis

The word "hepatitis" can be divided into two parts: "hepa" = liver and "itis" = inflammation. Therefore, hepatitis is literally defined as liver inflammation. There are five types of known hepatitis, including Hepatitis A, B, C, D, and E. **Table 9.3** compares Hepatitis A, B, and C. Note

TABLE 9.3 Description of Hepatitis A, B, and C

	Hepatitis A	Hepatitis B	Hepatitis C
Symptoms of Acute Infection	Symptoms of all types of viral hepatitis are similar and include • Fever • Fatigue • Loss of appetite • Nausea • Vomiting • Abdominal pain • Gray-colored bowel movements • Joint pain • Jaundice		
Routes of Transmission	Ingestion of fecal matter, even in microscopic amounts, from • Close person-to-person contact with an infected person • Sexual contact with an infected person • Ingestion of contaminated food or drinks	Contact with infectious blood, semen, and other body fluids primarily through • Birth to an infected mother • Sexual contact with an infected person • Sharing of contaminated needles • Needle sticks or other sharp instrument injuries	Contact with blood of an infected person primarily through • Sharing of contaminated needles Less commonly through • Sexual contact with an infected person • Birth to an infected mother • Needle sticks or other sharp instrument injuries
Persons at Risk	• Travelers to regions with high rates of Hepatitis A • Sex contacts of infected persons • Household members or caregivers of infected persons • Users of certain illegal drugs (injection and noninjection) • Persons with clotting-factor disorders	• Infants born to infected mothers • Sex partners of infected persons • Persons with multiple sex partners • Injection drug users • Household contacts of infected persons • Healthcare workers exposed to blood on the job • Hemodialysis patients	• Current or former injection drug users • Long-term hemodialysis patients • Persons with known exposures e.g., healthcare workers after needle sticks, recipients of blood or organs testing positive • HIV-infected persons • Infants born to infected mothers
Incubation Period	15 to 50 days (average: 28 days)	45 to 160 days (average: 120 days)	14 to 180 days (average: 45 days)
Treatment	• No medication available • Best addressed through supportive treatment	• Acute: No medication available; supportive treatment • Chronic: Regular monitoring for signs of liver disease progression; some patients are treated with antiviral drugs	• Acute: Antivirals and supportive treatment • Chronic: Regular monitoring for signs of liver disease progression; some patients are treated with antiviral drugs
Vaccination Recommendations	Hepatitis A vaccine is recommended.	Hepatitis B vaccine is recommended.	There is no Hepatitis C vaccine.

Modified from: The Centers for Disease Control and Prevention (2015). The ABCs of Hepatitis. Available from: http://www.cdc.gov /hepatitis/Resources/Professionals/PDFs/ABCTable.pdf. Accessed on September 14, 2014.[15]

that there are immunizations available for Hepatitis A and B, but not for Hepatitis C. Hepatitis D and E are less common.[14]

Lyme Disease

Lyme disease is caused by bacteria and is transmitted to humans through infected ticks. The major symptom is a rash. If the individual is not treated, the infection may spread to joints, the heart, and the nervous system. Most cases of Lyme disease are successfully treated with antibiotics for a few weeks. Lyme disease is prevented by using insect repellant, removing ticks promptly, applying pesticides, and reducing tick habitat.

© Dragisa/istockphoto

Malaria

Malaria is a mosquito-borne disease caused by a parasite. Individuals with malaria have symptoms of flu-like illness such as fever and chills. Left untreated, infected individuals can develop severe complications and die. In 2013, an estimated 198 million cases of malaria occurred worldwide with 500,000 deaths, mostly in children in poor tropical and subtropical areas of the world, such as Africa and Asia. In these areas, malaria is a leading cause of illness and death. The most vulnerable groups are young children and pregnant women.[16]

Treatment of malaria depends on many factors, including disease severity, the species of parasite causing the infection, and the part of the world in which the infection was acquired. The latter two characteristics help determine the probability that the organism is resistant to

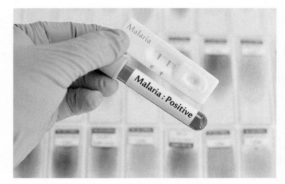

© jarun011/istockphoto

certain antimalarial drugs. Healthcare providers should always obtain a travel history, especially for individuals with a fever who have recently traveled in a malaria-endemic area. Such individuals should always be immediately evaluated using the appropriate diagnostic tests for malaria. Additional factors such as age, weight, and pregnancy status may limit the available options for malaria treatment.[17]

Methicillin-Resistant Staphylococcus Aureus (MRSA)

Methicillin-resistant Staphylococcus aureus (MRSA) is an infectious disease caused by a type of staph bacteria. It cannot be treated with the antibiotics that are usually prescribed for staph infections, because MRSA is resistant and does not respond to the usual prescriptions. MRSA is the result of decades of antibiotics being overprescribed for colds, flu, and other viral infections that don't respond to these drugs. Even when antibiotics are used appropriately, the prescriptions contribute to the rise of drug-resistant bacteria because the antibiotics may not destroy every bacteria or the antibiotics are not taken properly. For example, some individuals may not take the full prescription; others may share the prescription with a family member or friend; or others may start to feel better and forget to take the remainder of the prescribed pills. As a result, the bacteria may mutate. Misuse or overuse of antibiotics results in less-effective results the next time the antibiotics are used because the germs become resistant.[18] These examples reinforce the need to always remind patients and family members to take all of their prescribed antibiotics even if they begin to feel better.

Pertussis

Pertussis, also known as *whooping cough*, is a highly contagious respiratory disease. The symptoms include uncontrollable, violent coughing, which often makes it hard to breathe. Pertussis affects individuals of all ages, but it is very serious or deadly for babies less than a year old. The best way to prevent pertussis is with immunization.

Salmonella

Over the past 20 years, Salmonellosis has become the single most common cause of food poisoning in the United States. The salmonella virus infects chicken flocks without causing visible disease. Because chickens from one farm may be distributed across many states, the infection can spread rapidly through the population. After the infected chicken is consumed by a human, the salmonella passes from the stomach to the intestines, then spreads to the liver and spleen, and is expelled through diarrhea. In geographical regions with poor sanitation, the salmonella bacteria can survive in rivers; therefore, the bacteria can infect the individuals or animals that drink the contaminated water.

Sexually Transmitted Infections

Chlamydia: In the United States, chlamydia is the most frequently reported infectious disease and prevalence is highest in persons who are younger than 24 years.[19] Asymptomatic infection is common among both men and women. To detect chlamydial infections, healthcare providers frequently rely on screening tests. Annual screening of all sexually active women younger than 25 years of age is recommended, as is screening of older women at increased risk for infection (e.g., those who have a new sex partner, more than one sex partner, a sex partner with concurrent partners, or a sex partner who has a sexually transmitted infection).[19]

Gonorrhea: In the United States, gonorrhea is the second most commonly reported communicable disease.[20] For men, gonorrhea causes painful urination severe enough to seek medical treatment. Among women, gonorrhea infections are commonly asymptomatic (no symptoms) or the symptoms are not noticeable until there are complications, such as pelvic inflammatory disease (PID).[21]

HIV and AIDS: Human Immunodeficiency Virus (HIV) is spread by contact with infected bodily fluids. The most common modes of transmission include unprotected sexual contact with an infected individual, contaminated needles of drug users, contact with infected blood (e.g., healthcare provider not using personal protective techniques, such as gloves, gown, and face mask), and mother-to-child transmission during pregnancy, childbirth, or breast-feeding. Over time and without medication, HIV weakens the immune system. Acquired immunodeficiency syndrome (AIDS) is a chronic, potentially life-threatening condition caused by HIV. Although there is no cure for HIV and AIDS, medications are available that slow the progression of the disease. These medications are expensive, but have reduced AIDS deaths in many developed nations. However, HIV mortality rates continue to increase in Africa, Haiti, and parts of Asia.[22]

Human papillomavirus (HPV): HPV is a group of more than 200 related viruses.[23] About 40 HPV types are spread through direct sexual contact; skin and mucous membranes of infected individuals spread HPV to their partners. There are two main categories: low risk and high risk. Low risk does not cause cancer but does cause warts on or around the genitals, anus, mouth, and throat. Low risk is not controlled by the HPV vaccine. High risk can cause several types of cancer, including cervical cancer, anal cancer, and oropharyngeal (throat, soft palate, base of tongue, tonsils) cancers. Anyone who has ever been sexually active is at risk of acquiring HPV. The Food and Drug Administration has approved three vaccines to prevent high risk HPV infections. The three vaccine types are slightly different (e.g., number of required doses, cost, effectiveness, gender specific). It is recommended that females and males between the ages of 9 and 26 receive the vaccine.[24] The HPV vaccines are highly effective in preventing HPV infection for some high risk types of HPV when received prior to exposure to the virus. Although HPV vaccines are safe when given to individuals infected with HPV, the vaccines do not treat infection. The cost of the vaccines is expensive. Some health insurance companies cover the cost, while others do not. Some clinics offer a reduce rate for low-income individuals.[23]

Syphilis: Syphilis is a systemic infectious disease that is divided into four stages. Each stage goes away if not treated, but the syphilis infection remains in the body and the individual is infectious. Primary syphilis infection causes ulcers on the skin at the infection site, such as the genital area. These symptoms cause an individual to seek medical treatment. Secondary syphilis infection includes, but is not limited to, a skin rash; lesions on the mucous membranes; and swollen lymph glands. Tertiary syphilis infection includes cardiac conditions and several other vague symptoms. Latent syphilis infections are detected by blood tests; occur 10 to 30 years after infection; and involve the central nervous system (e.g.,

cranial nerve dysfunction, meningitis, stroke, acute altered mental status, auditory or ophthalmic abnormalities).[25]

Tuberculosis

Tuberculosis (also called *TB*) is caused by a bacterium called *Mycobacterium tuberculosis*. The bacteria usually attack the lungs. However, TB bacteria can attack any part of the body, such as the kidneys, spine, and brain. If not treated properly, TB can be fatal. TB remains a global public health problem and is one of the three leading causes of deaths worldwide due to infectious diseases.[26] TB is spread through the air from one person to another. Symptoms of TB include fever, chills, sweating at night, fatigue or weakness, coughing up blood, no appetite, and a bad cough that lasts 3 weeks or longer. Individuals with a weak immune system (e.g., HIV+, other serious health problems, diabetes, chemotherapy, alcohol and drug abuse) are especially susceptible to being infected with TB.

The TB bacteria are dispersed into the air when an individual with TB coughs, sneezes, speaks, or sings. Individuals near the infected individual inhale the TB bacteria and become infected. It is also important to know that TB is

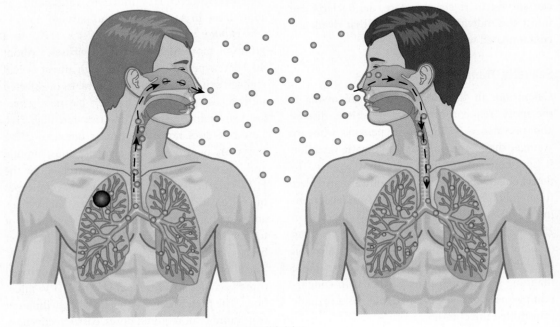

Reproduced from the CDC. Retrieved from http://www.cdc.gov/tb/topic/basics/default.htm

not spread by shaking someone's hand, sharing food or drink, touching bed linens or toilet seats, sharing toothbrushes, or kissing.[27]

It is possible to be infected with TB bacteria but not get sick. This is called *latent TB*. Such individuals do not feel sick, are not infectious, and do not spread the TB bacteria to other individuals. However, it is possible for the TB bacteria to become active and, thus, the individual moves from latent to infectious TB.

TB is diagnosed by a skin or a blood test. If individuals have a positive reaction, they are given more tests, such as a chest X-ray, to confirm the TB diagnosis. Once the diagnosis is confirmed, individuals take several types of drugs (multiple pills) per day for 6 to 9 months. It is essential for the individual to finish taking the prescription medication for two important reasons: (a) the individual may become symptomatic again because some of the bacteria were not killed; and (b) if not completely killed by the medication, the bacteria may mutate and may become resistant to the medication. If an individual with a mutated strain of the TB bacteria spreads the disease to another individual, TB remains resistant to medications and is more difficult to treat and more expensive to treat.[27]

New Emerging Infectious Diseases

An example of new emerging infectious disease was found in the 2003 outbreak of Severe Acute Respiratory Syndrome (SARS), which cost Asian economies between $11 and $18 billion, resulting in a GDP loss of between 0.5 percent and 2 percent.[26] Other infectious diseases requiring strict global monitoring include dengue fever, measles, yellow fever, and the Ebola virus. Strong health systems within countries, including effective surveillance systems and adequate human resources, are fundamental to curbing the spread of infectious disease and providing early warning of new disease outbreaks.[26] In summary, infectious diseases are more common in developing countries, and noncommunicable diseases are found primarily in high-income countries. However, the global pattern of disease burden is shifting away from infectious diseases and moving toward noncommunicable diseases.

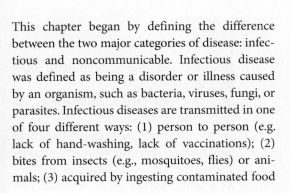

© Jim Barber/Shutterstock

Summary

This chapter began by defining the difference between the two major categories of disease: infectious and noncommunicable. Infectious disease was defined as being a disorder or illness caused by an organism, such as bacteria, viruses, fungi, or parasites. Infectious diseases are transmitted in one of four different ways: (1) person to person (e.g. lack of hand-washing, lack of vaccinations); (2) bites from insects (e.g., mosquitoes, flies) or animals; (3) acquired by ingesting contaminated food or drinking contaminated water; and (4) being exposed to organisms in the environment (e.g., swimming in a polluted lake). Today, infectious diseases remain a threat, but not to the extent as in the past. The discussion provided an overview of infectious disease prevention and control, including herd immunity and active and passive immunity. Finally, the chapter stressed that the need for primary prevention is important because, for many infectious diseases, no vaccine is available.

Case Study

Mark, age 38, and his wife, Cathy, age 34, have two children: Sam is 5 and Alex is 3. They decided that Cathy would stay home with the boys until they reached age 6 and were ready to attend first grade. Cathy's educational background is in early childhood education, so she feels comfortable staying home with the children. Mark is self-employed as an accountant, so he has a small office and two assistants. In addition, Gretchen, Cathy's mother, age 72, lives with the family. Gretchen has been battling breast cancer for several years and has received multiple chemotherapy treatments, causing her immune system to be weak. As for health insurance, Gretchen has Medicare and the recommended supplemental policies for cancer treatment and prescriptions. Mark, Cathy, and their children are enrolled in insurance they bought from the insurance exchange that was created through the federal Affordable Care Act. Generally, Mark and Cathy do not use their health insurance because they save money by only going to the doctor when it is necessary. They use the health insurance mainly for the children for annual physical examinations, vaccinations, and visits related to mild childhood illnesses, such as ear infections, vomiting, and sore throats. Mark and Cathy report that their children play outside daily, so the children remain healthy and active.

The family is involved in their faith-based community, and the children play soccer on the youth team sponsored by the community recreation center. Mark and Cathy are not opposed to having their children receive all of the recommended vaccinations for childhood illness, but they are opposed to receiving vaccines for themselves. For example, they have never received the flu vaccine. They believe that because they do not work in large corporate offices or travel on public transportation, they are not exposed to routine viruses. They also report that they have not had an upper respiratory infection or the flu in many years. As a result, Gretchen follows the beliefs of Mark and Cathy and does not receive prevention vaccinations, even though her oncology physicians recommend that she obtain the vaccines.

Over the past year, life in the household was stable and moving in a positive direction. Mark's accounting business increased profits, and he was able to hire another accountant to join his practice. Cathy started offering part-time day care to two young children in their neighborhood. Gretchen was in remission from breast cancer, but still suffering from a weak immune system.

After the holidays, things began to change for the family. Cathy got sick with flu symptoms and an upper respiratory infection. After 2 weeks, she went to the neighborhood urgent care clinic. The doctor told her that she had bronchitis and possible pneumonia and gave her a prescription for antibiotics and cough medication. She recommended that Cathy get a chest X-ray to verify her diagnosis. Although the urgent care offered chest X-ray services, Cathy refused the extra services. She filled the prescription, but once she started feeling a little better she stopped taking the medication and did not take the whole prescription. Within a week, Gretchen developed a severe cough and was admitted to the hospital for pneumonia. Cathy was unable to continue the day-care services. Mark shortened his work hours to care for their children, while Cathy went to the hospital to care for her mom for about 2 weeks. When Gretchen was discharged, her physician reminded her to rest, avoid stress, and eat healthy foods because her immune system remained weak. A few days later, she developed a painful rash and was diagnosed with shingles. Gretchen died 1 week later from a secondary infection caused by the shingles rash.

Student Activity

Answer the following questions:

1. How does this case study relate to infectious disease?
2. What are some prevention strategies that could have been used?
3. Write two more paragraphs about this family using information about infectious disease presented in this chapter.
4. As a health navigation professional, how would you assist this family?

References

1. The Mayo Clinic. *Infectious Diseases: Definition.* Retrieved September 14, 2014, from http://www.mayoclinic.org/diseases-conditions/infectious-diseases/basics/definition/CON-20033534; last updated July 23, 2014.

2. World Health Organization. *Noncommunicable diseases.* Retrieved September 14, 2014, from http://www.who.int/topics/noncommunicable_diseases/en; last updated in 2014.

3. Koo, I. *10 tips to prevent infections.* Retrieved October 5, 2015, from http://infectiousdiseases.about.com/od/prevention/a/prevention_tips.htm; last updated December 10, 2014.

4. Centers for Disease Control and Prevention. *Handwashing and nail hygiene.* Retrieved September 14, 2015, from http://www.cdc.gov/healthywater/hygiene/hand/index.html; last updated September 14, 2012.

5. Centers for Disease Control and Prevention. *Nail hygiene.* Retrieved September 14, 2015, from http://www.cdc.gov/healthywater/hygiene/hand/nail_hygiene.html; last updated December 30, 2009.

6. Centers for Disease Control and Prevention. *Keeping hands clean.* Retrieved September 14, 2015, from http://www.cdc.gov/healthywater/hygiene/hand/handwashing.html#handwashing; last updated February 1, 2011.

7. Department of Health and Human Services. *Community immunity.* Retrieved October 14, 2015, from: http://www.vaccines.gov/basics/protection/index.html; last updated April 16, 2015.

8. Szabo, L. *California measles outbreak linked to disneyland.* Retrieved October 28, 2015, from http://www.usatoday.com/story/news/nation/2015/01/07/measles-outbreak-disneyland/21402755; last updated January 8, 2015.

9. Badgett, M. R., Auer, A., Carmichael, L. E., Parrish, C. R., & Bull, J. J. (2002). Evolutionary dynamics of viral attenuation. *Journal of Virology, 76*(20), 10524–10529.

10. Centers for Disease Control and Prevention. *Diphtheria, tetanus, and pertussis (DTaP).* Retrieved October 4, 2015, from http://www.cdc.gov/vaccines/hcp/vis/vis-statements/dtap.html; last updated June 18, 2014.

11. Centers for Disease Control and Prevention. (2015). *Recommended immunizations for children from birth through 6 years old.* Retrieved October 15, 2015, from http://www.cdc.gov/vaccines/parents/downloads/parent-ver-sch-0-6yrs.pdf.

12. Centers for Disease Control and Prevention. *Infectious Disease.* Retrieved October 14, 2015, from http://www.cdc.gov/nchs/fastats/infectious-disease.htm; last updated May 14, 2015.

13. Johns Hopkins Medicine. *Health Library: Upper respiratory infection (URI or common cold).* Retrieved October 14, 2015, from http://www.hopkinsmedicine.org/healthlibrary/conditions/pediatrics/upper_respiratory_infection_uri_or_common_cold_90,P02966.

14. WebMD. *Hepatitis health center.* Retrieved September 14, 2015, from http://www.webmd.com/hepatitis/understanding-hepatitis-basics?page=1#0; last updated March 22, 2015.

15. Centers for Disease Control and Prevention. *The ABCs of hepatitis.* Retrieved September 14, 2015, from http://www.cdc.gov/hepatitis/Resources/Professionals/PDFs/ABCTable.pdf.

16. Centers for Disease Control and Prevention. *Malaria.* Retrieved September 15, 2015, from http://www.cdc.gov/malaria/index.html; last updated August 17, 2015.

17. Centers for Disease Control and Prevention. *Malaria diagnosis and treatment in the United States.* Retrieved September 14, 2015, from http://www.cdc.gov/malaria/diagnosis_treatment/index.html; last updated November 9, 2012.

18. The Mayo Clinic. *Diseases and conditions: MRSA infection.* Retrieved October 14, 2015, from http://www.mayoclinic.org/diseases-conditions/mrsa/basics/definition/con-20024479; last updated September 9, 2015.

19. Centers for Disease Control and Prevention. *Chlamydia: Fact sheet.* Retrieved October 30, 2015, from http://www.cdc.gov/std/chlamydia/stdfact-chlamydia.htm; last updated December 16, 2014.

20. Centers for Disease Control and Prevention. *Gonorrhea: CDC fact sheet.* Retrieved October 30, 2014, from http://www.cdc.gov/std/gonorrhea/stdfact-gonorrhea.htm; last updated October 14, 2015.

21. Centers for Disease Control and Prevention. *Gonococcal infections in adolescents and adults.* Retrieved October 14, 2015, from http://www.cdc.gov/std/tg2015/gonorrhea.htm; last updated June 4, 2015.

22. The Mayo Clinic. *Diseases and conditions: HIV/AIDS.* Retrieved September 14, 2015, from http://www.mayoclinic.org/diseases-conditions/hiv-aids/basics/definition/con-20013732; last updated July 21, 2015.

23. National Cancer Institute. *Human papillomavirus (HPV) vaccines.* Retrieved October 14, 2015, from http://www.cancer.gov/about-cancer/causes-prevention/risk/infectious-agents/hpv-vaccine-fact-sheet; last updated February 19, 2015.

24. Food and Drug Administration. *Patient information about GARDASIL®9.* Retrieved October 14, 2015, from http://www.fda.gov/downloads/BiologicsBloodVaccines/Vaccines/ApprovedProducts/UCM426460.pdf.

25. Centers for Disease Control and Prevention. *Syphilis.* Retrieved October 14, 2015, from http://www.cdc.gov/std/tg2015/syphilis.html; last updated June 4, 2015.

26. U.S. Department of State. *Infectious and chronic disease.* Retrieved September 14, 2015, from http://www.state.gov/e/oes/intlhealthbiodefense/id.

27. Centers for Disease Control and Prevention. *Basic TB facts.* Retrieved September 14, 2015, from http://www.cdc.gov/tb/topic/basics/default.htm; last updated March 13, 2012.

CHAPTER 10

Noncommunicable Disease

LEARNING OBJECTIVES

By the end of this chapter, students will be able to:

- Define infectious disease and noncommunicable disease
- Understand and apply a number of epidemiological terms
- Differentiate among different types of noncommunicable disease
- Describe the symptoms, diagnosis, and treatment of major noncommunicable diseases

CHAPTER OVERVIEW

This chapter introduces noncommunicable diseases. Unlike infectious diseases that are caused by organisms such as bacteria, viruses, fungi, or parasites, noncommunicable disease are not spread from person to person. *Noncommunicable diseases* are now the major cause of death and disability worldwide.[1] According to the World Health Organization (WHO), noncommunicable diseases are responsible for 63 percent of deaths worldwide, which is double the combined number of deaths from infectious diseases (including HIV/AIDS, tuberculosis, and malaria), maternal and perinatal conditions, and nutritional deficiencies.[2] After a brief description of the discipline of epidemiology (the study of the patterns, causes, and effects of health and disease conditions in defined populations[3]), the chapter discusses the various types of important noncommunicable diseases, including cardiovascular disease, cancer, diabetes, respiratory diseases like asthma and chronic obstructive pulmonary disease (COPD), and arthritis. For each noncommunicable disease, the chapter provides a description of the causes, symptoms, and treatment.

EPIDEMIOLOGY

Before discussing the types of noncommunicable diseases, it is important to learn about epidemiology, the science of public health. Epidemiology is the study of populations to understand the patterns, causes, and effects of health and diseases.[3] Epidemiology is used to develop methodology for clinical research, make decisions based on the understanding of data, identify risk factors, target ways to prevent the spread of disease, and create healthcare policies.[4] It is easier to understand by comparing epidemiology to clinical medicine. Epidemiology studies the small changes that have an effect on the population of interest; clinical medicine is interested in the health of individuals. For example, if your weight increased by 60 pounds over the next 12 months, you would increase your chances of developing coronary heart disease (CHD). However, if everyone in a given population gained 60 pounds over the next 12 months, there would be a big jump in the total number of CHD deaths in the population over time.

In addition, within the field of epidemiology, some vocabulary words are useful to learn to enhance your understanding of how epidemiology relates to disease.

Morbidity: Morbidity is another term for an illness or disease. The term "co-morbidity" is also used when an individual has several illnesses at the same time. For example, an individual may have diabetes, hypertension, and asthma; thus, the healthcare provider reports that the individual has several co-morbidities.

Mortality: Mortality is another term for death. A mortality rate is the number of deaths due to a disease for a population. Mortality rates are given as the number of deaths per year in a population per a consistent number (most often 100,000). This number is to standardize the death rate across different population sizes. For example, if there are 15 breast cancer deaths in one year in a population of 25,000, then the mortality rate for that population is 60 per 100,000. To understand this calculation, see **Box 10.1**.

Now test your skills with the scenario in **Box 10.2**.

Incidence: Incidence is defined as the number of newly diagnosed cases of a disease during a given period of time (e.g., 1 month, 1 year). For example, researchers investigate the national incidence rates of traumatic brain injuries among adolescent males that occur during a 12-month high school football season that were caused by allowable contact tackling procedures.

BOX 10.2   Test Your Mortality Rate Calculation Skills

In 2014, the town of Clarksville had a breast cancer mortality rate of 60 per 100,000. In 2014, the town of Fort Greene had a population of 50,000, and 25 individuals died of breast cancer.

Question: Is the mortality rate from breast cancer higher or lower in Fort Greene compared to Clarksville?

Answer: Look on the following page.

Answer to Box 10.2

Step 1: Because mortality rates are calculated on a standard population of 100,000 and Fort Greene has a population of 50,000, it is necessary to calculate 100,000/50,000 = 2. In other words, multiply 50,000 x 2 to reach the standard population of 100,000.

Step 2: Multiply 25 (individuals who died of breast cancer) x 2 = 50.

Step 3: The mortality (death) rate from breast cancer in Clarksville is 60 per 100,000, and the morality (death) rate from breast cancer in Fort Greene is 50 per 100,000.

Step 4: These two calculations allow researchers to determine that the mortality rate of breast cancer deaths is higher in Clarksville than in Fort Greene, based on a standard population of 100,000.

Step 5: The researchers would investigate the possible reasons why more individuals are dying from breast cancer in Clarksville than in Fort Greene.

BOX 10.1   Calculation for Mortality Rates

In 2014, the town of Clarksville had a population of 25,000. In that same year, 15 individuals died of breast cancer.

Step 1: Because mortality rates are calculated on a standard population of 100,000 and Clarksville had a population of 25,000, it is necessary to calculate 100,000/25,000 = 4. In other words, multiply 25,000 x 4 to reach the standard population of 100,000.

Step 2: Multiply 15 (individuals who died of breast cancer) x 4 = 60.

Step 3: The mortality (death) rate from breast cancer in Clarksville is 60 per 100,000.

Step 4: This calculation allows researchers to determine if the mortality rate of breast cancer deaths is higher or lower compared to other towns, because mortality rate calculations are based on a standard population of 100,000.

Prevalence: Prevalence is defined as the number of cases of disease existing in a population taken from the total population at any given time. For example, researchers investigate national prevalence rates of number of adults with a diagnosis of Alzheimer's disease who are living in assisted-living facilities.

By using the previously defined epidemiological terms and calculations, the Centers for Disease Control and Prevention (CDC) reports that noncommunicable diseases account for 10 out of the 15 leading causes of death (mortality rate) in the United States.[5] See **Table 10.1**.

Apart from the tremendous adverse effects on the quality of life of individuals involved, these conditions place enormous strains on family and community budgets. The overall economy suffers from both labor lost due to death (mortality) and illness/disability (morbidity) as well as the high direct medical costs. This phenomenon, during which health infrastructures already weakened by continuing battles with infectious disease are increasingly being taxed by rapidly growing noncommunicable diseases, is often referred to as the *double disease burden*.[2]

Generally, noncommunicable diseases have a long duration with a slow progression. The following section describes the most common types of noncommunicable diseases: cardiovascular diseases (e.g., heart attacks and stroke), cancer, diabetes, noncommunicable respiratory diseases (e.g., chronic obstructed pulmonary disease, pneumonia, asthma), and arthritis.[2]

TYPES OF NONCOMMUNICABLE DISEASES

Cardiovascular Disease

When studying cardiovascular (cardio = heart and vascular = arteries and veins) disease, it is important to know that the cardiovascular system encompasses a vast array of chronic conditions

TABLE 10.1 Fifteen Leading Causes of Death in the United States

Cause	Percent of Total	Noncommunicable Disease
Cardiovascular Disease	28.5	*
Cancer	22.8	*
Cerebrovascular Diseases	6.7	*
Chronic Lower Respiratory Diseases	5.1	*
Accidents (unintentional injuries)	4.4	
Diabetes Mellitus	3.0	*
Influenza and Pneumonia	2.7	
Alzheimer's Disease	2.4	*
Nephritis, Nephrotic Syndrome, and Nephrosis	1.7	*
Septicemia (blood poisoning)	1.4	
Suicide	1.3	
Chronic Liver Disease and Cirrhosis	1.1	*
Primary Hypertension and Hypertensive Renal Disease	0.8	*
Parkinson's Disease (tied)	0.7	*
Homicide (tied)	0.7	

Data from: The Centers for Disease Control and Prevention (2015). Leading Causes of Death. Available at: http://www.cdc.gov/nchs/fastats/leading-causes-of-death.htm. Accessed on September 14, 2015. Last updated August 21, 2015.[6]

and accounts for 48 percent of all deaths.[5] For a brief review of anatomy, the heart is a muscle. See **Figure 10.1**. There are four chambers in the heart: (1) the right atrium, which receives blood from the veins and pumps it to the right ventricle; (2) the right ventricle, which receives blood from the right atrium and pumps it to the lungs, where it is loaded with oxygen; (3) the left atrium, which receives oxygenated blood from the lungs and pumps it to the left ventricle; and (4) the left ventricle (the strongest chamber), which pumps oxygen-rich blood to the rest of the body. The left ventricle's vigorous contractions create our blood pressure. The coronary arteries are on the surface of the heart and provide oxygen-rich blood to the heart muscle. Throughout the heart, complex nerve fibers conduct the electrical impulses signaling the heart contractions and relaxation (heart pulse). Surrounding the heart is a sac called the *pericardium* (peri = around; cardi = heart). The pericardium protects the heart.

There are several types of cardiac (heart) disease, but the most common is **myocardial infarction (MI)** or **acute myocardial infarction (AMI)**. Both MI and AMI are the medical term for "heart attack." AMI occurs when the flow of oxygen-rich blood is blocked in a section of the heart. If the flow of blood is not restored quickly, a section of the heart muscle dies. Even though there are effective treatments to save lives and prevent disabilities, AMI remains the leading cause of death in the United States.

AMI occurs as a result of **coronary heart disease (CHD)** or **coronary artery disease (CAD)**. **CHD** is the result of waxy cholesterol (plaque) buildup in the coronary arteries. When

FIGURE 10.1 Anatomy of the Heart

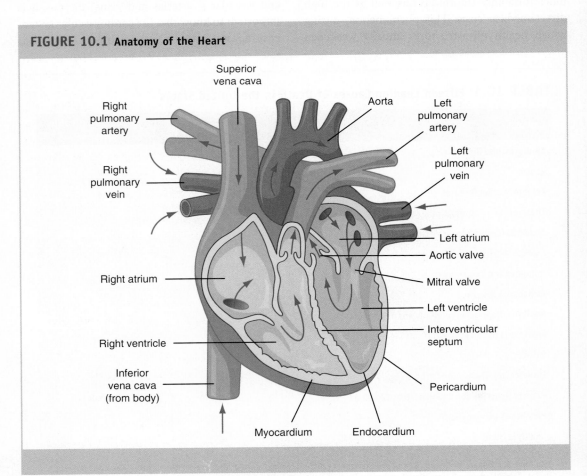

the plaque causes the arteries to narrow, thus causing a blockage, the disease is called *atherosclerosis*. Eventually, a piece of the plaque breaks off in the artery and forms a blood clot. If the blood clot is large enough, it blocks a portion or all of the blood flow within the heart, causing an AMI.

After surviving an AMI, the heart muscle may be damaged, so individuals may experience long-term health problems, including heart failure and arrhythmias (irregular heart beat). Heart failure is a condition in which the heart is unable to pump enough blood to meet the body's needs. Another name for heart failure is *congestive heart failure (CHF)*. Reasons the heart may be unable to pump enough blood include heart muscle damage caused by an AMI, hypertension (high blood pressure), and diabetes. When hypertension and diabetes are controlled, heart damage may be prevented or controlled.[7]

There are two types of CHF depending on the location of the heart muscle damage. First, left-sided heart failure occurs if the heart is unable to pump enough blood to the rest of the body. Second, right-sided heart failure occurs if the heart is unable to pump enough blood to the lungs to receive oxygen. Right-sided heart failure causes fluid to build up in the feet, ankles, legs, liver, abdomen, and the veins in the neck. In addition, both types cause shortness of breath and fatigue.[7] See **Table 10.2** for a list of common medications used to treat heart failure. Because health navigation professionals may need to explain medications to individuals, it is useful to become familiar with the common cardiovascular prescriptions.

In addition, heart damage may cause heart rate disorders: arrhythmias and fibrillation. Refer to Figure 10.1. First, arrhythmias are defined as the heart beating too fast (tachycardia), too slow (bradycardia), or with an irregular rhythm. The common causes of abnormal heart beats are congestive heart failure (CHF), heart damage from a previous acute myocardial infarction (AMI), abnormal levels of potassium in the body, overactive thyroid gland, and heart disease present at birth.[8]

Second, fibrillation is when the heart's two upper chambers (atrium) beat out of coordination with the two lower chambers (ventricles), and this chaotic heart rhythm causes poor blood flow to the body. There are two types of fibrillation: atrial and ventricular. Atrial fibrillation (AFib) is an irregular and often rapid heart rate that commonly causes poor blood flow to the body. The symptoms of atrial fibrillation include heart palpitations, shortness of breath, and weakness. Episodes of atrial fibrillation may

TABLE 10.2 Common Types of Medications Used to Treat Heart Failure

Medication	Action
Diuretics	Help reduce fluid buildup in lungs and swelling in feet and ankles
ACE (angiotensin-converting-enzyme inhibitor) Inhibitors	Lower blood pressure and reduce strain on the heart; may reduce the risk of future heart attacks
Aldosterone Antagonists	Trigger the body to get rid of salt and water through urine; lower the volume of blood that the heart must pump
Angiotensin Receptor Blockers	Relax the blood vessels and lower the blood pressure to decrease your heart's workload
Beta Blockers	Slow the heart rate and lower the blood pressure to decrease the heart's workload
Hydralazine Hydrochloride	Helps to relax the blood vessels so the heart does not work so hard to pump blood
Digoxin	Makes the heart beat stronger and pump more blood

Modified from: The National Library of Medicine (2015). NHLBI Health Topics – Heart Failure. Available at: http://www.ncbi.nlm.nih.gov/pubmedhealth/PMH0063056/. Accessed on September 14, 2015.

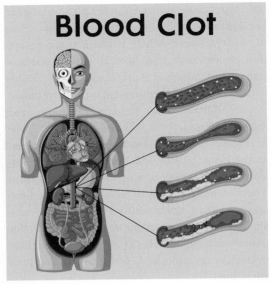

Blood Clot

© colematt/istockphoto

be sporadic or may need treatment. Atrial fibrillation is not usually life-threatening, but it can lead to complications due to blood clots forming in the heart that may circulate to other organs and lead to blocked blood flow (ischemia).[9]

On the other hand, ventricular fibrillation (VF) is a life-threatening arrhythmia that can cause death if not treated immediately. With VF, blood is not pumped from the heart and sudden cardiac death results. Even though the most common cause of VF is a heart attack, other conditions can lead to VF, including electrocution accidents

or injury to the heart (e.g., vehicle crash, athletic injury, cardiac surgery, narrowed coronary arteries, adverse effects of medications). Individuals with no history of heart disease can experience VF due to the risk factors of smoking, high blood pressure, and diabetes. VF episodes begin with chest pain, dizziness, nausea, rapid heartbeat, and shortness of breath. The symptoms can occur anywhere from several minutes to 1 hour prior. If medical intervention is not immediately available, the individual collapses, becomes unconscious, and dies due to lack of blood flow to the brain and muscles. If family, friends, or bystanders are present, they should call 911 for help and begin CPR (cardiopulmonary resuscitation) by doing chest compressions until help arrives. VF may also be treated by using a device called an *external defibrillator* that delivers a quick electric shock through the chest. This electric shock may restore the heartbeat to a normal rhythm and should be done as quickly as possible. Many public places (e.g., airports, restaurants, theaters) have such devices.[9] See **Table 10.3**.

Cancer

Cancer is a collection of related diseases. Normally, human cells grow and divide to form new cells as the body needs them. As cells age or become damaged, they die, and new cells take their place. When cancer cells develop, however, this orderly process breaks down. As cells mutate and become abnormal, the cells survive when they should die.

TABLE 10.3 Signs and Symptoms of an Acute Myocardial Infarction (AMI)

Common Signs and Symptoms	
Chest Pain or Discomfort	Involves center or left side of chest; may last a few minutes or go away and come back; feels like pressure, squeezing, fullness, or pain; can feel like heartburn or indigestion
Upper-Body Discomfort	Pain or discomfort in one or both arms, back, shoulders, neck, jaw, or upper portion of abdomen
Other Symptoms	Breaking out in a cold sweat, feeling tired for days for no reason (especially for women), nausea, vomiting, sudden dizziness

The symptoms of a heart attack vary from individual to individual. Some individuals have few symptoms, while others have multiple symptoms. If an individual has already experienced an AMI, the symptoms may not be the same for another one. When in doubt, call 911. Do not attempt to drive yourself to a hospital.

Modified from: The National Library of Medicine (2014). NHLBI Heatlh Topics – Heart Attack. Available at: http://www.ncbi.nlm.nih.gov/pubmedhealth/PMH0062989/. Accessed on September 14, 2015.[10]

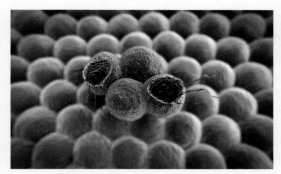

© Ugreen/ iStockphoto

BOX 10.3 The Seven Early Warning Signs of Cancer

Changes in the size, color, or shape of a wart or a mole
A sore that does not heal
Persistent cough, hoarseness, or sore throat
A lump or thickening in the breast or elsewhere
Unusual bleeding or discharge
Chronic indigestion or difficulty in swallowing
Any change in bowel or bladder habits

The mutated cells continue to divide and produce more mutated cells. These mutated cells multiply and may form growths called *tumors*. The mutated cells change to the point where the original function of the cell is lost. For example, mutated lung cells change over and over to the point that the mutated cells no longer functions as lung cells, but rather mutated cancer cells. On the other hand, normal lung cells divide and mature into very distinct cell types with specific functions. This is one reason that, unlike normal cells, cancer cells continue to divide without stopping. If the cancer cells are left unchecked, they eventually spread to surrounding tissues or organs.[11]

Cancer cells may form a solid tumor or create cancers within the blood (leukemia) or lymph system (lymphoma). There are two types of solid tumors: benign and malignant. Benign tumors do not spread into other tissues but may be quite large. Malignant tumors are cancerous and can spread into nearby tissues. Some of the cancer cells can break off and use the blood or lymph system to travel to distant organs and grow new tumors.[11] The remainder of this section discusses cancer from the standpoint of causes, type, stages, and treatment.

Causes of Cancer

Cancer is caused by changes to genes that control the way cells function, grow, and divide. Cell genes may be altered in different ways across the life span, including the following: (a) genetic changes inherited from parents; (b) gene damage due to environmental exposure (e.g., radiation, asbestos, ultraviolet rays from the sun); and (c) exposure to specific chemicals in tobacco products (e.g., inhaling smoke, secondhand smoke, oral tobacco use). Each individual with a cancer diagnosis has a unique combination of genetic changes. Even within the same cancerous tumor, different cells have different genetic changes.[11]

Because cancer is a progressive disease, there are many signs and symptoms. Some symptoms include a tumor growing within an organ or gland. As the tumor enlarges, the individual feels pain or pressure. These symptoms could be early warning signs of cancer. The American Cancer Society has established the seven warning signs of cancer. See **Box 10.3**.

In addition, laboratory tests of sputum, blood, urine, and stool are used to detect abnormalities that may indicate cancer. Blood tests can be used to check for cancer cells that release particular proteins. These cells are called *tumor markers*. Blood tests are also used to determine the effectiveness of the cancer treatment or to detect recurrent cancer. See **Table 10.4**.

Types

There are two types of tumors: benign and malignant. A benign tumor is not considered cancer, is slow growing, and does not spread or invade surrounding tissue. Once a benign tumor is removed, it does not usually recur. A malignant tumor (group of mutated cells) is cancer. Malignant tumors may be nonmetastatic or metastatic. Nonmetastatic means the cancer has not spread. When cancer spreads from one location in the body to

TABLE 10.4 Most Common Lifestyle Causes of Cancer

Tobacco	More than 80% of lung cancer cases occur in smokers. Smoking is also a contributing factor to cancers in the upper respiratory tract, esophagus, larynx, bladder, pancreas, liver, stomach, breast, and kidney. In addition, secondhand smoke increases the risk of developing cancer.
Alcohol	Excessive consumption of alcohol is a risk factor for liver cancer. When alcohol is combined with tobacco, there is an increase in the chances of developing mouth, pharynx, larynx, and esophageal cancers. See **Figure 10.2**.
Diet	Thirty-five percent of all cancers are due to dietary causes. Excessive intake of fat leading to obesity is linked to cancers of the breast, colon, rectum, pancreas, prostate, gall bladder, ovaries, and uterus.
Sexual and Reproductive Behavior	Human papillomavirus (HPV) is a common sexually transmitted infection and is the cause for cancer of the cervix, as well as other cancers. There is a vaccine available to prevent cancer caused by HPV.
Family History	Certain cancers like breast, colon, ovarian, and uterine cancer recur generation after generation in some families. Inheriting those particular genes makes individuals susceptible to certain cancers.
Occupational Hazards	Evidence shows that certain occupational hazards account for 4% of all cancer deaths: (a) asbestos workers have an increased incidence of lung cancer; (b) dye, rubber, and gas workers are more likely to get bladder cancer; (c) smelter workers, gold miners, and arsenic workers are at risk of skin and lung cancer; (d) varnish and glue workers are at risk of leukemia; (e) plastic workers are at risk of liver cancer; and (f) radiologists and uranium miners are at risk of bone and bone marrow cancer.
Environment	Radiation is the cause of 1%–2% of all cancer deaths. Ultraviolet radiation from the sun accounts for a majority of melanoma deaths, along with other sources including X-rays, radon gas, and ionizing radiation from nuclear material.
Pollution	It is estimated that 1% of cancer deaths are due to air, land, and water pollution. The main danger occurs when chemicals from the industries escape into the surrounding environment.

Data from: Anand P., Kunnumakara A. B., Sundaram C., Harikumar K. B., Tharakan S. T., Lai O. S., Sung B., Aggarwal B. B. (2008). Cancer is a preventable disease that requires major lifestyle changes. *Pharmaceutical research*, 25(9), 2097–2116.

another location, it is called *metastatic cancer*. In metastasis, cancer cells break away from the primary cancer site and travel through the blood or lymph system to a new body site and form new tumors (metastatic tumors) in other parts of the body. The metastatic tumor is the same type of cancer as the primary tumor. The metastatic cancer retains the same name and the same type of cancer cells as the original or primary cancer site. For example, when breast cancer spreads to the lungs, it is metastatic breast cancer, not lung cancer. There five categories of cancer.

First, *carcinoma* begins in the skin or in tissues that line or cover internal organs. Carcinomas are the most common type of cancer. They are formed by epithelial cells, which are the cells that cover the inside and outside surfaces of the body. There are four types of carcinomas: (a) adenocarcinoma forms in glandular (mucus-producing) tissues, including the breast, colon, and prostate; (b) basal cell carcinoma is a cancer that begins in the lower or basal (base) layer of the epidermis of an individual's outer layer of skin cells; (c) squamous cell carcinoma is a cancer that forms just beneath the outer surface of the skin as well as in the lining of the stomach, intestines, lungs, bladder, and kidneys; and (d) transitional cell carcinoma is a cancer found in the linings of the bladder, ureters, part of the kidneys, and a few other organs. Some cancers of the bladder, ureters, and kidneys are also *transitional cell carcinomas*.

Second, *sarcoma* begins in bone, cartilage, fat, muscle, blood vessels, or other connective or

FIGURE 10.2 Equivalence of Alcohol

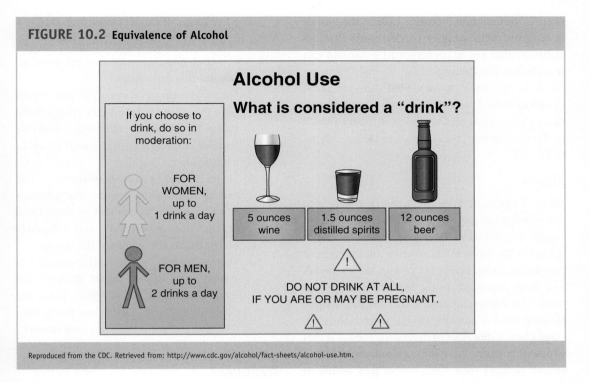

Reproduced from the CDC. Retrieved from: http://www.cdc.gov/alcohol/fact-sheets/alcohol-use.htm.

supportive tissues. Sarcoma is divided into two major categories: bone and soft tissue sarcoma. Bone sarcoma includes chondrosarcoma (rare; begins in cartilage around bones), Ewing's sarcoma (rare; affects children and young adults), and osteosarcoma (forms in cells within long bones, such as legs and arms). Osteosarcoma is the most common cancer of the bone. Soft tissue sarcoma includes gastrointestinal stromal tumor (forms in digestive tract; most often in stomach or upper part of the small intestine), liposarcoma (occurs in fat cells of the muscles of the limbs or abdomen), and rhabdomyosarcoma (rare; affects children and young adults; forms in the muscle and connective tissue). Treatments for sarcoma vary depending on tumor type, location, and other factors.

Third, *leukemia* starts in blood-forming tissue such as the bone marrow. The abnormal cells reproduce and enter the blood. Leukemia does not form into solid tumors but rather the abnormal white blood cells build up in the blood and bone marrow, thus crowding out normal blood cells. As the number of normal blood cells decreases, the body has to work harder to get oxygen to the muscles and tissues, control bleeding, or fight infections.

Fourth, *lymphoma* and myeloma cancer begin in the lymphocytes (T-cells and B-cells) of the immune system. Lymphocytes are also called *white blood cells*. Usually, the white blood cells fight infection as part of the immune system response to illness and injury. Lymphoma is a cancer that forms when abnormal lymphocytes turn into cancer cells, grow abnormally, spread beyond the lymphatic system to other organs, and compromise the body's ability to fight infection. Myeloma begins in the bone marrow and causes bone discomfort and bone weakness. Pain or discomfort in the back, ribs, legs, and arms is a common symptom and is usually more serious during the night.

Fifth, *central nervous system* cancers begin in the tissues of the brain and spinal cord. Unlike cancers that start in other parts of the body, tumors that start in the brain or spinal cord rarely spread to distant organs. Brain or spinal cord tumors cause damage by growing and damaging nearby normal brain tissue. Unless the tumor is removed with surgery or destroyed through radiation therapy, it continues to grow and can become life-threatening.[13]

It is important to note that different types of cancer have different signs and symptoms. All cancer types grow and spread at different rates.[11] In the next section, types of cancer treatments are discussed.

Stages

When a cancer is diagnosed, the first step is to determine what stage of the cancer it is. The term "stage" is defined as how much the cancer has spread in the body. Without knowing the stage of the cancer, a treatment plan cannot be developed. The stage also predicts the severity of the prognosis. The higher the stage level, the more serious the diagnosis. A cancer is always referred to by the stage given at the time of diagnosis, even if it gets worse or spreads. New information about how a cancer changes over time simply gets added to the original stage designation. The cancer stage designation does not change (even though the cancer itself might) because survival statistics and information on treatment by stage for specific cancer types are based on the original cancer stage at diagnosis.

Several methods are used to stage the cancer, including: (a) a physical exam to gather information about the cancer, such as size and location; (b) radiology imaging studies (e.g., X-rays, computed tomography (CT) scans, magnetic resonance imaging (MRI) scans, and positron emission tomography (PET) scans) to show size, location, and whether the cancer has spread; (c) laboratory tests, such as blood, urine, other fluids, and tissue samples taken from the body; and (d) pathology reports, which include information such the tumor size, spread of cancer cells, and type of cancer cells.[14] After all of the reports are reviewed, the staging is established. The common elements of staging include the site of the primary tumor, the grade of tumor (cell type), size of tumor, number of similar tumors, and presence or absence of lymph node involvement.

The five stages of cancer range from 0 to 4[15]:

1. Stage 0 (in situ): Earliest stage of cancer; it is probable that some cancers never go beyond this early stage.
2. Stage 1 (localized cancer): The cancer cells have the ability to invade the neighboring tissue. When cancer cells grow and divide without control, a tumor (lump) forms in a single area.
3. Stages 2 and 3 (regional spread): The cancer has spread beyond the primary site to nearby lymph nodes or tissues and organs. Staging between 2 and 3 depends on the organ and extent of the spread.
4. Stage 4 (distant spread): The cancer has spread to a distant organ through the lymph system or bloodstream. Once the cancer is in the blood, it can travel anywhere in the body and form new tumors.

Treatment

Because there are many types of cancers, there are also many types of cancer treatments. This section explores the most common types of treatments. However, it is important to note that cancer research is always developing new treatments with varying success rates. The type of treatment depends on the type and stage of cancer for each individual with a cancer diagnosis. The types of treatment that you receive will depend on the type of cancer you have and how advanced it is. Keep in mind that, depending on the type of cancer, the individual with cancer may undergo surgery first, followed by chemotherapy and radiation. In other cases, the treatment may begin with radiation to shrink the tumor and then surgery to remove the tumor. There are no exact treatment plans for each diagnosis. The treatment plan is established for each individual based on his or her age, gender, other noncommunicable diseases (e.g., diabetes, heart conditions, obesity), and their cancer diagnosis. See **Box 10.4**.

The main cancer treatments include:

A. Surgery: The tumor is removed by a surgical procedure.

B. Radiation therapy: Targeted radiation is used to destroy cancer cells and shrink tumors; radiation treatment may be 5 days per week over a few weeks or spread out over a few months.

C. Chemotherapy: Intravenous drugs are used to destroy cancer cells and shrink tumors; depending on the stage and type of cancer, the chemotherapy may be administered once per week up to once per month.

D. Immunotherapy: Helps the immune system fight the cancer; this therapy is also called a *biological therapy* because it uses living organisms (e.g., white blood cells) to boost the immune system to destroy the cancer. Immunotherapy is specially formulated for each individual and type of cancer. It is given as intravenous therapy over several months. Many immunotherapies remain in the research phase and are not available at all cancer treatment locations.

E. Other therapy treatments: Some treatment therapies change how cancer cells grow, divide, and spread; hormone treatment therapies slow or stop the growth of cancer cells that feed off of hormones, such as some types of breast cancer; and stem cell transplant therapies restore blood-forming stem cells after high doses of cancer treatments, such as chemotherapy and radiation.

F. Alternative treatments: Complimentary or alternative therapies are generally used in conjunction with medical treatments to minimize the side effects. For example, acupuncture may be useful in reducing cancer pain, nausea, and vomiting for some individuals. Massage eases muscle tension for others. Herbal remedies, such as tea, may help with other side effects. Other individuals may find vitamin supplements and exercise also reduce stress, improve energy, and decrease fatigue.

BOX 10.4 Questions to Ask about Cancer Treatment

What are the risks and benefits of each treatment option?

What treatment is best? When does the treatment begin?

How is it known if the treatment is working?

Is a second opinion recommended before starting the cancer treatment plan?

Will another specialist overview the cancer treatment plan?

Where will the treatment be given? How will treatment be given?

How many treatments are required? How long does each treatment take?

How will the side effects and pain be controlled? Are the side effects preventable?

What are considered to be serious side effects?

Are non-cancer medications taken during treatment?

Is it safe to continue taking supplements (e.g., vitamins, minerals, herbs) during treatment?

What support groups are available in this area?

Modified from: The National Cancer Institute (2012). Questions to Ask Your Doctor about Treatment. Available at: http://www.cancer.gov/about-cancer/treatment/questions. Accessed September 14, 2015.[16]

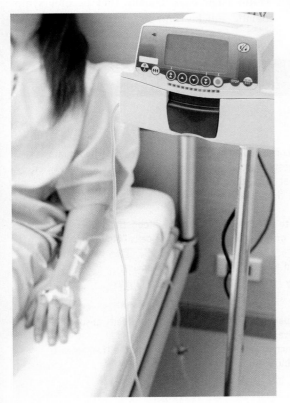

Diabetes

Before discussing diabetes, it is necessary to understand insulin and how it works in the body of an individual without diabetes. Insulin is produced in the pancreas, which is located behind the stomach near the small intestines. Within the pancreas, there are clusters of cells called the islets of Langerhans. The islets are composed of beta cells, which produce and release insulin into the bloodstream. Insulin is a hormone with the primary role of regulating bodily functions related to digestion. Each time an individual eats, the beta cells release insulin to convert the food into energy or to store the food for energy at a later time as needed. If the individual consumes more food than they need for energy, the body stores the energy. Over time, the excess stored energy results in weight gain. For individuals with diabetes, the body is unable to maintain a normal blood sugar level due to their insulin insufficiency. For this reason, individuals with diabetes must test their blood glucose levels daily to maintain their blood glucose, because their body is no longer regulating insulin production properly. See **Box 10.5** for a summary of how insulin works in the body.

In addition, insulin helps the body utilize fat, protein, and certain minerals. Because insulin is so essential, individuals with diabetes may experience widespread direct and indirect effects on all of their body's systems, tissues, and organs. See **Table 10.5** to learn the signs and symptoms of diabetes.

Even though there are two types of diabetes (Type 1 and Type 2), the long-term effects of organ damage are the same for both types of diabetes. Individual with diabetes must learn to how to maintain their blood glucose levels within normal limits; even then, they are at increased risk of organ damage over time. See **Table 10.6**. The distinct differences between Type 1 and Type 2 diabetes are presented in the following section.

Type 1 Diabetes

Type 1 diabetes is a type of autoimmune disorder that occurs when the body's immune system reacts improperly, attacking and damaging the body itself. Individuals diagnosed with Type 1 diabetes are generally children or adolescents. The progression of their disease is rapid and can occur within a few days. Usually, they become symptomatic quickly and are hospitalized, because

---

BOX 10.5   How Insulin Works in the Body

Insulin works to maintain the body's blood sugar levels within a normal range.

Mechanics of Insulin

- Blood sugar levels rise when most foods are consumed. When carbohydrates (e.g., whole grains, pasta, cereal, fruit, ice cream, candy) are ingested, blood sugar increases more rapidly than when protein (e.g., meat, fish, poultry, nuts) and fat (e.g., oils, butter) are consumed.
- The digestive system releases glucose (sugar) from foods, and the glucose molecules are absorbed into the bloodstream.
- The rising glucose levels signal the pancreas to release insulin into the bloodstream.
- In the bloodstream, the insulin acts as a key or receptor to open up the cells (blood, muscle, tissue) to receive glucose.
- Insulin receptors allow the glucose to be used as energy or stored for later use.
- If insulin is not present, the body has no way to convert the glucose into energy.

Insulin Utilization

- If blood sugar is high (hyperglycemia): The pancreas releases insulin to help cells absorb glucose from the bloodstream to lower blood sugar levels.
- If blood sugar is low (hypoglycemia): The pancreas releases glucagon to help the liver release stored glucose into the bloodstream to raise blood sugar levels.

TABLE 10.5 Signs and Symptoms of Diabetes

Signs and Symptoms	Explanation
Increased Thirst and Frequent Urination	As excess glucose builds up in the blood, the brain triggers a need to dilute the glucose concentration, so the individual becomes thirsty, which leads to frequent urination.
Increased Hunger	Without sufficient insulin, the glucose cannot move from blood to muscles for energy. This causes the individual to experience hunger in order to get more energy.
Weight Loss	Despite eating more, the body cannot use glucose for energy, so muscle and fat are used for energy. Excess calories from glucose are excreted in the urine, thus causing urine testing to reveal high levels of glucose.
Fatigue	Because the cells are deprived of energy (glucose), the individual feels tired and irritable most of the time.
Blurred Vision/Blindness	If the individual's blood sugar level remains too high, the tiny blood vessels in the eye become damaged.
Slow Healing and Frequent Infections	Diabetes affects the body's ability to heal and resist infections.
Areas of Darkened Skin	Patches of dark skin in folds and creases (e.g., armpits, neck) may be a sign of insulin resistance.

Data from: The Mayo Clinic (2014). Diseases and Conditions – Type 2 Diabetes Symptoms. Available at: http://www.mayoclinic.org/diseases-conditions/type-2-diabetes/basics/symptoms/con-20031902. Accessed on September 14, 2015. Last Updated on July 24, 2014.[17]

TABLE 10.6 Long-Term Organ Damage from Diabetes

Organ	Explanation
Cardiovascular (heart and blood vessels)	Diabetes increases risk of cardiovascular diseases (e.g., coronary artery disease, atherosclerosis, angina, hypertension).
Neuropathy (nerve damage)	Nerve damage causes tingling, numbness, burning, or pain at the tips of the toes or fingers and gradually moves up limbs.
Nephropathy (kidney damage)	Diabetes can damage this delicate filtering system. Severe damage can lead to kidney failure or irreversible end-stage kidney disease, which often eventually requires dialysis or a kidney transplant.
Diabetic Retinopathy (eye damage)	Diabetes can damage the blood vessels of the retina (diabetic retinopathy), potentially leading to blindness, cataracts, and glaucoma.
Podiatry (foot damage)	Nerve damage in the feet or poor blood flow to the feet increases the risk of various foot complications. Untreated, cuts and blisters can lead to serious infections and amputation of lower extremities (e.g., toes, feet, legs).
Loss of Hearing	Hearing problems are more common in people with diabetes.
Skin Conditions	Individuals with diabetes are more susceptible to skin problems (e.g., bacterial and fungal infections).
Alzheimer's Disease	Type 2 diabetes is thought to increase the risk of Alzheimer's disease. Additional research is currently being conducted.

Adapted from: The Mayo Clinic (2014). Disease and Conditions: Type 2 Diabetes Complications. Retrieved September 14, 2015, from www.mayoclinic.org/disease-conditions/type-2-diabetes/basics/complications/con-2003902. Last updated July 24, 2014. By permission of Mayo Foundation for Medical Education and Research. All rights reserved.[18]

DIABETES MELLITUS

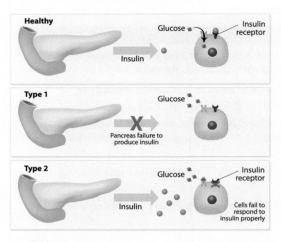

© ttsz/Thinkstock

suddenly their bodies are no longer able to make insulin because the beta cells in their pancreas are damaged or destroyed due to their autoimmune disease. Individuals with Type 1 diabetes must monitor their blood sugar and insulin levels for the rest of their lives. Therefore, they must prick their finger, test their blood sugar level, and inject insulin as needed, based on their blood glucose test results. If their hyperglycemia (high blood sugar) is not kept under control with insulin injections, over time the hyperglycemia can cause long-term complications, such as renal (kidney) failure, blindness, amputations due to poor circulation, neuropathy (painful continuous tingling in legs and feet), and cardiovascular conditions. Finally, advanced medical technologies are continually being researched and developed (e.g., internal and external insulin pumps, pancreatic transplants) to ease the burden of testing the blood glucose level and self-injecting insulin several times each day.[19] There is no cure for Type 1 diabetes, but there are advances in medical research related to internally and externally worn insulin pumps (small computers) that regulate blood glucose levels and pancreatic transplants.

Type 2 Diabetes

Type 2 diabetes is more common in adults (e.g., poor lifestyle choices, such as obesity, lack of adequate exercise, poor food choices). However, it is affecting more and more children as childhood obesity rates continue to increase. Type 2 diabetes develops very slowly over many years, as an individual can ignore its symptoms and not know to make lifestyle behavioral changes to decrease long-term damaging consequences such as renal (kidney) failure, blindness, amputations due to poor circulation, neuropathy (painful continuous tingling in legs and feet), and cardiovascular conditions.

Even though there is no cure for Type 2 diabetes, individuals with Type 2 diabetes can decrease the symptoms and long-term effects by learning to manage their diabetes, keeping their blood glucose levels within normal range by reducing their weight, making healthy food choices, and sustaining a regular exercise routine. When food choices and exercise do not normalize blood glucose levels, the individual may need oral diabetes medications or insulin injection therapy similar to a Type 1 diabetic. Keep in mind that oral diabetes medication is not insulin, but rather works with other body systems to regulate blood glucose, such as increasing the amount of glucose secreted through the kidneys. Insulin cannot be consumed as a pill and must be injected. Type 2 diabetes is a progressive and complex medical condition. The longer an individual has Type 2 diabetes and the blood glucose levels are not controlled within normal ranges, the more likely insulin is required to maintain blood glucose levels.[20] Keep in mind that research is not conclusive as to the reasons why some people acquire Type 2 diabetes and other individuals do not. However, certain factors increase the risk of developing Type 2 diabetes. See **Table 10.7**.

Early diagnosis of Type 2 diabetes is difficult, because it is easy for individuals to ignore. In the early stages of diabetes, individuals feel fine; may be overweight but not obese; and their blood glucose levels are slightly elevated. Their healthcare provider may advise them to increase their exercise, try to lose some weight, and retest the blood glucose levels in 6 to 12 months. However, even though there may not be any noticeable symptoms, Type 2 diabetes may already be starting to affect several major organs, including the heart,

TABLE 10.7 Factors That Increase the Risk of Developing Type 2 Diabetes

Risk Factor	Explanation
Weight	The primary risk factor for Type 2 diabetes is being overweight or obese. Excess fat tissue causes the cells to become resistant to insulin. However, individuals of normal weight may acquire Type 2 diabetes.
Fat Distribution	When there is increased fat accumulation in the abdomen, the risk of Type 2 diabetes increases.
Inactivity	Individuals with low activity levels are at greater risk of Type 2 diabetes. Physical activity controls weight, uses up excess glucose as energy, and makes the cells more sensitive to insulin.
Family History	Risk of developing Type 2 diabetes increases if a parent or sibling has Type 2 diabetes.
Race	Research shows that African Americans, Hispanics, American Indians, and Asian Americans are more likely to develop Type 2 diabetes than are whites.
Age	After age 45, the risk of Type 2 diabetes increases, especially if individuals do not exercise and gain weight.
Pre-Diabetes	Pre-diabetes is a state where a person's blood sugar is elevated, but not high enough for diabetes and left untreated. If left untreated, pre-diabetes may progress to Type 2 diabetes.
Gestational Diabetes	Gestational diabetes is a state where a pregnant woman experiences insulin and blood sugar problems during pregnancy. If gestational diabetes occurs in pregnancy or if the baby weighs more than 9 pounds at birth, the mother is at risk of developing Type 2 diabetes later in life.
Polycystic Ovary Syndrome	Women with a diagnosis of polycystic ovary syndrome (PCOS) are at increased risk of developing Types 2 diabetes.

Adapted from: The Mayo Clinic (2014). Disease and Conditions: Type 2 Diabetes Risk Factors. Retrieved September 14, 2015, from www.mayoclinic.org/disease-conditions/type-2-diabetes/basics/risk-factors/con-20031902. Last updated July 24, 2014. By permission of Mayo Foundation for Medical Education and Research. All rights reserved.[20]

blood vessels, nerves, eyes, and kidneys. Long-term organ damage causes disability and multiple other medical conditions.

By the time individuals are diagnosed with Type 2 diabetes, they may have gained additional weight due poor nutrition and inability to exercise and are starting to experience organ changes or damage, such as poor circulation in their lower legs and decreased vision. It is essential for individuals at risk of developing Type 2 diabetes to learn about diabetes and strive to control their blood glucose levels to prevent further organ damages and complications.

Respiratory Diseases

Two respiratory diseases are discussed in this section: asthma and chronic obstructive pulmonary disease (COPD). First, asthma is a common chronic condition that affects approximately 8%–10% of Americans.[21] Asthma is the leading cause of missed workdays and is responsible for 1.5 million emergency department visits annually, with numbers increasing.[21] Asthma is the chronic inflammation of the bronchial airway, causing it to narrow in response to various stimuli. This narrowing causes spasms, thus making it difficult for the individual to inhale. There are two types of asthma. Allergic asthma is triggered by inhaling allergens such as dust mites, pet dander, pollens, and mold. Non-allergic asthma is triggered by other factors, such as anxiety, stress, exercise, cold air, dry air, hyperventilation, smoke, or other irritants. In non-allergic asthma, the immune system is not involved in the reaction, as with allergic reaction. However, many of the symptoms of allergic and non-allergic asthma are the same (coughing, wheezing, shortness of breath or rapid breathing, chest tightness).

Treatment of asthma is linked to prevention and control. Individuals learn to recognize and control the triggers of their asthma flare-ups. For example, if cigarette smoke and pet dander cause asthma flare-ups, it is important to avoid such triggers. When the triggers are not avoidable (e.g., cold air, dry air, pollen), then control is needed with the use of preventive, long-term medications to reduce inflammation in the airways. For immediate symptoms, individuals use a quick-relief inhaler, such as albuterol, to reduce symptoms.[22]

Second, COPD is a progressive disease that makes it more and more difficult to breath. COPD begins with chronic bronchitis and inflammation and swelling of the bronchial tubes, which causes a narrowing and obstruction with symptoms of an unresolved cough. The next stage is emphysema and COPD with chronic shortness of breath. As the symptoms gradually become worse, individuals begin to avoid certain activities. Eventually, shortness of breath begins to interfere with all daily tasks, including resting. Other symptoms include chest pain, clubbing of the fingers and toes (thickening of the tissue beneath the nail

beds), fatigue, severe shortness of breath, blue or gray lips and fingernails upon exertion, and loss of mental alertness.[23]

The main cause of COPD is long-term exposure to substances that irritate and damage the lungs. Cigarette smoking is the leading cause of COPD, but other contributors include air pollution, chemical fumes, or dust. As symptoms progress, the cough produces lots of mucus, shortness of breath, wheezing, and chest tightness increases to the point that the individual has limited mobility and requires continuous supplemental oxygen. COPD is diagnosed with lung function tests, radiology imaging tests, and blood tests. There is no cure for COPD. Treatment objectives include slowing the accelerated decline in lung function, relieving symptoms associated with shortness of breath and cough, improving daily lung function, decreasing exacerbations, and improving quality of life, usually with medication and oxygen therapy. In contrast to asthma, the airflow reduction does not improve significantly with the administration of medication. This is due to permanent lung damage. If the individual smokes, COPD treatment begins with smoking cessation.[24, 25]

Arthritis

Arthritis is the leading causes of disability in the United States. Arthritis is defined as "arthr" = joint and "itis" = inflammation, so arthritis is a form of joint disorder that involves inflammation

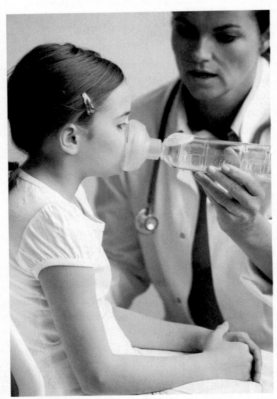

© Creatas Images/Thinkstock

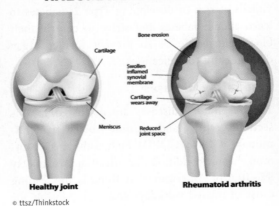

© ttsz/Thinkstock

TABLE 10.8 Common Types of Arthritis

Name	Description
Osteoarthritis	Osteoarthritis is the most common form of arthritis. Risk factors for osteoarthritis include being overweight, aging, and joint injuries. It causes pain, swelling, and reduced motion of the joints. Osteoarthritis breaks down the cartilage that covers the ends of the bones. When the cartilage is decreased, the bones rub together and cause pain and permanent damage. Treatment includes exercise, medicines, and surgery.[27]
Rheumatoid Arthritis (RA)	RA is a disease in which the immune system attacks the linings of the joints, which results in joint pain, stiffness, swelling, and destruction. The symptoms occur during flare-ups and then resolve after a period of time. The cause of RA is unknown, but research shows a possible genetic link. RA lasts many years and is treated with medications.[28]
Systemic Lupus Erythematosus (SLE) or Lupus	Systemic lupus erythematosus (SLE) is an autoimmune disease that attacks healthy tissue (e.g., skin, joints, kidneys, brain, other organs). The cause is unknown. SLE is more common among women, African Americans, and Asians. The main symptoms are joint pain and swelling. Other symptoms include fatigue, fever with no other cause, malaise (flu-like symptoms), hair loss, mouth sores, sensitivity to sunlight, skin rash, and swollen lymph nodes. SLE attacks most organs, including the brain and nervous system (headaches, seizures, vision problems, personality changes), digestive tract (abdominal pain, nausea, vomiting), heart (arrhythmias), lungs (coughing and difficulty breathing), skin (patchy skin color), and kidneys (weight gain due to fluid retention and end-stage renal disease).[29]
Fibromyalgia	Fibromyalgia is a disorder characterized by widespread musculoskeletal pain accompanied by fatigue, sleep, memory, and mood issues. Fibromyalgia may begin after physical trauma, surgery, infection, significant psychological stress, or be a gradual process over time. Women are much more likely to develop fibromyalgia. Symptoms include tension headaches, temporomandibular joint (TMJ) disorders, irritable bowel syndrome, anxiety, and depression. There is no cure for fibromyalgia, but treatment involves medications to control symptoms, exercise, and relaxation and stress-reduction techniques.[30]
Gout	Gout is a complex form of arthritis. It is more common among men. Symptoms include a sudden, severe attack of pain, and redness and tenderness in joints. Often, the big toe is affected, having intense pain, feeling hot, being swollen, and experiencing extreme tenderness. Gout is managed with medications, and there is risk for recurrence.[31]

of one or more joints. Many forms of arthritis affect the joints, including osteoarthritis, rheumatoid arthritis, lupus, fibromyalgia, and gout. See **Table 10.8**. The common symptoms are pain, aching, stiffness, and swelling in or around the joints. Arthritis may occur at any age, but it is more common among adults ages 65 years or older. Because it is more common among adults who are obese, it is estimated that 60% of people who are obese will develop osteoarthritis.[26] Arthritis limits the activities of individuals, such as preventing them from being able to climb stairs or walk more than short distances. Approximately 1 of 3 working adults (18–65 years) with arthritis has limitations due to the type and amount of work they can perform or perhaps whether they can work at all.[26]

Arthritis Management and Control

Individuals with a diagnosis of arthritis learn to manage and control their symptoms, because there are limited treatment options. The management and control of symptoms include self-management, education interventions, maintaining physical activities (e.g., walking, bicycling, swimming), maintaining a healthy weight to protect joints and prevent joint damage, and communicating with healthcare providers on a regular basis to improve quality of life.[32]

Summary

This chapter introduced noncommunicable diseases. Unlike infectious diseases that are caused by an organism, such as bacteria, viruses, fungi, or parasites, noncommunicable disease are not spread from person to person. After a brief description of the discipline of epidemiology, the chapter discussed the various types of important noncommunicable diseases, including cardiovascular disease, cancer, diabetes, respiratory diseases such as asthma and chronic obstructive pulmonary disease (COPD), and arthritis. Most noncommunicable diseases are associated with poor lifestyle and behavioral choices, such as obesity, poor nutrition, tobacco use, and lack of sufficient exercise. Other noncommunicable diseases are linked to genetic risk factors. For each noncommunicable disease, the chapter provided a description of the causes, symptoms, and treatment.

Case Study

Roger Jones, age 52, is a black male, is married to Elaine, and they have two male children, ages 9 and 13. Roger works as a computer software engineer and has excellent health insurance for himself and his family through his employer. Elaine, age 48, is an accountant and heads the billing department of a local law firm. Both Roger and Elaine are involved with their children's sport activities. Due to their full-time employment and parenting responsibilities, they have limited time for exercise and consistently cooking healthy meals. Roger and Elaine have never smoked. Both have a family history of heart disease and diabetes.

Last weekend, Roger was coaching his older son's soccer game. As he was running up and down

the field, he noticed some chest pain. Because it went away on the drive home, he did not think much about the pain. On Monday, Roger noticed some shortness of breath while walking up a flight of stairs at work. This concerned him, so he called his healthcare provider and requested an appointment for the following week because his calendar was busy for the next few days. The office medical assistant transferred his phone call to Cindy, the advanced registered nurse practitioner (ARNP). Cindy told Roger that he needed to come to the office that afternoon.

Roger called Elaine and told her the news. They left work and met at their healthcare provider for the 3:00 p.m. appointment. The medical assistant weighed Roger. He was about 30 pounds overweight. His blood pressure (138/88) and pulse (90) were slightly elevated. Roger does not take any prescription medications at this time, but he does take an over-the-counter (OTC) multivitamin each day. The physician, Dr. Sanchez, examined Roger. Because Roger had been going to this medical practice for the past 10 years, Dr. Sanchez was familiar with Roger's family history of heart disease and diabetes. He had Cindy run an electrocardiogram (ECG) to determine a possible cause of Roger's chest pain. The ECG determines if there are problems with the heart, including electrical activity problems, previous AMIs, pericarditis (inflammation of the sac surrounding the heart), or angina (chest pain caused by reduced blood flow to the heart muscle).[33]

After the ECG, Dr. Sanchez met with Roger and Elaine. He said that there were a few signs of heart disease showing on the ECG. While they were talking, Cindy made an appointment for

Roger to see a cardiologist, Dr. Cintron, the following day. When she came in the room, Roger said that he could not make the appointment tomorrow morning due to a quarterly meeting at work. Dr. Sanchez explained that Roger's health needed to be the top priority in his life and that Roger had to miss the morning meeting. Elaine agreed and said that she would take off for the appointment also. Dr. Sanchez ordered some blood work to be drawn prior to Roger's leaving the office. Cindy drew five tubes of blood and called the lab for a late pickup with overnight processing. The lab would enter the results into the electronic medical record prior to 8:00 a.m., so the cardiologist could review the results during Roger's morning appointment.

Finally, Dr. Sanchez introduced Roger and Elaine to the newest member of his office staff. Sharon, the health navigation professional, had been hired a few weeks to assist Cindy and Dr. Sanchez with patient education, insurance referrals, and case management. Sharon handed Roger the health navigation professional brochure and told them that if and when they had any further questions, she would be available to research and find the answers. Sharon suggested that before leaving the office, Roger and Elaine could schedule an appointment with her in a few days to go over their immediate questions. Sharon explained they would likely have more questions after visiting Dr. Cintron.

Questions

1. What questions (and answers) would you expect Roger and Elaine to have after their appointment with Dr. Cintron?
2. What are some of the labs that Dr. Sanchez ordered prior to Roger's leaving the office? *Note:* Keep in mind that Roger was not fasting at the time the labs were drawn.
3. Name at least three kinds of heart disease that Roger might have at this time, because the symptoms seem to be intermittent.
4. What questions might Elaine have when they meet with Sharon?
5. Name at least three topics that Sharon should cover in the first meeting with Roger and Elaine after answering their immediate questions and concerns.

References

1. U.S. Department of State. *Infectious and chronic disease.* Retrieved September 14, 2015, from http://www.state.gov/e/oes/intlhealthbiodefense/id.
2. World Health Organization. *Noncommunicable diseases.* Retrieved September 14, 2015, from http://www.who.int/topics/noncommunicable_diseases/en.
3. U.S. Department of Veteran's Affairs. *Public health: Epidemiology.* Retrieved October 14, 2015, from http://www.publichealth.va.gov/epidemiology/index.asp.
4. Porta, M. S., Greenland, S., Hernan, M., dos Santos, Silva I., & Last, J. M. (2014). A Dictionary of Epidemiology. Oxford, England: Oxford University Press.
5. Centers for Disease Control and Prevention. *FastStats: Death and mortality.* Retrieved September 14, 2015, from http://www.cdc.gov/nchs/fastats/deaths.htm; last updated August 21, 2015.
6. Centers for Disease Control and Prevention. *Leading causes of death.* Retrieved September 14, 2015, from http://www.cdc.gov/nchs/fastats/leading-causes-of-death.htm; last updated August 21, 2015.
7. National Library of Medicine. *NHLBI health topics: Heart failure.* Retrieved September 14, 2015, from http://www.ncbi.nlm.nih.gov/pubmedhealth/PMH0063056.
8. National Library of Medicine. *Medical Encyclopedia: Arrhythmias.* Retrieved September 14, 2015, from http://www.nlm.nih.gov/medlineplus/ency/article/001101.htm; last updated May 13, 2014.
9. The Mayo Clinic. *Diseases and conditions: Atrial fibrillation.* Retrieved September 14, 2015, from http://www.mayoclinic.org/diseases-conditions/atrial-fibrillation/basics/definition/CON-20027014; last updated May 18, 2015.
10. National Library of Medicine. *NHLBI health Topics: Heart attack.* Retrieved September 14, 2015, from: http://www.ncbi.nlm.nih.gov/pubmedhealth/PMH0062989; last updated June 11, 2014.
11. National Cancer Institute. *What is cancer?* Retrieved September 14, 2015, from http://www.cancer.gov/about-cancer/what-is-cancer; last updated February 9, 2015.
12. Anand, P., Kunnumakara, A. B., Sundaram, C., Karikumar, K. B., Tharakan, S. T., Lai, O. S., Sung, B., & Aggarwal, B. B. (2008). Cancer is a preventable disease that requires major lifestyle changes. *Pharmaceutical Research, 25*(9), 2097–2116.
13. American Cancer Society. *Brain and spinal cord tumors in adults.* Retrieved September 14, 2015, from http://www.cancer.org/cancer/braincnstumorsinadults/detailedguide/brain-and-spinal-cord-tumors-in-adults-types-of-brain-tumors; last updated January 7, 2014.

14. National Cancer Institute. *Cancer staging.* Retrieved September 14, 2015, from http://www.cancer.gov/about-cancer/diagnosis-staging/staging/staging-fact-sheet; last updated January 6, 2015.

15. National Cancer Institute. *Cancer staging.* Retrieved October 4, 2015, from http://www.cancer.gov/about-cancer/diagnosis-staging/staging/staging-fact-sheet; last updated January 16, 2015.

16. National Cancer Institute. *Questions to ask your doctor about treatment.* Retrieved September 14, 2015, from http://www.cancer.gov/about-cancer/treatment/questions; last updated February 14, 2012.

17. The Mayo Clinic. *Diseases and conditions: Type 2 diabetes symptoms.* Retrieved September 14, 2015, from http://www.mayoclinic.org/diseases-conditions/type-2-diabetes/basics/symptoms/con-20031902; last updated July 24, 2014.

18. The Mayo Clinic. *Diseases and conditions: Type 2 diabetes complications.* Retrieved September 14, 2015, from http://www.mayoclinic.org/diseases-conditions/type-2-diabetes/basics/complications/con-20031902; last updated July 24, 2015.

19. Hess-Fischl, A. *What is insulin?* Retrieved September 14, 2015, from http://www.endocrineweb.com/conditions/type-1-diabetes/what-insulin.

20. The Mayo Clinic. *Diseases and conditions: Type 2 diabetes risk factors.* Retrieved September 14, 2015, from http://www.mayoclinic.org/diseases-conditions/type-2-diabetes/basics/risk-factors/con-20031902; last updated July 24, 2014.

21. American Lung Association. *Lung health & diseases: Asthma.* Retrieved October 4, 2015, from http://www.lung.org/lung-health-and-diseases/lung-disease-lookup/asthma.

22. The Mayo Clinic. *Diseases and conditions: Asthma, treatments and drugs.* Retrieved October 4, 2015, from http://www.mayoclinic.org/diseases-conditions/asthma/basics/treatment/con-20026992; last updated February 16, 2014.

23. The Mayo Clinic. *Diseases and conditions: Emphysema symptoms.* Retrieved September 14, 2015, from http://www.mayoclinic.org/diseases-conditions/emphysema/basics/symptoms/CON-20014218; last updated April 4, 2015.

24. National Library of Medicine. *Health A–Z: Chronic obstructive pulmonary disease (COPD).* Retrieved September 14, 2015, from http://www.ncbi.nlm.nih.gov/pubmedhealth/PMHT0022631.

25. National Library of Medicine. *MedlinePlus: COPD.* Retrieved September 14, 2015, from https://www.nlm.nih.gov/medlineplus/copd.html.

26. Centers for Disease Control and Prevention. *Arthritis in general.* Retrieved October 4, 2015, from http://www.cdc.gov/arthritis/basics/general.htm; last updated November 13, 2014.

27. National Library of Medicine. *MedlinePlus: Osteoarthritis.* Retrieved September 14, 2015, from https://www.nlm.nih.gov/medlineplus/osteoarthritis.html.

28. National Library of Medicine. *Health A–Z: Rheumatoid arthritis (RA).* Retrieved September 14, 2015, from http://www.ncbi.nlm.nih.gov/pubmedhealth/PMHT0024678.

29. National Library of Medicine. *MedlinePlus: Systemic lupus erythematosus.* Retrieved September 14, 2015, from https://www.nlm.nih.gov/medlineplus/ency/article/000435.htm.

30. The Mayo Clinic. *Diseases and conditions: Fibromyalgia.* Retrieved September 14, 2015, from http://www.mayoclinic.org/diseases-conditions/fibromyalgia/basics/definition/CON-20019243; last updated February 20, 2014.

31. The Mayo Clinic. *Diseases and conditions: Gout definition.* Retrieved September 14, 2015, from http://www.mayoclinic.org/diseases-conditions/gout/basics/definition/CON-20019400; last updated November 25, 2014.

32. Centers for Disease Control and Prevention. *Arthritis: Self-management education.* Retrieved September 14, 2015, from http://www.cdc.gov/arthritis/interventions/self_manage.htm.

33. WedMD. *Heart Disease Health Center: Electrocardiogram.* Retrieved September 14, 2015, from http://www.webmd.com/heart-disease/electrocardiogram.

CHAPTER 11

Health-Related Quality of Life (HRQOL) and End-of-Life Planning and Decisions

LEARNING OBJECTIVES

By the end of the chapter, students will be able to:

- Define and discuss the impact of health-related quality of life (HRQOL)
- Explain patient rights and responsibilities and their impact
- Describe various end-of-life issues

CHAPTER OVERVIEW

This chapter covers the topics of quality of life and end-of-life planning and decision making. The first section explores various aspects of quality of life, including the definition, global rankings, assessment of stress, and considerations for elderly services and care. The second section introduces the concept of patients' rights and responsibilities and related terms. The third section involves the complex issue of end-of-life planning and decisions, including landmark end-of-life legal cases, legal documents, and termination of medical treatment. This section concludes with a discussion of end-of-life care options ranging from palliative care and pain management through hospice care.

QUALITY OF LIFE

Quality of life, a concept often used in relation to health and well-being, is defined in various ways: (a) the degree of satisfaction regarding a particular style of life; (b) general well-being, including mental status, stress level, sexual function, and self-perceived health status; (c) ability to function at a usual level of activity without, or with minimal, compromise of routine activities; (d) overall enjoyment of life, sense of well-being, freedom from disease; and (e) ability to pursue daily activities.[1]

In 1980, the Centers for Disease Control and Prevention (CDC) initiated the concept of health-related quality of life (HRQOL).[2] HRQOL includes all of the aspects of overall quality of life that affect physical and mental health. For example, on the individual level, physical and mental health perceptions include health risks and conditions, functional status, social support, and socioeconomic status. The community level includes resources, conditions, policies, and practices that influence a population's health perceptions and functional status. HRQOL measures demonstrate scientifically the impact of health on quality of life beyond the status of only disease and wellness.[2]

In 2013, the Organization for Economic Cooperation and Development (OECD), an international economic organization, developed the Better Life Index. This index explored the quality of life in member countries by using 11 categories. The categories included income, housing, jobs, community, education, environment, civic engagement, health, life satisfaction, safety, and work–life

TABLE 11.1 2013 Quality of Life Ranking of Top 30 Countries

Rank	Country or Territory	Score (out of 10)	Rank	Country or Territory	Score (out of 10)	Rank	Country or Territory	Score (out of 10)
1	Switzerland	8.22	11	Finland	7.76	21	Italy	7.21
2	Australia	8.12	12	Ireland	7.74	22	Kuwait	7.18
3	Norway	8.09	13	Austria	7.73	23	Chile	7.10
4	Sweden	8.02	14	Taiwan	7.67	24	Cyprus	7.10
5	Denmark	8.01	15	Belgium	7.51	25	Japan	7.08
6	Singapore	8.00	16	Germany	7.38	26	France	7.04
7	New Zealand	7.95	17	United States	7.38	27	United Kingdom	7.01
8	Netherlands	7.94	18	United Arab Emirates	7.33	28	Czech Republic	6.96
9	Canada	7.81	19	South Korea	7.25	29	Spain	6.96
10	Hong Kong	7.80	20	Israel	7.23	30	Costa Rica	6.92

Data from: Organization of Economic Cooperation and Development (2014). How's Life?: Measuring Well-Being. Paris, France: OECD Publishing. Available at: http://www.oecdbetterlifeindex.org/media/bli/documents/how_life-2015-sum-en.pdf.

balance. The report shows that even the wealthy countries have the opportunities to improve their quality of life or well-being.[3] Given this information, review **Table 11.1** to see where the United States ranks on the topic of quality of life. The higher the score, the higher the quality of life.

Now, let us explore some of the HRQOL details reported by the CDC regarding the U.S. population. See **Table 11.2**.

Table 11.2 shows the type and age of U.S. populations that experience lower degrees of health-related quality of life, but it does not illustrate specifically on a day-to-day basis what factors are causing their quality of life to diminish. For this answer, look at **Table 11.3**. Take a few minutes to rate your own personal life stress inventory to determine what is causing stress in your own life. Also explore in your own life the types of stress

TABLE 11.2 U.S. Health-Related Quality of Life

Americans say they feel unhealthy (physically or mentally) about 6 days per month.

Approximately one-third of Americans say they suffer from some mental or emotional problem every month—including 10% who say their mental health was not good for 14 or more days a month.

Younger American adults, ages 18–24 years, suffer the most mental health distress.

Older adults suffer the most poor physical health and activity limitation.

Adults with the lowest income or education report more unhealthy days than those with higher income or education.

Native Americans and Alaska Natives report the highest levels of unhealthy days among American race/ethnic groups.

Americans with noncommunicable diseases or disabilities report more unhealthy days than those without these diseases or disabilities.

Centers for Disease Control and Prevention (2011). Health-Related Quality of Life (HRQOL): Key Findings. Available at: http://www .cdc.gov/hrqol/key_findings.htm. Last updated on March 15, 2011. Accessed on October 30, 2015.

© michaeljung/iStockphoto

that are changeable and the types of stress that are not changeable. Finally, think about what activities you may be able to incorporate into your daily routine to decrease your own personal stress (e.g., increase exercise, eat healthy foods, stop smoking, find enjoyment, spend more time outside).

Now that you have identified your personal level of stress, let's explore how stress impacts health and quality of life. First, stress may be positive or negative. Positive stress motivates individuals to improve their performance (e.g., piano recital, final

TABLE 11.3 The Holmes-Rahe Life Stress Inventory (Social Readjustment Rating Scale)

Life Event	Mean Value
1. Death of spouse	100
2. Divorce	73
3. Marital separation from mate	65
4. Detention in jail or other institution	63
5. Death of a close family member	63
6. Major personal injury or illness	53
7. Marriage	50
8. Being fired at work	47
9. Marital reconciliation with mate	45
10. Retirement from work	45
11. Major change in the health or behavior of a family member	44
12. Pregnancy	40
13. Sexual difficulties	39
14. Gaining a new family member (e.g., birth, adoption, older adult moving in)	39
15. Major business readjustment	39
16. Major change in financial state (e.g., either a lot worse or better off than usual)	38
17. Death of a close friend	37
18. Changing to a different line of work	36
19. Major change in the number of arguments w/spouse (e.g., either a lot more or a lot less than usual regarding child rearing, personal habits)	35
20. Taking on a mortgage (for home, business)	31
21. Foreclosure on a mortgage or loan	30
22. Major change in responsibilities at work (e.g., promotion, demotion)	29
23. Son or daughter leaving home (marriage, attending college, joined military)	29
24. In-law troubles	29

Life Event	Mean Value
25. Outstanding personal achievement	28
26. Spouse beginning or ceasing work outside the home	26
27. Beginning or ceasing formal schooling	26
28. Major change in living condition (e.g., new home, remodeling, deterioration of neighborhood or home)	25
29. Revision of personal habits (dress manners, associations, quitting smoking)	24
30. Troubles with the boss	23
31. Major changes in working hours or conditions	20
32. Changes in residence	20
33. Changing to a new school	20
34. Major change in usual type and/or amount of recreation	19
35. Major change in church activity (e.g., a lot more or less than usual)	19
36. Major change in social activities (e.g., clubs, movies, visiting)	18
37. Taking on a loan (e.g., car, TV, freezer)	17
38. Major change in sleeping habits (a lot more or a lot less than usual)	16
39. Major change in number of family get-togethers (e.g., birth or adoption of children, wedding, reunion, graduation)	15
40. Major change in eating habits (a lot more or less food intake, or very different meal hours or surroundings)	15
41. Vacation	13
42. Major holidays	12
43. Minor violations of the law (e.g., traffic tickets, jaywalking, disturbing the peace)	11

Find Your Score	
Less than 150 points	Low amount of life changes and low susceptibility to stress-induced health breakdown
150 to 300 points	About a 50% chance of a major health breakdown in the next two years
300 or more points	Raises the odds to about 80% for a major health breakdown in the next two years

Data from The American Institute of Stress (2015). Holmes-Rahe Stress Inventory. Available at: http://www.stress.org/holmes-rahe-stress-inventory/; Accessed on October 30, 2015.

exam, athletic competition), while negative stress (e.g., fight with spouse or supervisor, traffic, constant noise, being late) diminishes an individual's energy and overall motivation. Negative stress may be short term (acute) or long term (chronic). Multiple studies have shown that sudden, intense stress, such as intense anger, may trigger heart attacks, arrhythmias, and even sudden death. Although these health outcomes happen to individuals who already have heart disease, many individuals are unaware of their health condition until the acute stress causes the medical diagnosis (e.g., heart attack).[6]

© andresr/istockphoto

© Pixsooz/istockphoto

On the other hand, long-term negative stress leads to chronic health conditions that influence quality of life. In some situations, the individual has limited control over the chronic stress due to life circumstances (e.g., poverty, poor air quality and noise pollution, lack of transportation or access to health care, unemployment, violence). However, if the individual is able to make a positive change in one aspect of his or her life situation, it may become less difficult to tackle other negative circumstances. Let us look at three possible scenarios of chronic stress and possible solutions.

Family

Situation: A family of four lives in a poor neighborhood. They experience chronic stress due to limited green space and safe outdoor space, excessive noise, lack of medical and transportation services, limited school choices, limited employment opportunities, and inadequate grocery stores.

Possible Solution: By going to a social service office, the parents learned about available, but limited, subsidized housing and services in a more desirable neighborhood. Although it is not a simple process and the waiting lists are long, the first step was investigating what was needed—improved housing—to change their life circumstances. The second step was making an appointment.

Caregiver

Situation: An elderly couple has lived in the same house for the past 38 years. Over the past 2 years, the wife has become a primary caregiver for her frail husband living with chronic obstructive pulmonary disease. She drives only for shopping and medical appointments. She no longer attends church. He suffers from chronic stress because the house has fallen into disrepair, he is incapable of fixing it, and has no money to pay for repairs. They have no children.

Possible Solution: At her husband's last medical appointment, she asked the nurse to take her blood pressure as a way to ask for help. When she saw the elevated numbers, she began to cry. Caregiving caused chronic stress and a cascade of health issues for her. The nurse referred the couple to the community elder care agency. Over time, they sold their home and moved into a subsidized retirement apartment complex. Her husband received home health services and she joined a few social groups. They both benefited from less stress.

Worker

Situation: A long-term employee falls into a cycle of negative attitudes about her work environment due to siding with coworkers who choose to complain about work issues such as scheduling, work load, lack of support, and poor equipment. When she begins to experience symptoms of chronic stress, her ability to maintain daily routines is interrupted. Her healthcare provider explains that the common symptoms of chronic stress are fatigue, inability to concentrate, irritability, and development of poor lifestyle habits, such as overeating, smoking, substance abuse, depression, headaches, lack of exercise, and low social support.[7]

Possible Solution: After agreeing to join a few coworkers for dinner, she realizes that these individuals with a positive attitude experience more enjoyment at work. She accepts an invitation to go to a free aerobic exercise class from a woman in this group. Over time, she recognizes how negativity breeds more negativity and appreciates the value of surrounding herself with positive and happy individuals. Her symptoms of chronic stress diminish, her habitual negative response is redirected into affirmative behavior, and the overall work environment improves.

As these examples illustrate, there are numerous causes of chronic stress even without a medical diagnosis. Also, how individuals respond to chronic stress varies by age, gender, culture, circumstances, and many other factors. However, for the purpose of this chapter, it is also important to explore how individuals living with a serious medical diagnosis cope with chronic stress. Although individuals respond to their diagnoses differently, there are some common experiences that affect the overall quality of life. For example, as a health navigation professional, it may be useful to ask questions about their quality of life. This type of conversation encourages the individuals and their caregivers to discuss how they are coping or are not coping with their symptoms of chronic stress.[8] This type of discussion allows

for improved and open communication among the individual, caregivers, family members, and healthcare providers. See **Table 11.4**.

So far this section has provided information about the quality of life of all age groups, but now the focus changes to the elderly. Because health navigation professionals are likely to work with the elderly, it is important to realize how their perception of quality of life changes over time. For example, the elderly may prefer a higher level of comfort rather than a longer life. Because many elderly adults are unable to advocate for their own care or have no family members or friends to advocate on their behalf, it is important for health navigation professionals to consider the special needs of the elderly when working with this population. See **Box 11.1**. The indicators for Assessing Care of Vulnerable Elders (ACOVE) provide a list of topics to explore when assessing

TABLE 11.4 Quality of Life Questions

What is your quality of life? What needs to change to improve your quality of life?
Are you able to take care of the daily activities of life (e.g., dressing, bathing, toileting, preparing food, eating, walking)? Do you have enough food in your home?
What is your level of pain? How would you describe your pain? Have you discussed your pain with your healthcare provider?
What about your level of fatigue? What have you tried to reduce your fatigue, such as short rest breaks, moderate exercise?
What is your level of stress? What causes your stress, such as financial, emotional, employment, or relationship issues? How would you describe your stress (e.g., pain, anxiety, panic, fear, depression)? What have you tried to reduce your stress (e.g., meditation, yoga, taichi, guided imagery, improved communication)? Have you discussed the cause of your stress with your healthcare provider and/or family?

© Purestock/Thinkstock

Who are the individuals in your life who provide physical, emotional, and spiritual support?
Do you feel connected to the important individuals in your life? Are there individuals whom you can contact if you need immediate or long-term assistance?
How often do you leave your home and go outside? Do you feel isolated?

BOX 11.1 Indicators for Assessing Care of Vulnerable Elders (ACOVE)

Appropriate use of medications	Hypertension
Chronic pain	Malnutrition
Continuity and coordination of care	Osteoarthritis
Dementia	Osteoporosis
Depression	Pneumonia
Diabetes complications	Pressure ulcers
End-of-life care	Preventive care
Falls and mobility problems	Stroke
Hearing loss	Urinary incontinence
Heart disease	Visual impairment
Hospital care	

Data from: The Rand Corporation (2004). Developing Quality of Care Indicators for the Vulnerable Elderly: The ALCOVE project. Available at: http://www.rand.org/pubs/research_briefs/RB4545-1/index1.html. Accessed on October 30, 2015.

the quality of care for the vulnerable elderly population. The ACOVE topics are not meant to evaluate individual healthcare providers, but rather to approach the systemic level of overall health care

provided to vulnerable elders by their healthcare plans or medical groups and thus could be used to identify areas in need of improvement.[9]

Finally, when considering quality of life for the elderly population, it is useful for health navigation professionals to explore the advantages and disadvantages for their clients and family members on the preferred location in which they will reside. Several residential options are available for the elderly, including (a) staying in their own home, also called *aging in place*; (b) living with family members or friends; (c) residing at a continuing care retirement community that offers a continuum of care from independent living through nursing care and end-of-life decisions; or (d) living in an assisted-living facility. The following section explores the advantages and disadvantages of these four options for the elderly. The case study is used to compare the same scenario in all four options. See **Box 11.2**.

a. *Aging in Place*: Mary would like to continue to reside in her own home. The American Association of Retired Persons (AARP) defines the phrase "aging in place" as the ability to live in one's own home and community safely, independently, and comfortably, regardless of age, income, or ability level.[10]

BOX 11.2 Case Study of Mary and James

Mary, age 75, and James, age 78, had been married for 52 years. Mary retired from the county school district after teaching Fourth Grade for many years, and James retired after being a welder and mechanic in the automotive industry for 32 years. They both have an adequate pension in addition to receiving their Social Security and Medicare benefits. They live in a suburb of a large city in the Midwest. Because Mary does not like to drive on the icy roads and James does most of the driving, they have downsized to one car. They are in good physical shape and go to the community recreational center 3 days per week for aerobics and swimming. Besides the exercise, it serves as a social gathering place. Mary and James volunteer at the community hospital 2 afternoons a week. Because they own their home and are in excellent health, they have never considered any option besides aging in their home. For the past 35 years, they have lived in the same home, where they raised their two children: Sarah and Wayne. Sarah, age 40, lives in San Diego, California, with her husband, Bill, and three children. She is employed as a tax accountant for a large university, and Bill is a general contractor for a land developer. Wayne, age 44, lives about 200 miles north of Mary and James. He is married to Susan, and they have two children. Wayne and Susan struggle with finances. Because Wayne and Susan had worked in the same vehicle manufacturing plant, they both lost their jobs when the factory closed. Wayne worked as a mechanical engineer to maintain the assembly

(continued)

line, and Susan worked in the finance department. They are living off of their savings while they search for employment in surroundings cities. They are willing to relocate but prefer not to sell their home.

A few months ago, James slipped on some ice in the driveway and fractured his hip. A few days after surgery, James was discharged from the hospital to home via a home health transportation service. The health navigation professional had arranged for in-home physical therapy and other home health equipment. The first week after discharge, Mary and James were pleased with his progress, but everything soon changed. Soon after dinner, James complained of a headache and asked Mary to help him get back into bed. She gave him two Tylenol and took his temperature. He did not have a fever, but within 30 minutes he was slurring his speech. When the ambulance arrived, James was unconscious but still breathing. James was admitted to the intensive care unit and died from a massive stroke 3 days after admission. Mary's life was shattered. After James' funeral, Mary realized that she needed help making decisions regarding where she will live for the remaining years of her life.

Although aging in place is considered to be the ideal, AARP recommends that individuals explore eight domains that are needed to age successfully in a community: (1) outdoor space and buildings—safe parks and sidewalks; (2) transportation—reducing the need to drive, safe and convenient bus routes, improved bus shelters and benches; (3) housing—intergenerational housing communities, affordable housing, small housing with low maintenance; (4) social participation—intellectual stimulation for older residents (e.g., book clubs, gardening, walking, eating meals with others); (5) respect and social inclusion—volunteering based on skills and experience from their lifetime; (6) civic engagement and employment—remaining employed as desired; cultural lifelong learning opportunities; (7) communication and information—access to social services such as Meals On Wheels, computer classes, and money management; and (8) community and healthcare services.[11] Mary must take into consideration how important these eight domains are to her when making a decision about where she will live in the future. See **Box 11.3**.

b. *Living with Family or Friends*: If Mary decides to move to California to live with her daughter, son-in-law, and grandchildren, she would need to evaluate the advantages and disadvantages of doing so. See **Box 11.4**.
c. *Continuing Care Retirement Communities (CCRCs)*: Mary is not familiar with the

CCRC concept, so she does some investigating. She discovers that there are more than 2000 CCRCs in the United States. The primary benefit of the CCRC is that it allows people to age in one community even if they need additional healthcare services over time.[12,13] Additionally, CCRCs provide a general sense of community to those who live there. CCRCs offer three levels of care:

1. *Independent Living*: Residents live in a villa or an apartment on the CCRC campus and have access to amenities including weekly laundry and housekeeping services; exercise classes and personal training; beauty and barber shop services; convenience store for small items; pharmacy services and walk-in non-urgent medical clinic a few hours per week; art, music, and cultural events within CCRC and the local community; group (e.g., shopping, special events) and individualized (e.g., medical appointments, airport shuttle) transportation; and meal services (e.g., menu choices served in the dining room or ala carte food services).
2. *Assisted Living*: Residents continue to live in a villa or an apartment on the CCRC campus, but they receive assistance with daily tasks such as bathing and dressing.

BOX 11.3 Mary's Decision: Eight Domains of Aging in Place

Outdoor Space and Buildings	Excellent	Mary lives in a beautiful, safe suburb with sidewalks, parks, and recreation centers.
Transportation	Poor	Mary's suburb offers poor and limited public transportation.
Housing	Good	Mary owns her home, but it is 35 years old and in need of constant repair, including more insulation to reduce her electric bills. Safety bars need to be installed in the bathroom.
Social Activity	Good	Mary has friends in the community, but only a few friends drive, so she feels isolated. She does not enjoy cooking for one or eating alone. Her diet is less than optimal.
Social Inclusion	Fair	Mary drives in the daytime during the warm months. She finds that more and more of her friends are moving away or are deceased.
Civic Engagement, Volunteering, Employment	Very Good	Mary volunteers at the hospital and her friend drives. Without James, she has limited interest.
Communication and Information	Good	Mary walks to the local library and recently joined the book club. She has no interest in learning about the computer beyond email.
Community and HealthCare Services	Fair	She is embarrassed to ask for help, because she has lived in the community for 35 years. She goes to her regular physicians, but she tries not to complain about little aches and pains.

3. *Nursing Home–Style Care*: As medically needed, residents move from a villa or an apartment to a medical facility on the CCRC campus to receive 24-hour nursing care. One spouse can remain independently in a villa or an apartment, while the other spouse moves to the medical facility for additional care. The medical facility also offers a memory care center and hospice services. As residents' health needs increase, they transition from one level to the next within the same CCRC community.

The cost of most CCRCs includes a one-time entrance fee and a monthly fee. These costs vary widely depending on several factors: the luxuriousness of the facility, the size and type of housing unit, whether the person enters alone or with a spouse, and how much future care is covered. Fees vary by community. It is essential to review contracts with an attorney. Additionally, residents should plan on a 3%–6% increase in monthly fees each year. CCRCs usually offer various payment plans.[14] Individuals and their families need to research various CCRCs before committing to one. CCRCs are also not located in all areas of the United States. Mary would likely need to relocate from her community to move into a CCRC. Keep in mind, residents buy into a CCRC. If they decide to move out, they are likely to forfeit all or a portion of their buy-in costs. For example, Mary

BOX 11.4 Mary's Decision: Eight Domains of Living with Daughter in San Diego

Outdoor Space and Buildings	Excellent	San Diego suburb offers safe sidewalks, parks, and recreation centers.
Transportation	Poor	San Diego suburbs offer limited public transportation. Mary is also not familiar with using public transportation.
Housing	Good	Sarah's home is large; Mary would be given the guest room and share the bathroom with the teenage grandchildren. Mary would not bring any of her furniture; safety bars need to be installed in bathroom. Mary thinks that she would miss her belongings and her home.
Social Activity	Good	Mary would have to leave her friends; her social activity would be participating in family activities; and she does not know how she will make friends her age. She loves her children, but does not want to intrude. She would enjoy eating breakfast and dinner with the family.
Social Inclusion	Fair	Mary would not take her car to San Diego. She is afraid to drive in strange places and fears getting lost.
Civic Engagement, Volunteering, Employment	Fair	Sarah is willing to find places for Mary to volunteer, but she is not sure about transportation due to the family's busy schedule.
Communication and Information	Fair	Mary does not know the new community and is intimidated about searching for community resources. She is not familiar with how to search for this type of information on the Internet.
Community and HealthCare Services	Fair	Mary does not know where to begin to find a physician. She decides that she will ignore her preventative health wellness visits until some new symptom develops. She does not wish to bother her busy daughter with minor health questions when she feels fine.

buys into a CCRC in San Diego near her daughter. After a few years, her daughter relocates to North Carolina for a career promotion. Mary would likely have to remain in San Diego or forfeit the money that she has already spent. See **Box 11.5**.

d. *Residing in an Assisted-Living Facility*: Mary is familiar with the concept of the assisted-living facility as an intermediate step for the elderly who need more help than they or their families can provide at home, but do not need 24-hour medical care. Generally,

the elderly prefer to remain in their own homes and live independently, because they have visited assisted-living facilities and did not like what they observed. However, as individuals age, independent living requires more services (e.g., home repairs, home healthcare services, transportation). As their health diminishes and the need for caregiving increases, the family is often called into service, when possible. Keep in mind that many elderly individuals do not have family members.

BOX 11.5 Mary's Decision: Eight Domains of Living in a CCRC

Outdoor Space and Buildings	Excellent	CCRC offers safe sidewalks, bike parks, and recreation activities.
Transportation	Excellent	Mary could keep her car or use the transportation offered by the CCRC.
Housing	Excellent	Mary would select the desired size of villa or apartment and bring her own furniture. All safety features and alarms are preinstalled.
Social Activity	Excellent	Mary would have to leave her friends, but she would be surrounded by new friends. She could try new activities, socialize, and eat in the dining room with others as desired.
Social Inclusion	Excellent	Mary could take the CCRC transportation to join friends for social activities and medical appointments without fear of getting lost.
Civic Engagement, Volunteering, Employment	Excellent	Mary could volunteer on the CCRC campus (e.g., library, gift shop, information desk, garden, faith-based groups) as a way of meeting people.
Communication and Information	Excellent	Mary could read the monthly newsletter to learn about activities and clubs.
Community and HealthCare Services	Excellent	Mary could use the physician who staffs the non-urgent walk-in clinic and visit her practice in the local community when more medical services are required. She could ask others for referrals to a dentist and other medical specialties.

Of those with family, the family members have numerous competing demands (e.g., employment, geographical location, parenting children). When the decision is made to have an elderly parent move into a family member's home for the purpose of caregiving support, the pressure increases and begins to strain relationships in families. The financial burden of hiring home healthcare services while family members are employed outside the home may or may not be acceptable. If family members are not able to afford outside home health services, the elderly individual may be isolated and home alone for long periods of time. Also, busy family members may not have time to prepare nutritious meals that meet the dietary needs of the elderly. Finally, a household with children and working parents may not be safe for the elderly due to clutter and lack of safety equipment. If the family determines

© Alija/Thinkstock

that this is the case, then the elderly parent would be less isolated and safer in an assisted-living facility than home alone for the majority of the day. This decision is never easy for the elderly individual or family members.

Each of the four options presented has advantages and disadvantages. The key to determining

BOX 11.6 Student Activity

Discussion Questions

1. As a health navigation professional, how would you assist James and Mary in retirement planning prior to being 70 years of age?
2. If you were the health navigation professional in the hospital where James was admitted prior to his death, what resources would have been useful to Mary?
3. As the health navigation professional, what type of resources do you need to investigate in your community for elderly patients?
4. As a health navigation professional, what questions are you going to ask when you conduct site visits of local assisted-living facilities?
5. As a health navigation professional, how would you go about conducting an Internet search related to what assisted-living facility costs are and are not covered by Medicare and/or Medicaid for elderly residents?

the best choice for each aging individual and his or her family is centered on planning for the future. Waiting until a health crisis occurs drastically limits these options. For example, Mary and James had no plans in place for a health crisis. If they had had a conversation with each other and with their children, they could have determined the pros and cons of each option for their family and financial situation (e.g., geographical location, repairing or selling their own home, downsizing into a small home near Sarah in San Diego, selling their current home, and helping Sarah purchased a larger home with a parent suite). Each family needs to plan ahead or they may be forced to make poor decisions due to lack of planning. For example, what would have happened if James had not died, but incurred severe disabilities from his stroke? Mary would not have been able to care for him at home, so at the time of hospital discharge, she would have to make immediate decisions for his care, such as 24-hour home healthcare services versus limited assisted-living facility choices based merely on the availability of a bed. Each choice has serious advantages and disadvantages for James as well as Mary.

Health navigation professionals have the opportunity to gather the pertinent resource information needed to assist elderly individuals and their families to plan for the future. Without an imminent health crisis forcing decisions, health navigation professionals can help

elderly individuals to plan, budget, visit, and make informed choices about where they choose to live as their health needs increase and greater assistance is needed. See **Box 11.6**.

HEALTHCARE DECISIONS

Now that you have an understanding of how health impacts an individual's quality of life, the chapter moves into a discussion about making healthcare decisions. For a patient to make decisions regarding his or her health care, a trusted partnership must be formed between the individual receiving the health care and the health professional providing the care. Both parties have rights and responsibilities. For example, if the healthcare provider delivers quality health care by examination, diagnosis, treatment, and prescriptions, but the individual refuses to follow the treatment plan, then it is unlikely that the individual will achieve improved quality of life. On the other hand, if the healthcare provider is negligent in providing quality care (e.g., communication, diagnosis, treatment), the individual has a right to complain and seek health care from another healthcare provider. For example, when the healthcare provider fails to communicate, the individual is unable to comply due to lack of understanding. Communication between the healthcare provider and the individual (and caregivers) is critical for understanding, compliance, and most importantly, trust. Both parties—the individual and the healthcare provider—have rights and responsibilities that must be upheld to form a successful and trusting partnership. Without trust, informed decisions are not possible. Because the rights and responsibilities of the healthcare provider are governed by legal statute, the following section focuses primarily on the patient's rights and responsibilities.

Patient's Rights and Responsibilities

In 2010, President Obama announced the Patient's Bill of Rights, which included a set of protections related to health coverage.[14] The basic definition of patient rights in health care includes, but is not limited to, access to care; assistance or aid (e.g., home health care, medical transportation, rental of medical equipment); an appeals process

when one has a grievance; choice in the selection of one's healthcare providers; confidentiality and privacy; freedom from discrimination; access to information; respectful treatment; safety; shared decision making; and respect for patient preferences and wishes. There are numerous examples of the Patient's Bill of Rights.

Along with patients having rights within the healthcare system, patients also have responsibilities. Rights and responsibilities are a two-way street. Communication between the individual and healthcare provider must be respectful, honest, and communicated at the correct literacy level for the relationship to be positive and beneficial. See Box 11.7.

So, how does the concept of patient's rights and responsibilities relate to a health navigation

---

BOX 11.7 Patient's Bill of Rights and Responsibilities

Patient's Rights

The patient has the right to:

- Respectful, considerate, quality care at all times.
- Informational and personal privacy in compliance with federal Health Insurance and Accountability Act (HIPPA) regulations.
- Be informed by the healthcare provider or doctor about his or her current diagnosis, treatment, and prognosis in language the patient can understand. When the patient is unable to comprehend, the information will be made available to an appropriate individual on the patient's behalf.
- Receive from the healthcare provider adequate information to give informed consent regarding the procedure or treatment. Also, the individual has the right to know who will be performing the procedure.
- Deny treatment and the consequences as allowed by law.
- Adequate follow-through of care after discharge.
- Be advised of any proposed experimental procedures or treatment.
- Request an itemized explanation of the total bill after services are rendered.
- Request personal medical information regarding care.
- File a complaint with the organization or the federal Department of Health and Human Services.

Patient's Responsibilities

The patient has the responsibility to:

- Provide all relevant health information to the best of his or her knowledge.
- Report any changes in health conditions.
- Follow the treatment plan as requested by the healthcare provider.
- Be compliant and involved in health care.
- Fulfill any financial obligation resulting from healthcare services rendered.
- Follow any policies and procedures regarding patient conduct.
- Be considerate of the rights of other patients and office personnel.

Modified from: The Johns Hopkins Hospital (2012). Patient Bill of Rights and Responsibilities. Available at: http://www.hopkinsmedicine .org/the_johns_hopkins_hospital/_docs/bill_of_rights.pdf. Accessed on October 30, 2015.

professional? First, let us define some terms that pertain to patient rights and responsibilities. Without understanding the terms, it is not possible for a health navigation professional to offer resources related to healthcare decisions. See **Table 11.5**.

Second, health navigation professionals have the opportunity to talk to individuals about their healthcare decisions, rights, and responsibilities. Although health navigation professionals are not licensed to provide medical advice, they may offer guidance based on the patient's rights.

TABLE 11.5 Glossary of Terms

Authorization	Authorization is the act of giving permission. For example, an individual gives the healthcare provider permission to share confidential medical records with a third party, such as the spouse of the individual, an attorney, or an employer. The individual has control over who may receive the personal information, what information is to be released, and the duration of the authorization (e.g., current injury or illness, medical records from the past 3 months, current diagnosis but not previous hospitalizations). The authorization form is also called a *waiver*.[16]
Autonomy	Autonomy is the right of an individual to determine what will or will not be done regarding his or her body, personal belongings, and personal information. Autonomy applies to any adult individual who is mentally competent. If the individual is a child or not mentally competent, the parent or legal guardian acts as the decision maker. In some situations, the court may intervene if the parent or legal guardian withholds potentially life-saving treatment that is clearly indicated for the child. In other situations, autonomy is overridden in the interest of protecting other individuals (e.g., if an individual has infectious tuberculosis but refuses treatment). This individual poses a significant health threat to other people and, therefore, the court mandates treatment. In rare situations, the individual is detained in a facility for the required treatment.[16]
Disclosure	Disclosure is the act of revealing personal information. An individual reveals all personal health information to the healthcare provider to receive an accurate diagnosis, appropriate treatment, and quality care. Individuals sign authorization forms so the healthcare providers can receive and share the individual's personal information to improve quality of care. For example, the healthcare provider may determine that the individual needs knee surgery. However, prior to scheduling the surgery, the surgeon wants to review the person's previous medical records regarding radiology tests (e.g., MRI, X-rays, CT scans) on the individual's knee. Without disclosure and authorization, the healthcare provider lacks the individual's medical history to determine if the surgery is required and if the surgery is safe given the individual's overall health status.[16]
Informed Consent	Informed consent is a legal written document that an individual signs to agree to a specific surgical or medical procedures or other course of treatment. Prior to signing of an informed-consent document, the healthcare worker must disclose and inform the individual about all potential benefits and risks involved in the medical procedure as well as any alternative treatments available. This information allows the individual to make an informed decision and, thus, given written consent. If the individual is not capable of making an informed decision, the parent or legal guardian provides consent. The informed-consent procedure is protected under federal and state medical consent laws.[16]
Statement of Disagreement	Statements of disagreement are requested by individuals when they learn that a portion of their medical record is incorrect (e.g., error in medical history, wrong medication is listed, allergy is omitted, medication is misspelled and thus noted as another medication). An individual has the right to request and review his or her medical records. This type of request must be approved by the healthcare provider or institution that maintains the individual's record. If the individual sees an error or omission, he or she can request a correction or amendment. If the healthcare provider or institution does not agree that the record should be corrected or amended, the individual may request a statement of disagreement that indicates the error or need for an amendment. An individual's medical record is important, and errors or omissions may lead to serious consequences (e.g., medication errors, known allergies, previous reactions to medications, omitted procedures) when there are inaccuracies.[16]

For example, an individual may seek the opinion of a health navigation professional regarding how to obtain a printed copy of his or her electronic medical record, seek the services of an interpreter if English is not the primary language, get answers about possible billing errors or a health insurance company's refusing to pay for a necessary medical test or treatment, or determine the process to file a complaint about a healthcare provider or institution with limited computer skills. On the other hand, the health navigation professional is able to reinforce the personal responsibilities of individuals in the achievement of improving their own quality of life (e.g., taking medication as prescribed, attending follow-up appointments for monitoring diagnoses, eating healthy food, smoking cessation, exercising as permitted). Whether the individual needs financial assistance in paying for their prescription medication, obtaining transportation to the follow-up visit, or trying to obtain health insurance, a health navigation professional is able to investigate each request and assist the individual to understand the terminology as well as obtain services or answers to their questions. Most importantly, the health navigation professional takes time to listen, while other healthcare providers may not have a schedule that allows for a thorough investigation of each request.

The next section moves from the general discussion of patient rights and responsibilities to an individual's right to make decisions and choices

© monkeybusinessimages/iStockphoto

regarding end-of-life plans. Although most individuals assume this topic can be avoided until old age, the evidence suggests that making end-of-life decisions is important for all ages to consider.

END-OF-LIFE ISSUES

Care of patients near the end of life is often emotionally and ethically challenging. Healthcare providers, patients, and families find certain concepts vague and hard to understand. Furthermore, there must be a balance between two extremes: a treat-at-all-cost and a too-rapid-withdrawal of potentially beneficial treatments. The glossary of terms in **Table 11.6** assists with the understanding of complex terms related to end-of-life issues.

With greater awareness of end-of-life terms, the following three legal landmark end-of-life cases demonstrate how unforeseen circumstances of individuals led their families, healthcare

TABLE 11.6 Glossary of Terms

Brain Death	There are no reflexes (e.g., absence of pupil dilation, no response to pain, no startle movement), no spontaneous breathing (the individual is ventilator dependent), and an electroencephalogram (ECG) (brain wave test) shows a flat line after two readings taken 24 hours apart. Under these circumstances, it may be ethically appropriate to discontinue life support or consider organ donation.[17]
Imminent Death	Death is likely to occur at any moment. Death is expected within a short time, usually days or weeks.
Persistent (permanent) Vegetative State (PVS)	A wakeful, unconscious state that lasts longer than a few weeks is referred to as a persistent vegetative state. Unlike brain death, in the United States, courts have required petitions before termination of life support that demonstrate that any recovery of cognitive functions above a vegetative state has been assessed as impossible by authoritative medical opinion. The vegetative state is a chronic or long-term condition. Unlike a coma (a state that lacks both awareness and wakefulness), patients in a vegetative state may have awoken from a coma, but still have not regained awareness. The chances of regaining awareness diminish considerably as the time spent in the vegetative state increases.[18]

providers, and the courts to change U.S. laws from 1975 to 2005. See **Box 11.8**.

End-of-Life Planning: Legal Documents and Termination of Medical Treatment

Several types of legal documents can guide and assist individuals and their families to plan end-of-life decisions. As noted in Box 11.8, life does

not always end in a preplanned scenarios, such as with a terminal cancer diagnosis. Each day individuals encounter unexpected events (e.g., vehicle crashes, pedestrian injuries, falls, fires, natural disasters) that lead to serious unplanned medical situations. Without some discussion and documents in place, families and health-care providers are left trying to agree on what

---

BOX 11.8 Landmark End-of-Life Cases

Three of the most widely discussed cases involving the termination of life-extending treatment were the cases of Karen Ann Quinlan, Nancy Cruzan, and Terri Schiavo:

Karen Ann Quinlan

In 1975, Karen Ann Quinlan, age 22, became unconscious after she consumed valium and alcohol while on a crash diet. She lapsed into a coma and remained in a persistent vegetative state with no hope of recovery. She was kept alive by a ventilator that sustained her breathing. In 1976, her parents wanted to discontinue treatment, but the hospital refused. In 1976, they persevered with their legal bills and appealed the ruling to the New Jersey Supreme Court. The Supreme Court of New Jersey decided that the hospital could legally discontinue treatment for a patient in a persistent vegetative state without fear of criminal or civil retribution. Although Quinlan was removed from mechanical ventilation in 1976, she lived on in a persistent vegetative state for almost a decade until her death from pneumonia in 1985.[19]

Nancy Cruzan

In 1983, Nancy Cruzan, age 25, lost control of her car and was thrown from the vehicle. Paramedics found her with no vital signs, but were able to resuscitate her. After 3 weeks in a coma, she was diagnosed as being in a persistent vegetative state. Surgeons inserted a feeding tube for her long-term care. However, when Cruzan's parents wanted to discontinue artificial nutrition and hydration several weeks after the crash, the hospital would not do so. In a 5–4 court decision, the Missouri State Court ruled in favor of the hospital, because there was no "clear and convincing evidence" of what Nancy Cruzan would have wanted before she died. Her case ended up before the U.S. Supreme Court, where it was decided that food and water could be withheld in cases where there is clear and convincing evidence that the patient would not have wanted to live. The case was returned to the Missouri State Court when Nancy's parents were able to present additional evidence of her wishes, and the court ruled in their favor. They then requested removal of the artificial nutrition and hydration tubes, and, subsequently, Nancy Cruzan died 11 days later on December 26, 1990. This decision has influenced many other cases.[20]

Terri Schiavo (1963–2005)

On February 25, 1990, Terri Schiavo, age 33, experienced cardiac arrest that was triggered by extreme hypokalemia (low potassium) brought on by an eating disorder. She was resuscitated, but suffered massive brain damage due to lack of oxygen to her brain and was left comatose. After 2½ months without improvement, her diagnosis was changed to that of a persistent vegetative state. For the next 2 years, doctors attempted speech and physical therapy in addition to other experimental therapy, hoping to return her to a state of awareness, without success. In 1998, Schiavo's husband, Michael, petitioned the Sixth Circuit Court of Florida to remove her feeding tube pursuant to Florida law. He was opposed by Terri's parents, Robert and Mary Schindler, who argued that she was conscious. The court determined that Schiavo would not have wished to continue life-prolonging measures, although there were no written directives from Terri Schiavo on the matter. April 24, 2001, her feeding tube was removed for the first time, only to be reinserted several days later. On February 25, 2005, a county judge again ordered the removal of Terri Schiavo's feeding tube. After appeals, the federal court system upheld the original decision to remove the feeding tube. The staff at the hospice facility disconnected the feeding tube on March 18, 2005, and Schiavo died on March 31, 2005.[21]

the individual would or would not wish to be included in his or her spectrum of medical treatment. The following discussion introduces the terms and definitions regarding end-of-life planning that guide such important decisions. First, the discussion introduces legal documents needed to make end-of-life decisions. Second, the discussion provides complex options available for individuals with a terminal medical diagnosis or those in a situation where a life-threatening condition occurs (e.g., vehicle crash, traumatic brain injury, unintentional poisoning) and the family must make end-of-life decisions for their loved one.

© Fuse/Corbis/Getty Images

Legal Documents

Because health navigation professionals serve as communication liaisons among healthcare providers, patients, family members, and significant others, they are able to assist with end-of-life decisions ranging from the most advanced medical care to enhanced quality of life. Communication is a key aspect of making healthcare decisions. The decision process remains difficult, but is less problematic and stressful when the patient is able to participate in his or her own healthcare decisions. However, when the patient is no longer able to communicate competently and end-of-life documents are not available, the health navigation professional serves as a decision-making guide to the family, based on what the family believes the patient would desire and in conjunction with the medical information provided by the healthcare providers. For the healthcare navigation professional, the following section defines terms and documents needed to guide families through end-of-life planning and decisions, including advanced-care planning, durable power of attorney, advanced health directives, and termination of medical treatment.

Advanced-Care Planning: Advanced-care planning is a conversation that allows individuals to express their desires concerning medical treatment options. This type of planning involves the individual and family members and is facilitated by a healthcare provider, such as a nurse or social worker. This planning conversation ensures that the family understands the individual's overall decisions. Once this planning conversation has occurred, the individual and family members may proceed with writing and signing the advanced directive that is used to ease the process and improve communication regarding medical treatment, if and when the situation occurs.[22]

Durable Power of Attorney: Durable Power of Attorney is a legal document that appoints a healthcare decision maker. This document is a better strategy than an advanced directive or living will. Durable Power of Attorney is more helpful to physicians when they need to know what an individual would want in a particular medical situation and who can legally make decisions.[23]

Advanced Health Directives: Advanced directives (also called *living wills*) are documents that state the individual's goals and wishes regarding medical care, including specific instructions about treatment (e.g., do not resuscitate (DNR)), organ donation, palliative care, feeding tubes, artificial breathing equipment). Unfortunately, advanced directives and living wills are tools that are underused. Many individuals who might benefit from such documents do not have them. Furthermore, when the documents are available, the written directives are frequently not followed or provide only limited value and instruction.[24] For example, the advanced directive states no artificial ventilation; however, the physician feels that the ventilator is a temporary treatment that could extend life and diminish suffering.[23] See **Box 11.9**.

BOX 11.9 Sample of an Advanced HealthCare Directive Document

Advanced Health Care Directive

INSTRUCTIONS: This form lets you give specific instructions about any aspect of your health care. Choices are provided for you to express your wishes regarding the provision, withholding, or withdrawal of treatment to keep you alive, as well as the provision of pain relief. Space is provided for you to add to the choices you have made or for you to write any additional wishes. This form also lets you express an intention to donate your bodily organs and tissues following your death. Finally, this form lets you designate a physician to have primary responsibility for your health care.

After completing this form, sign and date the form at the end. The form must be signed by two qualified witnesses or acknowledged before a notary public. Give a copy of the signed and completed form to your physician, to any other health care providers you may have, to any health care institution at which you are receiving care, and to any health care agents you have named.

I, _____, being of sound mind and at least 18 years of age, declare that:

(1) END-OF-LIFE DECISIONS: I direct that my health care providers and others involved in my care provide, withhold, or withdraw treatment in accordance with the choice I have marked below: (Initial only one box.)

- [___] (a) Choice NOT to Prolong Life. I do not want my life to be prolonged if (1) I have an incurable and irreversible condition that will result in my death within a relatively short time, (2) I become unconscious and, to a reasonable degree of medical certainty, will not regain consciousness, or (3) the likely risks and burdens of treatment would outweigh the expected benefits, OR
- [___] (b) Choice to Prolong Life. I want my life to be prolonged as long as possible within the limits of generally accepted health care standards.

(2) RELIEF FROM PAIN: Except as I state in the following space, I direct that treatment for alleviation of pain or discomfort should be provided at all times even if it hastens my death:

_____
_____
_____

(3) OTHER WISHES: (If you do not agree with any of the optional choices above and wish to write your own, or if you wish to add to the instructions you have given above, you may do so here.) I direct that:

_____
_____
_____

(4) PRIMARY PHYSICIAN: (OPTIONAL)

- I designate the following physician as my primary physician:

_____

(Name of physician)

_____

(Address) (City) (State) (Zip code)

_____

(Phone)

OPTIONAL: If the physician I have designated above is not willing, able, or reasonably available to act as my primary physician, I designate the following physician as my primary physician:

_____

(Name of physician)

_____

(Address) (City) (State) (Zip code)

_____

(Phone)

(5) DONATION OF ORGANS AT DEATH: (OPTIONAL)

Upon my death: (mark applicable box)

- [___] (a) I give any needed organs, tissues, or parts, OR
- [___] (b) I give the following organs, tissues, or parts only.
- [___] (c) My gift is for the following purposes: (strike any of the following you do not want)
  - (1) Transplant
  - (2) Therapy
  - (3) Research
  - (4) Education

In the absence of my ability to give directions regarding the use of such life-sustaining procedures, it is my intention that this declaration shall be honored by my family and physician(s) as the final expression of my legal right to refuse medical or surgical treatment, and I accept the consequences from such refusal.

I understand the full import of this declaration and I am emotionally and mentally competent to make this declaration.

I execute this declaration, as my free and voluntary act, on this _____ day of _____, 20__, in the City of _____, County of _____, State of _____.

_____

(Signature)

(INSTRUCTIONS: This advanced health care directive will not be valid for making health care decisions unless it is (1) either signed by two qualified adult witnesses who are personally known to you and who are present when you sign or acknowledge your signature, or (2) is acknowledged before a notary public.)

I declare under penalty of perjury under the laws of the state (1) that the individual who signed or acknowledged this advanced health care directive is personally known to me or that the individual's identity was proven to me by convincing evidence; (2) that the individual signed or acknowledged this advance directive in my presence; (3) that the individual appears to be of sound mind and under no duress, fraud, or undue influence; (4) that I am not a person appointed as agent by this advance directive; and (5) that I am not the individual's health care provider, an employee of the individual's health care provider, or the operator of a community health care facility.

I further declare under the penalty of perjury that I am not related to the patient by blood, marriage, or adoption, and, to the best of my knowledge, I am not entitled to any portion of the patient's

(continued)

estate upon the patient's death under a will existing when the advanced directive is executed or by operation of law.

Signed at _____ on this _____ day of _____, 20__.

_____
(Name and address of first witness)

_____
(Name and address of second witness)

State of _____

County of _____

On this the _____ day of _____, 20__, before me, the undersigned, a notary public in and for said County and State, personally appeared _____, personally known to me (or proved to me on the basis of satisfactory evidence) to be the person(s) whose name(s) is/are subscribed to the within instrument and acknowledged to me that he/she/they executed the same in his/her/their authorized capacity(ies), and that by his/her/their signature(s) on the instrument the person(s), or entity upon behalf of which the person(s) acted, executed the instrument.

WITNESS my hand and official seal.

_____
Signature of Notary

TERMINATION OF MEDICAL TREATMENT

The following definitions provide the health navigation professional with an overview of the complex choices that individuals and family members face when making critical end-of-life decisions. For ease of understanding, the terms are listed in alphabetical order.

Antibiotics Usage: Terminally ill and dying individuals are susceptible to infections.[25] In the final days of life, the purpose of giving antibiotics is to alleviate symptoms rather than cure any infection. However, there are ethical challenges related to providing or withholding antibiotics. Some physicians view antibiotics as part of treatment, while others believe that withholding antibiotics allows the natural process of death to occur.[25]

Cardiopulmonary Resuscitation (CPR) and Do Not Resuscitate (DNR): Cardiopulmonary resuscitation (CPR) improves an individual's chance of survival from sudden cardiac arrest. Although CPR is valuable for heart attacks, it may be an undesired procedure for terminally ill individuals. Such individuals must communicate this desire to the healthcare provider and request a do-not-resuscitate (DNR) order. If an individual is unable to speak, a family member may seek a DNR order on their relative's behalf.[26] Of course, there are ethical situations and medical conditions that make such legal decisions difficult in the field of health care for individuals, families, and healthcare providers.

Euthanasia and *Physician-Assisted Suicide*: The word "euthanasia" comes from the Greek for "good death." First, euthanasia is defined as an act where a third party, usually a physician, terminates the life of an individual involving, but not limited to, a diagnosis of living in a situation that the individual considers to be worse than death or existing in a coma or in a persistent vegetative state (PVS).[27]

Second, in a physician-assisted suicide, the physician provides an individual with a prescription for medications that the individual may use to end his or her life. Such a prescription is not given without lengthy counseling and discussion with the individual and family members, including an investigation of alternative choices and therapies. In addition, the individual requesting the medication must be conscious, mentally competent, and fully capable of making his or her own decisions.

The difference between euthanasia and physician-assisted suicide is that in euthanasia the physician ends the individual's life, while in the case of physician-assisted suicide, the physician provides the prescription, but the individual makes the decision to forego suffering and loss of control.[28] With either of these decisions, there are numerous ethical challenges and arguments. For example, some argue that physician-assisted suicide allows autonomy, self-empowerment, mercy, and compassion, while others contend that any form of euthanasia or assisted suicide is immoral. Some also debate that both actions involve a physician making decisions that are against their training.[29] However, some individuals and family members view suffering at the end of life

as worse than death. Euthanasia and physician-assisted suicide are considered to be the reasonable and merciful choices.

Assisted suicide is legal in the states of Oregon (Oregon Death with Dignity Act), Washington (Washington Death with Dignity Act), and Vermont (Patient Choice and Control at End of Life Act). In Montana (through the 2009 trial court ruling *Baxter v. Montana*), the court found no public policy against assisting suicide, so consent may be raised in court. Oregon and Washington specify some restrictions. It was briefly legal in New Mexico in 2014, but this verdict was overturned in 2015. See **Box 11.10**.

Kidney Dialysis: Kidney dialysis removes waste and fluids from the blood in individuals with kidneys that no longer function or have been surgically removed due to damage or injury. Kidney dialysis requires that the individual receive a dialysis treatment up to three times per week at home or at a licensed dialysis facility. Each dialysis treatment takes 4–6 hours depending on the weight of the individual and whether he or she retains the ability to urinate. Some individuals on dialysis retain the ability to urinate, but the kidneys are no longer able to remove toxins. Other individuals on dialysis are no longer able to urinate because their kidneys

BOX 11.10 Death with Dignity Act of Oregon

The Oregon Death with Dignity Act legalized physician-assisted suicide in Oregon. Though it was passed in 1994, it did not go into effect until October 27, 1997. The Act allows terminally ill individuals to end their lives through the voluntary self-administration of lethal medications, purposely prescribed by a physician.[30] When a prescription is written under the Act, the prescribing physician must either submit Death with Dignity forms to the Oregon Health Authority or make available relevant portions of the medical record showing that the physician and the individual followed the requirements of the Act. After the individual has died, the death certificate is matched with their Death with Dignity forms or copies of the medical record and are reviewed by Oregon Health Authority staff. The physician confirms whether the individual died from the lethal prescription or from the terminal illness. The information collected by the Oregon Health Authority includes characteristics of the individual; motivation for requesting the prescription; medical diagnosis and condition; end-of-life care issues (e.g., under hospice care); compliance guidelines of the Act; events surrounding the patient's death (e.g., type of medications used, time to death after taking the lethal medications); and characteristics of the physician who participated in the Act.[30] The Act requires the Oregon Health Authority to publish the data collected in an annual statistical report. According to the 2014 report, 105 terminally ill patients used the Oregon law to hasten their own deaths.

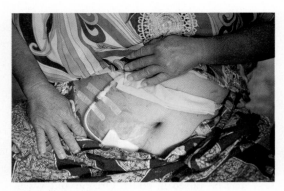

© Soda_02/Shutterstock

have been removed; therefore, the individuals retain fluid and toxins that must be removed three times per week. Without dialysis, fluid and toxins reach critical levels in the body and result in death within a few days. Dialysis is a time-consuming and physical burden for individuals with end-stage renal disease. Some individuals on dialysis decide that this burden outweighs the benefits and sometimes make the decision to discontinue any further dialysis treatment. The respect for the individual's autonomy (freedom to have voluntary choice and informed consent) allows their decision to be upheld by the medical and legal community. Once the individual makes the decision, the physician should provide sufficient information, including available treatment options, consequences of ending dialysis treatment, and other end-of-life care options, such as palliative care and hospice.[31, 32]

Mechanical Ventilation: Mechanical ventilation uses a machine to "breathe" for an individual by inflating and oxygenating the lungs. Mechanical breathing or ventilation is delivered through tubes inserted through the nose or mouth into the trachea. Approximately 75 percent of dying individuals experience breathlessness, or dyspnea ("dys" = difficult, painful; "pnea" = breathing).[33] Ventilation provides these individuals reduced anxiety and improved sleep.[34] Mechanical ventilation is the most common life support treatment

withdrawn in anticipation of death.[35] Some individuals consider mechanical ventilation a nonbeneficial treatment that delays the natural death process.[36]

Nutrition and Hydration: Nutrition and hydration provide nutrients, fluid, and water to individuals who are unconscious or cannot swallow. There are two methods: (a) enteral nutrition, which involves a feeding tube that is either inserted in the nose and down to the stomach or is surgically inserted into the individual's stomach or intestines; liquid nutrients are delivered via the feeding tube as a way to provide the individual with adequate nutrition; and (b) parenteral nutrition, which provides adequate daily nutrients directly into the bloodstream via intravenous catheter. Decisions concerning maintaining or withdrawing nutrition and hydration are among the most emotionally and ethically challenging issues in end-of-life care.[37]

Terminal Sedation: Depending on the diagnosis, some individuals with a terminal illness suffer profound pain near the last days of their life. Terminal sedation uses medication to make the individual unconscious until death occurs from the underlying illness.[38] Sedatives are medications that act on the brain and spinal cord and provide a calming or tranquilizing effect on the body. Depending on the circumstances, sedatives are given in small doses to relieve anxiety, and soothe coughing and nausea. When larger doses are given, the individual sleeps and may become unconscious. There are ethical challenges related to the use of terminal sedation due to the unknown effect of hastening death, rendering the individual unable to speak, and potential abuse of dying individuals.

Once these terms are understood by individuals and family members, they are able to have an informed discussion with their health-care providers regarding end-of-life planning decisions. As for the health navigation professionals, even though providing advice on end-of-planning is beyond their scope of responsibilities, it is important to know the definitions and be familiar with the state laws in their location of employment. This knowledge provides a greater understanding of the decisions faced by healthcare providers, individuals, and family members. Once the legal decisions have been finalized, the last and final care end-of-life care choices are enacted to keep the dying individual comfortable.

END-OF-LIFE CARE: OPTIONS

When individuals are asked to describe the type of death that they would prefer, the answers have some similarities. For example, most individuals wish to maintain the ability to control the situation or circumstances. In other words, they wish to participate in decisions about medical options at the end of life. For the individual to be involved with medical decisions, it is important to establish excellent communication with the healthcare providers. Communication at the end of life is key to good health care. When communication diminishes, mistrust and conflict increase. This results in inappropriate or unwanted treatment. When individuals have trouble communicating about their symptoms, the health navigation professional offer suggestion to assist family members and friends. The symptoms of pain and discomfort are complicated. The typical 0 (no pain) to 10 (extreme) pain scale does not always solve the problem of describing pain.

Healthcare providers must listen closely to gain a full understanding of their patients and to increase communication with the individual. Cultural differences can also affect communication with the individual and their family. Many cultures do not support the idea of full disclosure when it comes to illness, while others want disclosure to family members or community leaders. Finally, some healthcare providers find it difficult to tell the individual the complete truth about a terminal prognosis. The healthcare provider may feel that he or she is taking away all hope or that the treatment was not successful. Because proper communication takes time and advanced training, some healthcare providers are sharing that responsibly with other skilled providers, such as highly trained hospice workers (e.g., physicians,

> ### BOX 11.11 Common Elements of a Good Death
>
> Adequate pain and symptom management
> Avoiding a prolonged dying process
> Clear communication about decisions by patient, family, and physician
> Adequate preparation for death, for both patient and loved ones
> Feeling a sense of control
> Finding a spiritual or emotional sense of completion
> Affirming the patient as a unique and worthy person
> Strengthening relationships with loved ones
> Not being alone
>
> Data from: Steinhauser K.E., Clipp E.C., McNeilly M., et al. (2000). In search of a good death: Observations of patients, families, and providers. *Annals of Internal Medicine*, 132,825–832.

nurses, chaplains, social workers, healthcare navigation professionals).[39] See **Box 11.11**.

End-of-life planning may involve family members making decisions for their loved ones. The next section defines various terms and options that individuals or family members must consider during perhaps the most stressful time of their lives. For example, family members are asked to make end-of-life decisions following serious vehicle crashes. In other situations, the individual may be making such decisions regarding their own end of life because of a terminal diagnosis. Because end-of-life planning is difficult in the midst of the event, it is important for families to have these discussions prior to any such event occurring. It is always useful for the family to know what their loved one would have wanted rather than trying to make decisions without prior knowledge. Finally, if individuals plan for end of life by putting their wishes in writing, their family members will not quibble over or disagree about end-of-life decisions. Now, let us explore end-of-life decisions, starting with palliative care and pain management through hospice care.

© Cathy Yeulet/ iStockphoto

Palliative Care

The primary purpose of palliative care is to relieve symptoms with a focus on achieving the highest quality of life. Palliative care is an option for individuals with chronic pain or severe symptoms from a serious or terminal illness. Palliative care is similar to that of hospice care, except palliative care is not restricted to individuals near the end of life. Palliative care is available in a variety of settings, including home, outpatient clinics, hospitals, and long-term care facilities. Both palliative care and hospice use an interdisciplinary team approach of professionals, including physicians, nurses, social workers, psychologists, chaplains, and other healthcare therapists (e.g., massage, physical, occupational, art, music, pet therapists) to provide comprehensive care. Because traditional health care in the United States focuses primarily on curing illnesses and healing injuries, palliative care is becoming a positive alternative when medical treatment is no longer an effective option.

Pain: Management and Treatment

Healthcare providers face difficult decisions when managing the symptoms of pain. If they choose narcotic drugs like morphine and sedatives, the individual may experience relief from unwanted symptoms like pain and shortness of breath, while reducing depression and anxiety. However, medications may increase unwanted side effects, such as nausea, drowsiness, delirium, diarrhea, vomiting, and unconsciousness.

Because physicians are sometimes wary of prescribing excessive narcotics, the ideal situation is when the individual and the family are involved in the decision regarding the best method of pain and symptom management. Often times, the narcotic drug treatment is combined with complementary and alternative medicine (CAM) therapies for best results, such as hypnosis, massage therapy or aromatherapy to relieve pain and other symptoms. CAM is becoming a popular way to supplement medical treatment or decrease pain in nonterminal medical conditions and includes art therapy, music therapy, mindful meditation, yoga, and pet therapy. Finally, most individuals have used some form of CAM in their day-to-day lives for mild health conditions. Getting a massage for various aches and pains, drinking hot ginger tea or gargling with warm saltwater for a sore throat, using over-the-counter pain patches for sore muscles, and going to an acupuncturist to reduce inflammation and pain are all examples of CAM.

Hospice Care

The philosophy of hospice involves supporting both the individual and the family while restoring communication and control over the circumstances of death. The hospice team cares for the dying individual at home, in a nursing home, in a hospital, or in a separate hospice facility. In addition to medical care, the hospice team may provide emotional and spiritual support, social services, nutrition counseling, and grief counseling for both the patient and loved ones.[41]

Dying individuals may choose hospice care. A holistic and philosophical approach to end-of-life care, hospice brings doctors, nurses, social workers, and other professionals together as a care team. The hospice team's goal is to make the individual as comfortable as possible during his or her final days. Hospice emphasizes pain control, symptom management, natural death, and quality of life to comfort the individual's physical body, while also supporting the family members as needed. See **Table 11.7.**

TABLE 11.7 Hospice and Palliative Care Organizations

National Hospice and Palliative Care Organization (NHPCO), www.nhpco.org	This organization is an association of programs that (1) provide hospice care, (2) advocate for the rights of terminally ill patients, and (3) connect patients and families with hospice programs.
Hospice Association of America (HAA), www.hospice-america.org	This organization represents about 2800 home care and hospice programs and has a strong lobbying component.
Hospice Education Institute, www.hospiceworld.org	This organization focuses on educating, referring, and supporting people seeking hospice services for themselves or a loved one.

Summary

© Jim Barber/Shutterstock

This chapter covered the topics of quality of life and end of life. The first section explored the basic concept of quality of life from a global perspective for elder care. The second section investigated the concept of patient's rights and responsibilities, including the need for communication with healthcare providers. The third section involved the complex issues of end-of-life planning and decisions, including landmark end-of-life legal cases, legal documents, and termination of medical treatment. The chapter concluded with a discussion of end-of-life care options ranging from palliative care and pain management through hospice care.

Case Study

George, age 79, was diagnosed with congestive heart failure (CFH) about 3 years ago. Since his wife died 5 years ago, he has been living at his only daughter, Susan's, home. Susan has no other siblings and she is married to Jim. They have one teenage son, Rick, age 16. Susan and Jim work full-time. Recently, Rick got his driver's license and is gone most of the time with school and sport activities. When George was first diagnosed with CHF, he felt good most of the time and was still driving. He had plenty of friends and enjoyed playing bridge and cooking for the family. Within the past 6 months, George has been hospitalized twice and each time never had a full recovery. He is experiencing shortness of breath and edema (swelling) in both ankles and lower legs. He says that walking feels like slugging through knee-deep mud. Because he can no longer drive, his friends have mostly stopped calling. He can no longer stand long enough to cook dinner, so he feels like a burden to his daughter. He tries to fold the clothes and tidy the house while they are at work, but even these small tasks are becoming too difficult.

George has decided to call a family meeting to discuss his desires for the remainder of his life. He asked an attorney friend, Rose, to stop by the house for a conversation about advanced directives, living wills, and do-not-resuscitate medical orders. In addition, at his last cardiologist's appointment, George had the same conversation with his physician, Dr. Hendrik, but the conversation did not go as George had wanted.

Dr. Hendrik said that George was doing fine, and there was no need for such morbid conversations. He changed George's medication and told him to come back in 2 months. The medication made George feel worse, so he stopped taking it. George canceled his follow-up appointment with Dr. Hendrik; instead, he made an appointment with his primary care physician, Dr. Sanchez. When Rose visited, she was able to answer all of George's questions. She completed the documents for George per his request. Rose saved the files on her laptop and, per George's request, sent copies of the documents to Dr. Sanchez while she was visiting George. She left all of the documents on a thumb drive, so Susan could print the documents after the family discussion.

George told Susan about the visit with Rose when she got home from work, but they did not open the files for any further discussion. That night George took a turn for the worse, and he called to Susan from his room. His call woke her up, and she went to his bedside. He was slipping in and out of consciousness; she determined that it was necessary to call 9-1-1 and get George to the hospital. Susan did not know what George and Rose had written in the documents that afternoon.

Student Activity

Write 2–3 paragraphs to end the story.

References

1. The Free Medical Dictionary by Farlex. *Quality of life.* Retrieved October 30, 2015, from http://medical-dictionary.thefreedictionary.com/quality+of+life.
2. Centers for Disease Control and Prevention. *Health-related quality of life (HRQOL) concepts.* Retrieved October 30, 2015, from http://www.cdc.gov/hrqol/concept.htm; last updated March 17, 2011.
3. Organization for Economic Cooperation and Development. (2014). *How's life? Measuring well-being.* Paris, France: OECD Publishing.
4. Centers for Disease Control and Prevention. *Health-related quality of life (HRQOL): Key findings.* Retrieved October 30, 2015, from http://www.cdc.gov/hrqol/key_findings.htm; last updated March 15, 2011.
5. The American Institute of Stress. *Holmes-Rahe stress inventory.* Retrieved October 30, 2015, from http://www.stress.org/holmes-rahe-stress-inventory.
6. Krantz, D. S., Whittaker, K. S., & Sheps, D. S. (2011). Psychosocial risk factors for coronary heart disease: Pathophysiologic mechanisms. In *Heart and mind: The practice of cardiac psychology* (2nd ed.). Washington, DC: American Psychological Association.
7. Thorn, B. E., Pence, L. B., Ward, L. C., Kilgo, G., Clements, K. L., Cross, T. H., Davis, A. M., & Tsui, P. Q. (2007). A randomized clinical trial of targeted cognitive behavioral treatment to reduce catastrophizing in chronic headache sufferers. *The Journal of Pain, 8*(12), 938–949.
8. Ness, S. M. *Living with cancer blog: Quality of life issues key factor for cancer patients.* The Mayo Clinic. Retrieved October 30, 2015, from http://www.mayoclinic.org/diseases-conditions/cancer/expert-blog/cancer-and-quality-of-life/BGP-20056307; last updated June 4, 2014.
9. The Rand Cooperation. *Developing quality of care indicators for the vulnerable elderly: The ACOVE project.* Retrieved October 2015, from http://www.rand.org/pubs/research_briefs/RB4545-1/index1.html.
10. American Association of Retired Persons. *Livable communities: About us.* Retrieved January 20, 2016, from http://www.aarp.org/livable-communities/about.
11. American Association of Retired Persons. *Beyond 50.05: A report to the nation on livable communities: Creating environments for successful aging.* Washington, DC: American Association of Retired Persons. Retrieved January 20, 2016, from http://assets.aarp.org/rgcenter/il/beyond_50_communities.pdf.
12. Brecht, S. B., Fein, S., & Hollinger-Smith, L. (2009). Preparing for the future: Trends in continuing care retirement communities. *Seniors Housing & Care Journal, 17*(1).
13. Shippee, T. P. (2012). On the edge: Balancing health, participation, and autonomy to maintain active independent living in two retirement facilities. *Journal of Aging Studies, 26*(1), 1–15.
14. Executivegov.com. *Obama announces patients' bill of rights.* Retrieved October 30, 2015, from http://www.executivegov.com/2010/06/president-obama-announces-patients-bill-of-rights; last updated June 23, 2010.
15. Johns Hopkins Hospital. *Patient bill of rights and responsibilities.* Retrieved October 30, 2015, from http://www.hopkinsmedicine.org/the_johns_hopkins_hospital/_docs/bill_of_rights.pdf.
16. Centers for Disease Control and Prevention. *Self-study modules on tuberculosis: Protecting patients' rights.* Retrieved October 30, 2015, from http://www.cdc.gov/tb/education/ssmodules/module7/ss7reading2.htm; last updated September 1, 2012.
17. Sullivan, J., Seem, D. L., & Chabalewski, F. (1999). Determining brain death. *Critical Care Nurse, 19*(2), 37.
18. Laureys, S., Celesia, G. G., Cahadon, F., Lavrijsen, J., Leon-Carrion, J., Sannita, W. G., Sazbon, L., Schmutzhard, E., von Wild, K. R., Zeman, A., Dolce, G., et al. (2010). Unresponsive wakefulness syndrome: A new name for the vegetative state or apallic syndrome. *BMC medicine, 8*(1), 68.
19. Karen Ann Quinlan Memorial Foundation. *History.* Retrieved October 30, 2015, from http://www.karenannquinlanhospice.org/history.

20. Oyez. *Cruzan by Cruzan v. Director, Missouri Department of Health*. Retrieved October 30, 2015, from https://www.oyez.org/cases/1989/88-1503.

21. Quill, T. E. (2005). Terri Schiavo—A tragedy compounded. *New England Journal of Medicine, 352*(16), 1630–1633.

22. Thompson, T. D., Barbour, R. S., & Schwartz, L. (2003). Health professionals' views on advance directives: A qualitative interdisciplinary study. *Palliative Medicine, 17*(5), 403–409.

23. Hickey, D. P. (2002). The disutility of advance directives: We know the problems, but are there solutions? *Journal of Health Law, 36*(3), 455–473.

24. Winick, B. J. (1998). Foreword: Planning for the future through advance directive instruments. *Psychology, Public Policy, and Law, 4*(3), 579.

25. Pereira, J., Watanabe, S., & Wolch, G. (1998). A retrospective review of the frequency of infections and patterns of antibiotic utilization on a palliative care unit. *Journal of Pain and Symptom Management, 16*(6), 374–381.

26. Pellegrino, E. D. (1998). Emerging ethical issues in palliative care. *JAMA, 279*(19), 1521–1522.

27. Ashwal, S. (1994). Medical aspects of the persistent vegetative state (second of two parts). *The New England Journal Of Medicine, 330*(22), 1572–1579.

28. Coughennower, M. (2003). Physician-assisted suicide. *Gastroenterology Nursing, 26*(2), 55–59.

29. O'Brien, C. N., Madek, G. A., & Ferrara, G. R. (2000). Oregon's guidelines for physician-assisted suicide: A legal and ethical analysis. *University of Pittsburgh Law Review, 61*(2), 329–365.

30. Oregon Health Authority. Death with dignity act. Retrieved October 30, 2015, from http://public.health.oregon.gov/ProviderPartnerResources/EvaluationResearch/DeathwithDignityAct/Pages/index.aspx.

31. Cohen, L. M., Germain, M. J., & Poppel, D. M. (2003). Practical considerations in dialysis withdrawal: To have that option is a blessing. *JAMA, 289*(16), 2113–2119.

32. Galla, J. H. (2000). Clinical practice guideline on shared decision-making in the appropriate initiation of and withdrawal from dialysis. *Journal of the American Society of Nephrology, 11*(7), 1340–1342.

33. LaDuke, S. (2001). Terminal dyspnea & palliative care: Patient deaths are inevitable. "Bad deaths"—those accompanied by severe suffering—are not. *The American Journal of Nursing, 101*(11), 26–31.

34. Shee, C. D., & Green, N. (2003). Non-invasive ventilation and palliation: Experience in a district general hospital and a review. *Palliative Medicine, 17*(1), 21–26.

35. Cook, D., Rocker, G., Marshall, J., Sjokvist, P., Dodek, P., Griffith, L., Freitag, A., Varon, J., Bradley, C., Levy, M., Finfer, S., Hamielec, C., McMullin, J., Weaver, B., Walter, S., & Guyatt, G. (2003). Withdrawal of mechanical ventilation in anticipation of death in the intensive care unit. *New England Journal of Medicine, 349*(12), 1123–1132.

36. Singer, G. (1997). Disconnecting the ventilator: Life saving or death delaying? *The Journal of the Florida Medical Association, 84*(8), 498–501.

37. The American Medical Association. *AMA Policy E-2.20 Withholding or withdrawing life sustaining treatment*. Retrieved October 30, 2015, from http://www.ama-assn.org.

38. Loewy, E. H. (2001). Terminal sedation, self-starvation, and orchestrating the end of life. *Archives of Internal medicine, 161*(3), 329–332.

39. Singer, P. A., Martin, D. K., & Kelner, M. (1999). Quality end-of-life care: Patients' perspectives. *JAMA, 281*(2), 163–168.

40. Steinhauser, K. E., Clipp, E. C., McNeilly, M., Christakis, N. A., McIntyre, L. M., & Tulsky, J. A. (2000). In search of a good death: Observations of patients, families, and providers. *Annals of Internal Medicine, 132*(10), 825–832.

41. Steinhauser, K. E., Clipp, E. C., McNeilly, M., Christakis, N. A., McIntyre, L. M., & Tulsky, J. A. (2000). Factors considered important at the end of life by patients, family, physicians, and other care providers. *JAMA, 284*(19), 2476–2482.

PART 4

Accessing and Analyzing Health Information

CHAPTER 12

Health Literacy

LEARNING OBJECTIVES

By the end of this chapter, students will be able to:

- Describe the importance of health communication in assisting individuals and families in making desired behavioral changes
- Define and describe elements of health literacy and describe the poor health outcomes related to low health literacy
- Describe key principles in the development of health literacy materials
- Describe and discuss customer service in healthcare settings
- Describe patient responsibilities during clinical appointments

CHAPTER OVERVIEW

This chapter explores the topics of health communication and health literacy. First, communication is defined as the process of using words, sounds, signs, or behaviors to exchange information with another individual. This exchange occurs in person, on paper, through technology, or perhaps merely through touch or a facial expression. Regardless of the topic being communicated, proper expression is needed for understanding. For instance, everyone has had the experience of sending or receiving a text or email that included the correct words, but due to lack of facial expression or context, the message was misunderstood. The same is true in health communication. If the individual is not conveying the correct message for a variety of reasons, then the other individual is unable to receive and understand the message. Second, literacy is defined as the understanding and ability to use written text to participate in society to achieve goals and develop knowledge and potential.[1] Literacy is not only about understanding words, but also numbers. Numeracy is related to the use of numbers and is defined as the ability to use, interpret, and communicate mathematical information and ideas to manage mathematical demands in adult life.[2] This chapter explores health literacy with an emphasis on the consequences of inadequate communication (e.g., medical errors, hospital readmissions), ways to develop health materials, customer service enhancement, and responsibilities of the healthcare providers and patients. Let us begin with a closer investigation of adult literacy, specifically health literacy.

© REB Images/Getty

ADULT LITERACY AND NUMERACY

The U.S. National Assessment of Adult Literacy (NAAL) reports literacy levels based on the Basic Reading Score (BRS). The BRS score is a simple average of passage reading, word reading, and decoding scores presented as the number of words read correctly per minute. The U.S. adult population is categorized into the following health literacy levels: 14 percent with below basic skills (e.g., reading fewer than 60 words correctly per minute), 22 percent with basic skills (e.g., reading fewer than 98 words correctly per minute), 53 percent with intermediate skills (e.g., reading more than 99 words correctly per minute), and 11 percent with proficient skills.[3]

Reasons for limited literacy skills include: (a) lack of educational opportunity, such as individuals with less than a high school education; (b) individuals with developmental or learning disabilities; (c) individuals with cognitive decline due to aging or medical condition (e.g., stroke, Parkinson's disease, Alzheimer's disease); and (d) individuals with limited exposure to reading, because reading abilities are typically 3 to 5 years below the last year of education completed. For example, an individual with a high school diploma usually reads at a seventh or eighth grade reading level.[4] Adults with below basic or basic health literacy are more likely to obtain health information from radio and television. This verbal communication does not allow them to review the information or gain further understanding through additional written materials. Adults with higher health literacy obtain information about health issues from written sources (newspapers, magazines, books, brochures, the Internet).[3] By reading information, adults with higher literacy skills have the ability to compare and contrast information from several sources.

HEALTH LITERACY

The relationship between literacy and health is complex. Literacy is the ability to read (words or numbers) and understand the meaning, while health literacy involves a complex group of skills including reading, listening, analyzing information, decision making, and applying these skills to health situations.[4] For example, an individual must navigate the healthcare system to obtain an appointment, have transportation to arrive at the appointment on time, complete required forms, obtain health insurance, and bring proof of health insurance, money, or method of payment to appointments, explain symptoms to the healthcare provider, understand explanations of medical conditions, obtain a medical prescription, and understand where to fill the prescription, how

© goldy/ iStockphoto

to take the prescription, and make appointments for additional follow-up care. To accomplish such tasks, individuals are likely to need (a) visual literacy (ability to understand graphs and charts); (b) computer literacy (ability to use a computer); (c) information literacy (ability to seek appropriate information); and (d) numerical and/or computational literacy (ability to calculate and understand simple math).[4]

Health literacy impacts health knowledge, health status, and access to health services. Several socioeconomic factors impact literacy and health status, including income level, occupation, education, housing, and access to medical care. In addition, individuals working under hazardous conditions or be exposed to environmental toxins (e.g., coal mines, roofing, pesticide exposure).

Populations that are vulnerable to low health literacy include the following four groups. First, older adults use more medical services due to noncommunicable disease than any other segment of the population. For example, 71 percent of older adults have difficulty reading printed materials, and 80 percent have difficulty understanding forms and charts.[3] Second, immigrant adult populations that spoke a language other than English prior to starting school are more likely to have low health literacy levels.[3] Third, when comparing minority populations, 41 percent of Hispanics, 25 percent of American Indians and Native Alaskans, 24 percent of African

Americans, and 13 percent of Asians scored below basic literacy levels.[3] Finally, adults living below the poverty level have lower average health literacy levels than the general population as well as individuals with chronic mental and/or physical health conditions.[3] Therefore, individuals with low health literacy use more healthcare services, have a greater risk for hospitalization, and have a higher utilization of expensive services, such as emergency care and inpatient admissions.[3]

In addition to written health literacy, individuals must achieve verbal health literacy. Individuals must be able to explain their medical symptoms to healthcare providers accurately as well as understand the medical advice and directions for treatment, follow-up, and prescriptions. Verbal communication also includes the ability to ask appropriate questions to gain knowledge and understanding of medical condition. Without adequate health communication, the individual will likely encounter mild to serious health consequences.[4] The next section discusses the health outcomes related to poor health literacy.

Consequences of Inadequate Health Literacy

Without sufficient health literacy skills, individuals are unable to understand their medical conditions and may quickly fall into a downward spiral leading to poor health outcomes, increased hospital readmission, and eventually death. **Table 12.1**

TABLE 12.1 Research Related to Low Health Literacy and Poor Health Outcomes

Topic	Research Results
Prevention Care	Individuals with low health literacy are less likely to receive a seasonal flu shots, understand medical labels and instructions, and are at greater risk of taking medicines incorrectly compared to adults with higher health literacy[5] and are less likely to use preventative care.[6]
Healthcare Costs	Inpatient spending increases by approximately $993 for patients with limited health literacy.[7] The annual cost of low health literacy to the U.S. economy is $106 billion to $238 billion.[8]
Cancer	Merriman (2002) reported three results: (a) cancer screening information may be ineffective; as a result, patients may be diagnosed at a later stage; (b) treatment options may not be fully understood; therefore, some patients may not receive treatments that best meet their needs; and (c) informed-consent documents may be too complex for many patients and, consequently, patients may make suboptimal decisions about accepting or rejecting interventions.[9]

Topic	Research Results
Diabetes	Individuals diagnosed with Type 2 diabetes and have inadequate health literacy are likely to have worse glycemic control and higher rates of retinopathy. In addition, inadequate health literacy may contribute to the disproportionate burden of diabetes-related problems among disadvantaged populations.[10]
Asthma	Inadequate literacy was common and strongly correlated with poorer knowledge of asthma and improper metered-dose inhaler (MDI) use. More than half of patients reading at a sixth-grade level or less report they go to the emergency department when they have an attack compared to less than a third of literate patients. Less than one-third of patients with the poorest reading skills knew they should see a physician when their asthma was not symptomatic as compared to 90 percent of literate patients.[11]
Hypertension and Diabetes	Almost half (48%) of the patients with hypertension or diabetes in a study had inadequate functional health literacy, and these patients had significantly less knowledge of their disease, important lifestyle modifications, and essential self-management skills, despite having attended formal education classes.[11]
Poor Outcomes	Individuals with low levels of health literacy are more likely to be hospitalized and have bad disease outcomes.[10]

presents some of the research results related to low health literacy that affect poor health outcomes.

Even though the discussion has focused on individuals with low health literacy skills, it is also possible for adults with high literacy skills to encounter a health literacy challenge at some point in their lives because they are not familiar with a health condition or medical diagnosis. When individuals and their family members face such health challenges, they may attempt to increase their knowledge and understanding in hopes of making appropriate decisions. However, some individuals determine that their healthcare provider is the expert and only follow the advice without seeking additional information. Information-seeking individuals acquire facts in the following sequence:

- During the initial appointment when the diagnosis is given, the individual hears the diagnosis but becomes overwhelmed with fear, so only a limited amount of information is understood or retained.
- After the diagnosis is obtained, the individual begins to seek health information. This process may begin with an Internet search, if the individual is computer literate.
- Basic knowledge of the diagnosis leads to an attempt to understand the physiology of the health condition.
- With greater understanding and knowledge, the individual begins to ask specific questions about available treatment options and services.
- The healthcare provider may provide health statistics that the individual must interpret to make decisions about the risks and benefits of treatment options.
- The individual returns to the Internet to seek more in-depth information about the available treatment options. If the individual lacks access to a computer or computer literacy, friends and family members become the primary source of information clarification.

This cycle of seeking and understanding continues throughout the process of most health conditions or medical diagnoses. Each step of information acquisition provides the healthcare provider with an opportunity to answer questions. See **Scenario 12.1**.

SCENARIO 12.1 Mr. Bigelow

Mr. Bigelow is 89 years old, lives in a retirement community in independent living apartments, and exercises every day in the fitness center. His hypertension is controlled with one medication. He has never been overweight and eats a healthy diet in the community dining room with his friends. On Tuesday, when Mr. Bigelow got out of bed and walked to the bathroom, he noticed a slight numbness on the left side of his face. His wife of 58 years had died of a stroke, so he immediately called the nurse's station located within the retirement community. Robert, the nurse, arrived at his apartment within minutes and examined Mr. Bigelow.

While Mr. Bigelow waited for the nurse, he called his daughter, Elan. She is employed in banking, and her office is near her dad's retirement community. Elan, age 54, is Mr. Bigelow's only child. Mr. Bigelow put his daughter on speaker phone so she could hear what Robert was saying during the initial examination. Robert called for an ambulance during the initial assessment because he was uncertain about Mr. Bigelow's health status. Robert knew the signs + symptoms of a stroke. He assumed that Mr. Bigelow was having a stroke and did not waste calling an ambulance. See **Box 12.1** and **Box 12.2**. Elan agreed and told her dad that she would go to St. Mary's Hospital and meet him in the emergency department.

After arriving at St. Mary's Hospital, Mr. Bigelow connected with his daughter. The physician examined him and ordered a scan of his brain to determine the diagnosis. Soon after the scan was read by the radiologist, the physician came back to Mr. Bigelow's room. He explained that Mr. Bigelow had a brain tumor called a *glioblastoma* and wanted to admit Mr. Bigelow to the hospital for a neurological evaluation. Mr. Bigelow and Elan agreed with the physician's suggestion, and he was moved to the inpatient neurological unit. Even though Mr. Bigelow and Elan were scared, she remembered to ask for the name of the neurologist who would be treating her father. The hospital nurse told her that the neurologist who would be seeing her father was named Dr. Lee.

Elan called Dr. Lee's office and asked if she could schedule a phone appointment to discuss her father's medical diagnosis. In the meantime, she searched the Internet to gain information about the glioblastoma diagnosis. Elan wanted to prepare questions to ask Dr. Lee during their phone appointment. Although she had a phone appointment, Elan was fortunate to be visiting her dad when Dr. Lee stopped by his room. Because Elan had prepared her questions, she and her dad were able to gain more information about their treatment options.

After a long discussion with Elan after Dr. Lee's visit, Mr. Bigelow made it clear to Elan that he did not want any treatment. He stated that he was 89 and had lived a full life. He had learned from Dr. Lee that the radiation treatment would likely make him sick and may or may not extend his life by any more than perhaps a few months. Dr. Le explained that without any treatment, Mr. Bigelow would die with minimal pain within 3–6 months. Mr. Bigelow requested that Dr. Lee write a referral to hospice and was discharged the following day. He returned to his apartment and received 24-hour hospice care for 4 months prior to his peaceful death with Elan at his side. Over the course of those 4 months, Elan went from not being able to properly pronounce glioblastoma to feeling comfortable with this type of brain tumor. With some Internet research and asking Dr. Lee questions, Elan learned the physiology of how the brain tumor developed and how her beloved father would die. She was comfortable knowing that her father would not suffer pain prior to his death.

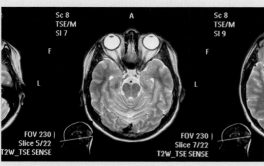

© Kondor83/iStock/Thinkstock

BOX 12.1 Signs of Stroke in Men and Women

Sudden **numbness** or weakness in the face, arm, or leg, especially on one side of the body

Sudden **confusion**, trouble speaking, or difficulty understanding speech

Sudden **trouble seeing** in one or both eyes

Sudden **trouble walking**, dizziness, loss of balance, or lack of coordination

Sudden **severe headache** with no known cause

Call 9-1-1 immediately if you or someone else has any of these symptoms.

The Centers for Disease Control and Prevention (2015). Stroke Signs and Symptoms. Available at: http://www.cdc.gov/Stroke/signs _symptoms.htm.[12]

BOX 12.2 Acting F.A.S.T. Stroke Test

Acting F.A.S.T. can help stroke patients get the treatment that they desperately need. The most effective stroke treatments are available only if the stroke is recognized and diagnosed within 3 hours of the first symptoms. Stroke patients may not be eligible for the most effective treatments if they don't arrive at the hospital in time.

If you think someone may be having a stroke, act F.A.S.T. and do the following simple test:

F—Face: Ask the person to smile. Does one side of the face droop?

A—Arms: Ask the person to raise both arms. Does one arm drift downward?

S—Speech: Ask the person to repeat a simple phrase. Is his or her speech slurred or strange?

T—Time: If you observe any of these signs, call 9-1-1 immediately.

The Centers for Disease Control and Prevention (2015). Stroke Signs and Symptoms. Available at: http://www.cdc.gov/Stroke/signs _symptoms.htm.[12]

DEVELOPING HEALTH MATERIALS

Now that you are aware of the basic concept of health literacy, the discussion moves into the development of appropriate written health materials for various types of audiences. In 2010, President Obama signed the Plain Writing Act, which requires federal agencies to write all government communications in language that the public can understand and use.[13] Let's explore each of the key points of the Plain Writing Act of 2010 by asking a few questions:[13]

a. Who is the audience?

b. How is it best to organize the information?

c. What information is being communicated?

Who Is the Audience?

Prior to writing health information for a specific audience, it is important to get to know the cultural background of the audience. An individual's culture affects how they communicate, understand, and respond to health information. Culture includes an individual's beliefs, values, attitudes, traditions, language preferences, and health practices. For example, the community healthcare clinic may be located in a neighborhood where many refugees seek a common support network with common values in their resettlement endeavor. Refugees seeking political or religious asylum may have college degrees with years of professional experience prior to the war-torn events in their home countries. Depending on their country of origin, refugees may have excellent literacy in their native language and a range of English competency skills. On the other hand, some migrant families come to the United States seeking a better life, but have limited literacy in their native language and inadequate English communication skills. In addition to language and education, it is important to learn other aspects of the various cultural healthcare practices. Keep in mind that there is sometimes a fine line between cultural beliefs and religious beliefs.

The following are a few examples of cultural and/or religious beliefs that influence healthcare behaviors:

a. The patient prefers a healthcare provider the same gender as himself or herself.
b. The female relatives are present at the birth instead of the infant's father.
c. Breastfeeding is preferred, while in other cultures bottle feeding is more common.
d. Some families use herbal remedies as the first line of treatment rather than going to a healthcare provider.
e. The family prefers to bring food to the patient rather than accepting hospital food.
f. Some religious beliefs are against receiving vaccines, blood products, and organ donations.
g. Some families call their own ministers to anoint and care for the body immediately after death instead of the hospital staff.
h. Some families are not comfortable with making end-of-life decisions for loved ones.

Regardless of the culture of the population, it is up to the healthcare provider to recognize cultural beliefs, values, attitudes, traditions, language preferences, and health practices and to apply that knowledge to produce positive health outcomes. Without the healthcare provider acquiring some level of cultural competency relative to the population that is served, health outcomes are compromised. Keep in mind that competency includes communicating in a manner that is linguistically as well as culturally appropriate. In addition, it is important to remember that healthcare providers have their own "culture." Healthcare providers have a language that is specialized and generally loaded with acronyms resulting from their training and work environment. As healthcare providers move through their day, it is important to remain aware of how their own culture and language

affect their communication and health literacy skills with their patients and the public.

One of the easiest ways to learn about a culture or religion is to simply ask the family or members of the community. In most situations, individuals are willing to exchange knowledge about their beliefs with the healthcare providers. In return, they are likely to ask questions about practices that they have observed but not understood within the U.S. culture. This opportunity opens the conversation to shared communication with greater knowledge and understanding. The worst approach is to act on a cultural assumption and to learn later the notion was incorrect.[14] Finally, here is a list of potential questions to ask regarding the audience when designing appropriate culturally competent health information materials: [13, 15]

- Who is the audience?
- What does the audience already know about the subject?
- What does the audience need to know?
- What questions will the audience have?
- What's the best outcome for the audience?
- What needs to be said to get this outcome?

How Is It Best to Organize the Information?

When deciding on how to organize the health information—whether in a brochure or on a website—it is best to present information in chronological order (e.g., general information first, exceptions, conditions, and specialized information later). It is also important to express only one idea in each sentence for ease of understanding. This helps to break up ideas into their parts and make each one the subject of its own sentence. This technique is called "chunking." If the brochure or website has a paragraph format, limit the information in each paragraph to one topic. Lists with consistent bullet points help to organize the information. For example, the bullet point should say "Take this medication with a glass of water" instead of "When taking this medication, it is recommended that you drink a glass of water." The first bullet point contains 8 words, while the second bullet point contains 14 words.

The list may provide an explanation for a step-by-step process or the list may be illustrated in two columns, such as one column for healthy food choices and a second column for unhealthy food to avoid. Using color (e.g., green for healthy foods and red for unhealthy foods) also helps to organize the information for the reader. It is important to remain consistent throughout the brochure. For example, always use the same bullet design and font style; use color sparingly so the brochure is not confusing. When the information contains a list of action items, each bullet point must be concise.

Finally, avoid using all capital letters at any time. ALL CAPS IS MUCH HARDER TO READ AND UNDERSTAND FOR A LOW LITERACY POPULATION. Think in terms of how a person acquires a second language. He or she learns the basic alphabet of the language and then simple words, commonly used phrases, verb tense, and finally sentence structure. When learning a new alphabet, it is difficult enough to learn the letters and sounds without having to work around learning capital letters. See **Box 12.3** and **Box 12.4** for additional information on organizing information.

What Information Is Being Communicated?

Information is communicated in a written (e.g., brochure or website) or verbal format. Information may also include numbers as well as words. Two categories of individuals struggle with written and verbal communication. First, as previously stated, vulnerable populations with low health literacy skills include older adults, immigrant populations, minority populations, and low income populations. People with low health literacy use more healthcare services, have a greater risk for hospitalization, and have a higher utilization of expensive services, such as emergency care and inpatient admissions.[4]

Second, there are also individuals with high literacy in their native language, but low literacy in the language of their current location. Regardless of their status, all individuals must have some knowledge of the language to understand any portion of the health information. See **Table 12.2**. If the individual's native language utilizes the same alphabet, he or she may recognize a few English words. This technique works only if the health information is provided in a written rather than verbal format. However, with a totally different

---

BOX 12.3 Written Information Tips

- Individuals scan instead of reading entire web pages.
- Begin with a short, clear statement. Put the most important information first.
- Individuals start at the top-left side of the page and then read headings or bulleted lists.
- On average, individuals read the first two words on each line.
- Individuals decide in as little as 5 seconds whether the site is useful to them.
- On websites, avoid posting PDF files. PDF files often cause difficulty and confusion, such as not knowing how to navigate back to the original website from the PDF file or not having the current version of the software to read PDF files.
- Write short headings in the form of a question (e.g., Are you interested in losing weight?).
- Use active verbs (e.g., Eat three serving of vegetables each day) and avoid passive voice (e.g., Three servings of vegetables should be eaten daily).
- Use pronouns (e.g., *you* and *we*), so the reader relates to the sentence.
- Use common, familiar words.
- Avoid jargon, technical terms, and unnecessary words.
- Use vertical lists to make clear the level of importance, order, or step-by-step process.
- Minimize abbreviations and, if used, always define the first time, such as "Chronic Obstructive Pulmonary Disease (COPD)."
- Omit unnecessary information.

BOX 12.4 The Three A's

The Centers for Disease Control and Prevention (CDC) suggests starting with the health information related to The Three "A"s:

Accurate: Health information needs to be accurate and written in a way that individuals can understand.

Accessible: Health information needs to be located where individuals see it even if they are not looking for information. For example, if a brochure about hypertension is placed at the sign-in window of a clinic, individuals may take it, read it while waiting, and ask the healthcare provider about their hypertension status. If the brochure is placed at the check-out counter, it is less likely that individuals will take it because they are eager to leave after their visit.

Actionable: It is important to provide health information in small segments. There is no point in giving an elaborate explanation of the physiology of the differences between Stage II and Stage III cancer prior to giving a cancer diagnosis. Individuals are only capable of hearing one segment of pertinent information. In this case, the individual only hears that the diagnosis showed cancer in a specific organ. Once the initial information is understood, the individual can hear the stage of the cancer. Each segment of information is followed by an action item. For this example, the action item would be a brochure explaining the type and stage of cancer. The second action item would be a referral to an oncologist for treatment.

Modified from: The Centers for Disease Control and Prevention (2014). Health Literacy-Develop Materials. Available at: http://www.cdc .gov/healthliteracy/developmaterials/index.html[16]

alphabet, it is impossible to decipher any words. Keep this activity in mind as you begin to work with families who are fluent and highly educated in their native language, but have not yet acquired adequate literacy in English. For instance, if you traveled to Korea and acquired an illness, how well would you navigate the healthcare system to receive treatment?

Finally, numerous computer software programs and smartphone apps are available to provide good-to-excellent translation services. Such programs make translation simple and easy for global travelers.

As for verbal communication, when providing health information to an individual with low literacy skills, it is best to also give written

TABLE 12.2 Same Information in Three Languages

Language	Similar Words	
English	Navigator medical attention clinic	Hello, my name is Linda. I am a health navigation professional. I will help you to understand how you can receive medical attention at this clinic. Do you have any questions before we get started?
Spanish	Navegador atención medica clinica	Hola, me llamo Linda. Yo soy navegador oficial de la salud. Le puedo ayudar a entender como puede recibir atención medica en esta clinica. ¿Tiene usted algunas preguntas antes de empezar?
Chinese		你好，我的名字是琳达。我是一个健康导航器。我将帮助您理解如何您可以收到这个诊所的卫生保健。在我们开始之前，你有任何问题吗？

materials with the same information to supplement the conversation. The supplemental material allows the individual to take the information to a family member or friend with higher literacy skills in order to assist with understanding the health information. See **Scenario 12.2**.

In addition to basic literacy skills, health literacy requires some knowledge of health topics. People with limited health literacy lack health knowledge or have misinformation about the human body and causes of disease. Without some health knowledge in their native language, individuals may not understand the need to take medications on time, the signs and symptoms of disease, or the relationship between lifestyle factors such as diet and exercise and various health outcomes. With this lack of understanding, individuals may revert to beliefs such as fatalism, where they believe that they have no control over the outcome of their disease. Health literacy is also influenced by the individual's age, education, language, culture, and access to resources.[17]

Keep in mind that health information, whether in a printed brochure or on a website, can overwhelm even those individuals with high literacy skills, but perhaps in a field outside of health care. For example, an individual trained in mechanical engineering may or may not have a thorough understanding of anatomy and physiology. When they seek information, the volume that they find may be intimidating. In addition, health information changes frequently. Whatever an individual learned in high school biology has changed drastically or has been forgotten. Finally, when a medical diagnosis is given to an individual, it is likely to cause stress and anxiety. During such times of increased stress, the health information provided is less likely to be retained.

So far, this discussion has investigated the verbal and written information that individuals receive from healthcare providers, but it is also important to consider the written and verbal information that the individual conveys to the healthcare provider. An individual's health literacy affects his or her ability to communicate with the healthcare system. For example, navigation of the healthcare system includes completing complex forms regarding one's medical history, completing health insurance forms for payment and reimbursement, finding the office location of healthcare providers, and discovering community support services.

The services of a health navigation professional would greatly serve an individual struggling to complete all types of forms, because completing forms incorrectly may lead to incorrect healthcare charges and potential medical errors that may be life threatening. For example, individuals are encouraged to bring the labeled containers of their daily medications to their medical appointments. If they do not bring the containers, they may fail to list each medication correctly. This error of omission could lead to serious consequences if the healthcare provider is unaware and prescribes a contraindicated medication.

SCENARIO 12.2 Mrs. Blackwell

When providing verbal action items, it is essential to use clear instructions along with the same instructions in written format for greatest comprehension. For example, Dr. Zimmerman tells Mrs. Blackwell, age 78, that he wants her to have some blood drawn in the lab. If Dr. Zimmerman hands her the paper prescription for the lab tests with no directions, she will likely skip going to the lab, struggle to locate the parking garage, and drive home. Dr. Zimmerman needs to clearly state the action item while providing the lab prescription and a paper map.

Dr. Zimmerman: "Mrs. Blackwell, the lab is located on the second floor. When you exit the elevator, you will see a big green sign on the right. That is the lab. They are waiting for you to draw your blood for the tests. Do you understand that you are going to the second floor for the lab?"

Mrs. Blackwell: "Yes, second floor and big green sign. I got it."

For example, warfarin is a commonly prescribed medication used for reducing blood clots. If the healthcare provider is unaware that the individual is taking warfarin, the provider may prescribe another type of anti-blood-clotting medication. This error of omission could result in a fatal overdose of two types of the same medication. Fortunately, the individual could avoid such serious consequences if he or she used the same national chain pharmacy (e.g., CVS, Walgreen's, Walmart) to fill all of his or her prescriptions. Each national chain pharmacy has a database that compares the prescriptions for safety. Unfortunately, the chain pharmacies are not linked to each other. Therefore, if the individual fills one prescription at CVS and the next at Walmart, there is no link for checking. It is wise for health navigation professionals to recommend that individuals use the same national chain pharmacy for all prescriptions to avoid serious consequences.

In addition to understanding words, it is important to have basic knowledge of numbers and mathematical equations. In health care, individuals need to use math skills to understand important concepts (e.g., how to measure liquid medications, count the number of pills needed over a 24-hour period, understand nutrition labels). Math skills are also needed to select health insurance plans when balancing the cost of monthly premiums and prescription drugs, calculating co-payments for office visits, and determining the out-of-pocket costs for annual deductibles. Finally, math skills are needed to

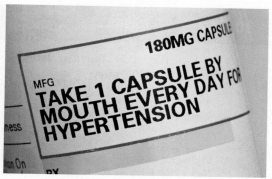

© Roel Smart/ iStockphoto

understand health concepts related to probability and risk. For instance, the healthcare provider may tell an individual that 1 in 4 individuals with the same medical diagnosis used Drug A and experienced improvement. Without adequate understanding of math skills, the individual may think that the healthcare provider is stating that Drug A is useful. However, upon further calculation, the individual would realize that 3 out of 4 individuals did not show improvement. As a result, math skills are essential when making informed decisions about health care.

In addition to the information presented, let us discuss the layout of a useful brochure or website by addressing a few questions:[16]

- Does the brochure or website have one main message statement?
- Is the information easy to skim and receive the main message?
- Is the font large enough to be read without reading glasses?
- Are subheadings and bullets used to divide the information into readable segments?
- Is there adequate white space to make the print appear clear and uncluttered?
- Are upper- and lowercase letters used appropriately? (*Hint*: Individuals with low literacy skills have difficulty reading all capital letters.)
- Do the graphics match the text and have useful captions?
- Is the readability level below an eighth grade reading level? See **Box 12.5** and **Figure 12.1**.

© AlexRaths/ iStockphoto

BOX 12.5 Readability Level in Word

1. Click the **File** tab and then click **Options**.
2. Click **Proofing**.
3. When correcting spelling and grammar in Word, make sure the Check Spelling & Grammar check box is selected.
4. Select Show Readability Statistics.

Or

1. Highlight the section that you wish to check for readability.
2. Click **F7** on the function keys.

Student Practice Activity

Practice your skills by downloading information describing Type 2 diabetes. Check the readability level. If it is higher than an eighth grade level, rewrite the information into a lower readability level. Check your skills by checking the readability level of the material that you have rewritten.

FIGURE 12.1 Readability Statistics

Readability Statistics	
Counts	
Words	214
Characters	1029
Paragraphs	1
Sentences	14
Averages	
Sentences per Paragraph	14.0
Words per Sentence	15.2
Characters per Word	4.6
Readability	
Passive Sentences	14%
Flesch Reading Ease	54.1
Flesch-Kincaid Grade Level	9.5

OK

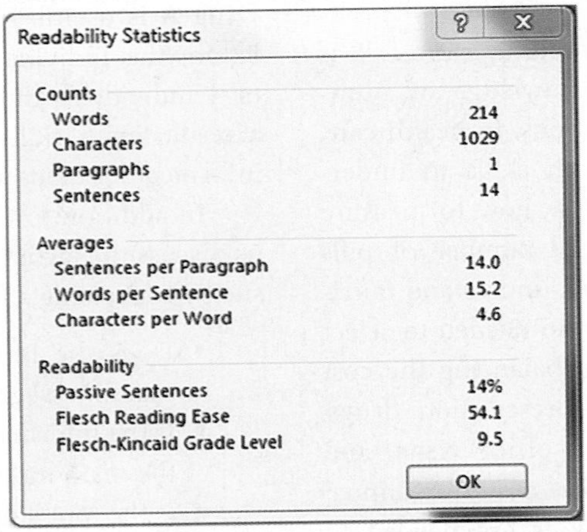

NUMBERS

Before moving onto the next topic, let us discuss ways to communicate numbers. As with words, individuals need a working knowledge of numbers and equations to make sense of health information that is conveyed by numbers. For instance, individuals may need to calculate whether they have enough pills to last until their next clinic appointment, read nutrition labels to adhere to their low sodium diet, estimate the cost of prescription medications, or rate pain on a 0 to 10 pain scale. It is important to simplify the message about numbers. Individuals with a poor understanding of numbers and

© monkeybusinessimages/ iStockphoto

calculations must rely on the help of others for accurate interpretation. In addition, some individuals may state their lab values or their blood pressure, but without medical knowledge, the numbers remain meaningless. For example, one individual's blood pressure may be 142/88 and the healthcare provider is pleased with the positive change due to prescribing a new medication, because at the previous visit the individual's blood was 179/98. However, if the individual's usual blood pressure has been about 120/60 during most recent visits, but at this visit it is 142/88 after two readings and for no apparent reason, this sudden increase would cause concern for the healthcare provider.

Charts and graphs are useful in some situations, but not in others. For example, a pediatrician plots the height and weight of a child on a graph to illustrate to the parent that the child is on target for his or her age. The healthcare provider explains to the parent that for the child's age, height and weight are appropriate. If the child is gaining weight too quickly, the growth chart illustrates that the child is gaining weight faster than he or she is growing. See **Figure 12.2.**

As for conveying statistical information, if the research report states that 410 out of 1000 study participants noticed improvement on Drug A, it is easier to understand that about 1 in 4 individuals reported an improvement after using Drug A. Another convenient method of

conveying numbers is to provide common examples. For instance, 4 ounces of chicken breast is about the size of a deck of cards; 1 ounce of hard cheese is about the size of an adult's thumb. Show the differences when measuring liquid by comparing four 8-ounce glasses of liquid side-by-side: ¼ cup (2 ounces), ½ cup (4 ounces), ¾ cup (6 ounces), and 1 cup (8 ounces). Also, one portion of cooked pasta is illustrated by filling an 8-ounce measuring cup and then placing the pasta portion onto a dinner plate. This portion size does not look like the typical portion served in most restaurants. Nevertheless, portion size is critical information for individuals to understand for medical compliance. There are endless ways to illustrate measurement by using common household items. It is important to ask individuals for a return demonstration or to teach it back to the provider, so it is clear that they comprehend the skills. Finally, numbers are often confusing to individuals, but also to health navigation professionals and healthcare providers. For instance, the U.S. numerical system is based on decimals, while most other countries utilize the metric system. In the past, school children learned formulas for such conversions, but now there are websites and apps for the formulas: www.metric-conversions.org/number/decimal-conversion.htm.

VISUALS

Visuals including pictures, charts, graphs, and diagrams are excellent tools for communicating health information. The phase "a picture is worth a 1000 words" is true. Visuals convey information to individuals with low literacy skills as well as individuals with limited English proficiency. Pictures may also be used to describe symptoms. **Figure 12.3** illustrates a headache; **Figure 12.4** shows a headache and abdominal pain.

When making health education brochures, it is also useful to use a limited amount of illustrations to explain a topic. Keep in mind that visuals do not speak for themselves and should be used to

FIGURE 12.2 CDC Growth Charts: United States

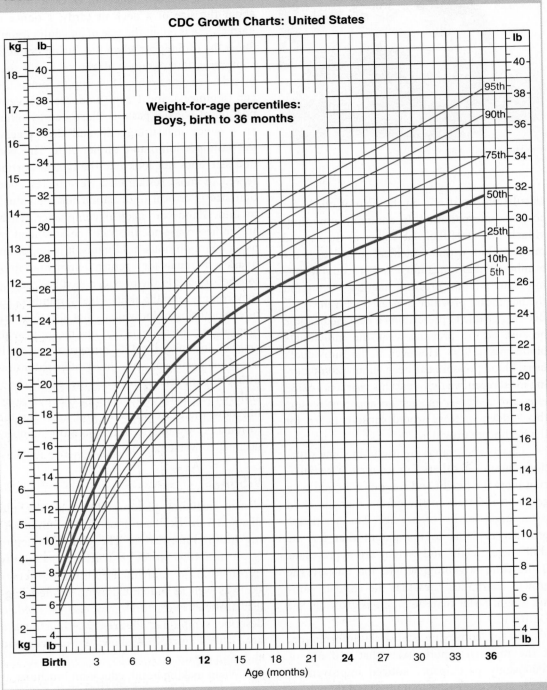

Developed by the National Center for Health Statistics in collaboration with the National Center for Chronic Disease Prevention and Health Promotion (2000).

FIGURE 12.3 Headache

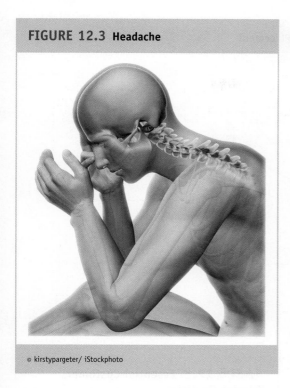

© kirstypargeter/ iStockphoto

support THE main message. Visuals are not used without an explanation, for this increases confusion in the health message.[18]

FIGURE 12.4 Headache and Abdominal Pain

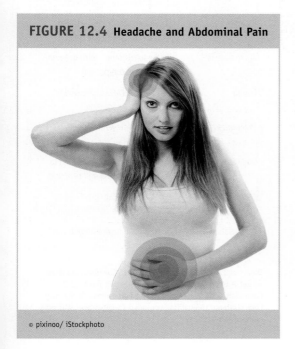

© pixinoo/ iStockphoto

FIGURE 12.5 Display of Organs without Labels and Placement

When using pictures and models to provide examples of body systems (e.g., cardiovascular system) or organs (e.g., heart, lungs, uterus), it is important to show the system or organ in relationship to the whole body. See **Figure 12.5**, **Figure 12.6**, and **Figure 12.7**. Figure 12.5 shows the uterus, fallopian tubes, and ovaries without any labels or connection to placement in the body. Figure 12.6 has appropriate labels and organ placement within the body. Figure 12.7 combines body placement and labels for clarification.

So far, this chapter has presented health literacy and the key points of the Plain Writing Act of 2010, including the audience, information organization, and communication through written and verbal text. The next section explores the aspects of health communication, including customer service and preparation for a conversation with a healthcare provider.

CUSTOMER SERVICE

First and foremost, customer service is essential for health communication. Without the basic qualities of customer service, any attempt at positive communication is likely to fail. In the field of health care, all team members (e.g., physicians, nurses, laboratory technicians, clerical and dietary staff) must exhibit quality customer

FIGURE 12.6 Display of Organs with Labels and Placement

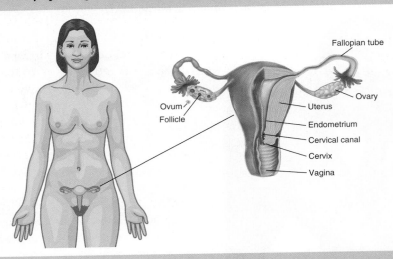

FIGURE 12.7 Display of Hip and Femur with Body Placement

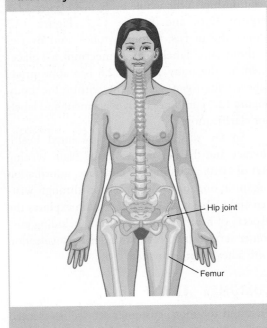

TABLE 12.3 Essential Customer Service Qualities

Quality	Definition
Self-Control	Control thoughts and comments.
Strong Work Ethic	Go above and beyond the job description to solve problems.
Patience	Listen and search for a solution with a slow and steady pace.
Relationships	Relate to customers with genuine concern and compassion.
Caring	Show a positive attitude while searching for a solution.
Willingness to Help	Assist in whatever manner is needed.
Knowledge	Know the answer or be willing to say that the answer will be found.
Team Member	Work with all team members to maintain customer satisfaction.
Appreciation	Show a genuine gratitude toward the customer.

Data from: Rudolph, Stacey (2012). 15 Qualities You Need To Get A Good Customer Service Job. From Business 2 Community. Available at: http://www.business2community.com/strategy/15-qualities-you-need-to-get-a-good-customer-service-job-0139217[19]

service skills to achieve adequate health communication. See **Table 12.3**.

Keep in mind that words alone are powerful, but attitude also influences the level of customer satisfaction. Try to remember a situation in which you received excellent customer service in a healthcare office and a time when you received poor customer service in a healthcare office. Was the poor quality due only to the words that were spoken? Was an individual ignoring you as you stood by the counter, waiting to schedule your next appointment? Did the healthcare provider ask with a genuine concern if you had any further questions at the end of the appointment or was his or her hand on the doorknob when the question was asked? If you had a poor experience, remember how you felt leaving the office. How likely are you to return for a similar experience at your next appointment? If the experience was positive, was your attitude different regarding your next appointment?

In a work environment, the attitude toward customers is also reflected among coworkers. If most employees are not enjoying their jobs, the negative attitude spreads quickly through the staff and thus is reflected in customer service. However, if the employer sets a tone of positive attitude and enjoyment, the staff reflect this congeniality to each other and the customers. Keep in mind that most individuals spend more hours per day at their place of employment than they do with their family members. If your place of employment feels like it is draining your energy due to a negative environment, it is time to search for another place of employment. See **Table 12.4** for ways to create a positive work environment.

CONFIGURATION OF A POSITIVE ENVIRONMENT

Now that a positive work environment has been defined, let us explore the configuration of a positive environment. Environment is composed of the people and the configuration (structure, location, décor, ambiance, sound, air quality). If the healthcare team is positive, they can work together even in a rundown location and make the interactions with individuals a positive experience. On the other hand, the best location with fancy furniture and a negative staff with bad attitudes will not lead to a positive interaction. Therefore, it is a combination of a positive healthcare team and a cheery work environment (even if the location is not new and ideally furnished) that leads to good outcomes.

Before delving deeper into this discussion, let us think about a typical day in a busy clinic. First, the office staff spend their time multitasking throughout the day, including answering phones, making appointments, checking-in patients, verifying insurance, collecting payments, ordering supplies—the list goes on and on. As for the clinic staff, they are interviewing, examining, teaching, ordering, explaining, and helping patients and families learn and cope with various illnesses. All employees are occupied with some day-to-day routine tasks, but most of their employment responsibilities are focused on customer service and working

TABLE 12.4 Ways to Create a Positive Work Environment

Quality	Definition
Empowerment	Train employees to make decisions to solve immediate problems.
Positivity	Avoid reasons for destructive gossip and speculation.
Transparency	Keep employees informed regarding pending changes and policies.
Feedback	Address the problem and work toward a mutual compromise.
Mistake	Admit to mistakes; move forward with changes to avoid same error again.
Pest	Identify personnel issue, remove the individual, and regain stability.

Data from: Forbes Magazine (2012). The 10 Keys of Excellent Customer Service. Available at: http://www.forbes.com/sites/aileron/2012/11/15/the-10-keys-of-excellent-customer-service/[20]

SCENARIO 12.3 Welcome to the Office

As Ms. Jeffery pulled into the tree-lined parking lot, she was surprised to see plenty of empty spaces. She entered a 1920-style bungalow home that had been converted into Dr. Sinclair's oncology office. At first glance, she noticed the hardwood floors, fireplace and multiple rattan chairs with inviting soft, flower-patterned cushions, and a few wooden rocking chairs. The sign-in window was not a window, but rather Lisa, a friendly clerk, in an alcove off to the left of the front door. Lisa greeted Ms. Jeffery, made a copy of her health insurance card, asked how Ms. Jeffery wished to pay the $40 co-payment, and took the CD scans and reports. Lisa mentioned that Dr. Sinclair would see Ms. Jeffery in about 10 minutes and invited her to pour herself a cup of spiced tea, which was available next to the fireplace.

SCENARIO 12.4 Office of Inefficiency

As Ms. Jeffery pulled into the parking garage of the medical office building, she wound her way up several floors before finding a parking place. After locating the parking garage elevator, she walked into the six-story medical building. She took the elevator to the fifth floor, exited, and found the appropriate office door. The large, tiled waiting room was cluttered with outdated magazines and had several rows of cushioned chairs bolted together and facing the flat-screen television, which was tuned to a local news station. Several clerks were at an open counter; one of them asked her to sign in on the clipboard and take a seat. After a few minutes, she was called to the counter. A nondescript female with no name tag asked Ms. Jeffery for her health insurance card, test results, and a credit card for the co-payment. She also handed Ms. Jeffery another clipboard with several pages of forms to complete prior to seeing the physician. Ms. Jeffery commented that she had completed these forms 2 weeks ago and nothing had changed. The clerk was obviously annoyed at the break in required protocol. As Ms. Jeffery sat down to complete the forms again, the clerk turned to her colleague and said, "Really, how hard is it to fill out a few forms?"

---

with individuals who may not feel well or are scared, confused, and lacking information. These individuals and their families and/or caregivers deserved a pleasant environment, a positive experience, and excellent customer service. See **Scenario 12.3** and **Scenario 12.4**.

Now that you understand the need for a positive customer service attitude and pleasing environment, let us investigate the actual patient and healthcare provider interaction. Both parties have a responsibility for their side of health communication during appointments.

PATIENT RESPONSIBILITIES

- Arrive on time for the health appointment.
- Provide identification and health insurance cards at check-in.
- Complete forms prior to appointment or complete forms upon arrival.

- Wear clothing and shoes that are easy to remove when asked to put on an examination gown.
- Bring a current list of all prescription and over-the-counter medications, vitamins, and herbal supplements, including purpose, dose, and strength of each medication.
- Bring a list of laboratory tests or medical procedures that were prescribed by other healthcare providers since the last visit with this healthcare provider. If possible, bring a copy of the results or provide a list of where the test or procedure was performed, so results may be obtained.
- Be prepared to describe the purpose of the appointment, including any symptoms or concerns that have changed since the last appointment.

- Bring a list of no more than five questions to ask the healthcare provider during the appointment.
- Ask all of the questions. Do not worry that the healthcare provider is too busy to answer the questions or that so many others are in the waiting room. Each patient deserves to gain understanding about health information at each appointment.
- Be willing to serve as a personal patient advocate. If the responses to the questions were not understood, then additional questions need to be asked. It is not useful to simply nod in agreement without adequate comprehension.
- Take responsibility for personal health care. If the patient does not understand and participate in medication compliance, positive behavioral lifestyle choices, treatment plans, and follow-up care, the healthcare provider has limited ways to improve his or her quality of life. Health communication is a partnership.
- Avoid falling into the trap of silence by thinking this healthcare provider is the best in this area, so remaining silent and not asking any questions are probably best. Fear of retribution leads to limited communication, misunderstanding, and a complete loss of empowerment for the patient and family.
- Have a personal calendar available so the next appointment can be scheduled prior to leaving to avoid needing to schedule it over the phone or changing it after consulting the calendar.
- Be willing to change healthcare providers if the overall interaction experience is negative or if there is a lack of mutual respect and health communication.

HEALTHCARE PROVIDER RESPONSIBILITIES

- Schedule appointments to avoid making individuals wait longer than 15 minutes.
- Maintain a clean, pleasant, and positive environment throughout the office.

- Train staff to provide excellent customer service for each encounter of the appointment.
- Design patient forms using the principles of the Plain Writing Act and health literacy research.
- Avoid asking patients to repeat the same information multiple times. For example, if the nurse asks and records the patient's response regarding the purpose of today's visit, the healthcare provider should read that information and not ask the same question when entering the exam room.
- Have a conversation with the patient prior to having the patient disrobe for an examination. The conversation should be at the same eye level. For instance, the patient should not be sitting on the exam table, while the healthcare provider is sitting and typing into an electronic medical record computer. Both parties should be sitting at the same level.
- Attempt to engage the patient in shared decision making. The patient looks to the healthcare provider for guidance, but the final decision for treatment is ultimately up to the patient. When the healthcare provider fails to disclose all treatment options, including no treatment, the communication fails and coercion persists.
- Explore the patient's story by simply repeating "go on" when the individual starts to talk. This technique is a simple and effective way of encouraging communication and understanding the complete scenario. For example, the individual complains of abdominal pain, but upon listening to the story, the healthcare provider realizes the patient is under extreme stress due to unemployment and fear of eviction. Without listening to the story, the healthcare provider may have misdiagnosed the patient.
- Explain the diagnosis and treatment plan in an appropriate verbal literacy level for understanding. Follow up verbal explanation with a brochure and information sheet for reference at home.

- Take more time if the diagnosis is serious. For some disciplines of medicine, healthcare providers give bad news to patients and families. Although it is routine for the healthcare provider, it is not for the patient. Time is required to show compassion and empathy.
- Ask the patient and caregiver if they have any questions. Ask the patient to describe the diagnosis, procedure, and treatment plan or medication regime to ensure understanding for compliance. This return demonstration is called a "teach-back" opportunity. If return "teach-back" omits vital information or lacks accurate details, the provider repeats the dialogue until adequate understanding through a "teach-back" demonstration is achieved for compliance.
- Admit not knowing the reason why the laboratory results and tests do not explain the patient's symptoms. Be willing to say "I do not know" and explore other options or consult with other healthcare providers to search for a possible explanation. Do not respond to patients with a flippant response or say their symptoms are not real.
- Ensure the check-out experience is satisfying and positive. For example, the office clerk may offer several options for the next appointment time rather than merely stating the time and date of the next appointment without any regard for the individual's availability. Or if today's appointment was in the morning, the office clerk may ask if a morning appointments is a convenient time for the follow-up appointment.

The concept of medication adherence and medical management often poses additional problems with communication between patient and provider. Sometimes providers assume this is the fault of patients, but this is not always the case. First, medication adherence is defined as the extent to which a patient continues with the agreed-upon mode of treatment under limited supervision when faced with conflicting or competing demands. For example, a patient may fail to adhere to the medication or treatment plan because of a lack of understanding or miscommunication with the healthcare provider. If the patient does not adequately understand aspects related to treatment, the failure of medical adherence is the fault of the healthcare provider rather than the patient. In addition, the patient may have a desire to adhere to the medication or treatment plan, but due to competing demands (e.g., lack of money for the prescription drug, transportation to the pharmacy, parenting or job responsibilities), they fail to do so. They may also be embarrassed to disclose this information to the healthcare provider, and the healthcare provider failed to ask the correct questions to achieve adherence. Second, medical management is a collaborative process that facilitates recommended treatment plans to assure the appropriate medical care is provided to sick, injured, or disabled individuals. It is up to the healthcare provider or a member of their team (e.g., health navigation professional) to manage and facilitate the treatment plan. For example, if an individual is unable to drive due to an injury, it is likely that transportation will be required to comply with the physical therapy sessions or, in some cases, home physical therapy sessions may be arranged. Without some minimal assistance with medical management from the healthcare team, the responsibilities are left to the patient or family and friends. Without assistance, the optimal health outcome is less likely to be achieved.

Finally, a new concept in health communication, patient portals, needs to be addressed in this discussion. Patient portals are a computer-technology software that allows healthcare providers to upload lab results, prescriptions, treatment updates, and follow-up appointments so that patients can access them from their home computers or mobile devices. From the patients' viewpoint, the portals allow easy access to their medical information without the need for an immediate follow-up phone call or appointment. However, as previously mentioned, many individuals do not have access to a computer, lack the computer literacy skills to access the patient portals, or have limited understanding of the medical information uploaded within the portal. With greater dependence on the convenience of patient portals, many individuals will fail to adhere to or comply with treatment plans for the simple reason of not opening their electronic medical patient portal.

As noted throughout this chapter, health communication is complex. Health communication is the responsibility of healthcare providers, public health professionals, and patients. Unfortunately, communication breaks down quickly when the patients do not ask questions and the healthcare providers assume that the patient understood the information due to lack of questions. There is no easy fix to the lack of health communication, but rather each conversation, healthcare form, written document, brochure, media advertisement, and website must aim to improve the understanding of health information and communication. Healthcare benefits from shared decision making through a partnership between patients and their healthcare providers. However, systemic changes are needed to restructure reimbursement schedules that allow healthcare providers the time for more meaningful conversations. Until this change takes place, healthcare providers and health navigation professionals must work together with patients to improve health communication to ensure greater understanding of and compliance to improve health conditions. See **Table 12.5** for further information.

TABLE 12.5 Useful Health Literacy Information

U.S. Department of Education, Office of Vocational and Adult Education, www2.ed.gov/about/offices/list/ovae/index.html	Administers and coordinates programs for adult education and literacy, career and technical education, and community colleges.
National Adult Education Professional Development Consortium, www.naepdc.org	The Consortium leads staff in adult education in the states and territories to increase literacy and prepare adults for success as contributing members of society.
National Coalition for Literacy, www.national-coalition-literacy.org	The Coalition advances adult education, family literacy, and English-language acquisition in the United States by increasing public awareness for the need to increase funding and programs; promoting effective public policy; and serving as a resource on national adult education issues.
ProLiteracy, www.proliteracy.org	ProLiteracy helps build the capacity and quality of programs that are teaching adults to read, write, compute, use technology, and learn English as a new language.
National Action Plan to Improve Health Literacy, www.cdc.gov/healthliteracy/planact/national.html	Find a blueprint for efforts to improve health literacy.
Participatory Materials Development, www.hsph.harvard.edu/healthliteracy/practice/participatory-materials-development	The Health Literacy Studies group from the Harvard School of Public Health examines literacy-related barriers to a variety of health services and care. Here you will find information on how to develop materials with input from the intended audience, as well as examples of materials developed through a participatory process.
Toolkit for Making Written Material Clear and Effective, www.cms.gov/Outreach-and-Education/Outreach/WrittenMaterialsToolkit/index.html?redirect=/WrittenMaterialsToolkit	The Toolkit for Making Written Material Clear and Effective is a health literacy resource from the Centers for Medicare and Medicaid Services (CMS). This 11-part Toolkit provides a detailed and comprehensive set of tools to help you make written material in printed formats easier for people to read, understand, and use.

Summary

The chapter began with a definition of communication as a process by using words, sounds, signs, or behaviors to exchange information with another individual. In today's world, information is communicated in person, on paper, or through technology. The same is true in health communication. If the healthcare provider or the individual is not conveying the correct message for a variety of reasons, then the individual (healthcare provider or patient) is unable to receive and understand the message. This breakdown of communication leads to medication errors, a misunderstanding of treatment options, noncompliance, missed appointments, and many other errors. This chapter explored all aspects of health communication and health literacy, including the consequences of inadequate communication in the healthcare system.

Case Study

Anthony, age 42, took his mom, Mary, age 72, to her medical appointment this week. His mom is overweight and was diagnosed with Type 2 diabetes several months ago. She has not enrolled in the diabetes education course offered at the local hospital because she wants to try to control without medication. Mary's social and behavioral background includes having a community college degree, working as an administrative specialist for a large car dealership for 28 years, and retiring at age 68. She drives a little and has many close friends from living in the same community for her entire life.

Most of the time, her blood glucose levels are maintained within normal ranges, so Anthony assumed that today's appointment would be routine. Mary's appointment was scheduled for 8:00 a.m. The clinic nurse had left a message on her cell phone yesterday that Mary should not eat any food or drink any fluids prior to her 8:00 a.m. appointment. Mary knew that it was important to fast to ensure that her blood glucose lab results would be as accurate as possible. The nurse, Cynthia, called Mary into the clinic room from the waiting room. She weighed Mary, recorded her blood pressure, and drew her blood for the glucose test. After a quick review of any changes in her medical condition, Cynthia asked if Mary had any specific questions or concerns that she wanted to speak about with the doctor at today's appointment. During the conversation with Cynthia, Mary had a few bouts of coughing. Because her blood had been drawn, Mary requested a cup of water. Cynthia asked her how long she had been coughing. Mary said just a few days, but she felt fine. Cynthia gave her a cup of water. Mary returned to the waiting room and the sandwich that she had packed for breakfast. While Mary was eating, Anthony noticed that his mom seemed to be coughing often. She said it was nothing and continued to enjoy her breakfast.

Soon the nurse called Mary back and directed her to the first exam room on the right. Cynthia told Mary that her fasting blood glucose level exceeded the normal range and her blood pressure was also higher than usual. Mary looked puzzled and did not recall eating or doing anything differently. Cynthia asked a few more questions but was unable to reach any conclusions. The physician, Dr. Williams, came into the room while Mary was coughing. She asked a few more questions after Mary stopped coughing. Dr. Williams listened to

Mary's heart and lungs. She heard some cracking in her lungs and a few irregular beats when listening to her heart. She told Mary that she needed to have a chest X-ray this afternoon to rule out pneumonia. In addition, Mary was told to make another appointment for next week with the nurse to recheck her fasting blood glucose levels. The office clerk scheduled the X-ray for Mary for 10:00 a.m. today and the follow-up appointment for the same day and time next week.

As Anthony was driving Mary to the hospital for the X-ray, Mary started coughing. She reached into her purse and pulled out a travel-size bottle filled with red liquid. Anthony saw her unscrew the cap and take a few sips of the red fluid. He asked what was in the bottle and Mary said cough syrup. She wanted to suppress her cough, so she could hold still for the chest X-ray.

Questions

1. List the resources in your community for newly diagnosed individuals with Type 2 diabetes.
2. Why it is important for Dr. Williams to know that Mary took cough syrup prior to her blood glucose test? Explain the physiology.
3. List a minimum of five over-the-counter medications that Mary could have ingested for her cough, but failed to report to her healthcare provider.
4. List a few additional questions that the nurse and the physician could have asked Mary.
5. As a health navigation professional, what factors need to be considered when providing Mary with health education information about her new diagnosis of Type 2 diabetes?

References

1. White, S., & McCloskey, M. (2009). *Framework for the 2003 national assessment of adult literacy (NCES 2005–531)*. Washington, DC: US Department of Education National Center for Education Statistics.
2. Centers for Disease Control and Prevention. *Understanding literacy and numeracy*. Retrieved August 8, 2015, from http://www.cdc.gov/healthliteracy/learn/understandingliteracy.html; last updated May 4, 2015.
3. Baer, J., Kutner, M., Sabatini, J., & White, S. (2009). *Basic reading skills and the literacy of America's least literate adults: Results from the 2003 national assessment of adult literacy (NAAL) supplemental studies (NCES 2009-481)*. Washington, DC: US Department of Education National Center for Education Statistics.
4. National Network of Libraries of Medicine. *Health literacy*. Retrieved August 8, 2015, from http://nnlm.gov/outreach/consumer/hlthlit.html; last updated June 2013.
5. Bennett, I. M., Chen, J., Soroui, J. S., & White, S. (2009). The contribution of health literacy to disparities in self-rated health status and preventive health behaviors in older adults. *The Annals of Family Medicine, 7*(3), 204–211.
6. Kindig, D. A., Panzer, A. M., & Nielsen-Bohlman, L. (2004). *Health literacy: A prescription to end confusion*. Washington, DC: National Academies Press.
7. Howard, D. H., Sentell, T., & Gazmararian, J. A. (2006). Impact of health literacy on socioeconomic and racial differences in health in an elderly population. *Journal of General Internal Medicine, 21*(8), 857–861.
8. Vernon, J. A., Trujillo, A., Rosenbaum, S. J., & DeBuono, B. (2007). *Low health literacy: Implications for national health policy*. Washington, DC: Department of Health Policy, School of Public Policy and Health Services, George Washington University.
9. Merriman, B., Ades, T., & Seffrin, J. R. (2002). Health literacy in the information age: Communicating cancer information to patients and families. *CA: A Cancer Journal for Clinicians, 52*(3), 130–133.
10. Schillinger, D., Grumbach, K., Piette, J., Wang, F., Osmond, D., Daher, C., Palacious, J., Diaz Sullivan, G., & Bindman, A. B. (2002) Association of health literacy with diabetes outcomes. *JAMA, 288*(4), 475–482.
11. Williams, M. V., Baker, D. W., Honig, E. G., Lee, T. M., & Nowland, A. (1998). Inadequate literacy is a barrier to asthma knowledge and self-care. *Chest Journal, 114*(4), 1008–1015.
12. Centers for Disease Control and Prevention. *Stroke signs and symptoms*. Retrieved August 9, 2015, from http://www.cdc.gov/Stroke/signs_symptoms.htm; last updated April 30, 2015.
13. Indian Health Service. *What is plain language?* Retrieved August 9, 2015, from http://www.ihs.gov/healthcommunications/index.cfm?module=dsp_hc_plain.
14. Indian Health Service. *Welcome to health communications!* Retrieved August 8, 2015, from http://www.ihs.gov/healthcommunications/index.cfm.
15. Osborne, H., & Sudbury, L. (2004). *Health literacy from A to Z: Practical ways to communicate your health message*. Sudbury, MA: Jones and Bartlett Publishing.
16. Centers for Disease Control and Prevention. *Health literacy: Develop materials*. Retrieved August 9, 2015, from http://www.cdc.gov/healthliteracy/developmaterials/index.html; last updated 2014.

17. Kutner, M., Greenberg, E., Ying, J., & Paulsen, C. (2006). *The health literacy of America's adults: Results from the 2003 national assessment of adult literacy (NCES 2006-483)*. Washington, DC: US Department of Education National Center for Education Statistics.

18. Centers for Disease Control and Prevention. *Visual communication*. Retrieved August 9, 2015, from http ://www.cdc.gov/healthliteracy/developmaterials/visual -communication.html; last updated June 23, 2014.

19. Rudolph, S. *15 qualities you need to get a good customer service lob*. Retrieved August 9, 2015, from http://www .business2community.com/strategy/15-qualities-you -need-to-get-a-good-customer-service-job-0139217; last updated February 28, 2012.

20. Forbes Magazine. *The 10 keys of excellent customer service*. Retrieved August 9, 2015, from http://www.forbes .com/sites/aileron/2012/11/15/the-10-keys-of-excellent -customer-service;\ 15, 2012.

CHAPTER 13

Accessing and Using Health Information

by Richard Riegelman

LEARNING OBJECTIVES

By the end of this chapter, students will be able to

- Describe how to evaluate the reliability of online health information
- Describe types and sources of public health information, including their access and uses
- Describe how health information can be used to measure the health status of a population
- Identify the uses and misuses of graphic presentations of health information
- Describe the requirements for establishing cause and effect relationships and the types of health research needed

CHAPTER OVERVIEW

Health information is available in a wide variety of forms, from newspapers and magazines to Internet websites and social media, to television advertising, and, of course, word of mouth. All of this and more is available in addition to health information offered by public health officials and providers of health care. This deluge of data can lead to information overload and a great deal of confusion. If used well, however, it can be the basis for educating individuals and groups and helping them to prevent disease and to share in their own health decision making.

A key role of health navigation professionals is to help individuals and groups access,
evaluate, and use health information. Increasingly, the Internet is the ultimate source of health information available to most if not all individuals and health navigators. Maximizing the use of the Internet requires a high level of health literacy and often a sophisticated understanding of health, disease, and the health system.

To facilitate the process of accessing health information on the Internet, it is important to learn how to identify websites that can be relied on to provide high-quality, unbiased, and easily understood health information. Therefore, this chapter starts with a set of criteria that can be used to evaluate the quality of a website and suggests a number of websites that meet all or most of these criteria.

The second section looks at public health information, including accessing and using public health information. The special uses of health information for measuring health status as well as documenting health disparities will also be examined.

Health information is often presented in graphical form. It is key for individuals to understand the uses and potential abuses of graphics. Therefore, the third section takes a look at the basic types of graphics and illustrates their strengths and limitations.

The goal of health information is often to draw conclusions about cause and effect relationships such as a relationship between a behavior or an exposure and the development of disease. Therefore, the final section examines the meaning of cause and effect in clinical medicine and public health and illustrates the types of health information needed to establish a cause and effect relationship.

ACCESSING HIGH-QUALITY HEALTH INFORMATION ON THE INTERNET

How do I know that I can rely on that website? If there are advertisements on the website, should I look any further?

What are some examples of websites providing high-quality health information?

These are the type of issues that health navigators face when trying to find high-quality information on the Internet. The role of the health navigator is often to help individuals and groups locate and understand reliable health information. Therefore, it is important to have a set of criteria for determining whether a website provides reliable health information.

A useful series of criteria and related questions to ask are summarized in **Table 13.1**.[1, 2] These are very helpful when using the Internet to search for high-quality health information. At the end of this section, a number of websites are recommended that meet all or nearly all of these criteria.

Let us examine in more detail what is meant by each of these criteria and why the answers are important.

- *Overall Site Quality*: When first looking at a website, it is important to determine if the site's purpose is to provide the type of information that is needed. The purpose of a website may vary from providing information to consumers to providing technical information, to promoting products, to soliciting donations, as well as a large number of other purposes. Quality health information is generally found on sites whose purpose is specifically to provide information. Advertising may be included in these sites but should be clearly separated from the information provided.

The sponsors of the site should be clearly and easily identified. If the user has to search for the sponsors of the site, this is a cause for concern. The site ideally should allow the user to easily find the information being looked for, including a search function that quickly brings up the needed information.

- *Authors*: The qualifications of the website content authors are important in determining the reliability of the information. The authors may be a sponsoring organization, such as the Centers for Disease Control and Prevention (CDC) or the National Institutes of Health (NIH). The authors may be individuals with or without qualifications relevant to the health information provided. Ideally, individual authors can be identified and their health credentials examined. Contact information for the authors or at least for sponsoring organizations should also be included in the website.

Government health websites such as CDC and NIH are often seen as reliable. Other national health organizations such as the American Cancer Society and the American Heart Association, which have representatives of the health professions as well as consumers, also are generally considered reliable. The credentials of individual authors can reinforce this initial assessment.

- *Information*: In addition to examining the qualifications or reliability of the authors, an evaluation of a website should include a look for references or citations for the information provided. Peer-reviewed research and information from respected sources help confirm the quality of the website.

Websites without citations and those that rely on individual opinions, testimonials, or endorsements by celebrities should be viewed with skepticism. Many health websites provide unverified assertions or the results of experience either from patients or providers of services.

TABLE 13.1 Questions to Ask When Accessing High-Quality Information on the Internet

Overall Site Quality

- Is the purpose of the site clear?
- Is the site easy to navigate?
- Are the site's sponsors clearly identified?
- Are advertising and sales separated from health information?

Authors

- Are the authors of the information clearly identified?
- Do the authors have health credentials?
- Is contact information provided?

Information

- Does the site get its information from reliable sources?
- Is the information useful and easy to understand?
- Is it easy to tell the difference between fact and opinion?

Relevance

- Are there answers to your specific questions?

Timeliness

- Can you tell when the information was written?
- Is the information current?

Links

- Do the internal links work?
- Are there links to related sites for more information?

Privacy

- Is your privacy protected?
- Can you search for information without providing information about yourself?

Data from: Evaluating Internet Health Information: A Tutorial from the National Library of Medicine; U.S. Food and Drug Administration: How to Evaluate Health Information on the Internet.[2]

These types of health information are often called *anecdotal information* and may not be typical of the types of results that can be expected from a recommended intervention on a reliable website.

Opinions and endorsements from reliable sources may be included in a website. However, it is important that the opinions and conclusions be separated from the factual or research information provided.

- *Relevance*: The health information provided may be very reliable, yet it may not be relevant. That is, the information may not be

applicable to the type of question or the type of individual or group to whom the user plans to apply the information.

For instance a website established by a specialized referral center may offer options that are not available at most outpatient or even hospital settings. Information on the newest advances in cancer therapy may have been used on patients with far advanced disease and may not be relevant to patients with early disease. Therefore, it is important to ask whether the information applies to the setting and type of patient of interest.

- *Timeliness*: High-quality websites include an indication of when the website was last updated. Regular updates are needed to keep a website current, especially for rapidly changing areas of health research. Ideally, recommendations on a website include an indication of when the recommendations were made and the planned timing for a review of the recommendations.

- *Links*: High-quality websites should include extensive links to provide additional information and referral to other sources. It is important that these links work and send the user to the expected source of high-quality information. Links to advertisements or individual testimonials suggest a low-quality website.

- *Privacy*: Websites designed to provide high-quality, reliable information do not generally require the user to provide personal information. At times, registration may be required for full use of the site, but the information needed to register should usually be limited to a name and email address. Sites that require disclosure of extensive personal information are often more interested in obtaining personal information than in providing high-quality information.

SUGGESTED WEBSITES

Following is a partial list of websites that meet most, if not all, of the previous criteria.

- Agency for Healthcare Research and Quality (AHRQ), U.S. Preventive Services Task Force: www.ahrq.gov/professionals/clinicians -providers/guidelines-recommendations /uspstf/index.html

- Centers for Disease Control and Prevention: www.cdc.gov

- http:nam.edu/ National Academy of Medicine (formerly Institute of Medicine): http://www.nationalacademies.org/hmd

- Kaiser Family Foundation: http://kff.org

- The National Institute for Occupational Safety and Health (NIOSH): www.cdc .gov/niosh

- The National Library of Medicine–Medline Plus: www.nlm.nih.gov/medlineplus /encyclopedia.html

- The National Library of Medicine–Environmental Health & Toxicology Specialized Information Services: http://sis .nlm.nih.gov/enviro.html

- Pan American Health Organization: www .paho.org/hq

- Partners in Information Access for the Public Health Workforce: https://phpartners.org

- Robert Wood Johnson Foundation: www .rwjf.org/en.html

- United Nations Millennium Development Goals: www.un.org/millenniumgoals

- United States Environmental Protection Agency (EPA): www.epa.gov

- USAID: www.usaid.gov

- The World Bank: www.worldbank.org/en /research

- World Health Organization: www.who.int/en

In addition, abstracts from research publications on health can be accessed using PubMed, which is available free of charge from the National Library of Medicine, www.ncbi.nlm.nih.gov /pubmed.

On their own or with some help from a health sciences librarian, health navigators now can have access to the world's health information including the latest research. When searching for high-quality research, it is important that the journal be "peer reviewed." That is, the articles have been evaluated by experts in the same field prior to publication. In addition, the journal should not have advertisements close to the articles; should provide information on potential conflicts of interest; and should clear the source of funding for the research.

ACCESSING AND USING PUBLIC HEALTH INFORMATION

A single case of totally drug resistant tuberculosis (TB) was recently reported to a state health department. What does this mean for other people with TB in the state?

African American men have lower life expectancy than African American women and white men. Is this evidence of health disparities?

Reporting of many communicable diseases to the health department is required by law. How is this information used for health purposes?

These are the types of questions that arise when looking at public health information. Public health information is health information collected by governmental agencies and freely available on the Internet. It plays important and unique roles. Public health information is collected by local, state, and federal health agencies, including the Centers for Disease Control and Prevention. The collection and reporting of public health information is often required by law. For instance, a great deal of data is obtained from birth certificates and death certificates as well as through the required reporting of many communicable and a small number of noncommunicable diseases.

A wide range of public health information is currently available on the Web. Web search engines such as Google and Bing have transformed the ability to access public health information. Public health data can be categorized into five basic types, each of which comes from a different source and has somewhat different uses. The five types of public health information can be called the *5-Ss* or five sources of public health information, as follows:

- Single case or a small series often reported by alert clinicians to their health department
- Statistics, or what are called *vital statistics* and *reportable diseases*, whose reporting is required by law
- Surveys or investigations of small numbers of individuals to draw conclusions about the larger population or groups within the larger population, such as women or racial groups
- Self-reporting or what are called *spontaneous reporting* systems
- Sentinel surveillance or systems that provide early warning

To understand public health information, it can be useful to summarize these 5-Ss of public health information, their uses, and how to access them on the Internet. **Table 13.2** summarizes the 5-Ss of public health information.

TABLE 13.2 5-Ss of Public Health Information

Type	Examples	Uses	How to access
Single Case or Small Series	Case reports of one or a small number of rare or serious cases of a disease such as SARS, anthrax, or mad cow disease New diseases, e.g., first report of AIDS Spread of disease such as drug resistant tuberculosis	Alert to new disease or resistant disease Alert to potential spread beyond initial area	Centers for Disease Control and Prevention (CDC) compiles local /state data and makes available on website www.cdc.gov and through CDC publication "Morbidity and Mortality Weekly Reports" (MMWR) www.cdc.gov/mmwr/publications /index.html
Statistics— "Vital Statistics" "Reportable Diseases"	Vital statistics: Birth, death, marriage, divorce Legally required reporting of specific communicable and noncommunicable conditions, e.g., elevated lead levels, child and spouse abuse	Birth and death certificates key to measuring death or mortality rates and defining leading causes of death Reporting of disease may be helpful for identification of changes over time to generate hypotheses about cause and to also to identify the occurrence of epidemics	National Center for Health Statistics www.cdc.gov/nchs and MMWR

Type	Examples	Uses	How to access
Surveys	National Health and Nutrition Examination Survey (NHANES) Behavioral Risk Factor Surveillance System (BRFSS)	Carefully constructed surveys of a sample of the entire U.S. population allow the investigator to draw conclusions about smaller groups within the United States	National Center for Health Statistics www.cdc.gov/nchs
Self-Reporting	Adverse effect monitoring of drugs and vaccines	Identification of events reported by those affected May help identify unrecognized or unusual events	"Package inserts" accompanying prescription drugs provide detailed FDA approved information for patients and for providers
Sentinel Monitoring (Early Warning Systems)	Influenza monitoring to identify start of outbreak and changes in virus type	Early warnings or warning of previously unrecognized events based on intensive investigation of high-risk sites	Information used by public health officials for specific purposes; may be included in MMWR

One key use of public health information is to create measures that summarize the health of populations and groups within the population. These are often called *measures of population health* or *health status measures*.

MEASURES OF POPULATION HEALTH[3]

"Life expectancy" and "infant mortality rate" are two important measures of the health of the population. The measurement known as "life expectancy" combines the death or mortality rates from each age group in a population in a particular year and comes up with a summary measurement. Life expectancy tells us the average number of years of life remaining for those of a particular age. When used alone, the term "life-expectancy" implies the number of years of expected life at birth. Life expectancies at birth of 80 years or more are now common and increasingly expected in developed and healthy societies.

Imagine that life expectancy at birth for females is 82 years. At 65 years of age, life expectancy might still be 20 years or more. This increase makes sense because women who have reached age 65 have escaped death during earlier years from complications of pregnancy, motor vehicle injuries, breast cancer, and other conditions that tend to be the causes of death among younger women.

Life expectancy is best used to compare the health status of countries and large groups such as racial groups within countries. For example, life expectancy at birth in a developing country such as Nigeria might be 55 years compared to 80 years for a developed country such as the United States. Within one country, life expectancy at birth for one racial group such as black males in the United States might be 70 years as compared to 80 years for white males. These differences in life expectancy at birth often provide the basis for establishing health disparities or group difference in health outcomes.

Using life expectancy to predict the future life span of a group or population assumes that nothing will change, which is very unlikely. In addition, you need to be careful in using life expectancy to predict the length of life for any one individual, especially an elderly person. A healthy 80-year-old women, for instance, may have a life expectancy of well over a decade—far greater than her not-so-healthy peers.

The second widely used measurement of population health status is known as the *infant mortality rate*. The infant mortality rate measures the chances of dying during the first year of life among those born alive in a particular year. U.S. infant mortality rates in the early 20th century were approximately 100 per 1000 live births per year. Today, infant mortality rates in the United States are approximately 6 per 1000 live births per year. In many other developed countries, however, the rates are now below 5 or even 4 per 1000 live births. The United States is not among the 20 countries with the lowest infant mortality rate. For some populations in the United States, such as African Americans, the rates are far greater than 6, indicating important health disparities.

Life expectancy and infant mortality remain two key measures of population health status. New measures incorporate and extend these older measures. As health status has improved around the world, the measure known as *under-5 mortality* has come to be widely used. Under-5 mortality goes beyond mortality rates during the first year of life to include mortality rates during the first 5 years of life. Under-5 mortality is now considered the standard measure of child health.

The measure known as *Health Adjusted Life Expectancy* or *HALE* has extended life expectancy measurement to include the quality of health and not just the existence of life. The following measures of the quality of health are incorporated into HALE:

- *Mobility*: The ability to walk without assistance
- *Cognition*: Mental function, including memory
- *Self-Care*: Activities of daily living, including dressing, eating, bathing, and using the toilet
- *Pain*: Regular pain that limits function
- *Mood*: Alteration in mood that limits function, such as depression
- *Sensory Organ Function*: Impairment in vision or hearing that limits function

The difference between HALE and life expectancy provides a measurement of the loss of healthy life that is due to these disabilities. Disabilities are not limited to the elderly. For example, young people in the United States have disabilities from injuries, drug abuse, mental illness, and post-traumatic stress syndrome.

Health information presented as numbers such as HALE or under-5 mortality is important to understand. Increasingly, numerical information is presented in graphic format because, for most people, pictures are much easier to understand than numbers. Let us see how graphics can inform as well as misinform in the next section.

DISPLAYING HEALTH INFORMATION[4]

This line graph suggests that cancer will soon surpass heart disease as the greatest killer.

This column graph is complicated to read; why not use a simpler line graph?

Does this attractive 3-D graphic provide a better view of the data than the 2-D graphic?

These are the types of issues that confront the user of health information presented as figures or graphics.

Graphics are used primarily to display and examine possible relationships, often called *association* or *correlations*. The wide array of graphical displays of data that are now available means that health navigation professionals need to have an understanding of how displays of data can help inform the user but can also mislead the user.[2]

This section looks at the uses and abuses of the three basic forms of graphical presentation: X-Y graphics, geometric graphics, and pie charts.

X-Y Graphics

X-Y graphics, or what are often called *line graphs*, are a popular and attractive method for presenting large amounts of information in a single figure. X-Y graphs use a horizontal scale called an *X-axis* and a vertical scale called a *Y-axis*. They are very useful for displaying possible associations or what are often called *correlations* when both measurements have a large number of potential levels.

Figure 13.1 provides data on a hypothetical country Z illustrating the way X-Y graphs should be used. This same data will be used for all of the graphics in this section.

FIGURE 13.1 X-Y Graph of the Deaths in Country Z per 100,000 Population

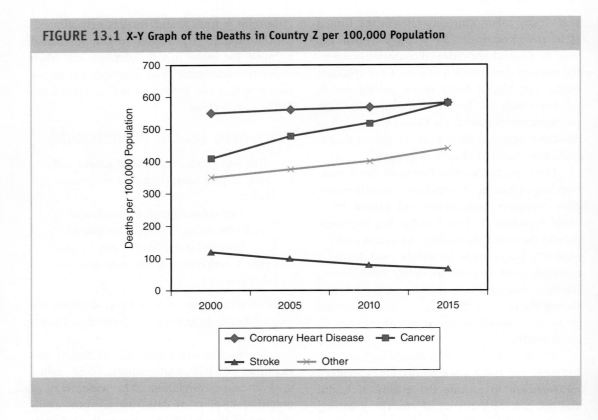

The geometric figures (diamond, square, triangle, X) represent the point when death rates are actually measured. Straight lines are then drawn to connect these points. Notice that the lines do not extend beyond the points in which actual data or information is available. Also notice that both the X-axis and the Y-axis go all the way to zero even though there is no data close to zero.

When X-Y graphics do not strictly follow this approach, they may produce misleading results. For instance X-Y graphs may be drawn with lines that extend far beyond the data. This is known as *extrapolation beyond the data*. It assumes that events will continue to increase (or decrease) at the same pace beyond the information provided. Here, if one extrapolates the rate of cancer, it might be concluded that, in the future, cancer will far exceed coronary heart disease. This may or may not turn out to be true. Predicting the future is always a difficult job and requires far more than expecting current trends to continue.

It is tempting when little or no data exist near the zero point on the X-axis or Y-axis to stop the data at a higher point. **Figure 13.2** illustrates how this type of display of health information can be misleading. Here, it looks like the rate of cancer deaths is increasing very rapidly, far more rapidly than in Figure 13.1. Yet, both figures come from the same data. By "cutting-off" the death rates at 350 per 100,000 instead of at zero in Figure 13.2, the apparent increase in cancer rates is magnified.

Notice the use of the symbol "~" on the Y-axis in Figure 13.2. It alerts the viewer that levels have been left out of the Y-axis. When not displaying the full scale on the X-axis or Y-axis, it is expected that a "~" will be inserted to alert the reader to this omission to try to avoid misinterpretation.

Geometric Graphics

Traditional geometric graphics are often called *column charts* or *bar charts* because they display data using rectangular columns or bars, as indicated in

FIGURE 13.2 X-Y Graph of the Deaths in Country Z with Rates "Cut Off" at 350

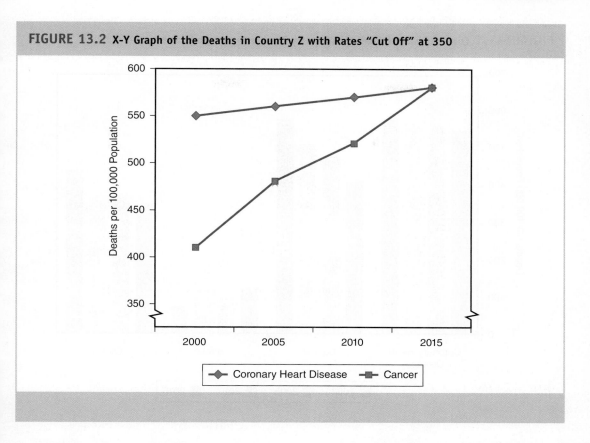

Figure 13.3. Once again Figure 13.3 comes from the same data used in the previous figures.

Column graphics are very good ways to display information, especially when there are only a limited number of potential categories of information such as coronary artery disease, cancer, stroke, and other. Column charts help avoid extrapolation beyond the data. In addition, they do not require drawing lines between points where data is actually measured. Therefore, column graphics are often the best presentation of the data because they are the least likely to be misleading.

As shown in Figure 13.3, a column chart allows side-by-side comparison between different groups. However, Figure 13.3 may look more complicated than Figure 13.1, despite the fact that it includes exactly the same data. Therefore, people may prefer X-Y graphics.

Pie Charts

Pie charts or percentage charts display the percentage of the total that is associated with each of the components that make up the whole at one point in time. **Figure 13.4** shows the same 2015 data that were used earlier. However, this time only the percentage who die from coronary artery disease, cancer, stroke, and other can be seen in Figure 13.4. Pie charts from different populations are often presented using the same size pie despite the fact that the actual rates may be very different in the two populations. Therefore, comparisons between these pies should talk about the "percentage of the pie" and not the "size of the piece of pie."

Pie charts are increasingly presented as 3-D graphics. Three-dimensional graphics are often more attractive and easier to produce using standard computer software. These 3-D graphics, however, may be misleading because they lead us to think that a pie chart has a front nearer to us and a back farther from us. Our eyes and brain automatically see things that appear closer as larger and see things that are farther away as smaller.

FIGURE 13.3 Column Chart of Deaths in Country Z per 100,000 population

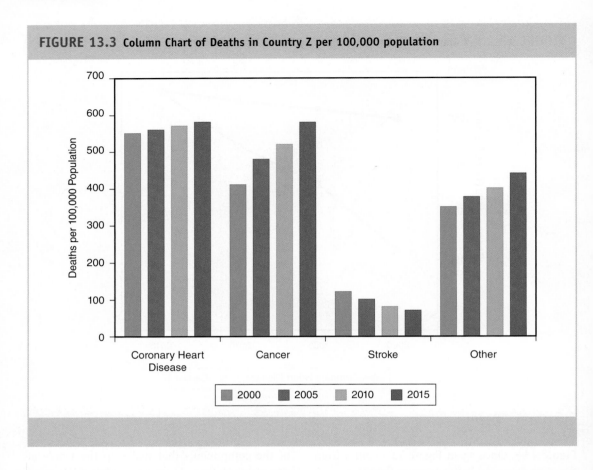

FIGURE 13.4 Pie Chart with Deaths in Country Z, 2015

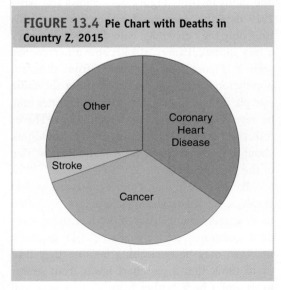

Figure 13.5 and Figure 13.6 are both 3-D pie charts using the same data that were used to construct the other figures. In all of these figures, the death rate for coronary artery disease and cancer in 2015 is the same. However, notice that in Figure 13.5 coronary artery disease is appears closer and appears larger than cancer.

In Figure 13.6 the situation is reversed. Now cancer appears closer and appears larger than coronary artery disease, even though their rates are actually the same. The eye can be fooled even when you know that the rates are the same. This type of problem can occur whenever 3-D graphics are used.

Graphics can be a very useful way to display and examine associations, providing a picture of what is happening. However, even when carefully constructed, graphics do not demonstrate that a cause and effect relationship is present. The following section focuses on what is necessary to establish the existence of a cause and effect relationship.

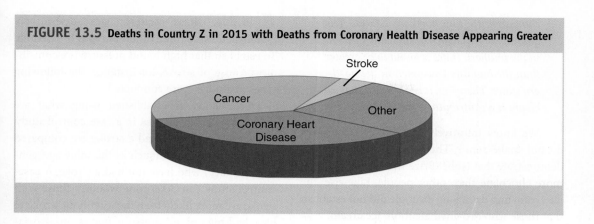

FIGURE 13.5 Deaths in Country Z in 2015 with Deaths from Coronary Health Disease Appearing Greater

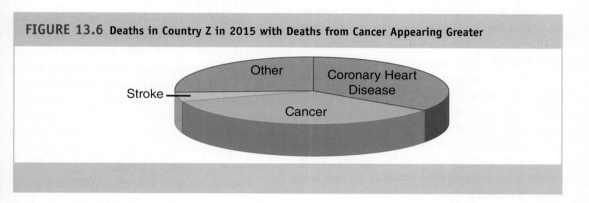

FIGURE 13.6 Deaths in Country Z in 2015 with Deaths from Cancer Appearing Greater

USING HEALTH INFORMATION TO ESTABLISH CAUSE AND EFFECT AS WELL AS EFFECTIVENESS AND SAFETY

Air pollution can't be a cause of heart disease because we don't know a mechanism that would explain how this can happen.

Cigarettes can't be a cause of lung cancer because not every smoker develops lung cancer.

Cell phones are likely to be a cause of brain tumors because most people spend hours with them up against their heads.

These are the types of assertions related to cause and effect or etiology that are often found on the Internet. In order to make sense of these types of statements, health navigation professionals need to have an understanding of what cause and effect means, what it does not mean, and how it is established.

Associations are often obtained by comparing groups rather than individuals. Sometimes, these associations are also true at the individual level, such as the association between high blood pressure and stroke, the relationship between high LDL or bad cholesterol and coronary artery disease, and the relationship between cigarettes and lung cancer.

However, not every true association between groups is due to a cause and effect relationship. Think about the following:

An article in a major medical journal reported that countries that consume more chocolate also produce more Nobel Prize winners. Therefore, it is suggested that eating chocolate contributes to intelligence.

Drowning is found to be associated with living in the southern United States

compared to the northern states. The quantity of ice cream consumed per person in the southern states is found to be greater than the quantity consumed in the northern states. Therefore, it is suggested that ice cream is a contributory cause of drowning.

We know intuitively that these conclusions do not make sense. The journal article did not demonstrate that Nobel Prize winners actually eat more chocolate than other people. Likewise, the ice cream and drowning example did not establish that those who drowned ate more ice cream.

Even if eating ice cream is associated with drowning at the individual level, it is much more likely that the association is present because the warmer weather in the southern states is related to both more ice cream consumption and more swimming. An association between ice cream and drowning is most likely due to warmer weather, which leads to more ice cream consumption and more swimming. In order to establish cause and effect relationships, we often need to perform a series of investigations. Let us examine more closely what is needed to establish a cause and effect relationship.

CRITERIA FOR DEFINITIVELY ESTABLISHING CONTRIBUTORY CAUSE

In clinical medicine and public health, the concept known as *contributory cause* is key to defining a cause and effect relationship.[5] Let us use the example of high blood pressure and strokes to examine the criteria that are used to definitively establish contributory cause. Three criteria must be met to definitively establish contributory cause.

1. *An association exists at the individual level.* In the example, those with strokes are more likely to have had high blood pressure than similar individuals who have not experienced a stroke.
2. The *"cause" precedes the "effect."* In this example, the high blood pressure precedes the development of a stroke
3. *Altering the "cause" alters the "effect."* In this example, reducing blood pressure reduces the subsequent chances or incidence rate of strokes

Ideally, these criteria are definitively established using three different types of research. To establish that high blood pressure is a contributory cause of stroke, for instance, the following types of studies were conducted:

Criteria #1 is established using what are called *case-control studies.* In a case-control study, individuals who have had a stroke are compared to similar individuals (such as the same age, gender, and race) who have not had a stroke. A case-control study can determine whether those with stroke are more likely than those without stroke to have had high blood pressure, that is, an association at the individual level.

Criteria #2 is established using what are called *cohort studies.* A cohort study of high blood pressure starts with a study group made up of individuals who have high blood pressure and a similar control or comparison group of individuals without high blood pressure. The individuals in both groups are followed for long periods of time, and the outcomes in the study group and the control group are compared to determine their chances of developing a stroke.

Criteria #3 is definitively established using what is called a *randomized controlled trial.* In a randomized controlled trial of high blood pressure, eligible individuals are assigned using a chance process, similar to rolling the dice, to a study group whose members are prescribed high blood pressure medication or to a control group whose members are not prescribed high blood pressure medication. In randomized controlled trials, ideally individuals and their clinicians are unaware of the treatment group to which they are assigned, though this may be unethical or impractical to achieve. Randomization is key to establishing criteria #3. That is, by successfully treating the study group for high blood pressure, the chances of subsequent strokes are reduced compared to the control group.

Now let us return to the chocolate and intelligence example. To definitively demonstrate contributory cause for the chocolate and intelligence example, investigators would need to start by conducting case-control studies to establish that individuals with greater intelligence actually consumed more chocolate. Cohort studies would then be needed to definitively demonstrate that the consumption of chocolate began early in life—well before the full development of intelligence. Finally, to definitively demonstrate that altering the "cause" alters the "effect," a well-conducted randomized controlled trial would be needed that randomly assigned participants to consuming or not consuming large quantities of chocolate. Those randomized to consuming large quantities of chocolate would need to be followed up and demonstrate higher levels of intelligence.

When examining these types of investigations, it is important to try to ensure that the results obtained in small groups or "samples" included in the investigations are what is called *statistically significant*. Statistically significant implies that the relationship is real in the larger populations from which the sample of individuals who actually participated in the investigation was obtained.

It is also important to be sure that the strength of the relationship is large or substantial. The strength of a relationship is most often measured by what is called the *relative risk*. A relative risk of 5 for high blood pressure and stroke would imply that those with high blood pressure have 5 times the chances of developing a stroke compared to those without high blood pressure. Although this is an ideal sequence of studies to definitively establish contributory cause, it may not be feasible or ethical. Image the situation with cigarettes and lung cancer. Randomizing patients to a study group in which individuals are encouraged to smoke cigarettes is not likely to be acceptable once there is evidence suggesting a relationship to lung cancer or other health conditions.

Therefore, for practical as well as ethical reasons, one or more of these criteria often cannot be fully established. In these situations, it is important to look at what are called *ancillary* or *supportive* criteria for establishing contributory cause. The most important and commonly used supportive criteria and their applications to the relationship between cigarettes and lung cancer are as follows:[4]

- *Strength of the Relationship*: For example, the relationship between cigarette smoking and lung cancer has a relative risk of at least 10.

That is, those who smoke cigarettes on average have 10 times the risk of lung cancer than those who do not smoke cigarettes.
- *Consistency of the Relationship*: For example, studies in a wide range of countries and groups within countries consistency demonstrate a strong relationship between cigarette smoking and lung cancer.
- *Dose-Response Relationship*: For example, the more cigarettes that are smoked and the longer cigarettes are smoked, the greater the chances that lung cancer will develop at least in the range of ½ pack per day to 3 packs per day.
- *Biological Plausibility*: Cigarette smoking exposes the lungs to a long list of chemicals that have been found to produce cancer in animals.

None of these criteria is essential to establishing causation, but they are useful in situations such our case with lung cancer and cigarettes. Though cigarette smoking has not been demonstrated to be a contributory cause of lung cancer based on a randomized controlled trial, the supportive or ancillary evidence is very strong that a contributory cause exists.

Despite the generally accepted existence of a cause and effect relationship or contributory cause between cigarette smoking and lung cancer, it is important to recognize what a contributory cause implies and what it does not imply. Cigarette smoking is a very strong contributory cause of lung cancer. Nonetheless,

- Smoking cigarettes does not always lead to the development of lung cancer. Cigarette smoking is not a "sufficient cause" of lung cancer. Other factors such as genetics must be at work because not every person who smokes cigarettes even for long periods of time develops lung cancer.
- Not smoking cigarettes does not always protect an individual from developing lung cancer. Cigarettes are not a "necessary cause" of lung cancer. There are other factors such as asbestos and radon exposure that may also contribute to the development of lung cancer.

Therefore, contributory cause implies that cigarette smoking greatly increases the chances of developing lung cancer. However, cigarette smoking is neither necessary nor sufficient to produce lung cancer.

Figure 13.7 diagrams the criteria used to establish the existence of a contributory cause and the types of research studies that often play a role.

ESTABLISHING EFFECTIVENESS AND SAFETY OF TREATMENTS

The same types of criteria that are used to establish contributory cause can also be used to demonstrate that a treatment or other intervention works under research conditions; that is, it has "efficacy." Randomized controlled trials are the "gold standard" or definitive criteria for establishing efficacy. Once two well-conducted randomized controlled trials demonstrate the efficacy of a new drug and suggest at least short-term safety of the drug, the Food and Drug Administration (FDA) may approve the drug.

The approval of a drug allows the drug to be advertised only for the use or indication for

which it was investigated. However, those with prescribing privileges may prescribe the drug for any reason, at any dose, and for any length of time that they choose. These uses of drugs are called *off-label* prescribing. It is important to recognize that off-label prescribing is very common in clinical practice but does imply that there is less research supporting its use.

Despite the importance of randomized controlled trials, treatments that work under research conditions will not always work under the conditions of clinical practice. In addition, even drugs that appear to be safe in randomized controlled trials may not be as safe when used in practice.

The limitations of randomized controlled trials include their relatively small size, their relatively short duration, and their conduct under ideal experimental conditions often excluding patients with complicated conditions. These limitations can be summarized by saying that randomized controlled trials are "too small, too short, and too simple" to definitively establish the safety of a treatment. This often means that the results may not be

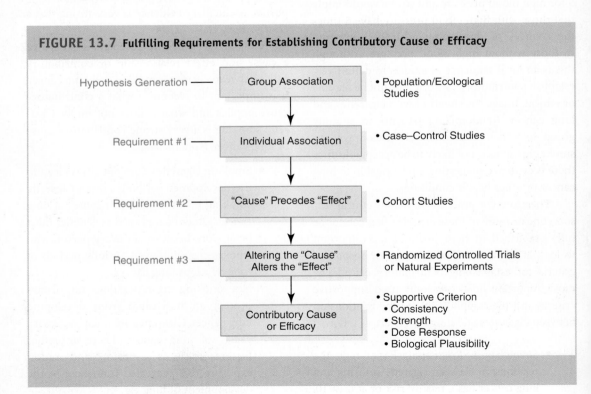

FIGURE 13.7 Fulfilling Requirements for Establishing Contributory Cause or Efficacy

as good when the drug is used in clinical practice as it appears from the randomized controlled trials.

In terms of safety, it is quite common for a new drug to be withdrawn from the market or have what is called a *black box warning label* placed on the drug information during the first few years after it is approved. Those who are the first to use a newly approved drug are participating in the research because there is still much to be learned after a new drug has been approved and made available to clinicians and patients.

A health information sheet known as a *patient insert* is usually included with a prescription drug.

This written material can alert a health navigator and the patient to the potential benefits as well as the potential harms of a drug. Information on the correct way to take the drug, the early warning signs of side effects, as well as the dangers of taking higher doses or stopping the drug abruptly are generally included in the patient insert. An important role for health navigators is to help patients understand their drugs and to actively participate in efforts to maximize the benefits and minimize the harms.

Understanding how to access and use health information is a central role for health navigators. It is key to helping patients help themselves.

Summary

© Jim Barber/Shutterstock

Discussion Questions

1. Identify a website and apply each of the criteria for reliability discussed in this chapter.

2. An active and healthy 85-year-old woman asks about how long she can expect to live. She hears that the life expectancy of women in the United States is now slightly greater than 80 years. She asks whether she has outlived her life expectancy.

   - Explain what life expectancy means and does not mean.
   - Explain the limitations of applying life expectancy figures to this woman.

3. Imagine that a recent newspaper article indicated that 25% of all deaths among children under 5 years of age are caused by injuries. The same article indicates

the only 5% of deaths among those over 70 year of age are caused by injuries. The article uses pie charts of the same size to show the dramatic difference between the percentage of the young and the old who die from injuries.

   - What are the limitations of using pie charts to present this data?
   - What additional information is needed to determine who has a greater chance of deaths from injuries—those over 70 or those under 5 years of age?

4. Assume that it has been established that LDL or bad cholesterol is increased among groups with higher incidence rates of coronary artery disease. What additional types of investigations are needed to definitively establish that LDL cholesterol is a contributory cause of coronary artery disease?

References

1. MedlinePlus. *Evaluating Internet health information: A tutorial from the National Library of Medicine.* Retrieved October 8, 2015, from https://www.nlm.nih.gov/medlineplus/webeval/webeval_start.html#.

2. U.S. Food and Drug Administration. *How to evaluate health information on the Internet.* Retrieved October 8, 2015, from http://www.fda.gov/Drugs/ResourcesForYou/Consumers/BuyingUsingMedicineSafely/BuyingMedicinesOvertheInternet/ucm202863.htm.

3. World Health Organization. *Health status statistics.* Retrieved October 8, 2015, from http://www.who.int/healthinfo/statistics/indhale/en.

4. Few, S. (2012). *Show me the numbers: Designing tables and graphs to enlighten* (2nd ed.). Burlingame, CA: Analytics Press.

5. Riegelman, R. K. (2013). *Studying a study and testing a Test: Reading evidence-based health research.* Philadelphia, PA: Williams and Wilkens.

CHAPTER 14

Analyzing Health Information for Clinical Practice

by Richard Riegelman

LEARNING OBJECTIVES

By the end of this chapter, students will be able to:

- Describe the uses of health information to diagnose health problems
- Describe the uses of testing as part of evidence-based decision making
- Describe the types of health information that need to be considered in making decisions about a treatment or other intervention
- Describe the development and uses of evidence-based recommendations/practice guidelines
- Describe electronic health records, including their uses, potential advantages, and potential disadvantages

CHAPTER OVERVIEW

Health information is used for a variety of purposes in clinical practice. This chapter examines key ways that health information is used for diagnosing disease, testing and screening, and evidence-based treatment decisions. Increasingly, health information is incorporated into evidence-based recommendations or practice guidelines, which can provide important tools for patients and practitioners. Personal health information is now often stored and used as part of the electronic health record (EHR), raising new issues for patients and health navigation professionals. This chapter examines each of these uses

of health information to understand principles that assist in navigating clinical practice.

USING HEALTH INFORMATION TO DIAGNOSE HEALTH PROBLEMS

The Institute of Medicine (IOM) of the National Academies of Sciences have issued a report on improving diagnosis in health care. The IOM found that "… the best estimates indicate that all of us will likely experience a meaningful diagnostic error in our lifetime." To address this issue, the IOM recognizes the "… need to establish partnerships with patients and their families to improve diagnosis."[1]

Therefore, there is an important role for health navigation professionals to play in working with patients and helping ensure that clinicians have the information they need for diagnosis. **Box 14.1** outlines the types of information that patients need to provide as part of the diagnostic process.

In order to help patients participate in diagnosis of their problem(s), it is important for health navigators to have a basic understanding of how physicians and, increasingly, nurse practitioners and physician's assistants use health information to come to conclusions we call *diagnoses*. To understand the basic approach and terminology used by clinicians in making a diagnosis, it is

BOX 14.1 Advice from the Institute of Medicine

Checklist for Getting the Right Diagnosis

1. *Tell Your Story Well*: Be clear, complete, and accurate when you tell your clinician about your illness.
   - *Be Clear*: Take some time to think about when your symptoms started, what made your symptoms better or worse, or if your symptoms were related to taking medications, eating a meal, exercising, or a certain time of day.
   - *Be Complete*: Try to remember all of the important information about your illness. Write down some notes and bring them with you. A family member may be able to help you with this.
   - *Be Accurate*: Sometimes you may see multiple clinicians during a medical appointment. Make sure your clinicians hear the same story regarding your illness.

2. *Be a Good Historian*:
   - Remember what treatments you have tried in the past, if they helped, and what, if any, side effects you experienced.
   - Think about how your illness has progressed over time.
   - Think about your family's medical history and if you may be at risk for similar illnesses.

3. *Keep Good Records*:
   - Keep your own records of test results, referrals, and hospital admissions.
   - Keep an accurate list of your medications.
   - Bring your medication list with you when you see your clinician or pharmacist.

Republished with permission of National Academies Press from: Balogh E. P., Miller B. T., Ball J. R. (eds.) Board on Health Care Services Institute of Medicine, 4–19; permission conveyed through Copyright Clearance Center, Inc.

useful to examine the steps that go into making a diagnosis using a mnemonic that has been called S.H.A.D.E.[2] The five letters stand for:

Symptoms
Hunch or hypothesis
Alternatives
Diagnosis
Explanation

Clinicians often follow this step-by-step process as follows:

Symptoms: After taking a history and doing a review of symptoms or checklist of other possible problems or symptoms as well as a physical examination, clinicians often identify a chief complaint or principal problem. The principal problem frequently represents the focus of the subsequent diagnosis process.

Hunch or Hypothesis: Clinicians often rapidly generate a likely diagnosis based on available data and medical knowledge. This hunch or hypothesis

often becomes what is called a *working diagnosis*, which needs to be either eliminated from consideration or confirmed.

Alternatives: Clinicians then try to identify possible alternative diagnoses and develop what is called a *differential diagnosis* or list of diseases that need to be ruled-in or ruled-out.

Diagnosis: The diseases in the differential diagnosis are then ruled-in and ruled-out using testing, which may be based exclusively on history and physical exam. This process leads to disease identification or diagnosis.

Explanation: The identification of a disease does not ensure that the disease is causing the patient's symptoms, especially when the patient has multiple diseases. Furthermore, disease identification may not be the end of the process; clinicians often need to establish the underlying cause or explanation for the disease.

A brief patient description or case can help illustrate the steps in the S.H.A.D.E. process.

George visits his doctor because of pain in the pit of his stomach. The pain does not move to his back and usually comes on when his stomach is empty. His physical examination is normal. His doctor immediately thinks of a stomach or duodenal ulcer but also considers gallbladder disease and inflammation of the pancreas. George's doctor sends him for an examination with a flexible scope or endoscopy of the stomach and duodenum to try to document the presence of an ulcer. She also does blood tests to help rule out gallbladder and inflammation of the pancreas.

The endoscopy confirms the diagnosis of duodenal ulcer. The tests of the gallbladder and pancreas do not indicate disease. She then tests George for H-pylori, a common bacterial cause of stomach and duodenal ulcers, which is positive. George's symptoms respond quickly to the treatment and do not return.

Symptoms: "George visits his doctor because of pain in the pit of his stomach. The pain does not move to his back and usually comes on when his stomach is empty." This description of George's symptoms may be considered his principal problem or chief complaint.

Hunch/Hypothesis: "His doctor immediately thinks of a stomach or duodenal ulcer." This hunch results from the location of the pain, occurrence on an empty stomach, and normal physical examination. This hunch or hypothesis produced a working diagnosis.

Alternatives: His doctor "also considers gall bladder disease and inflammation of the pancreas." These alternatives plus stomach and duodenal ulcers are often called the *differential diagnosis*.

Diagnosis: The fact that the pain does not radiate to the back helps the clinician rule out pancreatitis. The normal physical examination provides evidence against acute gallbladder disease. "George's doctor sends him for a flexible endoscope of the stomach and duodenum to try to document the presence of an ulcer. She also does blood tests to help rule out gallbladder and inflammation of the pancreas." The endoscopy

confirms the diagnosis of duodenal ulcer. The tests of the gallbladder and pancreas help rule out these alterative conditions.

Explanation: "She then tests George for H-pylori, a common bacterial cause of stomach and duodenal ulcers, which is positive. George's symptoms respond quickly to the treatment and do not return." This describes how the clinician looked for an underlying cause or explanation for the duodenal ulcer and how she and George followed up.

The S.H.A.D.E. process is a useful framework for understanding the complex thinking process of clinicians. It captures the need to rapidly focus on a small number of symptoms; make an educated guess well before all the data is in; constantly keep an open mind to other alternatives; draw conclusions even when doubt remains; and act while continuing to learn from the outcome.

By understanding this diagnostic process, health navigation professionals can help patients provide helpful information and actively participate in the diagnostic process. Health navigation professionals can help make this happen in a number of ways.

The tendency for clinicians to focus-in rapidly on a chief complaint is often an efficient habit reinforced by years of experience. Once the chief compliant is identified, it often becomes the focus of subsequent questioning designed to understand its history, timing of occurrence, severity, precipitating factors, and impact on the patient.

The very process of rapidly focusing in may have the inherent disadvantage of preventing the clinician from seeing the big picture and recognizing the patient's real reason for seeking medical care. Therefore, it is important to help patients think through before the visit why they are seeing the doctor and what they hope to accomplish.

In theory, physicians pick up the full range of symptoms by doing what is called a *review of systems*, asking check lists of questions about each body system. Increasingly, physicians are using paper or computer forms to identify other related or unrelated symptoms, past history, or data that may affect the outlook for the future or best type of treatment. Although these are often useful in providing important clues, they do not necessarily help physicians step back and see the big picture or the real reason for seeking medical care.

Thus, it is important for all of a patient's symptoms to be known to a physician, allowing him or her to recognize as early as possible what needs to be taken into account. A classic problem called the *doorknob syndrome* occurs when the real reason for a patient's visits comes to light just as the clinician is opening the door at the end of the visit. The doorknob syndrome may be the result of a physician who is not listening or a patient who is not talking. The doorknob syndrome can be prevented by making a full list of symptoms before the visit, whether or not they are believed to be important by the patient.

When the clinician is receptive, it can be helpful to give him or her the list at the beginning of the visit, thus giving the clinician a chance to prioritize. If a patient wants to be sure certain symptoms are addressed or questions answered, it can be most efficient to make this clear right at the beginning of the visit. At times, this may lead to follow-up visits to deal with less pressing problems or problems that do not seem to be directly related to the chief complaint. That, however, may be a reasonable way to deal with the reality of limited time.

Patients increasingly visit a doctor believing that they have a particular condition, one that has come to their attention through the media or perhaps a search on the Internet. Letting the clinician know about these concerns helps ensure that these possibilities will be considered. If possible, a patient should outline why he or she is concerned about a particular diagnosis. Often it will relate to a family history or friend who experienced similar symptoms or was diagnosed with a particular disease. This will often help the clinician focus on the issues that are of most concern to the patient.

Therefore, health navigators can help clinicians accurately and reliably achieve their aim of identifying and clarifying the principal problem. In preparation for a visit, a patient can think about and write down the details of what they see as the principal problem or problems. Remember that although a clinician may not focus on all the patient's problems, the clinician will want a great deal of information on the principal problem(s).

Physicians will want to know when the symptoms began; when they occur if they are intermittent; how long they last; what types of activities or situations bring on their occurrence; what other symptoms occur at the same time; and any other related information that will provide a clear and complete picture of the principal problem. It may be helpful for a patient to keep a diary to track symptoms and to provide these types of information. Thus, health navigators can assist by helping patients prepare a list of their concerns and questions as well as the details of the problem or problems that they bring to the clinician.

George's case also illustrates the role that the patient needs to play in implementing treatment and evaluating the results. Here, the treatment for *H-pylorie* played an important role in explaining the symptoms and ensuring that the *H-pylorie* was the underlying cause of the duodenal ulcer. Most diagnoses require patient involvement in recording their response and following up with additional tests and visits. A diagnosis should be considered a tentative diagnosis. That is, it needs to be confirmed by the patient's response to treatment and/or follow-up testing. Health navigators can help patients understand the need for follow-up visits and at times follow-up testing.

In practice, diagnosis is not always an orderly process of laying out all the facts, collecting all the data, and drawing logical conclusions. Rather, it is a very selective process that depends heavily on focusing on and clarifying key symptoms and fitting them together to explain the patient's problem. By understanding the steps in the S.H.A.D.E. process, health navigators can help patients contribute to and benefit from the diagnostic process.

USING INFORMATION FROM TESTING IN CLINICAL PRACTICE

When a patient has symptoms, testing is an important part of the diagnostic process. In fact, the history and physical examination are themselves tests. In this section we will see that testing also plays other important roles in clinical medicine. Testing includes information gathered from blood testing and other bodily fluids such as urine or saliva; imaging tests such as X-rays and MRIs;

and functional tests such as exercise stress tests and what is called *cognitive testing* for dementia or Alzheimer's disease.

The exercise stress test a good example of what can be gained from testing as well as the limitations. Exercise stress tests are not perfect. The perfect test for coronary artery disease is the coronary arteriogram. This gold standard test is assumed to be correct every time. In a coronary arteriogram, dye is injected into the coronary arteries, and X-rays are taken to visualize the inside of the arteries, looking for narrowing or blockages, the hallmark of coronary artery disease. Coronary arteriograms carry some danger and considerable expense, so they should not be conducted unless they provide information that is quite important to the diagnosis or care of a patient.

In comparison with coronary arteriograms, exercise stress tests for coronary artery disease can result in falsely negative results, i.e., false negatives, as well as falsely positive results, i.e., false positives. Tests that are less than perfect, as most tests are, can and do help rule-out or rule-in a diagnosis. However, the potential for false positives and false negatives needs to be kept in mind.

When assessing information gained from a test, clinicians use the concepts known as *sensitivity* and *specificity*. For instance, imagine that the sensitivity of exercise stress testing is 95 percent and the specificity is 90 percent, compared to a perfect or gold standard test that has 100 percent sensitivity and specificity. A sensitivity of 95 percent means that 95 percent of those with coronary artery disease will have a positive exercise stress test. A specificity of 90 percent means that 90 percent of those without coronary artery disease will have a negative exercise stress test.

That is, sensitivity measures the chances that the test is "positive-in-disease"; specificity measures the chances that the test is "negative-in-health." Notice that both sensitivity and specificity are about the test itself and do not in-and-of-themselves tell us about the chances that a disease is present or absent.

Clinicians really want to be able to estimate the chances that a specific patient has or does not have a particular disease. To achieve this

goal, more than sensitivity and specificity of the test are needed. The clinician needs to estimate the chances that the disease is present BEFORE the results of the test are known, based on the patient's symptoms and what they know about the frequency of the disease. By combining the chances of disease before the test results are known with the test results, the clinician can estimate the chances of disease if the test is positive and if the test is negative.

For instance, if coronary artery disease is very unlikely, as is the situation with young women with chest pain, even a positive exercise stress test does not make the diagnosis of coronary artery disease. On the other hand, when coronary artery disease is very likely, as in the situation of a 65-year-old man with chest pain and multiple risk factors, then even a negative test is not enough to rule out the disease.

SCREENING FOR ASYMPTOMATIC DISEASE

Screening can be thought of as testing when the patient does not have symptoms of the disease. That is, screening is conducted when patients are what is called *asymptomatic*, as opposed to the previous discussion of the use of testing when patients have symptoms. Screening for asymptomatic disease has become central to prevention. Screening is widely used to detect a number of cancers, common sexually transmitted diseases including HIV, as well as congenital diseases among newborns.

Screening often takes place when the chances of disease are low, perhaps 1 percent or even less. When the chances of the disease are this low, a large number of false positive results can be expected. Therefore, when screening for asymptomatic disease, it is almost inevitable that more than one test will need to be conducted. A single positive screening test is NOT the same as having the disease. Screening requires a strategy, including follow-up testing for those with an initial positive screening test.

In order to determine whether a screening strategy works well, it is helpful to have a list of characteristics of an ideal screening strategy. An ideal screening strategy would fulfill the following criteria:[2]

- The disease causes substantial deaths and/or disabilities.
- Screening for early detection of disease is possible and improves the health outcome.
- There is high-risk population to be screened and a feasible testing strategy.

- Screening is acceptable in terms of safety, costs, and patient acceptance.

Few screening tests perfectly meet all of these criteria, but ones that are recommended and paid for under health insurance need to be reviewed by experts and be found to be highly rated. **Table 14.1** presents a series of commonly used screening tests that meet most, if not all, of these criteria.[3]

TABLE 14.1 **Common Screening Tests That Meet Most, if Not All, of Criteria**

	Substantial Mortality and/or Morbidity	Early Detection Possible and Improves Outcome	Screening Is Feasible (Can Identify a High-Risk Population and a Testing Strategy)	Screening Is Acceptable in Terms of Harms, Costs, and Patient Acceptance
Hypertension (High Blood Pressure)	Strokes, myocardial infarctions, kidney disease	High blood pressure precedes often by decades, and effective treatment is available	Test children and adults as part of routine health care	Screening itself is free of harms, low costs, and is acceptable to patients; treatments have harms, costs, and side effects
Breast Cancer	Second most common fatal cancer among women and most common for women under age 70	Early detection improves outcome	For those 50 and over, combination of mammography and follow-up biopsy shown to be feasible; screening under 50 is controversial	Harms due to false positives, low risk of harm from radiation, good patient acceptance; earlier screening increases costs and false positives
Cervical Cancer	If undetected and untreated may be fatal	Early treatment dramatically reduces the risk of death	PAP smear and follow-up testing have been extremely successful	PAP results in substantial number of false positives; new DNA testing may be used to separate true and false positives
Colon Cancer	Second most common fatal cancer in men and third in women	Early detection of noncancerous growth or polyps reduces development of cancer and early detection of cancer improves survival	Men and women 50 and older plus those with high-risk colon disease; multiple options for screening	Patient acceptance has been major barrier but improving; low probability of harm from procedure; substantial cost of procedures now often covered by insurance
HIV Testing	Common disease especially in high-risk areas; progression to AIDS and potentially fatal complications	Early detection may lead to treatment to delay onset of AIDS and reduce transmission	Excellent screening and diagnostic tests; high risk patients and all patients in high-risk areas	Testing inexpensive and accurate even in relatively low-risk populations; false negatives with early testing when transmission risk high
PKU (Newborn testing for genetic disease)	Relatively low incidence but severe mental effects without treatment	Early detection possible and alters outcome	All newborns must receive screening test by law with follow-up testing of positives	Testing low cost, generally acceptable to patients

OTHER USES OF TESTING

Diagnosis and screening for asymptomatic diseases are not the only uses of testing in clinical medicine and public health. Other uses of testing include the following:[3]

- *Testing for Risk Factors*
Risk factors are characteristics such as smoking cigarettes, physical exam findings such as high blood pressure and obesity, or test results such as high LDL cholesterol or bad cholesterol and elevated blood sugar, which when present increase the chance of developing a disease such as coronary artery disease.

  Screening for risk factors is usually most important when the factor can be improved though actions by the patient and/or interventions such as drugs. Many people with the risk factor will never develop the disease. Therefore, screening for risk factors requires that the factor scores very highly on the screening criteria before being widely applied. Screening for high blood pressure is one of the few risk factors that is recommended for nearly universal screening.

- *Testing for Prognosis or Outlook for the Future*
Increasingly, clinicians are testing for genetic factors that may help predict the future occurrence of a disease like Alzheimer's disease, even when this information does not help in altering the course of the disease. This remains a very controversial use of testing because there is little that can be done once the diagnosis is made.

  Testing for prognosis, or to predict the future course of a disease, however, can be of great importance once a disease is diagnosed. Diseases such as cancer, heart disease, and Alzheimer's disease are increasingly being categorized into stages. For instance, cancers such as breast and prostate cancer are categorized as stage 1, 2, 3, or 4 depending on the extent of their spread. Alzheimer's is increasingly categorized as early, moderate, and advanced. Staging of disease is increasingly being used to make specific treatment recommendations and to tailor treatment to the individual.

- *Testing for Response to Treatment*
Testing to determine an individual's response to treatment including both the benefits and the harms is an important use of testing. Whenever a treatment is prescribed, whether it is surgery or medicine or another type of treatment, it is important to ask: How will the results be known? Sometimes, the outcome is merely determined by whether the patient feels better or can perform better, such as walking farther, breathing better, or having less pain. Often, however, specific tests are needed to assess the success of treatment as well as the side effects.

  With diabetes, for example, short-term outcomes can be judged by the blood sugar under fasting conditions, but longer term response requires measuring the Hemoglobin A1c, which provides a measure of control of high blood sugar over approximately a 2-month period. At other times, such as with treatment of high LDL cholesterol with statin medications, the level of LDL needs to be measured as well as periodic checks on liver function due to the potential for statin medications to damage the liver.

  Even when symptoms are improved, such as improvement in breathing, a physician may want to objectively establish that improvement has occurred and measure the extent of improvement by conducting breathing tests or what are called *lung function tests*. Follow-up evaluation through testing is an important part of the treatment and provides useful health information on both the benefits and the harms of a therapy. Health navigators can help patients understand and accept the recommended follow-up testing.

- *Testing for Causation*
Treatment itself can be viewed as a test. Often called a *therapeutic trial*, the response to treatment can help in establishing that a disease is the cause of a

patient's symptoms. In George's case, his response to treatment supported duodenal ulcer as the cause of his symptoms.

Issues of causation are becoming increasingly important as patients young and old have a long list of disease diagnoses. The elderly, those on multiple medications and treatments, and seriously ill patients with multiple complications can be very complex patients. Often the question is more than diagnosis; it is causation. That is, which of the many diagnoses or large number of medications is causing or producing the current symptoms?

When physicians are looking for underlying causes, it is important to consider the social determinants of health. Patients with asthma may have their conditions worsened by contact with air pollution, mold, cockroaches, and a variety of other environmental exposures. Alternatively, their inability to afford medications may be the underlying cause of their worsening condition. Health navigators can encourage clinicians to focus on these underlying causes of disease.

Health navigators can help patients interpret the reason for and the meaning of test results. At times, they can help clinicians recognize the underlying causes of disease, the social determinants of health. The social determinants of health may be thought of as the "causes of causes," which can help explain the development of disease and at times the less-than-ideal response to treatment as in the case of asthma.

Testing has become a central feature of clinical medicine. It is connected to diagnosis, screening, prognosis, causation, treatment, and assessing the outcome of treatment. It is therefore important that health navigators understand the uses of testing and the terminology used by clinicians when discussing testing and test results.

USING HEALTH INFORMATION TO MAKE TREATMENT DECISIONS

Once a disease diagnosis is established, a wide range of health information is needed to make decisions on the best way to treat the disease. At times, it is best to merely observe the disease and to carefully follow up. For early disease, what is called *watchful waiting* may be the best course of treatment. For some diseases, including early prostate cancer as well as Alzheimer's disease, this is often the recommended treatment because early treatment does not lead to better outcomes.

Frequently, however, clinicians will recommend a treatment that might range from medication, to surgery, to radiation, and/or chemotherapy. Treatment may also include rehabilitative efforts such as physical therapy or what are called *palliative efforts* designed to help a patient live with a worsening condition. The term "intervention" is increasingly used to describe the full range of possible therapies from prevention to medication to physical therapy to palliation.

When considering the options for intervention. A number of types of information are needed. This section identifies these types of information and explores how they can be used in practice to reach a decision on a recommended treatment.

In current practice, the treatment decision is increasingly becoming a joint or shared decision between doctors and patients. Physicians may recommend a treatment, but increasingly patients are seeking active participation in the decision-making process. It is well established that the patient has the final say on whether or not to proceed with a recommended intervention. Health navigators can help patients make the most of the decision-making process.

Clinicians usually engage in a process known as *informed consent*. Clinicians often start by explaining why an intervention is needed and what will happen. As part of this process, they also need to explain benefits and harms. Benefits are the desirable outcomes that clinicians and patients seek from treatment. These may range from relief of pain, to better function, to cure of disease, to prevention of complications, and to reduced anxiety while the disease progresses. It is important that patients understand the goal(s) of therapy.

Harms are the undesirable outcomes of treatment. Some of these undesirable outcomes are an inherent and inevitable result of the intervention itself. Surgery carries with it the known potential for infection, pain, and the need for rehabilitation as well as a small or not so small possibility of death.

Other harms are considered side effects. They are not an inherent part of the process and may occur in a part of the body far removed from the site of treatment. High blood pressure medicine may cause impotence, sleepiness, and even shortness of breath. Therefore, patients need to know and be on the lookout for the most common side effects that are known to occur with a treatment.

In addition to the known harms and side effects of treatment, there is always the possibility of unknown and unexpected harms. The longer a treatment has been used and the more commonly it is used, the less often surprises occur. However, with relatively new treatments it is important to be on the lookout for previously unknown or unrecognized harms.

Thus, it is important to understand what treatment is being recommended, why it is being recommended, and the probability of good outcomes (benefits) and the probability of bad outcomes (harms). It is also important to know when a patient is on a new medication. Health navigators can help patients understand and be on the lookout for the benefits and the harms of treatment.

Knowing the potential benefits and harms of a treatment is not enough to make good decisions. Two additional key pieces of information are needed. The first is the timing of the benefits and harms. Benefits that occur far into the future are often given less importance than benefits that occur immediately. The opposite is true of harms. The longer into the future the harms occur, the better. For instance, surgery is often feared because the harms are often immediate while the benefits may take time. Likewise, vaccinations are often underappreciated because their harms often occur soon after administration while their benefits may occur years into the future.

In addition to the chances or probabilities of benefits and harms and their timing, it is important to decide on the importance that a patient places on a particular benefit and/or a particular harm. A health navigator can work with a patient to help determine the importance placed on loss of vision, or regaining use of an arm, or retaining the ability to live independently, or losing

the right to drive a car. The importance or value placed on these types of benefits and harms will vary from person to person. The only way to know the answer for any particular person is to ask them!

Therefore, when assessing an option for intervention, it is important to consider:

- The chances of potential benefits
- The chances of potential harms
- The timing of the potential benefits and the potential harms
- The importance or value placed on the potential benefits and the potential harms

Putting this health information together is a complicated process. For many decisions, the benefits and the harms may seem to balance each other. In these situations, disagreements between clinicians and patients over the choice of treatment are quite common. When a patient is faced with a difficult choice, he or she may want to get a second opinion. When the patient has difficulty accepting the recommendation of clinicians, health navigators can help patients explore the reason(s) for the disagreement.

Even assuming that the patient accepts the information on the benefits and the harms of treatment, he or she may not accept the recommendation of the clinicians. When this is the situation, the patient may have a number of important and legitimate reasons that need to be explored:

- Patients are often understandably focused on the process of care, not just the outcomes. Issues like how long they will be in the hospital, how much pain to expect, and what will be involved in follow-up and recovery are important consideration that patients often use when making decisions, especially when they are dealing with difficult decisions.
- Patients, and at times clinicians, may be *risk takers* or *risk avoiders*. A risk taker often seeks an intervention that may improve the health outcome even when the odds are against him or her. A risk avoider often refuses a treatment if it has the potential to make his or her health worse.

Risk-avoiding is very common when patients feel they can tolerate their current state of health. Risk-avoiding may also be affected by the social determinants of health, such as fear of unemployment, lack of adequate financial resources, or a history of discrimination leading to lack of trust in the healthcare system. Risk-taking, on the other hand, is very common when patients feel their health is deteriorating or they cannot tolerate their current state of health.

Risk-taking and risk-avoiding attitudes are very common in these situations, but there are a small number of individuals who are risk takers much of the time and a roughly equal number of individuals who are risk avoiders much of the time. There is nothing inherently wrong with being a risk taker or a risk avoider, but it is important to recognize these types of behaviors.

It can be helpful to ask patients about their risk-taking attitudes. Risk avoiders will often say that they do not like to take chances, while risk takers are often proud of their willingness to "go for it" even when the odds are stacked against them.

Having explored the types of health information that are needed to make decisions on treatment and other interventions, it should be helpful to look at an example of how the pieces fit together.

Laura is faced with a choice of treatment for her knee injury. Her physician recommends that she undergo immediate surgery, which has a 90 percent chance of success but also a 1 percent chance of infection, which would make her knee problem worse. There is also a very small chance of death. The recovery period will require daily physical therapy, and Laura will be unable to engage in her usual physical activities for several months.

Alternatively, she can use a knee brace and have once-a-week physical therapy for the next 2 to 3 months. If she is not responding well at that point, the same surgery can be conducted. However, the outcome of the surgery is not likely to be as good as immediate surgery, while the chances of infection should be the same.

Laura wants to continue her new job in an office and thinks she can tolerate not being able to engage in high levels of physical activity in the coming months. She says she does not want to "take any more chances than absolutely necessary" and decides to go with the knee brace and physical therapy.

Laura's situation illustrates many of the issues involved with using health information to make treatment decisions. Laura's physician recommends immediate surgery on the basis of data showing that the benefits are high while the harms are low. The recommended treatment, however, is accompanied by the potential for harm in the near future from infection and even death. For Laura, these potential harms may be more important than the possibility of a less successful outcome at a future time.

Laura's decision to try a knee brace and physical therapy may have been influenced not only by the timing of possible outcomes. Laura seems to have placed a great deal of importance on being able to continue to work in her new job. The time away from work for surgery may give her understandable fear of unemployment. This may be an example of the impact of the social determinants of health.

Laura's natural risk-taking tendencies may also have played a role in her decision. She indicates that she does not want to "take any more chances than absolutely necessary." These are the words of a risk avoider. This risk-avoiding attitude may have played an important role in her decision.

HEALTH INFORMATION ON TREATMENT WITH PRESCRIPTION AND NONPRESCRIPTION DRUGS

Using health information to improve clinical practice is not limited to major decisions such as whether or not to undergo surgery. Obtaining and using health information is part of the day-to-day practice of clinical medicine. Because patients generally take medication on their own, health navigators can have a major influence on medication use and abuse.

To illustrate the types of health information that are used in health care, let us look at the increasingly common use of prescription and nonprescription drugs.

Today, prescription and nonprescription drugs are the most common form of treatment. Despite the fact that written informed consent is rarely required before prescribing and taking a prescription drug, drug treatment carries the same basic issues as other treatments such as surgery.

The use of drugs presents a special need for and special opportunities for patient involvement in care. Because drugs are treatment that patients usually administer on their own, there is a great need for patients to have key health information and to provide important information to their clinician. Drugs treatments are increasingly common, and over-the-counter drugs are increasingly powerful. Thus, it is very possible for patients to be taking a large number of medications prescribed by several clinicians as well as additional over-the-counter or nonprescription medications.

Box 14.2 provides a list of 10 key principles and information on medication use for

---

BOX 14.2 Advice on Getting the Most out of Medications

- Keeps a list of all medications, including over-the-counter medications, vitamins, and dietary supplements such as nutritional and herbal treatments. The list should include the medications as well as the timing and quantity of medications. Keep a copy of the list easily available in case of an emergency.
- Know the history of drug allergies or other side effects. New medications may be related to drugs previously taken.
- Understand what each medication is designed to do. Keep the quantity of medications to a minimum to avoid potential interactions and to minimize the number of side effects.
- Ask about the chances of side effects due to other medical conditions that may be present, such as kidney or liver disease. Some drugs such as blood thinners or anticoagulants and a number of asthma medications have a small margin of safety. That is, side effects often appear at doses only slightly above those that are beneficial and intended. Special attention for side effects is essential when taking a medication with a small margin of safety.
- Before taking a new medication, be sure that a pharmacist checks whether there are any known interactions between the new medication and other medications being taken. Interactions are very common and do not necessarily preclude taking the medication. However, they may require altering the dose or the timing of the medications.
- Understand how long the medication needs to be taken and if there are dangers when suddenly stopping the medication. For instance, it is generally important to take the full course of antibiotics, and it may be dangerous to suddenly stop certain high blood pressure medications.
- Ask what side effects to watch for and whether there are any side effects that will not be obvious and will require testing to adjust the dose or detect side effects. Distinguish between side effects that are likely to occur in the first few days of treatment, such as allergies or low blood pressure, and longer term side effects, such as depression or liver or blood problems.
- When taking a new medication, be sure to know when to take it and whether it can be taken with meals and with other medications. Ask whether there are any special precautions when beginning a medication. These may include being alert for allergies or taking the first dose sitting down or before going to bed at night.
- Understand whether the new medication is a well-established medication with well-known side effects or a new medication for which safely is still being assessed. Before taking a newly approved medication, be aware that early users are participating in the assessment of safety. When on new medications, be especially alert to and report changes in health.
- Be aware that even well-established drugs may not be safe over long periods. There is often very little data on long-term use of medications. When taking medication for years, it is often worth asking a clinician whether it is still needed and whether there are any newly recognized concerns about the treatment.

patients and health navigators that can greatly improve the safety and, at times, the effectiveness of medications:

EVIDENCE-BASED RECOMMENDATIONS/ PRACTICE GUIDELINES

Evidence-based recommendation or practice guidelines are a way of putting together—in one place, using a standard format—what is known about an intervention or treatment from research and clinical practice. Rapid increases in potential interventions have left many clinicians as well as patients at a loss to decide which intervention is the best for them. In response, the Institute of Medicine (IOM) put forth recommendations for the development and use of practice guidelines.[4]

These guidelines have been expanded to include the full range of interventions. As the use of practice guidelines has broadened and expanded in recent years, they are now often more generically referred to as *evidence-based recommendations*.

The IOM identified a series of goals for practice guidelines or evidence-based recommendations, many but not all of which have been successfully achieved. They include:

1. Assisting clinical decision making by patients and practitioners
2. Educating individuals or groups
3. Assessing and assuring the quality of care
4. Guiding which interventions should be covered by insurance
5. Reducing the risk of liability for negligent care

The order of this list is the same as the order of success in implementing evidence-based recommendations. They have been most successful in assisting with clinical decision making by patients and practitioners. Their availability online has enabled them to educate individuals and groups, including patients and health navigators, which is goal #2.

A wide array of carefully developed practice guidelines is now available. The Agency for Healthcare Research and Quality (AHRQ) maintains a National Guideline Clearinghouse (www.guideline.gov/browse/by-topic.aspx). The Clearinghouse includes a wide range of high-quality practice guidelines. The website allows the user to compare the available guidelines. This website can be very useful to patients and health navigators.[5]

Practice guidelines or evidence-based recommendations are increasingly being used by healthcare accreditors of hospitals and group practices to assess their quality of care, which was goal #3. The use of evidence-based recommendation for determining which interventions should be covered by insurance, goal #4, is in its early phases. However, provisions in the Affordable Care Act (ACA) have led to coverage without co-payment for clinical prevention efforts given high grades as part of the evidence-based recommendations process.

Finally, though widely discussed, there is little to suggest that evidence-based recommendations have reduced negligent care or provided malpractice protection to clinicians who adhered to them; this is goal #5. The reasons for negligent health care go far beyond the choice of treatment. Lawsuits are often related to how treatment was implemented and how the clinician relates to the patient. It is often directly related to communications. Adhering to evidence-based recommendations, however, is increasingly being seen as a standard for high-quality clinical practice, and failure to follow these recommendations may be an issue raised in a malpractice suit.

In addition to knowing how to access evidence-based recommendations and how they are used, health navigators need to know who develops practice guidelines, how they are graded, and what the grades mean in order to help patients understand these important sources of health information.

Evidence-based recommendations are often developed by the following types of groups, including:

- *A governmental task force.* These groups are appointed based on specific qualification by a governmental health agency such as the Centers for Disease Control and Prevention (CDC) or the Health

Resources and Services Administration (HRSA). Once appointed, the individuals give their own advice. The recommendations are those of the task force and are not controlled by the governmental agency.

- *Societies of health professionals* such as cardiologists, surgeons, pediatricians, or public health professionals. Recommendations from these groups may benefit from the special expertise of their members, but they may also reflect their own professional biases and vested interest.
- *Organizations with consumer representation as well as health professionals* such as the American Cancer Society and the American Heart Association. These organizations seek to take into account the perspectives of both health professionals and consumers or patients.

A range of other types of organizations may attempt to develop or fund the development of evidence-based recommendations ranging from large healthcare delivery systems to pharmaceutical companies. Thus, it is important to examine not only who develops the recommendations but also which group(s) fund the development.

Evidence-based recommendations should include the date on which they were approved. High-quality recommendations should be reviewed periodically, often every 5 years. Ideally, an evidence-based recommendation should have a termination data after which it is not considered valid unless reviewed and reapproved or revised.

Evidence-based recommendations do not always provide definitive answers, and they often change over time as more information is obtained or better methods are developed. The recommendations about what age to begin screening for breast cancer remain controversial, with recommendations from different groups coming to different conclusions. Recommendations about how often to perform a PAP smear have changed several times in recent year, and new tests for the papilloma virus, which has been shown to cause cervical cancer, have altered the approach to screening.

GRADING OF EVIDENCE-BASED RECOMMENDATIONS

Evidence-base recommendations have been widely used for preventive interventions. The United States Preventive Medicine Task Force (www.uspreventiveservicestaskforce.org) has developed a frequently used system for grading evidence-based recommendations on a scale of A, B, C, D, and I.[6] It is important for health navigators to appreciate how each of these grades is obtained and what they mean.

The process of grading recommendations for interventions relies on combining what is known from the health research literature. In grading a recommendation, two major factors are taken into account: (1) quality of the evidence, and (2) magnitude or strength of the impact of the intervention. The quality of the evidence is scored on a very simple scale of "good," "fair," and "poor." The quality of the evidence is addressed first because if the quality of the evidence is poor, the overall grade is I, which stands for incomplete or insufficient information and can be thought of as "I don't know."

In judging the quality of the evidence, the authors need to consider three factors:

1. *Type of Research and the Quality of Research*: Evidence-based recommendations generally assume that well-conducted randomized controlled trials are the best form of evidence, followed by well-conducted observational studies (i.e., case-control studies or cohort studies).
2. *Relevance of the Research*: To be scored as "good," the research needs to be relevant to the recommendation. That is, if the recommendations are being made for women age 65 and older, the research should be conducted on women 65 years and older, ideally from a population similar to the one on which the recommended intervention is being used.
3. *Clinical Importance of the Outcome*: For the evidence to be considered "good," the outcome being measured should also include an important clinical outcome

such as a cure, longer survival, or better function. Outcomes that are limited to better test results do not generally fulfill the criterial for "good" evidence.

In contrast to "good" evidence, "poor" evidence implies that there is a fatal flaw in achieving one or more of these criteria. When evidence cannot be scored as "good" or "poor," the commonly used default score is "fair."

Once an evidence-based recommendation is graded as "good" or "fair," the next step is to look at how much impact the intervention can be expected to have on individuals or groups of people. A "substantial" impact may imply a large impact on a small group of people or a smaller impact on a larger group of people. For instance, coronary artery bypass surgery may result in a substantial impact by having a large impact on a small number of people. Regular strenuous exercise may have only a modest impact on any one individual, but because it can be applied to large numbers of people, its impact on groups or populations may also be scored as substantial.

In addition to substantial, other scores for the magnitude of the impact can be "moderate," "small," and "zero or negative." The distinction between "moderate" and "small" may be subjective and potentially controversial. "Zero or negative" implies that the intervention's harms are equal to or exceed the benefits for the average person. Therefore, an intervention whose impact is "zero to negative" should not be recommended

and should receive a grade of D, which means "do not use."

Table 14.2 shows how the U.S. Preventive Services Task Force[6] recommends combining the score from the quality of the evidence with the scores from the magnitude of the impact. First identify the quality of the evidence at the left of the chart. Then identify the magnitude of the impact at the top of the chart. The grade is where the two scores come together. Note that there is only one way to obtain an A but three ways to achieve a B.

For preventive interventions such as vaccinations, behavioral change, and screening for disease, an A or a B is considered a good or very good recommendation. "A" recommendations can be regarded as a "must," while a "B" recommendation can be seen as a "should." Under the ACA, preventive recommendations that receive an A or B need to be covered by all ACA-affected insurance policies without any co-payment or deductible.

Let us look at a few examples of evidence-based recommendations for clinical prevention and see how they can be graded.

A preventive intervention has been shown through a long-term randomized controlled trial and clinical follow-up on relevant patients to greatly reduce deaths from coronary heart disease among patients in primary care practice. The harms are infrequent and not life-threatening.

TABLE 14.2 Classification of Recommendations

	Magnitude of the Impact			
	Net Benefit Substantial	Net Benefit Moderate	Net Benefit Small	Net Benefit Zero/Negative
Quality of the Evidence				
Good	A	B	C	D
Fair	B	B	C	D
Poor	I	I	I	I

Data from: Agency for Healthcare Research and Quality, U.S. Preventive Services Task Force Guide to Clinical Preventive Services. Vol 1 AHRQ Pub No. 02-500.

This recommendation for a preventive intervention would receive a grade of "A." The evidence is "good" because the research is (1) a long-term randomized controlled trial, (2) conducted on relevant patients, and (3) reduces deaths from coronary artery disease—a clinically important outcome. In addition, the intervention greatly reduces deaths with infrequent and not life-threatening harms; thus, the size or magnitude of the impact can be scored as "substantial." Combining a score on the evidence of "good" with a score on the magnitude of the impact as "substantial" produces an overall grade of "A."

Here is another example:

Two well-conducted randomized controlled trials of a new breast cancer test performed on a relevant population demonstrated that it is less effective than mammography in detecting breast cancer.

When grading recommendations, we first score the quality of the evidence. This evidence would have a score of "good" because the evidence comes from two well-conducted randomized controlled trials on relevant populations. The outcome being measured is detecting breast cancer, which is an important clinical outcome. Unfortunately, this good evidence indicates that the outcome is less effective; that is, the outcome is actually negative or worse than mammography. Thus, this is "good" evidence indicating that the screening test should not be used. This is an example of a "D" or "do not use the screening test."

And here is one last example:

Expert opinion by a well-respected group of surgeons indicates that a new treatment for lung cancer improved length of survival.

Evidence-based recommendations rely on research studies to establish the quality of the evidence. Expert opinion even by a respected group of experts whose experiences suggest that the treatment improves an important outcome is not enough to establish "good" or even "fair" evidence. Thus, the quality of the evidence here would

be considered "poor" and the recommendation would be give an "I" or insufficient information.

This approach to expert opinion represents a major change from the past, when expert opinion was often the basis for clinical recommendations. Some have called this a change from "eminence-based" to "evidence-based" recommendations.

ELECTRONIC HEALTH RECORD (EHRs)[7]

Imagine the following situation:

As a health navigation professional, you are asked to help a patient who does not speak English well to maximize the benefit of his visit to a clinician. You find that much of your time is spent helping the patient deal not just with the language but also with the technology. You help him make an appointment online, fill out the health information forms online, follow up on his laboratory tests online, and obtain a copy of his medical records that have been stored in an electronic health record (EHR). You are surprised how fast clinical medicine is moving to computerized practice and the importance of health navigation professionals in helping patients maximize the advantages and minimize the disadvantages of EHRs.

Health care is, in fact, rapidly moving to computerize practice. The electronic health record or EHR is central to that process. The EHR stores health information in digital format for easy retrieval, transfer, and integration of health services. EHRs are rapidly replacing paper medical records. EHRs can integrate personal health information with the full range of clinical activities, including asking patients to enter their own health information and health problems, scheduling appointments, and coordinating health care between different clinicians, different settings, and different institutions. They also potentially provide health information for health research.

Clinicians using EHRs may record personal health information on a computer or handheld device while they are in the examining room or at the bedside. Unfortunately, at times clinicians may focus on entering data into EHRs rather than interacting with patients.

EHRs generally include the same types of information that were previously included in paper records. Specifically, they usually include:

- Basic information, such as name, address, phone number, and emergency contact
- Medical history
- List of medications, allergies, and vaccinations
- Laboratory test results, such as blood work
- Radiology images, such as X-rays, CAT scans, and MRIs
- Advanced directives, living wills, and healthcare power of attorney

There are a number of potential advantages of a successfully operating EHR system.

Reduces Errors

- Eliminates errors caused by illegible handwriting
- Checks to make sure the drugs being prescribed are not harmful when taken with other drugs

Improves Security

- Allows clinicians to make a backup copy of all medical records; if the office catches fire or floods, medical records are safe
- Allows clinicians to keep track of, and to limit, who looks at a medical record

Saves Time and Money

- Ends searching for lost medical information and unnecessary duplicate testing
- Ends thumbing through the pages of medical charts to find information

Improves Care

- Reminds clinicians when it is time for you to get tests and vaccinations, such as a yearly influenza shot
- Reminds clinicians when to follow up on lab tests or reminds a patient to follow up on an important return visit

EHRs are designed for sharing information, often on the Internet. Increasingly, this means that when another clinician, such as a specialist, physical therapist, or nurse, is involved in care, they have access to the EHR. Ideally, this helps coordinate care by reducing duplication; reducing waiting for information, especially in an emergency; and ensuring that all clinicians have the same information.

In addition to sharing information, the EHR is now key to prescription and laboratory ordering, which is increasingly being done electronically. Ideally, this increases accuracy and speed as well as reducing costs. The ease of ordering tests and prescriptions, however, can also increase the number of orders placed, especially for laboratory tests.

Privacy and security concerns also arise whenever health information is shared. A federal law called the *Health Insurance Portability and Accountability Act* (*HIPAA*) provides a set of protections for EHRs. The HIPAA security rule requires healthcare providers to make reasonable efforts to protect the privacy of medical records so that they cannot be accidentally or illegally read, altered, shared, or destroyed.

Although breaches of security are an ongoing concern, HIPAA and other federal laws help protect the privacy of personal health information by giving patients more control over their health information, including the right to access information and request corrections. HIPAA also sets boundaries on the use and release of health records. State and federal laws offer increased protection for the confidentiality of records dealing with mental health and addiction treatment. These records may not be disclosed without specific authorization from the patient.

EHRs are increasingly requiring input from patients and allowing access by patients. Many patients are likely to turn to health navigation professionals with questions, including how to provide accurate information and how to obtain more information on the meaning of their EMRs. Helping patients record their health information and also gain an understanding of the meaning of information in their EHR is likely to become a major activity of health navigation professionals in the future.

EHRs are becoming one-stop shopping for the full range of health information, including patient history, physical examinations, laboratory tests, diagnoses, consultations, personal health directives, and even patient preferences. As EHRs become a central part of clinical medicine, they are also likely to be central to the future of the health navigation professions. EHRs are here to stay, and it is important that health navigators learn to help patients make the most of this key technology.

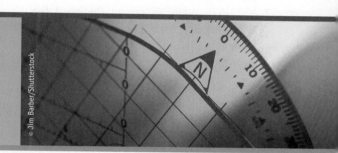

Summary

© Jim Barber/Shutterstock

Discussion Questions

1. Identify how the steps in the S.H.A.D.E process are illustrated in the following case:

   Dianne, a 30-year-old part-time receptionist, has been experiencing chest pains in the center of her chest for more than 2 months. The discomfort lasts from 5 to 10 minutes. These pains seem to occur after dinner if she lies down but not with exercise or at work. Dianne is concerned about whether these are due to her heart because her father died of a heart attack at age 62. She also worries because she is a bit overweight, being 5'4" and 170 pounds, and does not exercise regularly.

   After asking about the exact location, timing, and frequency of her symptoms and determining that Dianne has not been a cigarette smoker, her doctor did a physical examination. The doctor examined Dianne's heart, stomach, and lungs; took her blood pressure; and did not find any abnormalities. Finally, the doctor checked Dianne's previous records and found that her LDL, or bad cholesterol level, was within the normal range.

   Because of the concern about her heart, Dianne was sent for an exercise stress test in which she was hooked up to an electrocardiogram and ran in place on a treadmill. The doctor asked Dianne to report if she experienced any chest pain. Before, during, and after the examination, her blood pressure was taken.

   Noting that her stress test and examination were negative for any abnormalities, the doctor asked Dianne to help him by taking liquid antacid immediately whenever the pain occurs, recording what happens and how long it takes. Dianne found that on three occasions, within 30 seconds of taking the liquid antacid, the pain disappeared. After telling her doctor this information, the doctor confidently said: "There is no evidence of heart disease. Your symptoms are caused by acid reflux or heartburn."

2. Colon cancer is the second most common cause of death due to cancer in both males and females. Early detection of the disease often leads to cure as opposed to waiting until symptoms appear. Age over 50 is a strong risk factor for the disease and is

the recommended age to start screening procedures. A number of methods for screening, including colonoscopy and sigmoidoscopy plus testing of stool for blood, have been shown to be effective screening tests. These procedures are considered generally safe and cost-effective. Patients are increasingly accepting the need for screening and undergoing recommended screening examinations paid for by health insurance.

Indicate how this description addresses each of the four ideal criteria for a screening test, specifically:

- Substantial death and/or disability.
- Early detection is possible and improves outcome.
- A feasible testing strategy is available.
- Screening is feasible in terms of safety, cost, and patient acceptance.

3. Isabel is faced with the decision of whether to have eye surgery. She has already totally lost vision in her left eye, and now her right eye is losing vision as well. She is advised to have surgery on her right eye as soon as possible because delaying surgery would decrease the chances of success from 90 percent to 70 percent. Surgery would require Isabel to have a patch over her eye for a month and there is a 5 percent chance of infection after surgery, which, if it occurs, is likely to make her vision worse. There is a very small chance of death from the surgery.

Identify and explain the factors that Isabel might consider in making the decision whether or not to have the surgery.

4. Screening with mammography for breast cancer in a representative group of women 50 years old and older has been shown in two well-conducted randomized controlled trials to reduce the chance of death

from breast cancer. The reduction in the chance of death is considered large.

- What score for quality of the evidence and also what score for the magnitude of the impact would you give a recommendation to screen all 50-year-old women for breast cancer using mammography?
- What grade would you give a recommendation to screen all women 50 years and older for breast cancer using mammography?
- What does the grade you gave screening with mammography for women over 50 mean for health insurance coverage under the ACA?

5. You are working as a health navigator helping patients receive health care for complex health conditions such as advanced cancer. You make an appointment for a patient online and help him fill out an online history form before coming to the appointment. The patient is asked to sign forms including HIPAA forms, allowing release of information to other healthcare providers and informing the patient of the protections provided for their health records. Once in the examining room, the clinician asks questions while focused on the computer screen, entering information as he asks the patient questions. At the end of the appointment, the physician orders a series of laboratory tests as well as prescriptions electronically. His staff makes a consultation referral appointment and allows access to the EHR by the consulting physician's office.

- How does this situation illustrate the impacts of EMR and computerization on medical practice?
- What are the potential advantages of the use of EHR illustrated in this situation?
- What are the potential disadvantages of the use of EHRs illustrated in this situation?

References

1. Balogh, E. P., Miller, B. T., & Ball, J. R. (eds.). (2015). Board on Health Care Services Institute of Medicine. *Improving diagnosis in health care.* Washington, DC: National Academies Press, 4–19.

2. Riegelman, R. K. (1991). *Minimizing medical mistakes: The art of medical decision making.* Boston, MA: Little, Brown and Company.

3. Riegelman, R. K., & Kirkwood, B. (2013). *Public health 101: Healthy people–healthy populations.* Burlington, MA: Jones & Bartlett Learning.

4. Institute of Medicine (1992). *Guidelines for clinical practice: From development to use.* Washington, DC: National Academy Press.

5. Agency for Healthcare Research and Quality. *Clinical guidelines and recommendations.* Retrieved October 3, 2015, from http://www.guideline.gov/browse/by-topic.aspx.

6. U.S. Preventive Services Task Force. *Methods and processes.* Retrieved October 3, 2015, from http://www.us preventiveservicestaskforce.org.

7. Quality Insights of Delaware. *Electronic health records: What you need to know.* Retrieved October 2, 2015, from http://dehitrec.org/SiteAssets/resources/Consumer _EHR_Brochure.pdf.

GLOSSARY

CHAPTER 1

Advanced registered nurse practitioner: A health care professional possessing a degree required for a licensure who may work independently depending on the state licensure requirements or in collaboration with physicians.

Allied health positions: A segment of the workforce that delivers services involving the identification, evaluation, and prevention of diseases and disorders; dietary and nutrition services; and rehabilitation and health systems management.

Anesthesiologist: A physician who is certified and legally qualified to administer anesthetics and related techniques.

Certified nursing aide: A health care professional who works under supervision, assisting patients with eating, bathing, and dressing; taking some vital signs; making beds; noticing any changes in the physical or emotional state of a patient; and notifying a nursing supervisor.

Colonoscopy: A test done by inserting a flexible tube called colonoscope through the rectum to view and detect changes or abnormalities in the inner lining of the colon.

Co-payment: A fixed fee or cost that individuals must pay prior to receiving specific medical services or treatments covered by their health insurance plan.

Health navigation professional: A health care professional who provides services to patients and those supporting them, by assisting them in their search for resources, information, and answers to specific questions.

Hearing therapist: A health care professional who provides support and rehabilitation of individuals experiencing difficulties in hearing and communicating.

Hospital billing clerk: A hospital office staff having knowledge on computer software and insurance and billing practices and is responsible for administrative tasks like updating medical records, communicating with insurance companies, and billing patients.

Kinesiology and exercise science professional: A health care professional who studies the basics of mechanics and anatomy related to the movement of the body and helps individuals to learn better exercise and training habits.

Massage therapy: Manual manipulation of the soft-tissue muscles throughout the body to reduce stress, improve circulation, treat injuries, and promote general health in a patient.

Medical and clinical laboratory science professions: Health care professions responsible for carrying out laboratory tests and operating laboratory equipment under the supervision of a certified medical laboratory technologist to discover the presence or absence of disease and provide data that helps physicians determine the best treatment for the patient.

Medical ethics and bioethics: The basic ethical principles to be used when conducting biomedical and behavioral research involving human subjects, human dignity, and the sanctity of life.

Medical facilities management: It ensures that health care facilities are properly cleaned, maintained, and supplied and also oversees implementation of new technology and energy efficiency initiatives.

Medical office assistant: A staff who performs a variety of administrative tasks key to the overall functioning of a doctor's office, including office administration, insurance billing, and basic back-office clinical duties.

Medical record and information technician: A staff responsible for organizing and maintaining medical records by collecting information about patients, including test results, diagnoses, exam results, recommended treatments, prior medical history, and other relevant data.

Medical staff services: A position that ensures health care staff are compliant with regulatory requirements and is responsible for coordinating credentialing processes and maintaining databases of physician information, as well as other administrative duties.

Medical transcriptionist: A person who transcribes recordings made by physicians and other health care workers to produce medical records, regulatory documents, and other pieces of correspondence.

Mental health services: A health care professional who assists individuals with mental and/or behavioral disabilities by teaching them daily living skills and assisting them with social, recreational, educational, and occupational activities.

Occupational therapist: A health and rehabilitation professional who helps patients improve or maintain skills for day-to-day activities and well-being.

Ophthalmic laboratory technician: A technician who makes glasses and contact lenses based on the optometrist's instructions.

Pharmacist: A health care professional who distributes drugs prescribed by physicians and provides information to patients about medications and their use.

Physician: A health care professional qualified and licensed with clinical experience to practice medicine specializing in diagnosis and medical treatment.

Physical therapist: A health care professional who teaches patients a few basic exercises to improve their quality of life and strength.

Physician's assistant: A health care professional qualified and licensed to practice medicine under physician supervision.

Registered nurse: A health care professional who is trained and has clinical competence to provide services that are essential in the promotion, maintenance, and restoration of health and well-being of patients.

Speech therapist: A health care professional who helps individuals having speech defects and disorders by training them especially using exercises and audio-visual aids.

CHAPTER 2

Arteriosclerosis: A disease marked by degenerative changes in the arteries caused by buildup of plaques made up of fat, cholesterol, calcium, and some other substances found in blood, resulting in thickening, hardening, and loss of elasticity of the walls of the arteries.

Calculated risk: The risk of acquiring a disease or being exposed to danger that is undertaken after its probability is assessed or calculated.

Cardiovascular disease (CVD): A dysfunction of the heart and blood vessels that can be caused by controllable and non-controllable factors.

Endocarditis: An infection of the inner lining of the heart known as endocardium caused when bacteria or germs enter the bloodstream and lodge on the damaged areas of the heart valves or heart lining.

Evidence-based recommendations: A procedure or treatment used for a specific health condition based on research and the latest scientific findings.

Framingham Heart Study: An ongoing cardiovascular cohort study that began in 1948 with 5,209 adult subjects from Framingham, Massachusetts; a project of the National Heart, Lung, and Blood Institute, in collaboration with Boston University.

Health navigation professional: A professional who provides services to patients and those supporting them, by assisting them in their search for resources, information, and answers to specific questions.

Observable risk: A verifiable and predictable risk of acquiring a disease or being exposed to danger.

Primary prevention: An intervention or an activity that reduces health risks by protecting healthy individuals from illness or disease before it even occurs.

Risk assessment: The process of evaluating the likelihood of acquiring a disease or being exposed to danger.

Secondary prevention: An intervention to stop or slow the progress of risk factors by early screening or treatment of the disease or injury.

Tertiary prevention: An intervention to prevent further damage or injury, reduce pain, slow the progression of the disease or injury, prevent the disease or injury from causing further complications, and rehabilitate as much as possible to improve quality of life.

Victim-blaming: An act of blaming an individual for his or her circumstances without taking into account the surrounding contexts.

CHAPTER 3

Assessment: A regular and systematic investigation of the health problem to determine possible risks and hazards within the community.

Assurance: The provision of services to the public either directly or through regulation of other entities.

Botulism: A serious illness caused by eating foods that are contaminated with a nerve toxin produced by *Clostridium botulinum* bacteria.

Centers for Disease Control and Prevention: A federal agency under the umbrella of the U.S.

Department of Health and Human Services that investigates, diagnoses, and tries to control or prevent diseases, especially new and unusual diseases.

Chlamydia trachomatis: A common sexually transmitted infection (STI) that can infect both men and women. If left untreated, it can cause serious, permanent damage to a woman's reproductive system, making it difficult or impossible for her to conceive later on.

Communicable diseases: Diseases that get transmitted from one infected person to another through direct contact with an infected individual or indirectly through a vector.

Dengue virus: An acute mosquito-borne flavivirus disease characterized by headache, fever, pains in the joints, and skin rash.

Department of Health and Human Services: The U.S. principal agency with a mission to enhance and protect the health and well-being of all Americans and provide essential human services, especially for those least able to help themselves.

Department of Homeland Security: The department of the U.S. Federal Government with responsibilities in public security by protecting U.S territory from terrorist attacks and providing a coordinated response to large-scale emergencies.

Diphtheria: A respiratory disease that is transmitted from person to person, usually through respiratory droplets caused by coughing or sneezing.

Disease surveillance: An ongoing systematic collection and analysis of data with confirmed influenza-associated cases in children and adults and state and territorial reports of influenza activity and degree of severity.

Environmental Protection Agency: An independent agency within the federal government structure with the mission to protect human health and the environment by writing and enforcing regulations based on laws passed by Congress.

Epidemic (also called *Outbreak*): The occurrence of cases of a disease spreading rapidly in excess of what would normally be expected in a defined community, geographical area, or season.

Giardiasis: A diarrheal illness caused by a microscopic parasite and contracted by drinking untreated water contaminated with feces of infected animals.

Gonorrhea: A sexually transmitted disease (STD) caused by the bacterium *Neisseria gonorrhoeae* that can infect both men and women.

Hepatitis: A disease caused by a virus in which the liver is damaged by the presence of inflammatory cells in the tissue of the organ.

Human immunodeficiency virus: A non-curable infection transmitted through bodily fluids. If left untreated, HIV can cause severe illness and eventual death.

Influenza: An acute respiratory viral infection commonly known as 'the flu' that spreads from individual to individual through respiratory droplets from coughs and sneezing.

Legionellosis: A disease caused by any species of Gram-negative aerobic bacteria belonging to the genus *Legionella* found naturally in the environment, usually in water.

Listeriosis: A serious infection usually caused by eating food contaminated with the bacterium *Listeria monocytogenes*. It affects older adults, pregnant women, newborns, and adults with weakened immune systems.

Malaria: A mosquito-borne life-threatening disease caused by parasites transmitted to humans through the bite of the *Anopheles* mosquito.

Mandatory reportable disease: A health care provider is mandated by federal law to report the disease diagnosis to the U.S. Centers for Disease Control and Prevention (CDC) for tracking.

Measles: A highly contagious virus that spreads by air through coughing and sneezing.

Meningococcal disease: An acute infectious disease caused by bacteria and includes infections of the lining of the brain and spinal cord (meningitis) and bloodstream infections (bacteremia or septicemia) usually spread through the exchange of respiratory and throat secretions like phlegm.

Mumps: A contagious disease caused by a virus and starts with a few days of fever, headache, muscle aches, tiredness, and loss of appetite, followed by swelling of the salivary glands.

Pandemic: The occurrence of cases of a disease that has spread throughout an entire country, continent, or the whole world.

Pertussis: Also known as whooping cough. A highly contagious respiratory disease characterized by uncontrollable, violent coughing that often makes it hard to breathe.

Policy development: It includes the creation of comprehensive public health policies based on scientific evidence in service to the public.

Public health: It refers to the overall health and safety of the U.S. population achieved by preventing disease, monitoring, regulating, and promoting health through organized efforts, including core functions and essential services by several federal departments and agencies.

Rabies: A preventable viral disease of mammals that causes acute inflammation of the brain. It is most often transmitted through the bite of a rabid animal.

Reportable disease: A diagnosed disease from a list of diseases (called a reportable disease) that must be mandatorily notified by a health care provider to the CDC and the state health office so investigators are aware of the disease in a specific location.

Rubella: A contagious disease with symptoms of mild fever and rash caused by a virus usually transmitted by droplets from the nose or throat.

Salmonellosis: An infection caused by the bacteria *Salmonella* found in contaminated, undercooked food and poor kitchen hygiene.

Severe acute respiratory syndrome: A viral respiratory illness caused by a coronavirus which causes fever, cough, and other symptoms.

Shigellosis: A foodborne infectious disease caused by bacterium of the genus *Shigella*, especially *S. dysenteriae*, most often through improperly handled food and preparation. It is characterized by diarrhea, fever, and stomach cramps.

Syphilis: A sexually transmitted infection caused by *Treponema pallidum*, a microscopic organism called a spirochete that can cause long-term complications if not treated correctly. A person can get syphilis by direct contact with a syphilis sore during vaginal, anal, or oral sex. It can also be spread from an infected mother to her unborn baby.

Tetanus: An acute, often fatal, disease caused by an exotoxin produced by the bacterium *Clostridium tetani*, which usually enters the body by close contact with bacteria-harboring animals or by experiencing a cut or puncture by a rusty metal object (like a nail). It is characterized by muscle stiffness, generalized rigidity, and convulsive spasms of skeletal muscles.

Toxic shock syndrome: A potentially fatal disease caused by a bacterial toxin. The illness can be caused by the use of an infected contraception sponge, diaphragm, or tampon after a surgery; or a cut or burn to the skin. It is characterized by sudden onset of high fever, vomiting, and profuse watery diarrhea, sometimes accompanied by sore throat and headache.

Tuberculosis: A disease caused by bacteria that usually attack the lungs, but may attack any part of the body such as the kidney, spine, and brain. If not treated properly, TB can be fatal.

Typhoid fever: A life-threatening illness caused by the bacteria *Salmonella typhi* spread by eating or drinking food or water contaminated with the feces of an infected person.

Vancomycin-Resistant *Staphylococcus aureus*: An infection caused by bacteria strain of *S. aureus* that are resistant to vancomycin, the drug often used to treat infections caused by enterococci that are normally present in the human intestines and in the female genital tract and are often found in the environment.

Whooping cough: Refer **Pertussis**.

CHAPTER 4

Assisted living facility: A housing facility that provides non-medical services to individuals who are no longer able to live independently.

Cancer research institution: An institute that conducts research while treating individuals with cancer diagnosis. Many of these cancer institutions have the "National Cancer Institute" (NCI) designation in the title and get substantial amount of federal grant to fund the research being conducted.

Hospice: A holistic and philosophical approach to end of-life care to make the individual as comfortable as possible during his or her final days, with an emphasis on pain control, symptom management, natural death, and quality of life to comfort the individual's physical body, while also supporting the family members as needed.

Hospital: An institution with an organized medical staff offering in-patient health care service for individuals in need of medical care.

In-patient health care facility: A facility that provides medical care for individuals for diagnosis or treatment that requires overnight stay.

Long-term acute care hospital: A hospital with specialty-care for patients with serious medical problems that require special and intense treatment for an extended period of time.

Memory care center: A specialized type of assisted-care facility to protect individuals with Alzheimer's disease and other memory loss diagnoses, where the staff provides assistance with the activities of daily living as needed.

National Cancer Institute: It is part of the federal National Institutes of Health (NIH) which provides substantial amount of grant dollars to conduct and support research, training, health information dissemination, and other activities related to the causes, prevention, diagnosis, and treatment of cancer.

Nursing homes: A privately operated establishment providing health care for persons who are unable to take care of themselves.

Palliative care: Specialized medical care for people with serious illness, providing relief from the symptoms and improving the quality of life for individuals who have chronic long-term pain.

Pediatric hospitals: A hospital which offers medical services solely to children and adolescents in the age group from birth up to the age of 18.

Rehabilitation facility: A facility that provides residential treatment for individuals who sustained an injury or surgical procedure requiring short-term convalescence, physical therapy, and occupational therapy.

Shriner's Hospital: A national philanthropy organization that conducts research and provides specialized pediatric hospital care at no cost for children from the United States and around the globe.

Skilled nursing facility: A privately operated establishment offering a full range of nursing services, including 24-hour medication dispensing, wound care, diaper changes, nutritional supplements, extensive assistance with activities of daily living, as well as therapies.

St. Jude's Children's Hospital: A nonprofit medical corporation founded in 1962 that offers a vast array of inpatient and outpatient services for children and their families, including clinics for long-term survivors of childhood cancer and other life-threatening diseases.

Ventilator: A type of machine that helps patients who cannot breathe sufficiently on their own by supplying oxygen into the lungs and removing carbon dioxide from the body.

CHAPTER 5

Case manager: A health navigation professional who assists the individual in comprehensive planning and evaluation of medical services.

Debride: A procedure for removing dead, contaminated, or adherent tissue and any foreign material from a wound to avoid infection.

Dialysis: An artificial kidney medical treatment that filters blood through a machine to remove excess fluid and toxins.

Dialysis treatment center: A facility where dialysis treatment is provided to the individuals whose kidneys are no longer functioning to remove toxins from the blood.

Disordered eating treatment facility: A facility where the focus is on treating obesity, anorexia nervosa, and bulimia nervosa. The purpose of the treatment is weight loss or weight gain, and includes individual, group, and family therapy sessions; exercise and

yoga; healthy food choices; and a range of art, music, and meditation.

Drug treatment facility: A facility similar to mental health treatment centers in that they offer inpatient and outpatient services. Drug treatment centers offer services for addiction of alcohol, street drugs, or prescription drugs. The goal is to assist the individual in moving from addiction to a life free of addiction.

Electrocardiogram (ECG): A test that determines if there are problems with the electrical activity of the heart by detecting the abnormal heart rhythms recorded by the machine.

End stage renal disease: A permanent kidney failure and the individual must remain on dialysis for the remainder of their life.

Fee-for-service: A type of payment paid for health care providers for each service.

Federally Qualified Health Centers (FQHC): A unique reimbursement designation from the Bureau of Primary Health Care and the Centers for Medicare and Medicaid Services of the U.S. Department of Health and Human Services.

Formulary: A list of prescription drugs that are covered by a specific health care plan.

Free community clinic: These types of clinics have limited hours of operation, but do provide services with free or reduced rates.

Group practices: The practice of medicine by a group of physicians who share the premises and overhead costs. In addition, partners also share responsibility in responding to all patient calls after hours.

Hospital owned outpatient clinic: These are outpatient clinics operated by the hospitals to offer primary care to individuals with or without health insurance instead of having the individuals rely on the emergency department for nonemergency medical services.

Infusion center: A facility to allow patients to be discharged from the hospital and still continue their intravenous (IV) antibiotic medications.

Medicaid: A social protection program rather than a social insurance program. Eligibility is determined largely by income. It is the largest source of funding for medical and health related services for U.S. citizens living in poverty.

Mental health treatment facility: A facility owned by corporations, hospitals, community, organizations, or private physician groups where eligibility of services is divided by the individual's ability to pay for the services. Most treatment centers serve adolescents and adults.

Necrotic: The death of tissues due to severe injury or disease especially in a localized area of the body which may lead to amputation.

Out-patient ambulatory surgical center: A center owned and operated by a corporation, a local hospital, or a group of physicians where many surgical procedures are performed as outpatient services and it is no longer necessary to be admitted to a hospital.

Out-patient health care facility: A facility offering health care for individuals needing services that do not require an overnight stay under clinical supervision or long-term care.

Peritoneal dialysis: The second type of dialysis treatment generally performed at home with a caregiver and requires the patient to be lying flat. For that reason, it is usually done during the night while the patient sleeps.

Pharmacy: A shop or a dispensary where the most basic and simple type of outpatient health care service occurs over-the-counter (OTC).

Physical therapy: A rehabilitative health service offered to patients in the hospital, in the home, and in outpatient facilities providing therapy treatments to assist individuals with injuries or illness to improve the ability to move and manage their pain.

Private health insurance: An insurance protection policy often offered through employers or other organizations.

Subspecialties: A narrow health care service often called as sub-specialization within a specialty field of medicine.

Urgent care clinic: These are walk-in clinics and are usually owned by national, for-profit corporations offering ambulatory care in a dedicated medical facility outside of a traditional emergency room.

Wound care clinic: This type of clinic serves patients with specific wound management needs. Physicians who work in wound care clinics are generally dermatologists specializing in complex wound care.

CHAPTER 6

Children's Health Insurance Program (CHIP): A partnership between the Federal and State governments providing health coverage to uninsured children of those families who earn too much to qualify for Medicaid, but too little to afford private coverage.

Co-payment: A fixed fee or cost that individuals must pay prior to receiving specific medical services or treatments covered by their health insurance plan.

Consolidated Omnibus Budget Reconciliation Act (COBRA): A law passed by the U.S. Congress in 1985 that required most employers with group health insurance plans to continue to offer temporary group health insurance for their employees in special circumstances for a period of up to 18 to 36 months depending on the situation.

Deductible: A set amount of medical charges each individual enrolled in a health insurance plan must pay each year before the health insurance benefits begin.

Diagnostic-related groups (DRG): A unit of description to classify patients by diagnosis, average length of hospital stay, and therapy received; the units are used to determine the payment received by health care facilities and providers to cater to current and future inpatient procedures and services.

Employment-based health insurance: If individuals work for a company for a designated period of time (usually 90 days), then they are eligible to select a health insurance policy through their company.

Explanation of benefits (EOB): Each individual enrolled in a health insurance plan receives, via email or postal mail, a document that explains the health care benefits, deductibles, co-payment responsibilities, and reasons for non-coverage of claims.

The Family and Medical Leave Act (FMLA): It protects an employee's job while ill or caring for a family member.

Federal Bureau of Prisons (BOP): A United States federal law enforcement agency responsible for confining federal offenders in prisons. It is also responsible for delivering medically necessary health care to inmates in accordance with applicable standards of care.

Fee-for-Service: A type of payment paid for health care providers for each service.

Flexible spending account: A tax-advantaged account maintained by the employer where each year some amount is subtracted as a pretax deduction and added to a health savings account to be used for health expenses not covered by the employees' health insurance policy.

Gross domestic product (GDP): It represents the total value of all goods and services produced within a nation's geographic borders over a specified period of time.

Gross national product (GNP): It represents the total value of all goods and services produced within a nation's geographic borders over a specified period of time by the citizens of US.

The Health Insurance Portability and Protection Act (HIPPA): It assures that personal health information is protected from unlawful review, but still allows the information to be shared with other health care providers to promote quality health.

Health Maintenance Organization (HMO): An organization that provides health coverage with providers under contract where individuals who enroll pay a fixed-price payment without concern for the amount or kind of services received.

The Human Genome Project: An international scientific research project that was completed and has identified all of the more than 100,000 genes in human DNA. The project changed how health care identified, diagnosed, and treated certain disease and medical conditions.

Hypertension: A major health problem also known as high blood pressure which refers to the force of blood pushing against the walls of the arteries.

Indian Health Services (IHS): An agency within the U.S. Department of Health and Human Services that is responsible for providing federal health services to American Indians and Alaska Native members of the 566 federally recognized Tribes across the United States.

In-network: When individuals enroll in a health insurance policy plan, they receive a website that lists the contact information for health care providers in the health care plan network.

Medicaid: A social protection program rather than a social insurance program where eligibility is determined largely by income. It is the largest source of funding for medical and health related services for U.S. citizens living in poverty.

Medical errors: These are mistakes in health care referring to inaccurate or incomplete medicines, lab reports or diagnosis and treatment of a disease, injury, syndrome, behavior, infection, or other ailment which could be harmful to the patient.

Medicare: A health insurance program for people age 65 or older, people under age 65 with certain disabilities, and people of all ages with end stage renal disease.

Organization for Economic Cooperation and Development: An international economic group composed of 34 industrialized developed countries that works with 70 non-member economies to promote economic growth, prosperity, and sustainable development.

Out-of-network: It refers to a health care provider who is considered as non-approved in an insurance plan as they do not have contract with that insurance company.

Out-of-pocket: The amount of money that individuals must pay for health services or equipment that is not covered by the health insurance policies.

The Patient Protection and Affordable Care Act (PPACA): It is commonly known as the Affordable Care Act (ACA) enacted to increase the quality and affordability of health insurance, lower the uninsured rate by expanding public and private insurance coverage, and reduce the costs of healthcare for individuals and the government. It introduced mechanisms like mandates, subsidies, and insurance exchanges.

Preferred provider organization (PPO): A type of health insurance arrangement where individuals will have greater health care options within a large network of health care providers and services in discounted prices in hospitals, and pharmacists.

Prison health services: The Federal Bureau of Prisons employs licensed and professional staff to provide essential medical, dental, and mental health services in a manner consistent with accepted community standards for a correctional environment.

Single payer: A system in which the government provides insurance for all citizens and pays all health care expenses except for co-payments and co-insurance costs. Health care providers may be public, private, or a combination of both.

Socialized medicine: Also known as universal health care in which the government provides complete medical care through government subsidization and regularization of medical and health services.

TRICARE: A health care program of the United States Department of Defense Military Health System that provides insurance coverage to current and retired members of the U.S. armed forces.

Veteran's Administration: The largest integrated health care system in the United States which is administered under the Department of Veterans Affairs. It provides health care to all seven branches of uniformed services and is serving 8.76 million veterans in 1700 health care locations.

World Health Organization: A specialized agency of United Nations established in 1948, headquartered in Geneva, Switzerland concerned with international public health.

Worker's compensation: A form of health insurance that provides replacement wages and pays medical expenses to employees injured while performing their job.

CHAPTER 7

Accreditation: A process of validation for professional associations, nongovernmental organizations (NGOs), and nonprofit organizations.

Bioethics: The basic ethical principles to be used when conducting biomedical and behavioral research involving human subjects, human dignity, and the sanctity of life.

Bioethics committee: A committee with members representing various departments within the hospital and an ethicist to advice on matters pertaining to ethical considerations within the hospital and provides forums for discussion regarding ethical policy.

Certification: A process through which an organization recognizes that accreditation eligibility requirements have been met.

Healthcare Effectiveness Data and Information Set (HEDIS):   These measures have been adopted for use by about 90 percent of U.S. health insurance corporations to measure performance on specific areas of care and service.

Individual licensure: The process of granting permission by a government agency to legally engage in a practice or activity.

Institutional licensure: It is granted to any agency or organization providing a professional service to the public.

Institutional review board (IRB) committee: It is formally designated to assure, both in advance and by periodic review, that appropriate steps are taken to protect the rights and welfare of humans participating as subjects in the research.

Insurance fraud: A fraud that occurs when an insurance company, agency, adjuster, or consumer intentionally commits a deliberate deception to obtain an illegitimate gain.

Joint commission: A private, nonprofit organization that continues to improve the safety and quality of U.S. health care provided and assesses performance improvement and provides accreditation to health care organizations.

Licensure: The process of obtaining permission from a government agency to legally engage in a practice or activity.

Malpractice: An improper, unskilled, or negligent treatment of a patient by a health care provider.

National Committee of Quality Assurance (NCQA):   A non-profit organization created in 1990 dedicated to improving health care quality that provides accreditation for health insurance companies.

National Association of Insurance Commissioners: The U.S. standard-setting and regulatory support organization created and governed by the chief insurance regulators from all 50 states, the District of Columbia, and 5 U.S. territories.

Nongovernmental agencies (NGOs):   These are commonly established non-profit organizations by ordinary citizens and are funded by grants, foundations, businesses, or private individuals.

Quality assessment: It determines whether data were collected and analyzed accurately.

Quality assurance: A broad plan for maintaining quality in all aspects of a program, such as staff training, written protocols and procedures, data management, and data analysis.

Quality improvement: It involves utilizing systematic actions over time for the improvement of health care services and the health status of patients.

Quality control: The procedure intended to ensure that step-by-step processes in protocols and procedures are used within an organization.

Risk management: The process to improve safety and well-being for patients and staff and identify financial risks.

Risk assessment: The process of evaluating the likelihood of acquiring a disease or being exposed to danger.

CHAPTER 8

Body mass index (BMI):   A measure of body fat based on weight in relation to height, and applies to most adult men and women aged 20 and over.

Centers for Disease Control and Prevention (CDC):   A federal agency under the umbrella of the U.S. Department of Health and Human Services that investigates, diagnoses, and tries to control or prevent diseases, especially new and unusual diseases.

Cultural and social norms: These are norms defined as behavior patterns, values, attitudes, and beliefs of specific groups (e.g., ethnicity, age group, common language, geographical location).

Demographic information: It refers to statistical information such as marital status, race/ethnicity, religious preference, and type of health insurance.

Electronic medical records (EMRs):   A systematized collection of patient health information in digital version saved on computer hard disks for ease of access.

Equity: It refers to the absence of systematic disparities in health between groups with different levels of underlying social advantages/disadvantages.

Health disparity: the preventable differences in the burden of disease, injury, violence, or opportunities to achieve optimal health that are experienced by socially disadvantaged populations. The differences in health status between one population group in comparison to a more advantaged group due to issues of social justice and equity.

Life story: An individual's life story, which explores all aspects of health disparities and social determinants of health that influence him or her.

No known allergies (NKA): It infers that the patient does not know of any known drug allergies, and this is very important information that goes into the medical records.

Religious practice: A concept closely associated to cultural norms and has various meanings, including spiritual views, faith-based community, or mindfulness meditation. It influences how individuals go through their day-to-day lives as well as how they make decisions related to their health care decisions.

Social determinants of health: It may be thought of as the "causes of causes," which can help explain the development of disease and at times the less-than-ideal response to treatment.

Social justice: A framework to secure care for uninsured individuals prompting physicians and healthcare professionals to provide charity care.

Social support: It is one of most important factors in predicting an individual's overall well-being, physical health, mental health, and well-being across an individual's life span from childhood through old age.

Transient ischemic attack: It is often labeled as mini stroke and is more accurately characterized as a warning stroke.

CHAPTER 9

Active immunity: The immunity that occurs naturally when individuals come into contact with the virus and their bodies create antibodies to defend the virus.

Antibody: A blood protein produced in the body, which when combined chemically with substances, fights off specific antigens such as bacteria, viruses, and foreign substances present in the blood.

Attenuated virus: The attenuated virus is given usually by injection and multiplies in the body

to provide continuous antibody stimulation over a long period of time.

Centers for Disease Control and Prevention: A federal agency under the umbrella of the U.S. Department of Health and Human Services that investigates, diagnoses, and tries to control or prevent diseases, especially new and unusual diseases.

Chlamydia: The most common sexually transmitted bacterial infection and frequently reported infectious disease in the United States, where the prevalence is highest in persons who are younger than 24 years.

Chronic (non-communicable) disease: Diseases associated with poor lifestyle and behavioral choices, such as obesity, poor nutrition, tobacco use, and lack of sufficient exercise. It includes cardio vascular diseases (e.g., heart attacks, stroke), cancers, diabetes, chronic respiratory diseases (e.g., chronic obstructive pulmonary disease, asthma), diabetes, and arthritis.

Community immunity: A form of indirect protection from infectious disease that occurs when a large percentage of a population has become immune to an infection. This supports in providing a measure of protection for individuals who are not immune.

Common cold: Also known as the upper respiratory infection, and is among the most common illness. There are more than 200 different viruses that cause a URI, where the symptoms include inflammation of the membranes in the lining of the nose and throat.

Giardiasis: It is caused by Giardia, a microscopic parasite that causes the diarrheal illness, including symptoms of abdominal discomfort and prolonged intermittent diarrhea. It is commonly spread by drinking untreated water contaminated with feces of infected animals.

Gonorrhea: Gonorrhea is a sexually transmitted disease (STD) that can infect both men and women causing infections in the genitals, rectum, and throat. A very common infection, especially among people ages 15–24 years.

Hand hygiene: A simple and effective way to prevent infections, which includes diligently cleaning and trimming fingernails, which may harbor dirt and germs and can contribute to the spread of some infections, such as pinworms.

Herd immunity: Refer **Community immunity**.

Hepatitis: A disease caused by a virus in which the liver is damaged by the presence of inflammatory cells in the tissue of the organ.

HIV/AIDS: A non-curable infection transmitted through bodily fluids through sexual contact, sharing of needles, and breast milk. If left untreated it progresses to AIDS, reclassified as "HIV Stage III." This virus cannot be cured and is deadly. With effective treatment and management, individuals with HIV may live long, productive lives.

Immunocompromised: A person who has an immunodeficiency of any kind is said to be immunocompromised. An immunocompromised person may be particularly vulnerable to opportunistic infections, in addition to normal infections that could affect everyone. It may also decrease cancer immunosurveillance.

Immunization: The most effective way to prevent the spread of infectious disease by administering vaccines.

Infectious disease: It is defined as being a disorder or illness caused by an organism, such as bacteria, viruses, fungi or parasites. Infectious diseases are transmitted either from person to person or bites from insects/animals or acquired by ingesting contaminated food/drinking contaminated water or being exposed to organisms in the environment.

Inactivated immunity: The transfer of active humoral immunity when ready-made antibodies are transferred from mother to fetus during pregnancy or when administered by injection of an inactivated virus, in which the antibodies or specific elements of a virus are transferred to an individual so that the body does not need to produce these elements. Also known as Passive immunity.

Latent tuberculosis: Occurs when a person affected by TB bacteria does not show any symptoms of disease, but slowly there is a risk of getting affected by active TB when the immune system of the person is weakened.

Lyme disease: It is caused by bacteria and is transmitted to humans through infected ticks. The major symptom is a rash. If the individual is not treated, the infection may spread to joints, the heart, and the nervous system but can be treated successfully with antibiotics for a few weeks.

Malaria: A mosquito-borne life-threatening blood disease caused by parasites transmitted to humans through the bite of the *Anopheles* mosquito.

Methicillin-resistant *Staphylococcus aureus*: An infectious disease caused by a type of staph bacteria which cannot be treated with the antibiotics that are usually prescribed for staph infections, as it is resistant and does not respond to the usual prescriptions.

Passive immunity: Refer **Inactivated immunity**.

Pertussis: Also known as whooping cough. A highly contagious respiratory disease and is known for uncontrollable, violent coughing that often makes it hard to breathe.

Salmonella: An infection caused by the bacteria *Salmonella*, which is found in contaminated, undercooked food and spreads due to poor kitchen hygiene.

Severe acute respiratory syndrome: A viral respiratory illness caused by a coronavirus which causes fever, cough, and other symptoms.

Syphilis: A sexually transmitted infection caused by *Treponema pallidum*, a microscopic organism called a spirochete that can cause long-term complications if not treated correctly. A person can get syphilis by direct contact with a syphilis sore during vaginal, anal, or oral sex. It can also be spread from an infected mother to her unborn baby.

Tuberculosis: A disease caused by bacteria that usually attack the lungs, but may attack any part of the body such as the kidney, spine, and brain. If not treated properly, TB can be fatal.

Upper respiratory infection: Also known as the common cold, and is among the most common illness. There are more than 200 different viruses that cause a URI where the symptoms include inflammation of the membranes in the lining of the nose and throat.

Vaccine: It contains an agent that is similar to a disease-causing micro-organism made from weakened or killed forms of the microbe. Immunization with a vaccine involves a biological preparation to provide active acquired immunity to a particular disease.

CHAPTER 10

Accidents: Something which is unintentional, unintended, and undesirable that damages something or injures someone.

Acute myocardial infarction (AMI): A life-threatening condition that occurs when blood flow to the heart is abruptly cut off, causing tissue damage. It is usually the result of a blockage in one or more of the coronary arteries.

Adenocarcinoma: A cancer that forms in the glandular (mucus producing) tissues of the body, including the breast, colon, and prostate.

Arrhythmia: A condition in which the heart beats with irregular or abnormal rhythm either the heart beating too fast or too slow.

Arthritis: A form of joint disorder that involves inflammation of one or more joints. Many forms of arthritis affect the joints, including osteoarthritis, rheumatoid arthritis, lupus, fibromyalgia, and gout.

Asthma: The chronic inflammation of the bronchial airway, causing it to narrow in response to various stimuli. This narrowing causes spasms, thus making it difficult for the individual to inhale.

Atrium: The upper cavity of the heart which receives blood from the veins and from which the blood is passed to the ventricles.

Atherosclerosis: A disease characterized by degenerative changes in the arteries caused by buildup of plaques made up of fat, cholesterol, calcium, and some other substances found in blood. It results in thickening, hardening, and loss of elasticity of the walls of the arteries.

Alzheimer's disease: A physical disease that affects the brain, named after Doctor Alois Alzheimer, who first described it. A chronic neurodegenerative disease that usually starts slowly and gets worse over time and is the most common cause of dementia.

Basal cell carcinoma: A cancer that begins in the lower or basal (base) layer of the epidermis of an individual's outer layer of skin cells.

Benign tumor: A mass of cells that lacks the ability to invade neighboring tissue or metastasize. Benign tumors are not cancerous. They can often be removed, and, in most cases, they do not come back. Cells in benign tumors do not spread to other parts of the body.

Bradycardia: A condition in which the heart beat is slower than the normal rate and becomes a serious problem if the heart beat falls below 50 bpm as it does not pump enough oxygen-rich blood to the body.

Benign cancer: A mass of cells (tumor) that lacks the ability to invade neighboring tissue or metastasize. Benign tumors are not cancerous. They can often be removed, and, in most cases, they do not come back. Cells in benign tumors do not spread to other parts of the body.

Biological therapy: This therapy uses living organisms (e.g., white blood cells) to boost the immune system to destroy the cancer. It is specially formulated for each individual and type of cancer and is given as intravenous therapy over several months. Also known as immunotherapy.

Cardiovascular disease: A dysfunction of the heart and blood vessels that can be caused by controllable and non-controllable factors.

Cancer: A disease caused by mutated cells that continue to divide and produce more mutated cells. These mutated cells multiply and may form growths called tumors that may spread throughout the body.

Carcinoma: These are the most common type of cancer. They are formed by epithelial cells, which are the cells that cover the inside and outside surfaces of the body.

Coronary heart disease (CHD): The result of waxy cholesterol (plaque) buildup in the coronary arteries. When the plaque causes the arteries to narrow, thus causing a blockage, the disease is called atherosclerosis.

Coronary artery disease (CAD): It develops when the major blood vessels that supply blood, oxygen, and nutrients become damaged or diseased. It is caused by atherosclerosis, an accumulation of fatty materials on the inner linings of arteries.

Congestive heart failure (CHF): A condition in which the heart is unable to pump enough blood to meet the body's needs. Another name for it is heart failure. The reasons the heart may be unable to pump enough blood include heart muscle damage caused by an AMI, hypertension, and diabetes.

Chronic liver disease and cirrhosis: Chronic liver disease involves a process of progressive destruction and regeneration of the liver parenchyma leading to fibrosis and cirrhosis. Cirrhosis is caused when the scar tissue replaces healthy liver tissue and slows the flow of blood through the liver, which stops the liver from working normally.

Central nervous system: The part of the nervous system which consists of the brain and spinal cord. It integrates sensory impulses it receives from, and coordinates and influences the activity of, all parts of the body.

Chemotherapy: A category of cancer treatment using anti-cancer drugs administered to destroy malignant cells or tissues. It may be administered once per week up to once per month depending on the stage and type of cancer.

Chronic disease: A disease that persists for more than three months, as per U.S. National Center for Health Statistics. These diseases have a long-term impact on an individual, including quality of life and social and economic effects.

Chronic obstructive pulmonary disease (COPD): A progressive disease that makes it more and more difficult to breathe. It begins with chronic bronchitis and inflammation and swelling of the bronchial tubes, which causes narrowing and obstruction with symptoms of an unresolved cough.

Communicable disease: A disorder or illness caused by an organism, such as bacteria, viruses, fungi or parasites. Also known as Infectious disease, it is transmitted either from person to person or by bites from insects/animals or acquired by ingesting contaminated food/drinking contaminated water or being exposed to organisms in the environment.

Congestive heart failure: A condition where the heart fails to pump enough blood with normal efficiency. It usually occurs slowly after an injury like heart attack, too much strain on the heart due to years of untreated high blood pressure, or a diseased heart valve.

Cerebrovascular diseases: A disease condition in which blood circulation to the brain is affected which causes poor blood flow or no blood flow at all to affected areas in the brain.

Chronic lower respiratory diseases: These diseases are characterized by shortness of breath caused by obstruction of airways leading to the lungs. The most prevalent are COPD, emphysema, chronic bronchitis, and also smoking-related disorders.

Diabetes mellitus: The most common diabetes and is a metabolic disorder characterized by the presence of hyperglycemia, the pancreas no longer produces enough insulin or cells stop responding to the insulin that is produced, so that glucose in the blood cannot be absorbed into the cells of the body.

Double disease burden: A phenomenon often referred to as double burden of communicable and non-communicable diseases, during which health infrastructures already weakened by continuing battles with infectious disease are increasingly being taxed by rapidly growing non-communicable diseases.

Epidemiology: The study of populations to understand the patterns, causes, and effects of health and diseases, used to develop methodology for clinical research, make decisions based on the understanding of data, identify risk factors, target ways to prevent the spread of disease, and create health care policies.

External defibrillator: A lightweight, portable device that delivers an electric shock through the chest to the heart. The shock can stop an irregular heart rhythm and allow a normal rhythm to resume following sudden cardiac arrest.

Fibrillation: Fibrillation is when the heart's two upper chambers (atrium) beat out of coordination with the two lower chambers (ventricles), and this chaotic heart rhythm causes poor blood flow to the body.

Fibromyalgia: A disorder characterized by widespread musculoskeletal pain accompanied by fatigue, sleep, memory, and mood issues. It may begin after physical trauma, surgery,

infection, significant psychological stress, or be a gradual process over time.

Gout: A complex form of arthritis. Symptoms include a sudden, severe attack of pain, and redness and tenderness in joints. Often, the big toe is affected, with intense pain, feeling hot, being swollen, and experiencing extreme tenderness. Gout is managed with medications, and there is a risk of recurrence.

Hypertensive renal disease: A medical condition that damages the kidney due to chronic hypertension and results in chronic kidney disease.

Homicide: Killing of one person by another.

Hyperglycemia: A condition that refers to high blood glucose where the pancreas releases insulin to help cells absorb glucose from the bloodstream to lower blood sugar levels.

Hypoglycemia: A condition that refers to low glucose levels where the pancreas releases glucagon to help the liver release stored glucose into the bloodstream to raise blood sugar levels.

Incidence: The number of newly diagnosed cases of a disease during a given period of time.

Insulin: A peptide hormone produced by beta cells of the pancreatic islets, which helps the body utilize fat, protein, and certain minerals. Because insulin is so essential, individuals with diabetes may experience widespread direct and indirect effects on all of their body's systems, tissues, and organs.

Ischemia: The condition of inadequate and proper supply of blood to a local area due to blockage of blood vessels, causing a shortage of oxygen and glucose needed for cellular metabolism.

Influenza and pneumonia: Influenza is an acute respiratory viral infection commonly known as 'the flu' spread from individual to individual caused by influenza A or B viruses. Most people who get the influenza recover completely in 1 to 2 weeks, but some people develop serious and potentially life-threatening medical complications of influenza that may include viral pneumonia, secondary bacterial pneumonia and sinus infections.

Leukemia: A cancer that starts in blood-forming tissue such as the bone marrow. It does not form into solid tumors but rather the abnormal white blood cells build up in the blood and bone marrow, thus crowding out normal blood cells.

Lymphoma: A cancer that forms when abnormal lymphocytes turn into cancer cells, grow abnormally, spread beyond the lymphatic system to other organs, and compromise the body's ability to fight infection.

Malignant cancer: Cancer where cells continue to divide and produce more mutated cells. These mutated cells multiply and may form growths called tumors that start invading nearby tissues and can also spread to other parts of the body through the blood and lymph systems.

Metastatic cancer: A condition where the cancer spreads from one location in the body to another location. The metastatic tumor is the same type of cancer as the primary tumor. The metastatic cancer retains the same name and the same type of cancer cells as the original or primary cancer site.

Morbidity: Another term for an illness or disease. The term "co-morbidity" is also used when an individual has several illnesses at the same time.

Mortality: Another term for death. A mortality rate is the number of deaths due to a disease for a population. Mortality rates are given as the number of deaths per year in a population per a consistent number (most often 100,000). This number is to standardize the death rate across different population sizes.

Malignant tumor: These tumors grow out of control and start invading nearby tissues and can also spread to other parts of the body through the blood and lymph systems.

Myocardial infarction (MI): Also known as heart attack, which occurs when the flow of blood to the heart becomes blocked. This is usually the result of a blockage in one or more of the coronary arteries. It can cause tissue damage and can even be life-threatening.

Non-communicable disease: A disease that does not spread from person to person and are now the major cause of death and disability worldwide. Generally these diseases have a long duration with a slow progression.

Non-metastatic cancer: The opposite of metastatic cancer, it is a cancer that has not spread beyond the primary site to other sites in the body.

Nephritis: The inflammation of kidneys often caused by infections, and toxins, but is most commonly caused by autoimmune disorders that lead to impairment of kidneys.

Nephrotic syndrome: A kidney disorder that occurs because of the damage to the tiny blood vessels known as the glomeruli in the kidney. This allows protein to leave the body in large amounts through urine. Nephrotic syndrome causes swelling (edema), particularly in the feet and ankles, and increases the risk of other health problems.

Nephrosis: A degenerative disease of the kidney tubules, the tiny canals that make up much of the substance of the kidney. Nephrosis can be caused by kidney disease, or it may be a complication of another disorder, particularly diabetes.

Osteoarthritis: The most common form of arthritis, it breaks down the cartilage that covers the ends of the bones. When the cartilage is decreased, the bones rub together and cause pain and permanent damage. Treatment includes exercise, medicines, and surgery. Risk factors for osteoarthritis include being overweight, aging, and joint injuries.

Prevalence: It is defined as the number of cases of disease existing in a population taken from the total population at any given time.

Parkinson's disease: A neurodegenerative brain disorder that is caused due to malfunction and death of vital nerve cells in the brain, called neurons, damaging the nervous system. It progresses slowly, meaning that the symptoms continue and worsen over a period of time.

Pericardium: A sac surrounding the heart which protects the heart (peri = around; cardi = heart).

Primary hypertension: The form of hypertension or high blood pressure that does not have any known secondary/identifiable cause. Also known as Essential Hypertension.

Radiation therapy: A cancer treatment therapy using ionizing radiation. Targeted radiation is used to destroy cancer cells and shrink tumors. It may be 5 days per week over a few weeks or spread out over a few months.

Rheumatoid arthritis: A disease in which the immune system mistakenly attacks the linings of the joints, which results in joint pain, stiffness, swelling, and destruction. The symptoms occur during flare-ups and then resolve after a period of time.

Sarcoma: The tumors of the connectivity tissue are called as 'sarcomas'. It begins in bone, cartilage, fat, muscle, blood vessels, or other connective or supportive tissues. Sarcomas are divided into two main groups, bone sarcomas and soft tissue sarcomas. Treatments for sarcoma vary depending on tumor type, location, and other factors.

Staging: It is defined as how much the cancer has spread in the body. Without knowing the stage of the cancer, a treatment plan cannot be developed. The stage also predicts the severity of the prognosis.

Squamous cell carcinoma: A cancer that forms just beneath the outer surface of the skin as well as in the lining of the stomach, intestines, lungs, bladder, and kidneys.

Systemic lupus erythematosus: An autoimmune disease that attacks healthy tissue like skin, joints, kidneys, brain, and other organs. The cause is unknown.

Septicemia: A serious infection of the blood, also known as bacteremia or blood poisoning. It occurs when the bacterial infection enters the blood stream and is dangerous because the bacteria and the toxins can be carried to entire body through the blood stream.

Suicide: The act of deliberately killing oneself.

Tumor: As cells mutate and become abnormal, the cells survive when they should die. The mutated cells continue to divide and produce more mutated cells. These mutated cells multiply and may form growths called tumors.

Tumor markers: These are cells that help in detecting abnormalities that may indicate cancer by conducting a blood test to check for cancer cells that release particular proteins.

Type 1 diabetes: A type of autoimmune disorder that occurs when the body's immune system reacts improperly, attacking and damaging the body itself. Individuals diagnosed with Type 1 diabetes are generally children or adolescents.

Type 2 diabetes: A progressive and complex medical condition that develops very slowly over many years, as an individual can ignore its symptoms and not know to make lifestyle behavioral changes to decrease long-term damaging consequences.

Tachycardia: A condition in which the heart beat is faster than the normal resting rate and pumps less efficiently and provides less blood flow to the rest of the body.

Transitional cell carcinoma: A cancer found in the linings of the bladder, ureters, part of the kidneys, and a few other organs.

Ventricular fibrillation: A life-threatening arrhythmia, a condition where blood is not pumped from the heart, and sudden cardiac death results if not treated immediately.

Ventricles: These are the two lower chambers of the heart which pump the blood to the body. The right ventricle pumps blood into the lungs and the left ventricle pumps blood into the circulation of the body to deliver oxygen to organs.

White blood cells: These are colorless cells of the immune system that circulate mainly in the blood and lymph and are also known as lymphocytes. Usually, the white blood cells fight infection as part of the immune system response to illness and injury.

CHAPTER 11

Acute stress: The physical response to sudden, intense stress, such as intense anger or a traumatic event, that may trigger heart attacks, arrhythmias, and even sudden death.

Advanced care planning: A conversation that allows individuals to express their desires concerning medical treatment options.

Advanced health directives: A document that states the individual's goals and wishes regarding medical care, including specific instructions about treatment.

Aging in place: Defined by the American Association of Retired Persons (AARP) as the ability to live in one's own home and community safely, independently, and comfortably, regardless of age, income, or ability level.

American Association Of Retired Persons (AARP): A nonprofit, nonpartisan organization that works to address the needs and interests of people aged 50 and above in the United States by providing information, education, research, advocacy, and community services through a nationwide network of local chapters and experienced volunteers.

Assessing Care of Vulnerable Elders (ACOVE): A project that endeavors to develop a comprehensive set of quality-assessment tools and indicators that provide a list of topics to explore when assessing the quality of care for the vulnerable elders who are at high risk for serious decline in health and function.

Assisted living facility: A facility alternative to a nursing home providing personalized resident-centered support services and health care according to individual preferences and needs for those who require assistance with everyday activities.

Authorization: The act of giving permission to the health care provider to share confidential medical records with a third party, such as the spouse of the individual, an attorney, or an employer.

Autonomy: The right of an individual who is mentally competent to determine what will or will not be done regarding his or her body, personal belongings, and personal information.

Better life index: An index designed to explore the quality of life in member countries using 11 categories that include income, housing, jobs, community, education, environment, civic engagement, health, life satisfaction, safety, and work–life balance.

Brain death: An irreversible brain damage and loss of brain function evidenced by lack of reflexes, cessation of spontaneous breathing, and absence of muscle activity, and when an electroencephalogram shows a flat line after two readings taken 24 hours apart.

Cardiopulmonary resuscitation: An emergency procedure performed to improve an individual's chance of survival from sudden cardiac arrest. The procedure involves heart massage and mouth-to-mouth resuscitation or electric stimulation to the heart.

Chronic stress: The response to a situation resulting from prolonged and repeated emotional pressure or tension suffered by an individual resulting fatigue, inability to concentrate, irritability, and development of poor lifestyle habits, such as overeating, smoking, substance abuse, depression, headaches, lack of exercise, and low social support.

Complementary and alternative medicine (CAM): An approach to supplement medical treatment or decrease pain in nonterminal medical conditions. It includes art therapy, music therapy, mindful meditation, yoga, and pet therapy, which are not part of standard medical care.

Continuing care retirement communities (CCRCs): These are retirement communities offering a combination of independent living, assisted living, and nursing home-style care options allowing people to age in one community even if they need additional health care services over time.

Disclosure: The act of revealing personal health information to the health care provider to receive an accurate diagnosis, appropriate treatment, and quality care.

Do not resuscitate (DNR): An order set up by the individual to choose whether or not a CPR can be performed during emergency. If an individual is unable to speak, a family member may seek a DNR order on their relative's behalf.

Durable power of attorney: A legal document that appoints a health care decision maker more helpful to physicians when they need to know what an individual would want in a particular medical situation and who can legally make decisions.

End-of-life planning: A discussion that introduces the terms and definitions regarding end-of-life planning using several types of legal documents that can guide and assist individuals and their families to take important end-of-life decisions.

Euthanasia: It is defined as an act where a third party, usually a physician, terminates the life of an individual involving, but not limited to, a diagnosis of living in a situation that the individual considers to be worse than death or existing in a coma or in a persistent vegetative state.

Health-related quality of life: A concept that includes all of the aspects of overall quality of life that affect physical and mental health.

Imminent death: It refers to death likely to occur at any moment and is expected within a short time, usually days or weeks.

Independent living: A facility on the CCRC campus where individuals have access to amenities, pharmacy services, walk-in non-urgent medical clinic, cultural events within CCRC and the local community, group and individualized transportation and meal services.

Informed consent: A legal written document that an individual signs to agree to a specific surgical or medical procedures or other course of treatment. The procedure is protected under federal and state medical consent laws.

Kidney dialysis: A treatment that removes waste and fluids from the blood in individuals with kidneys that no longer function or have been surgically removed due to damage or injury.

Mechanical ventilation: A life support treatment by inflating and oxygenating the lungs delivered through a machine by inserting tubes through the nose or mouth into the trachea of an individual.

Nursing home facility: A privately operated facility providing health care for persons who are unable to take care of themselves.

Nutrition and hydration: A method to provide nutrients, fluid, and water to individuals who are unconscious or cannot swallow either by feeding tube or intravenous catheter.

Palliative care: An approach to medical care that improves the quality of life for individuals who have chronic long-term pain.

Persistent vegetative state: A chronic wakeful, unconscious state that lasts longer than a few weeks in which the patients may have awoken from a coma, but still have not regained awareness.

Physician assisted suicide: The voluntary termination of life by an individual where a physician provides with a prescription for medications that the individual may use to end his or her life.

Quality of life: A concept often used in relation to health and well-being defined in various ways as the degree of satisfaction, general well-being, ability to function, overall enjoyment of life, and ability to pursue daily activities.

Statement of disagreement: A request by the individuals indicating the error or need for an amendment in their medical record.

Stress: The response to a situation resulting from mental or emotional strain, anxiety or tension caused by adverse or demanding circumstances.

Terminal sedation: A medication to make the individuals with a terminal illness suffering profound pain near the last days of their life unconscious until death occurs from the underlying illness.

Termination of medical treatment: A situation where treatments are no longer of benefit and the patient or family no longer wants to continue the treatment. The patient has the right to make decisions if they fully understand the consequences of their decision, and states they no longer want a treatment.

Waiver: The act of giving permission by an individual to the health care provider to share confidential medical records with a third party, such as the spouse of the individual, an attorney, or an employer. This is also called as Authorization.

CHAPTER 12

Computer literacy: It denotes familiarity with the concepts and components of a computer and ability to work on computers and related technology.

Co-payment: A fixed fee or cost that individuals must pay prior to receiving specific medical services or treatments covered by their health insurance plan.

Culture: An individual's beliefs, values, attitudes, traditions, language preferences, and health practices.

Contraindicated medication: A condition in which a drug, procedure, or surgery should not be prescribed to a patient because it may be harmful and lead to serious consequences.

Fatalism: A belief that a person has no control over the outcome of their disease, subjugating all events to fate.

Glioblastoma: The most common and malignant type of astrocytoma that usually occurs in the brain.

Health care provider responsibilities: These are certain responsibilities that have to be assumed by the health care provider to protect the best interests of the patients.

Health literacy: A complex group of skills including reading, listening, analyzing information, decision making, and applying these skills to health situations.

Jargon: A technical terminology used in a context usually of a particular profession or a field of subject not easily understood by people outside of it.

Literacy: It is defined as the understanding and ability to use written text to participate in society to achieve goals and develop knowledge and potential.

Medication adherence: It is defined as the extent to which a patient continues with the agreed upon mode of treatment under limited supervision when faced with conflicting or competing demands.

Medical management: A collaborative process that facilitates recommended treatment plans to assure the appropriate medical care is provided to sick, injured, or disabled individuals

National Assessment of Adult Literacy (NAAL): The first national assessment of adult literacy sponsored by the National Center for Education Statistics (NCES) providing information on adult's literacy performance based on the Basic Reading Score (BRS).

Numerical literacy: It is related to the use of numbers and is defined as the ability to use, interpret, and communicate mathematical information and ideas to manage mathematical demands in adult life.

Patient portal: It is computer-technology software that allows health care providers to upload lab results, prescriptions, treatment updates, and follow-up appointments so that patients can access them from their home computers or mobile devices.

Plain Writing Act: A United States federal law which requires all federal agencies to write all government communications in language that the public can understand and use.

Patient responsibilities: These are certain responsibilities of a patient which have to be adopted so that quality health care can be provided.

Readability: The ease with which a reader can read and understand a written text.

Teach-back method: A methodology to ensure that the patient has understood what has been explained to them by asking them to describe all of it. This process is to ensure understanding for compliance.

Verbal communication: The ability of the individuals to explain their medical symptoms to health care providers accurately as well as understand the medical advice and directions for treatment, follow-up, and prescriptions.

Visual literacy: The ability of an individual to interpret and make meaning of information provided in the form of an image, graph, or chart.

CHAPTER 13

Association: The process of displaying health information using graphics to examine and establish possible relationships.

Ancillary or supportive criteria: A criterion that may be used to establish contributory cause by applying the relationship when the definitive requirements have not been fulfilled.

Anecdotal information: The information that is not reliable because it is completely based on casual observations and personal account rather than scientific facts.

Black box warning label: A type of warning placed on the drug during the first few years after it is approved to warn those who are using it or participating in the research because there is still much to be learned before making it available to clinicians and patients.

Case-control studies: A study in which an individual who had stroke is compared to similar individuals who have not had a stroke to determine whether those with stroke are more likely than those without stroke to have had high blood pressure, that is, an association at the individual level.

Cognition: A mental function of being conscious or being aware of intellectual activity like knowing, remembering, thinking, reasoning, or learning.

Cohort studies: A type of prospective medical study conducted on two similar groups of people with and without a particular disease to investigate the causes of disease by examining links between risk factors and outcomes.

Column charts: These charts display data using rectangular columns or bars.

Contributory cause: The concept of causation which is neither necessary nor sufficient but must be contributory.

Correlations: The process of displaying health information using graphics to examine and establish possible relationships.

Efficacy: The capacity of a specific medical intervention to produce a desired effect under ideal conditions.

Extrapolation beyond the data: It assumes that events will continue to increase or decrease at the same pace beyond the information provided.

Health adjusted life expectancy (HALE): The measure of population health status considering mortality and morbidity. The measurement extends to include the quality of health and not just the existence of life.

Health information: The information used for diagnosing disease, testing and screening, and evidence-based treatment decisions. Increasingly, health information is incorporated into evidence-based recommendations or practice guidelines, which can provide important tools for patients and practitioners.

Health status measures: These are the measures created using the public health information used to summarize health of population and groups within the population.

Infant mortality rate: The second widely used measurement of population health status that measures the chances of dying during the first year of life among those born alive in a particular year.

Life expectancy: The measurement of mortality rates from each age group in a population in a particular year that gives summary of average number of years of life remaining for those of a particular age. It implies the number of years of expected life at birth.

Line graphs: A popular and attractive method also known as X-Y graphics for presenting large amounts of information in a single figure. It is very useful for displaying possible associations or what are often called correlations when both measurements have a large number of potential levels.

Mobility: The ability to walk without assistance.

Measure of population health: These are the measures created using the public health information used to summarize health of population and groups within the population.

Mood: A temporary state of mind often referred as internal, subjective state of emotions, feelings or affects having positive or negative valence. Long-term disturbances of mood such as clinical depression or bipolar disorders are called as mood disorders.

Off-label: These are drugs with prescribing privileges that may be prescribed for any reason, at any dose, and for any length of time that the health care provider chooses.

Patient-insert: The health information sheet usually included with a prescription drug with written material that can alert a health navigator and the patient to the potential benefits as well as the potential harms of a drug.

Peer-reviewed: An evaluation of a website or any content by respected sources to help confirm the quality of the website or content.

Pie charts: The charts that display the percentage of the total that is associated with each of the components that make up the whole at one point in time.

Randomized controlled trials: They are considered as the gold standard or definitive criteria for establishing efficacy of a new drug and suggest at least short-term safety of the drug.

Relative risk: A measurement of probability of an event occurring by comparing the strength of a relationship but although this is an ideal sequence of studies to definitively establish contributory cause, it may not be feasible or ethical.

Relevance: The quality of health information provided that makes it very reliable and also meaningful or purposeful and is applicable to the type of question or the type of individual or group to whom the user plans to apply the information.

Reportable diseases: These are diseases that are of great importance to public health and have to be mandatorily reported if diagnosed by the health care provider to the US Centers for Disease Control and Prevention for tracking.

Self-care: An important self-initiated function to maintain good physical or mental health by doing activities of daily living, including dressing, eating, bathing, and using the toilet.

Sensory organ function: The receptivity function of sensory organs, eye, ear, tongue, nose, or skin, which are receptors for specific stimuli.

Spontaneous reporting: A method of collecting public health information in which the patient reports any adverse effect of drugs and vaccines. It helps in identifying unrecognized or unusual events.

Statistically significant: It implies that the relationship is real in the larger populations from which the sample of individuals who actually participated in the investigation was obtained.

Supportive criteria: A criterion that may be used to establish contributory cause by applying the relationship when the definitive requirements have not been fulfilled.

Timeliness: The indication on the website displaying when the website was updated, when the recommendations were made, and planned timing for review of the recommendations.

Under-5 mortality: The measure that goes beyond mortality rates during the first year of life to include mortality rates during the first 5 years of life and is now considered as the standard measure of child health.

Vital statistics: The required data such as birth, death, marriage, divorce etc which is very important to measuring death or mortality rates and defining leading causes of death.

X-axis: The horizontal scale on an X-Y graph.

Y-axis: The vertical scale on an X-Y graph.

CHAPTER 14

Asymptomatic: It refers to a situation where the patient may be the carrier of a disease or infection but does not experience any symptoms which make it difficult to identify.

Cognitive testing: A test conducted to the individuals with memory concerns or other cognitive complaints to detect possible cognitive impairment or early dementia.

Diagnoses: The process of examining and identifying the nature and cause of a disease, infection, illness or any other problem.

Differential diagnosis: The process of distinguishing and determining which disease is causing the patient's illness when two or more diseases with similar signs and symptoms are presenting.

Doorknob syndrome: Refers to a situation when the real reason for a patient's visits comes to light just as the clinician is opening the door at the end of the visit. It may be the result of a physician who is not listening or a patient who is not talking.

Electronic health record: The digital version of the patients' medical records and information which is saved on computer hard disks for ease of access.

Evidence-based recommendations: A procedure or treatment used for a specific health condition based on research and the latest scientific findings.

Health Insurance Portability and Accountability Act: This act provides a set of protections for Electronic Health Records. The HIPAA security rule requires health care providers to make reasonable efforts to protect the privacy of medical records so that they cannot be accidentally or illegally read, altered, shared, or destroyed.

Informed consent: A legal written document that an individual signs to agree to a specific surgical or medical procedures or other course of treatment. The procedure is protected under federal and state medical consent laws.

Lung function tests: These tests are also called Pulmonary Function Tests, designed to measure the function of lungs. The tests determine the causes of breathing problems and shortness of breath.

Palliative efforts: The efforts put forward by the health care providers to provide specialized medical care for people with serious illness, providing relief from the symptoms and improving the quality of life for individuals who have chronic long-term pain.

Review of systems: An inventory performed by the physician with the patient to pick up the full range of symptoms by asking checklists of questions about each body system.

Risk avoider: A patient who often refuses a treatment if it has the potential to make his or her health worse. It is very common when patients feel they can tolerate their current state of health. It may also be affected by the social determinants of health, such as fear of unemployment, lack of adequate financial resources, or a history of discrimination leading to lack of trust in the health care system.

Risk factors: Any attribute, characteristic, or exposure of an individual that increases the likelihood of developing a disease or injury.

Risk taker: A patient who often seeks an intervention that may improve the health outcome even when the odds are against him or her.

Screening: A strategy used to identify the possible presence of a disease or infection that has not yet been diagnosed and the individual does not show any noticeable signs or symptoms.

Sensitivity: It measures the chances that the test is "positive-in-disease."

S.H.A.D.E.:   A mnemonic useful to examine the steps that go into making a diagnosis. The five letters stand for Symptoms, Hunch or hypothesis, Alternatives, Diagnosis, and Explanation.

Specificity: It measures the chances that the test is negative-in-health. About the test itself and do not in-and-of-themselves tell us about the chances that a disease is present or absent.

Testing for causation: It refers that the treatment itself can be viewed as a test, often called a therapeutic trial, the response to treatment can help in establishing that a disease is the cause of a patient's symptoms.

Testing for prognosis: It is to predict the future course of a disease which can be of great importance once a disease is diagnosed.

Testing for response to treatment: It is testing to determine an individual's response to treatment including both the benefits and the harms is an important use of testing.

Therapeutic trial: It means that the treatment itself can be viewed as a test. The response to treatment can help in establishing that a disease is the cause of a patient's symptoms.

Watchful waiting: It means that it is best to merely observe the disease and to carefully follow up after a disease diagnosis is established. It may be the best course of treatment and this is often the recommended treatment because early treatment does not lead to better outcomes.

Working diagnosis: The hunch or hypothesis which needs to be either eliminated from consideration or confirmed as the clinicians often rapidly generate a likely diagnosis based on available data and medical knowledge.

INDEX